SLAVERY IN THE HISTORY OF MUSLIM BLACK AFRICA

Cover Bagirmi slave raid against the Pagan Kimre. From Gustav Nachtigal, *Sahara and Sudan*, vol. III (London, 1987), p. 342.

HUMPHREY J. FISHER

Slavery in the History of Muslim Black Africa

NEW YORK UNIVERSITY PRESS
WASHINGTON SQUARE, NEW YORK

© Humphrey J. Fisher, 2001
All rights reserved.

First published in the U.S.A. by
NEW YORK UNIVERSITY PRESS
Washington Square
New York, NY 10003
Printed in India

Library of Congress Cataloging-in-publication Data
Fisher, Humphrey J.
  Slavery in the history of Muslim Black Africa / Humphrey J. Fisher
    p. cm
  Includes bibliographical references and index.
  ISBN 0-8147-2715-8 (cloth : alk. paper) – ISBN 0-8147-2716-6
  (pbk. : alk. paper)
  1. Slavery—Africa—History. 2. Slavery and Islam—Africa—History.
  I. Title.
HT1321.F57 2000
326,096'0902—dc21   00-040219

For M.

ACKNOWLEDGEMENTS

Work on the English translation of Gustav Nachtigal's *Sahara und Sudan* began in the early 1960s, and has continued, with various intermissions and many ramifications, ever since. The present volume derives ultimately from those first steps nearly four decades ago. To thank all those who have helped in the work during that long span of time is manifestly impossible. The work itself would have been manifestly impossible, without that help. Four names, however, most directly connected with the immediate preparation of this book should be mentioned. Hannah Lloyd (then aged 12), who helped first launch me upon a radical reconsideration of *Slavery* 1970, dismembering the pages of that volume; Liazzet Bonate, who helped me lay the foundations for the index; the Research Committee of the School of Oriental and African Studies, which contributed towards the initial costs of indexing; and my wife, Helga, who has borne with me the burden and heat of the long day.

CONTENTS

ACKNOWLEDGEMENTS	*page* vii
FOREWORD	xvii

Chapters

I. INTRODUCTION	1
Population mobility	1
The Islamic factor	14
The enslavement of Muslims	18
II. THE SIZE OF THE SLAVE POPULATION	33
III. SLAVE STATUS AND RELIGION	40
Pagan slaving	40
Jihad and slave-raiding	46
Slave and free status	54
The contribution of slaves to religious activity	59
Religious conversion and commitment	64
Emancipation	70
The return of the slaves	83
IV. EXPORTS AND MARKETING	98
Slave exports and their relation to the home market	98
The arms trade	111
Selection of export models	115
Slaves on the march	122
V. THE DOMESTIC SCENE, I: GENERAL TREATMENT	138
General treatment	138
Slave revolts	152
Runaway slaves	158

CONTENTS

VI. THE DOMESTIC SCENE, II: SLAVES IN THE FAMILY ... 177
    Domestic demand for slaves ... 177
    Concubines ... 177
    Cooks and cooking ... 202

VII. THE DOMESTIC SCENE, III: SLAVES AT WORK ... 208
    Free and slave labour ... 208
    Agricultural workers ... 211
    Artisans ... 218
    Caravan workers ... 222
    Luxury slaves ... 231

VIII. THE DOMESTIC SCENE, IV: SLAVES AND THE STATE ... 238
    Colonists ... 238
    Soldiers ... 242
    Royal and other government slaves ... 256
    Eunuchs ... 280

IX. THE DOMESTIC SCENE, V: SLAVES AS A MEANS OF EXCHANGE ... 295
    Tribute ... 295
    Alms and presents ... 307
    Slaves as currency ... 316

X. THE SLAVE MARKET IN KUKA ... 322

XI. CONCLUSION: ANTI-SLAVERY MEASURES ... 332

APPENDIX A. Outline Chronology of Nachtigal's Travels ... 344
APPENDIX B. 'Slave Raids April to July 30, 1872' ... 347
STUDENTS' BIBLIOGRAPHY ... 383
INDEX ... 389

ILLUSTRATIONS

The attack on Musfeia, 1823	24
Reception by Abu Sekkin, 4 April 1872	51
An ivory porter	110
A slave caravan	129
Foot-irons, manacles, slave stick	169
A black African woman in Morocco	178
A slave in the block	232
A Ghadames bill of sale, including gold, male and female slaves, hides, pillow-cases, ivory, senna, perfume, camels, sacks and household slaves	325
Nachtigal's first grave, in Liberia	343
Tree-dwellings under siege in Kimre	350
Battle for Koli	364

MAPS

North and West Africa	xiv-xv
Tropical Africa	xvi

MAPS

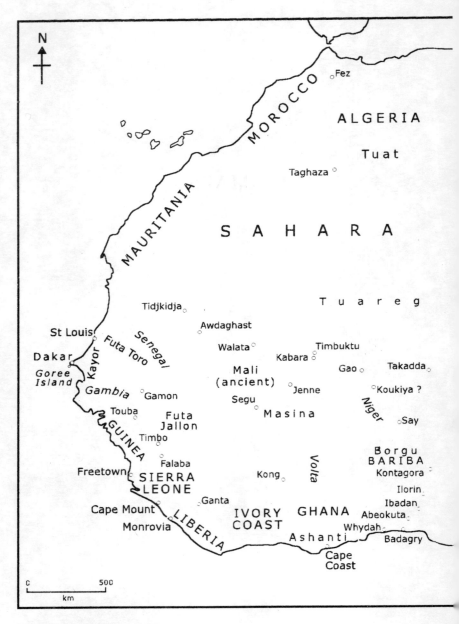

North and West Africa

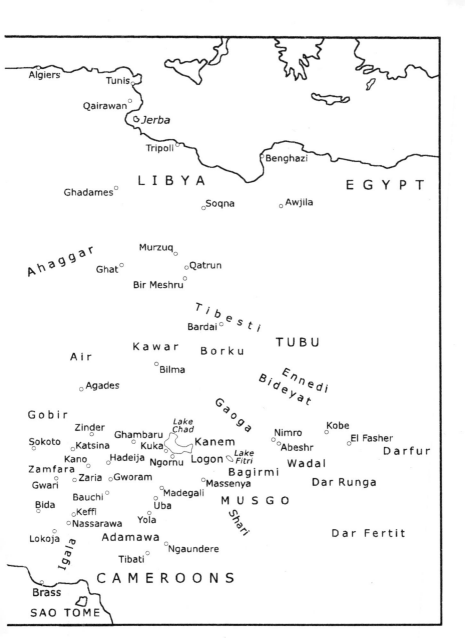

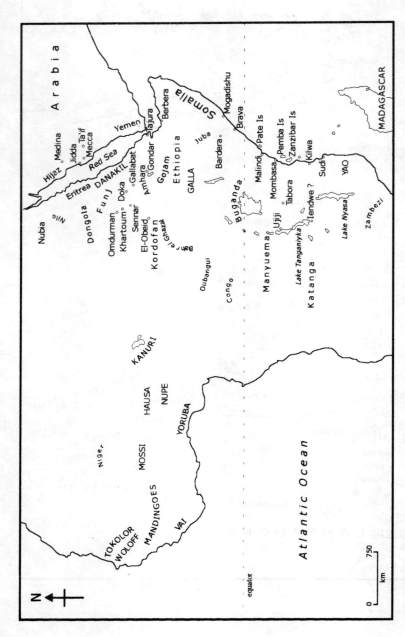

Tropical Africa

FOREWORD

'Let him who pauses to regard this writing know...' (*The diary of Hamman Yaji: chronicle of a West African Muslim ruler,* James H. Vaughan and Anthony H.M. Kirk-Greene, eds, Bloomington and Indianapolis 1995, p. 121, 5 January 1926; hereafter Hamman Yaji).

This book attempts to describe slavery in the history of Muslim black Africa. To this end, pride of place is given to eye-witness evidence, by observers, even participants. We hear the voice of the slaving chief, Hamman Yaji, quoted just above, through his own diary. And of Dorugu, erstwhile slave but later freed.[1] And the voices of local authorities, engaged in (among many other things) the administration of slavery, voices heard in their letters, written before the British conquest, and then translated and published by the British.[2] Or of a more recent dignitary, the late Alhaji Sir Abubakar Tafawa Balewa, whose short Hausa novel, *Shaihu Umar,* is driven fundamentally by the vicissitudes of slavery.[3] And many other voices, over centuries, of Muslim visitors like Ibn Battuta in the 14th and Leo Africanus in the 16th century, of local Muslims themselves, of Muslim lawyers addressing us through reference to standard Muslim legal texts.

One of the most moving statements comes from a slave with, literally, no voice. In 1823-4 a southbound caravan, including some thirty freed slaves, crossed the Sahara from Tripoli to Borno. The ex-slaves left the caravan shortly before Borno, turning east to Kanem, their native land. One was deaf

---

[1] Anthony Kirk-Greene and Paul Newman, eds, *West African travels and adventures: two autobiographical narratives from Northern Nigeria,* New Haven and London, 1971.

[2] H. F. Backwell, ed., *The occupation of Hausaland 1900-1904: being a translation of Arabic letters found in the house of the Wazir of Sokoto, Bohari, in 1903,* Government Printer: Lagos 1927, reprinted by Cass, London 1969.

[3] M. Hiskett, tr., Longmans: London 1967, reprinted Wiener, New York 1997.

and unable to speak. An Englishman, Dixon Denham, also in the caravan, speaks for her:

> She had left two children behind her [in Kanem]; and the third, which was in her arms when she was taken by the Arabs, had been torn from her breast after the first ten days of her journey across the desert, in order that she might keep up with the camels. Her expressive motions in describing the manner in which the child was forced from her, and thrown on the sand, where it was left to perish, while whips were applied to her, lame and worn out as she was, to quicken her tottering steps, were highly eloquent and interesting.[4]

European observers too: one of these, Gustav Nachtigal (1834-85), a young German physician, is our principal eye-witness in the present volume. In 1862, just qualified, and still in his twenties, he arrived in North Africa. He lived there six years, serving as a military doctor with Tunisian forces on campaign, and as private doctor to the Dey of Tunis. He acclimatised, learnt Arabic, became familiar with African and Muslim life-styles. In 1868, when Nachtigal was not yet thirty-five, on the eve of his proposed final return to Europe, the opportunity arose to carry presents from the Prussian King to Shaykh Umar, ruler of Borno, an ancient and powerful kingdom adjoining Lake Chad. Nachtigal seized this chance.

Something else, however, other than acclimatisation and experience, had happened to Nachtigal in North Africa. As a boy, he had seen his father and brother die of tuberculosis, then believed to be hereditary. As a doctor just graduating, he recognised the same symptoms in himself, and knew the gloomy prognosis. He went to North Africa ill, perhaps dying. He went in search of recovery, and found it. Africa, for Nachtigal, was resurrection. He would never have spoken with such hyperbole about himself: but surely the fact that Africa had given him back his life coloured and directed all his subsequent dealings with, and observations of, Africa and Africans.

In the Sahara, Nachtigal visited Fezzan, Tibesti, Borku; in

---

[4] E. W. Bovill, ed., *Missions to the Niger*, Hakluyt Society: 1964-6, II, 233. Three sisters were in the party, two freed by their owner in Tripoli, the third he had sought out, purchasing her freedom. See p. 87 below.

the Sudan belt below the desert, Borno, Kanem, Wadai, Darfur, Kordofan; further south, Bagirmi. His scientific training, turned in Africa to myriad subjects, history and anthropology, geology and meteorology, language and linguistics, flora and fauna, trade and taxation, disease and treatment, sociology and government, architecture, dress, even hair-styles; his access as a doctor to homes, families, individuals; his six years preparation (albeit unintended) in North Africa; the fact that his nearly six years of travel after North Africa were almost wholly without European companionship; his equable temperament—he never fired a shot in anger, and left friends everywhere (except maybe in Tibesti); his courage in danger, endurance in illness; all this equipped him as certainly among the very best of the early European travellers in Africa. Frank alike in commendation and criticism, never condescending, dismissive or derogatory, the chronicle of his odyssey may be read today by African scholar and European colleague alike, without embarrassment on the one hand or resentment on the other.

Nachtigal's magisterial travel report Sahara und Sudan: *Ergebnisse sechsjähriger Reisen in Afrika* (Sahara and Sudan: Results of six years travel in Africa), was published between 1879 and 1889.[5] This edition became rare, and a fragmented, unsatisfactory French version rarer still. In 1967 *Sahara und Sudan* was reprinted in facsimile by Akademische Druck-u.-Verlagsanstalt, Graz; this is still in print. In English a few pages appeared in *Harper's new monthly magazine*, 1874 (see below, 347 note), but nothing more.

Finally, a century after the original *Sahara and Sudan* in German, a complete, annotated English version followed.[6] The final volume of four appeared in 1987. There is thus an excellent reason for special interest in Nachtigal now as a

---

[5] I, Berlin 1879; II, Berlin 1881; III (posthumous), Leipzig 1889

[6] Volume I, *Tripdi and Fezzan, Tibesti or Tu*, 1974; II, *Kawar, Bornu, Kanem, Borku, Ennedi*, 1980; III, *The Chad basin and Bagirmi*, 1987; IV, *Wadai and Darfur*, 1971 [sic]; all published initially by Hurst, London, with a different American co-publisher for each, Barnes & Noble, Holmes & Meier, Humanities Press and the University of California, respectively. Tr. and ed. Allan G. B. and H. J. Fisher.

prolific, very high quality, effectively brand-new source for the study of the heart of Africa.

Sahara and Sudan is a treasure-trove of slavery data, not because Nachtigal went as an 'independent counsel' looking for this specifically, but because slavery confronted him at every turn. He travelled with slave-raiders: Appendix B below gives his eye-witness account of such operations, an almost unique record in the annals of slaving within Africa. He accompanied slave caravans, sometimes under horrifying conditions, sometimes more comfortably. He attended slave markets. He fended off gifts of slaves, finally accepting two after having failed to organise his household with free paid labour. He rubbed shoulders with high-ranking slaves in the top echelons of political society and national governments. Once he was nearly enslaved himself, in exchange for half a camel (see pp. 235-6 below). All this precisely because slavery was so pervasively important in those countries at that time.

As a by-product of the ongoing translation of *Sahara und Sudan*, a slim volume, *Slavery and Muslim society in Africa*[7] appeared in 1970, combining Nachtigal's material with comparative data. In 1998 a second edition was mooted, but what has emerged is a new book. Nothing of substance in *Slavery* 1970 is omitted, but the Nachtigal material has more than doubled, as has the supporting evidence, including now other independent voices. Analysis has been deepened, presentation tightened.

In the interval, the study of Africa and slavery has changed greatly. In 1970, the Atlantic trade was the crux, a tradition still maintained for example by Hugh Thomas's *The slave trade: the history of the Atlantic slave trade 1440-1870* (1997). Immense new progress has been made in studying slavery within Africa. Paul Lovejoy's *Transformations in slavery: a history of slavery in Africa* (1983) and Patrick Manning's *Slavery and African life: Occidental, Oriental, and African slave trades* (1990), both from Cambridge University Press, are excellent examples of this more Africa-centred approach. Both consider Muslims, but within a broader context; neither takes more than fleeting

---

[7] Allan G. B. and H. J. Fisher, *Slavery and Muslim society in Africa: the institution in Saharan and Sudanic Africa and the trans-Saharan trade*, Hurst, London, 1970; Doubleday, Garden City, NY, 1971.

notice of Nachtigal. Other, more precisely defined projects, such as *The human commodity: perspectives on the trans-Saharan slave trade* (1992), conference papers edited by Elizabeth Savage, and Lovejoy and Jan S. Hogendorn's *Slow death for slavery: the course of abolition in Northern Nigeria, 1897-1936* (1993), inevitably involve Muslim data. But none of these is an exercise in Islamic studies. The only explicit concentration is *Slaves and slavery in Muslim Africa* (1985), the two-volume collected papers of a 1977 conference at Princeton, edited by John R. Willis.

Slavery 1970 was then alone in looking specifically at the Muslim black African evidence. The present volume replaces it as, still, the only unitary overview of this field.

CHAPTER I

INTRODUCTION

Population mobility

'The drum rhythm said "Come in, come in, come in..." ' (Mary F. Smith, ed., *Baba of Karo: a woman of the Muslim Hausa*, London 1954, reprinted 1981, 69)

This is a book about slavery in African history. Slavery itself, however, is but a sub-heading of a broader and deeper African context, the context of demographic resources and of population mobility. First of all, that larger context needs to be briefly sketched.

The fundamental consideration upon which the entire argument of this book is based, fashioning the picture which is here presented, is: that people have been the fundamentally scarce resource, almost throughout the history of sub-Saharan Africa, in almost every location. There have been many exceptions: but the shortage of population has existed often enough to make it a basic, underlying, informing causative factor. The reasons for this recurrent demographic shortfall include disease and malnutrition of humans and of animals; drought and locusts and other causes of crop failure; the relative poverty, or paucity, of natural resources and fertile soils; the depredations of livestock, especially goats; raiding, slaving and warfare; polygamy; infant mortality and the perils of childbirth; an often all-too-abbreviated life expectancy; the relative slowness of rebuilding human stock compared with animals; and so on.

If this hypothesis be correct, then slaving and slavery seem tailor-made to enhance faltering demographic resources wherever a power centre is able to exercise the necessary force. Some scholars have argued precisely this.

INTRODUCTION

> Probably because, by and large, in West Africa land was always more abundant than labour, the institution of slavery played an essential role... *without it there were really few effective means of mobilizing labour for the economic and political needs of the state.*[1]

This is from John Fage, a pioneer modern analyst of the Atlantic slave-trade, and of slavery in West Africa.

But is it true? This view is certainly not simply the arm-chair musing of western academics. The same message is expressed in the approved rhetoric of jingoistic reciters of African oral traditions, or of scholarly (but no less jingoistic) local chroniclers. It has also been the received wisdom of innumerable black African states and societies, a received wisdom which has inflicted incalculable cost in suffering, destruction, and waste.

Despite this concurrence of opinion, from so many sides, Fage's dictum is not, I believe, more than a half-truth: for there were, nearly always, and nearly everywhere in black Africa, alternative, non-violent, 'effective means of mobilizing labour'. So fascinated, so obsessed even, has modern scholarship become with slavery studies,[2] that we often miss the wider scenario of demographic mobility, including more-or-less voluntary, even fully voluntary, movement.

'More-or-less', in the case of refugees fleeing an enemy, starving people fleeing drought, panic-stricken survivors fleeing an epidemic—or, to take a specifically European-colonial example, migrant workers in search of employment in order to earn money for tax—none of these were, or are, voluntarily

---

[1] J. D. Fage, 'Slavery and the slave trade in the context of West African history', *Journal of African history*, *10*, 1969, pp. 393-404, especially p. 400; my italics. See also Robin Law, *The Oyo empire c. 1600 - c. 1836*, Oxford, 1977, 207, for an approving citation of this article.

[2] Is there, perhaps, even today, hidden deep within the subconscious of slavery studies, hardly perceived if perceived at all, a measure of disdain for Africans, that is, for these unfortunate, limited people, who as slave-owners themselves could not conceive of any better means of marshalling demographic resources and organising a labour supply, even within Africa, other than through the tyranny of slavery—or again, for Africans who as labourers or as units of demographic resource of any kind (whether food producers, taxpayers, wives, army recruits, colonists, or whatever) would not respond, or were incapable of responding, to any inducement or incentive other than that same tyranny?

on the move. But, unlike captives in the hands of slave-raiders, or chattels in the hands of slave-traders, they did have some command over where and when they went, and to whom.

Sometimes slave-raiding itself contributed indirectly to the consolidation of population resources, amongst those targetted victims who managed to preserve their freedom, seeking refuge in numbers, and behind city walls. To cite but one example, tiny but vivid, amongst many: Baba of Karo, a Hausa woman of northern Nigeria, born about 1890, tellingly describes slave-raiding and kidnapping against the people of her area. When reports came in of raiders nearby,

> then the chief would order the drummer to climb up on a high place and beat the deep drum (nowadays [about 1950] we only use it for farming and dancing) so that the villagers and people in the surrounding hamlets should come inside the town walls. The drum-rhythm said 'Come in, come in, come in...'[3]

Severe raiding against them had involved Baba's family in heavy ransom payments to recover at least some of the captives; one of Baba's father's wives, for whose release 400,000 cowries had been paid, died just as she was about to return home. The money was forfeit.

> After this our father didn't go back to the hamlet [Karo], he lived inside the town walls; at that time our slaves ran away, and in the morning he went to Karo to farm, and at night he came back to our compound inside Zarewa town.[4]

The options in some instances, certainly amongst the 'more-or-less' voluntary movers, may have been exceedingly limited: but there was some choice, to go or not to go, or, if to go, to go here, or there: and it is precisely this choice, this space for individual and group initiative, which needs to be stressed. In other cases, of course, such movement might be more fully voluntary.

What evidence is there for such peaceful mobility (mainly migrant-led), for the non-violent marshalling of demographic resources (often at the behest of prospective hosts), on a scale comparable to slaving operations? An immediate problem:

[3] Mary Smith, 1954/1981, 69; see also 70-1.
[4] *ibid.*, 73.

non-violence is not news, whether for newspaper reporters and television news-readers today, or for reciters or chroniclers in the past. Regardless of the proportions of historical reality, it is not to be expected that there will be as much explicit evidence, as much emphasis in our sources, given to peaceful mobility, as to violent, imposed mobility. But, as so often happens, once one begins consciously looking for something which has not been much attended to previously, it is surprising how often just that something crops up. A few examples, one or two of a general, generic kind, and one or two quite specific.

First, legends of origin. These are widespread and well-known. Their exact formulation often responds, rather sensitively, to the current preferences and priorities of public opinion. At a time when there was a general belief in some kind of external superiority, whether racial, religious, cultural, imperial, or some combination of these, the legends of origin were likely to lead back to some source distant in place as well as in time, perhaps (there are many West African examples of this) a source somewhere in the Middle East, usually though not invariably a Muslim source. More recently, as more attention has come to be given to national identity, local achievement, and the like, many of the legends have been re-interpreted (often, for example, in the light of linguistic evidence—not always a reliable indicator, since migrants may sometimes change over entirely from one language to another), and such reinterpretation tends to focus upon origins much closer to home. What tends to be overlooked, in the argument about whether the immigrants came from the opposite side of the continent, or from the other side of the hill or behind the forest or across the river, is the fact that they did come. Whencesoever they came, over whatever distance, their coming illustrates, except of course in legends of conquest, the peaceful mobilisation of demographic resources. Indeed, scholars might profitably shift some of the concentration hitherto lavished on origins of immigrants, over instead to the absorptive capacity and facilities of the receiving societies.

Legends of origin may sometimes be misleading about the actual place from which the founding fathers came: such legends may be equally misleading in suggesting that the influx was a one-off affair, necessary to get the state or society started, but not needing to be repeated. Three quotations from early local chronicles will illustrate the theme of subsequent, recurrent, peaceful migration inwards.

The first passage comes from the *Tarikh al-sudan*, a seventeenth-century Timbuktu chronicle. This passage relates to Jenne, a major, and ancient, city on the upper Niger river, southwest of Timbuktu. At first a non-Muslim establishment, Jenne later—this may have been as early as the thirteenth century—adopted the new faith. The first Muslim ruler of the city gathered together the Muslim *ulama*, or clerics, of Jenne.

> He asked them to offer three prayers for that town: let everyone who emigrated from his own country out of distress and poverty be given by Allah wealth and prosperity, so that he will forget his home country; let the foreigners in the town be more numerous than its local people; let patience be taken away from those who come to the town for trade, that they will be tired of it and will sell their merchandise to its people cheap, so that the latter make great profits.[5]

The third prayer, about traders losing patience and selling cheap (before, presumably, returning home disappointed), while it may be a very useful prayer, is hardly a contribution to building up the demographic resources of the municipality: but obviously marshalling manpower, or people-power, was not the only aim of such authorities. The other two prayers, however, fit the demographic hypothesis perfectly: how many cities in the world today would offer the same petition, for no new arrivals ever to leave, and for strangers to outnumber the original citizens? The clerics of Jenne, busy at their orisons, represent the implementation of conscious local government policy: and, even if the precise event did not take place exactly as described, such policy was clearly in people's minds.

The same result of population inflow might sometimes materialise more or less unintentionally. In the *Kano Chronicle* for the reign of Yakubu about the middle of the fifteenth century, the

[5] The English is from N. Levtzion, *Ancient Ghana and Mali*, London 1973, 159-60; the original is by al-Sadi, ed. and tr. O. Houdas, *Tarikh es-soudan*, Paris 1913-4, reprinted by UNESCO, 1964, Arabic pp. 12-13, French p. 24.

whole entry heaves with immigration. Individual Hausa notables came in. Fulani scholars arrived, 'bringing with them books on Divinity and Etymology'—some of the scholars moved further east, but some stayed, 'together with some slaves and people who were tired of journeying'. Saharan salt became common in all of Hausaland, as Asbenawa traders penetrated southwards. Merchants from Gonja, kola country far to the west, began coming, as did 'Beriberi'. Arabs settled in Kano. Even eunuchs came in from Nupe to the south, as trade goods. And, in the midst of this swirling sea of population mobility, the chronicler tucks this tiny, enabling, clause: 'There was no war in Hausaland in Yakubu's time.'[6]

A later passage in the same chronicle, for Mohamma Yaji in the mid-eighteenth century, reverses the emphasis, dwelling primarily upon internal conditions within Kano:

> He was a just and good Sarki [ruler], and a man of mild disposition. On account of this his wives called him 'Mallam Lafia' ['blessing': see also pp. 135 and 151 below]. In his time there was no trouble. He ruled in harmony with his brothers, the sons of Bauwo. There was no difficulty either with his Sarkis or his chief slaves, or his household, or any one.

But there is again an 'arrow phrase' slipped in, which completes the fifteenth-century equation once more, the peaceful and profitable flow of population in the absence of violence: 'Many men came and settled in Kano-land in his reign.'[7] Happy the age without a name. Had Mallam Lafia been a swashbuckling warrior and slave-raider, like many who preceded or came after him, he might have had a chronicle entry ten times as long. And yet, would any swashbuckling *sarki* have brought as many men to Kano-land as came to Mallam Lafia? And would those whom others brought by force have worked as willingly, have settled in as peacefully, as those who came to Mallam Lafia, freely and of their own accord? 'Effective means' indeed.

Of course, conditions that were unfavourable might lead

---

[6] The *Kano Chronicle* in English is in Palmer, 1928/1967, III (see p. 19 n. 35, below), here pp. 110-11; see also below, pp. 241-2.

[7] *ibid.*, III, 126.

contrariwise to an outflow of population. An unusually well-documented instance of both outflow and inflow is provided in the career of a single individual, Lamino, in nineteenth-century Borno. In mid-century, when the traveller Heinrich Barth was there, Lamino was the deputy of a more senior Borno official: Lamino carried out the orders of his superior with complete loyalty and ruthless efficiency, and people moved out to escape his heavy-handed authority. Later, when Nachtigal visited Borno, Lamino had risen further: he was now his own boss (albeit under the king or *shaykh*), and had emerged as an immensely powerful, and immensely popular man (see p. 35 below, and other index references). It is reported that the population of Lamino's own fief, or district, had now more than doubled, as people moved in, resettling themselves in order to reside under his jurisdiction. An extraordinary fluidity of population, in response to local government policies.[8] Lamino reappears in this 'Introduction' (p. 12 below), providing more evidence of his awareness of demographic priorities.

Slavery itself supplies a further illustration of voluntary mobility. One of slavery's drawbacks is that it may encourage resistance; and a frequent form of that resistance is escape. Paul Lovejoy, a foremost slavery scholar, has written enlighteningly about this, in a paper significantly entitled 'Fugitive slaves: resistance to slavery in the Sokoto caliphate'. Lovejoy is fascinated by the property nexus 'as a fundamental component of slavery'. He argues that flight 'was an effective means of destroying property because flight struck directly and thoroughly at the property element of slavery'. Lovejoy hopes that his analysis will re-insert 'the property element into the equation'.[9]

There is manifest truth in this; but what is not so much

[8] L. Brenner, *The Shehus of Kukawa: a history of the al-Kanemi dynasty of Bornu*, Oxford, 1973, 81-2. For further examples of such mobility, petty traders flocking into frontier areas and founding towns, and for Muslim communities, often with royal charters, tax-free, centres 'of peace and learning in troubled times', havens for fugitive debtors (but surely also for so many others!), see R. S. O'Fahey and J. L. Spaulding, *Kingdoms of the Sudan* [notably Sennar and Darfur], London 1974, 83-5.

[9] In Gary Y. Okihiro, ed., *In resistance: studies in African, Caribbean and Afro-American history*, University of Massachusetts Press, Amherst 1986, 71-95.

stressed is that one man's fugitive slave is quite likely—provided, of course, that he or she escapes the perils of being re-enslaved by some other predator—to become someone else's voluntary immigrant. And indeed many state authorities have at one time or another, under one set of conditions or another, sought deliberately to recruit such volunteers. The leaders of the Muslim *jihad*'s, or reforming wars, in West Africa appealed to the slaves of their enemies to run away (offering sometimes surprising incentives—see below, pp. 173-4). Similarly (and for the 'strange pairing' between Islamic theocracies and western colonialists, in the matter of runaway slaves, see below, pp. 172 and 175-6), European colonial authorities, responding partly to their own needs for workers or soldiers or whatever category of people it might be, sometimes welcomed fugitive slaves: that on the other hand such volunteers were often an embarrassment, leading to ructions with neighbouring African societies which were thus losing slaves, underlines the independent initiative shown by the runaways—who, alas, in such cases were sometimes simply handed back to their aggrieved owners. Again, Christian missions might gladly receive fugitive slaves. Groups of runaways, already established in their own sanctuaries, themselves welcomed replenishment of their demographic resources. All along the slave-trade routes local people encouraged slaves to run away. (For further data about all this, see 'Runaway slaves' below, pp. 158-76.)

The list of examples of the voluntary mobilisation of people might be extended almost indefinitely. The few instances cited above suffice at least to suggest that slavery was not the only way to mobilize labour for the state. Not the only, maybe not the best either.

Admittedly, in order to make the point that non-violent alternatives existed, some of the preceding examples have been taken somewhat out of context, and have been presented simplistically. For example, slaves were surely flowing into Jenne, as well as various groups of prayer-induced volunteer immigrants; and slaves surely played an important part in bulking up Jenne society. How many slaves were brought into Kano in Mallam Lafia's time may be indeed more problematic, but certainly there was free immigration also under the *sarki*'s who were militarily successful—volunteers for their slave-raiding forces, merchants attracted by the prospect of cheap slaves in abundance, and various other categories of migrants. A balanced, overall picture would assess all these interwoven, contributory strands.

To conclude this brief discussion of slavery and voluntary mobility, three general points. First, although slavery was, to be sure, in black Africa one important means of enhancing demographic resources, it was in many ways an unsatisfactory policy. Slave-raiding was, much more often than not, a messy business. It could be dangerous. It was destructive of neighbouring societies which might otherwise have become trading partners, tribute-payers, conceivably even contributing voluntary immigrants. Even within the slaving society itself, the uncertainty engendered by kidnapping and the like might dislocate trade, travel, and other productive activities. Slaving, as will appear clearly later in this Introduction, might even rend asunder, with self-inflicted wounds, the theoretically seamless garment of Muslim society in Black Africa. Slavery often involved flagrantly extravagant wastage amongst slaves, especially during capture and in transit. And slavery itself—Lovejoy has shown this for even so highly organised a state as Sokoto—required constant surveillance and discipline even after the slaves had arrived.

Second, in contrast to these and other debit points, the pragmatic benefits to the host society of peaceful immigration stand out. Although this deduction is not made explicitly in the surviving records, it seems no more than reasonable that many states and leaders, like the first Muslim king of Jenne, and Sarki Yakubu and Mallam Lafia of Kano, and Lamino of Borno ruling his own fief, may have eschewed the blood-and-thunder glory of slaving for precisely such benefits. The pull factor, represented by the facilities and general welcome offered to newcomers—the use of land, for example, opportunities for marriage, lower taxes, stable justice—all this could be of crucial importance. Was a state or society or city willing in the first place to receive such people, including refugees—even the founding fathers in the legends of origin briefly considered above were in certain instances refugees themselves—and was the receiver thereafter able to provide security and protection, particularly for sanctuary-seekers?

Third, and most important, many Africans were quite enterprising enough to go of their own accord to Jenne because it was a boom town, or to Hausaland in Sarki Yakubu's time, a land flowing with salt and kola, with pious learning and seasoned with eunuchs, or to Mallam Lafia's Kano-land where 'there was no trouble', or to Lamino's fief in Borno because he was a powerful and popular patron. This is the point about 'space for individual and group initiative' urged above. Africans are everywhere on the move today, seeking to better themselves: people flood into cities, stranger-farmers come to Senegambia for the peanut seaon, Ghanaians pour into Nigeria (until Nigeria expels them in their thousands). There seems no reason why somewhat similar patterns of voluntary migration, often on a much smaller scale, should not have occurred in earlier periods.

Safer and more saving; responding to the welcoming incentives of prospective host societies; and giving scope to individual and group initiative, enterprise and even a sense of adventure: in all these aspects, voluntary migration was part of the life-blood of healthy development in black Africa, in contrast to the 'quick fix' surges of slaving.

We are embarked in this book upon a study specifically of Muslim black Africa. In the discussions so far we have already touched again and again on Islamic elements in the argument; Muslim slave raiders and traders, legends of Muslim origins, even-handed Muslim rulers such as Mallam Lafia and Lamino welcoming immigrants, Muslim clerics praying for an influx of newcomers, Muslim reformers encouraging fugitive slaves, and so on. One could build an entire study of Islam in black Africa around the theme of demographic growth. Muslim societies in black Africa were, and still are, often peculiarly well fitted for the mobilisation of demographic resources. And the importance of such mobilisation is graphically demonstrated by the anxiety shown over just those points at which mobilisation seems most threatened.

Slavery and *jihad* both bring in people. Further, how precisely the marvellously potent doctrine of *hijrah*—separation, or emigration, derived ultimately from the example of the Prophet's *hijrah* from Mecca to Medina—fulfils just this function, stealing people away from unworthy circumstances, and grouping them together in the new (or reformed) Muslim community. Pupils gather at the feet of their teacher, disciples at the feet of their shaykh. Everywhere, within Muslim black Africa, people gather together.

With one exception: the pilgrimage to Mecca, the *hajj*. There, people go out. The *hajj* is a fundamental requirement of Islam, a central pillar of the faith. It is inconceivable that any earnest and serious Muslim should argue, much less act, against the pilgrimage, should seek to prevent pilgrims from setting out upon their manifest holy duty. Inconceivable, almost. To find just one or two examples of Muslim authorities acting to block the pilgrimage, to stop people going out, that would tell us something very significant about the importance of demographic resources.

Such examples are unlikely to be blazoned proudly abroad. Despite this, we can in fact find considerably more than one or two of them, certainly more than the handful which limited space here allows. A fifteenth-century ruler of Mali first implored a large group of intending pilgrims, including clerics and others, to stay; when they refused, he forbade boat crews to ferry them across the river. The pilgrims escaped only when the power of their united prayer facilitated a Moses-style crossing.[10] Again, in the sixteenth century, a Timbuktu cleric tried to go on *hajj* with his family, intending to settle permanently in Medina: but the *qadi*, or judge, the effective ruler of Timbuktu, gave him permission to leave only if he went alone, his family remaining behind as hostages for his return.[11] Again, in the early nineteenth century, Muhammad Bello, son and successor of Usuman dan Fodio founder of the Sokoto caliphate, wrote an extensive and highly learned treatise giving all sorts of reasons why one should not go on pilgrimage—at least not from his state, not immediately.[12]

[10] Muhammad Al-Hajj, 'A seventeenth-century chronicle on the origins and missionary activities of the Wangarawa', *Kano studies*, 1/4, 1968, p. 10.

[11] al-Sadi, Arabic p. 32, French p. 53.

[12] This document has not been published, but is discussed in some detail by Umar al-Naqar, *The pilgrimage tradition in West Africa: an historical study with special reference to the nineteenth century*, Khartoum, 1972, 55-61. A full English translation is included with al-Naqar's PhD thesis at the University of London (O. el-Nager, *West Africa and the Muslim pilgrimage*, 1969); regrettably, this translation has never been published.

The demographic cost of the pilgrimage could be unacceptably high, not so much to the pilgrim himself, as to those who were depending upon his special services at home. Yet not everyone would go at once; and, though many might not return, some would. Mahdism—the apocalyptic expectancy that the end of the world, heralded by the *mahdi*, was imminent—changed this. If the *madhi* appeared in the East, everyone should go to him, and no one would expect to return. In the second half of the nineteenth century the Sokoto authorities intervened several times to control Mahdism, which threatened not only unrest within the caliphate but also population haemorrhage towards the east.[13] And it is, it seems manifest, for fear of sparking off a massive mahdist exodus that, in the nearly two centuries since the sultanate was established—the largest, most secure, wealthiest, most devout Muslim state in black Africa—no ruler of Sokoto has yet been on *hajj*.

Nachtigal's *Sahara and Sudan* provides a particularly clear instance of pilgrimage-related anxiety, from the 1850s. A huge pilgrimage caravan from further west passed through Borno, emptying villages and depopulating whole regions as people flocked to join it. Lamino, with his own intimate experience of population flows, suggested that discreet arrangements be made for the holy man leading the caravan (who may have seemed to some as the *mahdi* himself) secretly to disappear. Shaykh Umar, the pious ruler of Borno, scandalised at this suggestion, refused to sanction any such act. The caravan moved on towards Bagirmi. Borno, a huge sprawling empire teeming with immigrants of every kind, voluntary and involuntary, might be able to write off demographic losses on the scale which it had just suffered. Bagirmi, a small state, could not. The ruler of Bagirmi, a serious Muslim, negotiated with the pilgrims, he begged them to go round, bypassing his territory, he offered them gifts. The pilgrims were adamant: they would march through Bagirmi. It came to war: a Muslim king fighting against a pilgrimage caravan leader. The royal troops had no stomach for such an unholy fight: they were defeated, the king was killed. But by now the pilgrimage caravan was far too

---

[13] See, for example, R. A. Adeleye, *Power and diplomacy in northern Nigeria 1804-1906*, London 1971, 103-9.

large. Discipline, having increased in harsh severity, disintegrated; supplies and logistics became impossible; the leader himself was slain. The whole enterprise broke up in disorder and disaster. Many pilgrims were reduced to slavery, or killed; others returned home destitute.[14]

A remarkable parallel emerges from the material which we have just been examining. Lovejoy describes all manner of violent measures adopted in Sokoto to prevent slaves from running away. He argues that this shows how important the property nexus was: and so it was indeed, in a measure. But we have also seen somewhat similar measures, including violence (admittedly, in extreme situations), taken to prevent pilgrims from leaving. Pilgrims were not by any stretch of the imagination property: they were demographic resources, albeit of a particular, and often highly valued, kind. Slaves too were demographic resources—again of a particular, different kind.

The comparison might be carried further. Just as one man's runaway slave might be another's volunteer immigrant, so was the pilgrim a volunteer immigrant, wherever he or she might choose to stop along the way.[15] The frustrated Timbuktu cleric had intended to settle with his family in Medina: the pilgrims from Mali, who crossed their Red Sea in order to escape, never got to Mecca even so, being spiritually hi-jacked—very gently, of course, but effectively—further along the way, chiefly in Kano.[16] In a somewhat similar way, some of those who began their journeying as refugees, ended it as the founding fathers of a new society. The same unit which figures as a debit entry

[14] III, 418-21; see also Sherif ed-Din in the index of that volume.—Another instance of a local, seriously Muslim, state acting to bar the road to a pilgrimage caravan occurred in 1900, when the ruler of Darfur refused to grant rights of passage to a major Sanusi party *en route* for Mecca (A. B. Theobald, *Ali Dinar: last sultan of Darfur: 1898-1916*, Longmans, London 1965, 58-9). It may be, however, that the sultan's reservations stemmed more from the prospect of religio-political repercussions within Darfur, than of non-sustainable emigration as his subjects flocked to join the Sanusi party.

[15] For an interesting recent study of Hausa pilgrims in particular, and of their settled lives in the Republic of Sudan midway between home and Mecca, see C. Bawa Yamba, *Permanent pilgrims: the role of pilgrimage in the lives of West African Muslims in Sudan*, Edinburgh 1995.

[16] Al-Hajj, 1968, pp. 10-14.

in the demographic accounts of the sending (or losing) society, comes to safe lodging on the credit side of the corresponding accounts of his or her new hosts.

What binds all this material together, from slaves to pilgrims, from utterly forced mobility to free choice, with innumerable gradations between the two poles, is, I suggest, the fundamental scarcity of people.

The Islamic factor

'Be kind to those you possess [these might be animals and/or slaves], and do not demand of them work beyond their capacity.' (Ibn Abi Zayd al-Qayrawani, *La Risâla: ou épître sur les éléments du dogme et de la loi de l'Islâm selon le rite mâlikite*, L. Bercher, ed. & tr., Algiers 1945, reprinted 1949, 323.)

We have seen how admirably suited are Muslim doctrine and practice, what excellent 'effective means' they provide, for the non-violent stimulation of population mobility. But at the same time enforced, imposed mobility—particularly through slavery, for the immediate purpose of this book—is by no means excluded. Slavery is very closely woven into the fabric of Islamic religion and society. This is clear in the Quran, in the *sunnah* or traditions of the Prophet, and in the religious law or *shari'ah* which has been built up chiefly upon these two foundations. Two legal texts are of especial importance in this present study, since both have been most highly esteemed in west and central Muslim black Africa: the *Risala* of Ibn Abi Zayd from the tenth century, and the *Mukhtasar* of Khalil bin Ishaq from the fourteenth. These are standard works of the Maliki school of law, which predominates in north and west Africa, and in Upper Egypt. Details from these two books—some of which details are cited immediately below—will give some indication of the ubiquitous presence of slavery in the religious law. Other such details are cited here and there, at relevant points throughout this work. All these details are by no means rare curiosities of the law: they are representative of some of the central portions of constantly used texts. But, while the details cited are not rarities, neither, taken all together, do they make up a complete picture of Muslim Maliki law relating to slaves. For the most part, only legal points having direct relevance to the African material here are cited.

To slaves as slaves, as a separate topic requiring specific and extensive attention, a chapter to themselves, the two texts do not allocate much space. The quotation from Ibn Abi Zayd, at the opening of this section, barely two lines, satisfies the tenth-century author by way of general overview. The incidental references to slaves, on the other hand, are practically innumerable. In some cases, for example in the relationship of emancipation to inheritance and wills, slaves figure largely; in others, they may receive only passing mention. Yet at almost every point some special provision has to be made for them, since the law for slaves is so often slightly different from that relating to free people. The fifty oaths for homicide do not apply in the case of a slave;[17] may the trustee marry the female slaves in an orphan's estate?[18] if slaves are promised liberation on their master's death, is this set against the whole patrimony, or only against that third of it which is properly at the disposal of the testator?[19] The evidence of a slave is not admissible in court, but his confession, in cases not touching his master's property, may be;[20] the legal penalties inflicted on slaves differ somewhat from those which free persons suffer (and are, at first glance surprisingly, in some cases lighter); and so on.[21]

In some respects the position of the slave, acknowledged at so many points, and with special provision, albeit of inferior status, made for him, or her, resembles the position of the tolerated non-Muslim. Calumnious imputation of fornication against a slave or a non-Muslim does not entail the legal penalty of 80 strokes with the whip, which would punish such a slander against a free Muslim.[22] A free Muslim is not killed

[17] Ibn Abi Zayd, 242.
[18] ibid., 272.
[19] ibid., 220-2.
[20] ibid., 258, 262.
[21] ibid., 252-4. Illustrations of this kind of thing may be found in African practice: for certain misdemeanours, for instance, free Tuareg are fined domestic animals, while slaves—on the order of the senior chief, or *amenokal*, for it is rare for a slave to be so punished by his own master—may be flogged (J. and I. Nicolaisen, *The pastoral Tuareg: ecology, culture, and society*, London 1997, II, 600-1).
[22] Ibn Abi Zayd, 256.

for murdering a slave or a non-Muslim, though the same offence in the opposite direction means, in either case, death; the *lex talionis* does not apply between free and slave, or between Muslim and infidel.[23] Neither a woman, a slave, nor a non-Muslim, is able to give away in marriage a Muslim woman.[24] And just as a slave does not inherit (presumably from anyone, though Ibn Abi Zayd does not spell this out here), so a non-Muslim may not inherit from a Muslim, or *vice versa.*[25]

Just as slavery is deeply ingrained in historical, mainstream Islam, so there is evidence that it has been significant from the earliest days of Islam in black Africa. Two examples, from Hausaland, may serve here as introductory illustrations. One origins legend of the Hausa states says that these derived from the first founder's six children, each of whom received special gifts: Kano and Rano were dyers and weavers, Katsina and Daura were traders, and Zaria and Bauchi were slave-dealers.[26] And again, in the traditional spirit, or *bori,* possession dances of the Hausa—which are often regarded with suspicion by stricter Muslims—there is represented one character called Son Bawa, the desirer of a slave, who walks about weeping, looking for a slave, and calling upon other spirits for help.[27]

It is clear from such references as these, and from various others throughout this study, that slavery was part of the Muslim context in black Africa from the earliest arrival of the new faith there. It is less easy to see just how far slavery, in any precisely recognisable form, pre-dated Islam in black Africa. The brief discussion below on 'Pagan slavery' shows that there was a *non-*Muslim phenomenon; but was this in any absolute sense also *pre-*Muslim?

Certainly there was overlap and intermingling, in slave

---

[23] Ibn Abi Zayd, 248; whoever kills a slave owes his estimated value to the slave's owner (250).

[24] *ibid.,* 180.

[25] *ibid.,* 280. A non-Muslim slave suffers a further disability: he may not be freed as legal expiation for those offences for which his owner may atone by freeing a Muslim slave (*ibid.,* 228). Neither may a blind slave, nor one promised his freedom after his master's death, nor a slave who has had a hand amputated or has suffered other mutilation.

[26] A. J. N. Tremearne, *Hausa superstitions and customs,* London 1913, 141; his collection of Hausa stories is full of incidental references to slaves.

[27] *ibid.,* 536.

matters as in many other respects, making it difficult in some cases to draw a sharp line between local survivals and Muslim imports. Let us look again at the matter, mentioned just above, of inheritance. Slaves, according to the clear teaching of the *shari'ah*, do not inherit. This disability seems to have been generally true of slaves in Muslim black Africa; in Borno, for example, it was proverbial that slaves do not inherit property.[28] However, one observer, noting the same situation among the Tuareg, has attributed it not to Muslim law but rather to Tuareg traditional inheritance practice. Among the Tuareg, parents stand first in the line of inheritance from their children; slave owners are usually in the position of parents to their slaves; and, as a slave always has a master, so the property of any slave dying will pass to his master, *in loco parentis*, not to the slave's own children.[29]

Such a situation, in which local custom, perhaps even older than Islam itself in black Africa, and the more recently arrived *shari'ah* are mingled, has many precedents, even in Arabia at the time of the Prophet. The newly revealed Muslim law then was rooted in Arab custom, which custom however was being subjected to considerable change under the new dispensation: in the matter of slaves, the new law, for example, attempted to raise their moral status.[30]

That the institution of slavery, in one form or another, may have had deep roots in many parts of black Africa well before Islam became a significant social influence in this or that locality there—and that even in thoroughly Islamised black African regions there were many pre- or non-Islamic survivals, demonstrate how misleading it would be to suggest a hard-and-fast distinction between Muslim and traditional slavery. Nevertheless, the general pattern of slavery in the Muslim countries of black Africa, including those through which Nachtigal travelled, can fairly easily be recognised as different from that in areas unaffected by Islam. This present book is primarily concerned with Muslim masters and Pagan[31] or

---

[28] P. A. Benton, *Primer of Kanuri grammar*, London 1917, 105-6.
[29] Nicolaisen, 1997, II, 604.
[30] M. Khadduri, *War and peace in the law of Islam*, Baltimore 1955, 130.
[31] The word 'Pagan' is used for convenience, being shorter than 'traditional African religious' and more precise than 'non-Muslim'. The term

Muslim slaves. And, since Muslim law is quite specific in defining slavery, however lax administration may sometimes have been, we are spared the difficulties which arise when such an institution is found in an exclusively traditional society, of deciding whether it should be called slavery, or serfdom, or even the extended family, or whatever. How happily or unhappily slavery worked out in Muslim black Africa, this volume attempts to give some indication.

The enslavement of Muslims

'I was left behind among the remainder, the liars...whose purpose is...the collecting of concubines, and fine clothes....They showed the dissimulation of wicked people...and of *the sellers of free men in the market*. Some of them posing as *qadis*, in the clothing of foxes!' (Abdullah ibn Muhammad [Abdullahi dan Fodio, brother of Usuman dan Fodio], *Tazyin al-waraqat*, ed. and tr. M. Hiskett, Ibadan 1963, 121-2—my italics first).

No matter how well equipped Muslim society was, particularly though not exclusively through its religion, to draw people in, in a pattern of peaceful population mobility, we shall see in detail throughout this book, with what rigorous severity, ofttimes with what whips and scorpions, some elements of the Muslim community in black Africa pursued also the pathway of enforced population mobility, the mobility of slavery.

The prominence of slavery in all this is a destabilising force. Amid the tumult and the shouting of slaving, the wrong people may be enslaved, just as NATO rockets sometimes struck the wrong targets in Yugoslavia. Even when the victims are properly, in the eyes of the *shari'ah*, enslaved, many will become Muslim, blurring the distinction between slave and free by making both co-religionists. Throughout the millennium just ending, there have been millions of slaves within the black African Muslim community, people who have been born slaves, or who have converted *after* enslavement, for conversion does not necessarily lead to emancipation.

---

* does not, of course, imply a unity among Pagan peoples and beliefs corresponding to that among Muslims; nor is any derogatory connotation intended in the least.

Problems of determining whether an individual, or maybe a group of captives such as King Ali of Wadai's thousands of prisoners brought from the defeated nation of Bagirmi (see below, pp. 54-7, 136-7), or a whole tribe or nation, are slave or free, or, if not slaves, are they enslavable or not, such problems as these can be intractable.

The lynchpin, the lighthouse amid this sea of troubles, should be the fundamental rule, that no free Muslim can be made into a slave. This ruling ring-fences the Muslim community within black Africa: none of its free members may be enslaved. In the sole work known to have survived from al-Hajj Jibril, Usuman dan Fodio's most respected teacher, the selling of free men ranks with adultery, wine drinking and manslaughter, among the things which 'our people' forbid.[32] How significant in fact in black African history has this concept been, no enslavement of a free Muslim? Does the lighthouse always work? Barth had some justification for his view in 1857 that the Anti-Slavery Society in London was over-optimistic in believing Muslims to be adequately protected by their faith against the risk of being enslaved.[33] Nevertheless, even if the protection enjoyed by a Muslim were sometimes, perhaps often, limited and uncertain, historical incidents do show that local conduct could be influenced by scruples about enslaving fellow-Muslims. Here are some examples, ranging over several centuries.

It was noted as a sign of virtue in Askiya Muhammad I of the Songhay empire in the early sixteenth century that he liberated from slavery those who could prove their right to freedom.[34] Sultan Alooma of Borno released Muslim prisoners of free status after an expedition to Kanem in 1572-3.[35]

---

[32] A. D. H. Bivar and M. Hiskett, 'The Arabic literature of Nigeria to 1804', *Bull. School of Oriental and African Studies*, 1962, 143.

[33] H. Barth, *Travels and discoveries in north and central Africa*, 3 vols., New York 1857-9, reprinted London 1965, I, 553.

[34] Mahmud Kati ibn al-Hajj al-Mutawakkil Kati, *Tarikh el-Fettach*, eds. and trs. O. Houdas and M. Delafosse, Paris 1913-14, reprinted 1964, 115.

[35] Ibn Fartua in H. R. Palmer, *Sudanese memoirs, being mainly translations of a number of Arabic manuscripts relating to the central and western Sudan*, Lagos 1928, reprinted Cass, London 1967, I, 36; For the date see p. 14. J.-C. Froelich, *Les Musulmans d'Afrique noire*, Paris 1962, 50, adds that the release of the

After an internal quarrel in Timbuktu in 1730 had ended in violence, the victorious general allowed free women to return to their families.[36] Bello, the son and successor of Usuman dan Fodio creator of the Sokoto *jihad* at the beginning of the nineteenth century, after defeating the rebel Abd al-Salam's supporters, released those who knew the *fatiha* (the short opening chapter of the Quran, comparable to the Lord's Prayer of Christians) and the ritual of ablution, enslaving the rest.[37] When a combined Arab, Borno, and Mandara slave-raid was proposed in 1823 the sultan of Mandara havered, saying that the Pagan tribes round about were all converting without force.[38] In the same year al-Kanemi, a pious Muslim who saved (Muslim) Borno from (Muslim) Fulani attacks in the early nineteenth century, released prisoners taken on an expedition against a rebel cleric, 'a *fighi* of great power', not wishing, as he said, to make slaves of the wives and children of Muslims.[39] Nachtigal, who thought that some of the near-Muslim tribes in Borku got a raw deal from raiders who were no better Muslims than they were, believed that the 'exhaustive discussions' which he had with the king of Wadai on behalf of the Borku people were not without effect.[40] Nachtigal was himself with the Awlad Sulayman, renowned (or notorious) nomadic Arab warriors, in June 1871, when a raid into Ennedi was planned by them to fill in the time while they were waiting

---

prisoners occurred because Alooma, very scrupulous, did not regard this particular campaign canonically as holy war. Froelich does not give a specific source for this detail; and in any case the simple fact of *jihad* does not legitimate the enslavement of free Muslims. Astonishingly, Froelich goes on to say that Alooma 'showed himself humane and generous even towards the Pagans'. Please read this rather blood-curdling chronicle.

[36] *Tedzkiret en-Nisian*, tr O. Houdas, Paris 1913-4, reprinted 1966, 209.
[37] Haj Said, *Histoire du Sokoto* (attched to *Tedzkiret en-Nisian*), 313.
[38] Bovill, *Missions*, III, 334.
[39] *ibid.*, III, 359 and 374. The rebels had at one point been accused of 'kaffering, and not saying their prayers! the dogs'—*i.e.* of having apostasised, but as hundreds of captured women and children were brought in, al-Kanemi seems to have reconsidered. He was the father of Shaykh Umar, Nachtigal's principal patron.
[40] II, 421. 'All Borku people are Muhammadans, whatever the neighbouring tribes, who by alleging their Paganism seek a further excuse for their hateful and cruel persecution, might maintain.'

for the date harvest. The raid was a failure, and among the raiders whom the Awlad Sulayman left behind, prisoners in the hands of the enemy, was a neighbour of Nachtigal's, a *murabid*, a cleric or holy man. After a few days, however, and quite unexpectedly, this man, because of his religious status, was allowed to return on the mere promise of a ransom, the amount of which was left undetermined, to be paid later.[41]

In almost every case, however, an alternative explanation of the privileges of Muslim captives is possible. Askiya Muhammad I, a usurper seeking Muslim support, was anxious to curry clerical favour. The people of Kanem were kin to Alooma's Borno, and Alooma's principles did not protect the people of Kano, Muslim but not kinsmen, against whom Alooma also warred. Quarrels within Timbuktu were almost family affairs. Abd al-Salam, an early and prominent supporter of Usuman dan Fodio, clearly merited some special handling despite his subsequent rebellion. Mandara and Borno were probably trying to manipulate the 1823 raid for their own anti-Fulani political purposes. Al-Kanemi may have had some hesitation about crossing too harshly a cleric, even a rebellious cleric, whose supernatural powers were notorious (a consideration which may have contributed also to the return of the unransomed *murabid*). And any influence that Nachtigal may have had over the king of Wadai cannot be interpreted as purely Islamic.

In some instances scruples about enslaving members of a particular group appear to have had a tribal or ethnic basis, which might or might not correspond with the general distinction between Muslim and Pagan—for example Alooma's Kanem wars, just mentioned. A European slave-trader on the West African coast in the nineteenth century was told by a prince of Futa Jallon (now a part of modern Guinea) that Muslim courts there rescued Muslims from slavery, for the Fulani of that country detested the institution among themselves and among members of 'their caste', by which may have been meant a religious or an ethnic category; the same courts inflicted, for even the slightest offences, enslavement, as right

---

[41] II, 377-8; see also below, p. 79.

and reputable, upon non-Muslims.[42] Of the Fulani on the Gambia in the eighteenth century it was said:

> As their Humanity extends to all, they are doubly kind to People of their own Race, insomuch that if they know of one of them being made a Slave, all the Pholeys [Fulani] will redeem him.[43]

The writer, Francis Moore, thought that all the Fulani were strict Muslims, but this seems unlikely as there were still Pagan Fulani on the Gambia in the twentieth century. The Budduma of Lake Chad observed the unwritten understanding that no Kotoko, Arab or Fulani might be enslaved, but the Kanuri, also Muslims, were not exempt from Budduma raids.[44]

There are, moreover, numerous references explicitly to the enslavement of Muslims. In 1391-2 a letter came to Cairo from the ruler of Borno, complaining that Arab tribes from the east were enslaving free Borno Muslims, keeping some, selling others to Egypt, Syria and elsewhere. The letter pleaded for help to secure the release of those wrongfully traded eastwards: 'restore them to their freedom and Islam'.[45] Sonni Ali, ruler of Songhay in the later fifteenth century, though a

---

[42] T. Canot, *Adventures of an African slaver: being a true account of the life of Captain Theodore Canot...his own story as told in the year 1854 to Brantz Mayer...*, London 1928, 95-6. Canot gives another example of differential punishment: goods in the possession of an absconding debtor may be sequestrated to pay his creditors, 'but if their value is not equal to the debt, the delinquent, if a pagan, is sold as a slave, but is let off with a *bastinado* if he proves to be one of the faithful' (93).

[43] Francis Moore, *Travels into the inland parts of Africa...* London 1738, 32-3.

[44] Olive MacLeod, *Chiefs and cities of central Africa*, Edinburgh and London 1912, 227-8.

[45] N. Levtzion and J.F.P. Hopkins, eds, *Corpus of early Arabic sources for West African history*, Cambridge 1981, 347-8. Early in the nineteenth century, Muhammad Bello wrote to the two Holy Cities, and to the people of the east, justifying the Fulani *jihad* in northern Nigeria, and ending with these words: 'We also inform you that all those captured by the enemy from among the communities that followed us, and who were sold to the merchants who sold them to you, are free Muslims whose enslavement is forbidden. You are to do your utmost to rescue their necks from bondage.' (Umar al-Naqar, 1972, 142) Over 400 years between the two letters, but the final message is unchanged.

THE ENSLAVEMENT OF MUSLIMS

Muslim of some sort himself, sometimes took free Muslims and gave them as slaves, adding insult to injury by pretending thus to bestow pious alms on illustrious local clerics: the more upright married their gifts, the more pliable accepted them as concubines.[46] Between Askiya Muhammad I, usurping successor to Sonni Ali, and a Muslim cleric there had been an agreement that the cleric's descendants should not be sold, but the chronicler Kati saw great numbers of them offered in the Timbuktu market despite their protestations.[47]

Mansur, pasha of Timbuktu, before attacking Deba, a Pagan town, in the early eighteenth century, observed the strict rules, first sending a messenger to offer the peaceful alternatives of conversion or taxation. The inhabitants agreed, submitting to the authority of God and the pasha; but a warlike officer of the pasha, unwilling to lose the opportunity for a raid, intercepted the messenger, and persuaded him to report a contrary answer. Deba was then attacked, the men killed, the children enslaved, and of the women some were killed and some enslaved. The town became a desert. Despite the patent irregularity of these proceedings, Kati felt no embarrassment in quoting, for an illustrative parallel, the Quranic verse (1xix.7) describing the fate of some who ventured to deny God's prophets: 'and as for Ad, they were destroyed by a fierce roaring wind.'[48] In the seventeenth and eighteenth centuries, raid and counter-raid between Timbuktu and the Tuaregs led to the enslavement of Muslim prisoners by both sides.[49]

In the early years of the nineteenth century, Abdullahi, brother of Usuman dan Fodio, charged some of his colleagues with (among a great many other misdeeds) 'selling free men in the market'; a fragment of this colourful denunciation is quoted at the opening of this section (see above, p. 18). The combined expedition of 1823 (see above, pp. 20 and 21) wound up in an attack on a Muslim Fulani town, Musfeia, in which the assailants were thrashed and Denham nearly lost his life. Denham noted that, had the fortunes of battle swung the other way, while the Muslim Fulani could not have been enslaved,

[46] Kati, 84; al-Sadi, 109-10.
[47] Kati, 139-42; see also 15 note.
[48] *Tedzkiret*, 35-9.
[49] *ibid.*, 9-10, 11, 142.

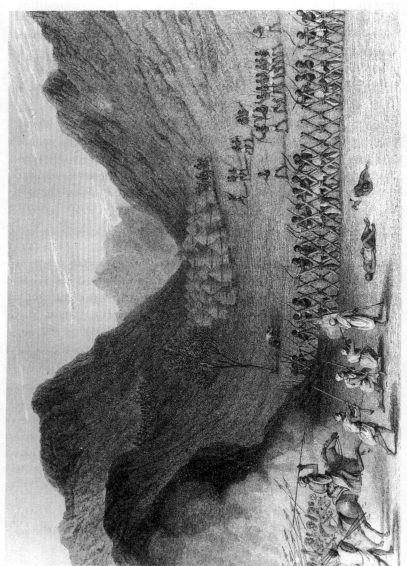

The attack on Musfeia, 1823. Bovill, *Missions*, III, facing p. 339.

their male and female slaves could have been appropriated, and the Arabs might have been rewarded for their help against the Fulani by being allowed to raid some local Pagans.[50] (It was a slave of the Arab leader who restored to Denham his horse, and also rescued the flag of the pasha of Tripoli from the stricken field.)[51] Barth found that in the borderlands between the Fulani and Borno it was hard even to get guides, so risky had it become for anyone to venture outside his own town.[52] Bokari, the rebel governor of Hadeija, which was technically a part of the Sokoto empire, devastated the country to the gates of Kano, and thousands of slaves, Muslim and Pagan, passed to dealers through his hands.[53] Hausa traders in Adamawa handled, among other slaves, some Fulani sold to them by Pagan raiders.[54] After his accession, Zubayr, emir of Adamawa 1890-1901, failed in an attack on an outlying district to secure slaves which might be sent to Sokoto in exchange for his robe of office. When he came home he found the collector from Sokoto, to whom on such an occasion he might have to surrender all the fruits of his foray, waiting for the slaves; he then took the people of Fali, near the capital of Adamawa, both free men and clerics, and gave them to the collector. A month later he followed the collector to Sokoto and received investiture and a flag.[55] At the end of the nineteenth century the emirs of Kontagora were enslaving Zaria Muslims.[56] The reign of Umaru, fourth emir of Bauchi, culminated in 1900 in a massacre in the town of Gworam, which

[50] Bovill, *Missions*, III, 344-53.
[51] Clapperton, 1829, 194.
[52] Barth, 1965, I, 548, 549-51.
[53] *ibid.*, I, 543-5.
[54] P.-F. Lacroix, 'Matériaux pour servir à l'histoire des Peul de l'Adamawa', *Études camérounaises*, 1952, 34.
[55] R. M. East, *Stories of old Adamawa*, Zaria 1934, reprinted 1967, 91ff. For a later instance of Zubayr again sending slaves to Sokoto, see below, p. 297, but on p. 308 Zubayr is momentarily indignant when he is himself offered, by one of his own subordinates, some wrongfully enslaved victims.
[56] M. G. Smith, 'Historical and cultural conditions of political corruption among the Hausa', *Comparative studies in society and history*, 1964 (hereafter M. G. Smith, 1964 A), 177.

had resisted a slave levy on its Muslim population.[57] As late as 1915 Ali Dinar, ruler of Darfur, accused the Muslim Kababish tribe of selling as slaves free Muslims, refugees from the French in Wadai.[58]

Baba of Karo, the Hausa woman who in 1949-50, at about the age of 60, told the story of her life to Mary Smith, recalled then the days of her youth: 'there was always fear; war, war, war—they caught a man and they made him a slave, or else they killed him'. She remembered that, before the British came and 'the world was settled', even Muslim clerics 'dared not travel freely, they would be kidnapped and sold in the market'. Baba gave not the slightest hint of any assured protection on which Muslims might rely against these risks.[59] Even more recently, similar memories live on here and there: in Segu, a local family was still being derided because the father was enslaved while on pilgrimage; and in Ibadan the story was told of Malam Harun who set out for Mecca with some of his students, only to have the party broken up near Lake Chad, some of the students being killed and their teacher falling into slavery.[60]

Some of this maltreatment of Muslims arose from an aggressive disregard of the requirements of religious law. Such action, however, sometimes aroused serious qualms of conscience. A good deal of discussion has been reported of the implications of the curse of Ham, Genesis ix. 20-7, which might appear to condemn to slavery the descendants of Ham, identified with the blacks.[61] Might this not, some were inclined to ask, be regarded as overruling the general prohibition of the enslavement of Muslims? This question was discussed at length early in the seventeenth century by Ahmad Baba, a scholar of Timbuktu of a Berber family, and to whom an enquiry had come from Tuat about the propriety of enslaving black Muslims, as was apparently happening frequently as a

[57] S. J. Hogben and A. H. M. Kirk-Greene, *The emirates of northern Nigeria*, London 1966, 462.
[58] Theobald, 1965, 144-5.
[59] Mary Smith, 1954/1981, 47, 132.
[60] el-Nager, 1969, 334n.
[61] See, for example, Willis, 1985, I, chapter 4 and other 'Hamitic hypothesis' references in the index.

result of war amongst the Muslim rulers of the states in the western Sudan. Ahmad Baba's petitioners explained that there was sometimes difficulty in distinguishing between Muslim and Pagan prisoners of war, who differed from each other in no respect save in their religion. Ahmad Baba had no doubt that a black African who had voluntarily embraced Islam should not later in any circumstances be enslaved. 'The reason for enslavement,' he said, 'is unbelief. The position of unbelieving Negroes is the same as that of other unbelievers, Christians, Jews, Persians, Turks, etc.' For this reason he firmly rejected the view that the curse of Ham could be regarded as justifying the enslavement of Muslim Negroes. 'On the contrary, any unbeliever, if he persists in his original unbelief, may be made a slave, whether he is descended from Ham or not. In this respect there is no difference between the races.' Conversion after enslavement arising from unbelief does not affect the continuation of possession in any way.[62]

The fact that these questions were raised at all and were then so seriously discussed indicates clearly enough that the practice of slave traders and of those who purchased slaves often diverged from the strict principles of the law.[63] Both Usuman dan Fodio and his son Muhammad Bello, in the Sokoto empire some 300 years later, cited Ahmad Baba respectfully though not slavishly as they examined the same and similar problems.

Usuman and his son were perhaps more meticulous than western scholars of our days in deciphering Ahmad Baba's message for modern times. A recent UNESCO publication, referring to Ahmad Baba, claims that it is

> a crime for a Muslim to buy a Muslim. Slavery, he goes on

[62] G. Rotter, *Die Stellung des Negers in der islamischarabischen Gesellschaft bis zum XVI. Jahrhundert*, Bonn 1967, 49-52; Bivar and Hiskett, 1962, 111. There is a not altogether satisfactory translation of Baba's principal treatise on slavery, with skimpy annotation, in Willis, 1985, I, chapter 7. For a more up-to-date and admirably painstaking discussion, see J. O. Hunwick, 'Islamic law and polemics over race and slavery in north and west Africa (16th-19th century)', in Shaun E. Marmon, ed., *Slavery in the Islamic Middle East*, Princeton 1999, 43-68.

[63] See also J. O. Hunwick's much earlier paper, 'A new source for the biography of Ahmad Baba al-Tinbukti (1556-1627)', *Bull. School of Oriental and African Studies*, 1964, 588n.

to say, is admissible in the context of the Holy War if the slaves are non-Muslim, but the forms must be respected. First, pagans must be called upon to embrace the Muslim religion. If they refuse, they have the option of paying capitation, in exchange for which they are allowed to keep their religion. Only if they refuse to comply with either of these alternatives can they be taken as slaves.[64]

It was however certainly not a crime for a Muslim to buy or sell a Muslim. Ahmad Baba is speaking specifically and exclusively of originally free Muslims, wrongfully enslaved: to buy and sell these was indeed forbidden. He is not concerned with non-Muslims captured in wars other than holy wars, or without the offer of the three options. The omission of these procedures—and, as will become clear throughout the present volume, they were almost always omitted in black Africa—might be regrettable, but it did not affect the legal status, as slaves, of the captives.

Hugh Thomas, in 1997, citing this UNESCO publication, goes further. He identifies Ahmad Baba incorrectly as an ex-slave. He too focusses on all Muslim slaves going north, not distinguishing between those legally and those illegally held.

> Ahmad Baba then wrote a study concluding that slavery was certainly permissible if the slaves were captured in a just war, but all captives had to asked before being enslaved whether they would accept Islam. If they did they should be freed.[65]

This is fantasy. Thomas, however, cannot resist a sarcastic comparison: 'A free man, therefore, might just have supposed in 1620 that Islam was a more tolerant faith than Christianity.'

Even for those who were fully persuaded by such arguments as were adduced by Ahmad Baba, the definition of a Muslim 'in good standing' might present delicate problems to pious believers confronted by others who professed to be Muslims but who in the practice of their religion were found to be deplorably lax. Amongst the categories against whom *jihad*—

---

[64] I. B. Kake, 'The slave trade and the population drain from Black Africa to North Africa and the Middle East', in *The African slave trade from the fifteenth to the nineteenth century*, UNESCO 1979, vol. 2 of *Studies and documents* of *The general history of Africa*, 165.

[65] Thomas, 1997, 149.

leading often to enslavement—might legally be waged some were quite clear, such as Jews and Christians, or polytheists, but others were more or less dependent upon definition, including apostates, deserters, highway robbers, and those who cause dissension.[66] To what extent did lapses from the true faith deprive a nominal Muslim of the immunity against slave-raiding which the *shari'ah* appeared to confer upon him—and make it legitimate, perhaps even obligatory, to launch a *jihad* against him? Heresy or apostasy might be regarded as an even more heinous offence than Pagan unbelief, for the example of a heretic might lead ignorant Muslims astray. Usuman dan Fodio considered the problem carefully, implicitly at least with special reference to the west African situation, and decided that in most cases the punishment meted out to erring Muslims must stop short of enslavement. Even he, however, admitted it under certain circumstances for apostates (*jama'at al-murtaddin*),[67] and if this doctrine were accepted there would be an obvious temptation to impute apostasy to anyone whom, for quite other reasons, one might wish to attack. Denham thought that any people against whom war was intended was stigmatised, almost as a matter of routine, as being guilty of apostasy—kaffering, he called it.[68]

Whether enslaved originally by Pagans or by other Muslims, or enslaved as Pagans and subsequently converted, Muslim slaves frequently turned up in export markets. They were, for example, passing through lower Dahomey in the early eighteenth century.[69] Many domestic slaves in eighteenth-century St Louis and Goree were Muslim.[70] In Borgu, Hausa Muslim slaves were

[66] Khadduri, 1955, 74 ff.

[67] A. D. H. Bivar, 'A manifesto of the Fulani jihad', *Journal of African history*, 1961, 241. For a fascinating discussion of the definition of a true Muslim, with the text and translation of a crucial local source c. 1500, see J. O. Hunwick, *Shari'a in Songhay: the replies of al-Maghili to the questions of Askia al-Hajj Muhammad*, Oxford 1985; not centrally focussed on slavery, but with interesting slavery details, many more than appear in the index.

[68] Bovill, *Missions*, III, 359 (see above, p. 20, note 39).

[69] Paul Marty, *Etudes sur l'Islam au Dahomey*, Paris 1926, 11.

[70] J. D. Hargreaves, *Prelude to the partition of west Africa*, London 1963, 180-1. Hargreaves, with the Atlantic trade dominating his slavery horizon, and noting the persistence of vast inland slaving operations as late as the 1870s, remarked that 'slaves were still a highly marketable commodity in

allowed freedom of worship.⁷¹ In Yorubaland, near the Atlantic coast, Clapperton received an account of the local Paganism from a Borno Muslim slave.⁷² An eighteenth-century report mentioned that among the slaves in a slave-yard on the Sierra Leonean coast was 'a Mahometan [who] could read and write Arabick', who had been put in irons for the first time the day before; an American slave captain told of the loss of another Muslim slave who, in despair at his enslavement, had died by 'the sulks', despite beating and being offered the tastiest meals available.⁷³ In Bahia in Brazil there were large numbers of Muslim slaves, many of whom were able to read and write Arabic, and who engaged in proselytizing activity among other slaves who had come to Bahia earlier.⁷⁴ Certain peoples, such as Mandingoes and Fulani, who were in Africa mainly Muslim, commanded higher prices from slave traders on the Liberian coast than the average slave; Mandingoes were much in demand in Cuba as the smartest type of domestic servant.⁷⁵ Some slaves rescued by the British and sent to Freetown were Muslims, including even Fulani who had fallen prey to their intended victims on slave-raids which did not go according to plan.⁷⁶

---

the Sudan, especially for the Saharan trade' (245), apparently overlooking the vast domestic market within black Africa.

⁷¹ Clapperton, 1829, 74.

⁷² *ibid.*, 51.

⁷³ C. P. Wadstrom, *An essay on colonization...*, London, Part 2, 1795, reprinted 1968, 83.

⁷⁴ P. Verger, *Trade relations between the Bight of Benin and Bahia from the 17th to 19th century*, Ibadan 1976, 327-8; first published 1968, in French. *Cf.* V. Monteil, 'Analyse des 25 documents arabes des Males de Bahia (1835)', and R. Reichert, 'L'insurrection d'esclaves de 1835 à la lumiere des documents arabes des Archives publiques de l'Etat de Bahia (Brésil),' both in *Bull. Institut fondamental d'Afrique noire*, series B, Jan.-Apr. 1967, 88 ff. Also R. K. Kent, 'Palmares: an African state in Brazil', *Journal of African history*, 1965, 161-76.

⁷⁵ Sir Harry Johnston, *Liberia*, London 1906, I, 174.

⁷⁶ P. E. H. Hair, 'The enslavement of Koelle's informants', *Journal of African history*, 1965, 197; S. W. Koelle, *Polyglotta Africana*, London 1854, reprinted 1963, 18. For a somewhat speculative argument that the enslavement of free Muslims may have been a significant stimulus to the rise of Usuman dan Fodio and to the outbreak of the Fulani *jihad* early in the nineteenth century, see my 'A Muslim William Wilberforce? the Sokoto jihad as anti-slavery crusade: an enquiry into historical causes' in S. Daget, ed., *De la traite à l'esclavage. Actes du Colloque International sur la traite des noirs:*

There were also large numbers of Muslim slaves in the Mediterranean area, usually taken through direct action by Christians. Malta was a centre for harrying the shipping of Tunis and Tripoli, and there are estimated to have been 10,000 Muslim slaves on the island in 1720.[77] These, being allowed considerable freedom, were able to meet together for prayers. In 1749 an alleged slave plot in Malta led to trials, followed by torture and executions.[78]

Nachtigal recorded several episodes which illustrated the uncertainty of the protection which their faith conferred upon Muslims in black Africa, as well as the confusion which sometimes arose in distinguishing between slave and free man,[79] or between the slave and the Muslim prisoner of war not yet exchanged or ransomed. In Tibesti, the fact that a man was a Muslim was not a decisive reason for not wanting to make a slave of him. The case of Sa'ad, one of Nachtigal's original servants, is mentioned just below (p. 38). Also in Tibesti an effort was made to kidnap another of Nachtigal's servants, indubitably a free man and a Muslim, on the ground that he was really a slave of the kidnapper's father.[80] And this in the presence of two other members of the travelling party, who had known Muhammad since childhood and could easily have borne witness, had they dared, to his free status. The wilder marauding peoples of the desert were also not particularly precise in distinguishing between Muslim and non-Muslim when they were considering whom to plunder and take prisoner. Bu Aisha, the official leader of the caravan with which Nachtigal travelled from Murzuq, capital of Fezzan, south to Borno, had once served the government of Fezzan before it became a Turkish province; the successful efforts which he made at that time to restore to the inhabitants of the

Nantes 1985, Paris 1988, vol. 2, 537-55.

[77] J. Godechot, 'La course Maltaise', *Revue africaine*, 1952, 106.

[78] T. Zammit, *Malta: the islands and their history*, 2nd edn, Valletta 1929, 247-8.

[79] That such difficulties were not confined to the less settled frontiers of the Muslim world, such as tropical Africa, appears from the provision, in standard legal texts, of advice about what to do in the case, for example, when you have married a slave woman under the impression that she was free (Ibn Abi Zayd, 266).

[80] I, 269; see also below, pp. 57 and 236.

Kawar oasis south of Fezzan their women and children, illegally captured by raiding Arabs, were still gratefully remembered by the Kawar people when Nachtigal passed through.[81] In Wadai, there was it seems no suggestion that Muslims were exempt from the condemnation to slavery whereby King Ali tried to protect foreign merchants against delinquent debtors:

> When in Wadai the time has come for the departure of a caravan to the north, and some of those who want to travel have not succeeded in collecting their debts, they turn to the king who does not delay in announcing clearly to the negligent debtor, whether a high official or a slave, 'If you have not satisfied your creditor by such and such a date, you will go with him as a slave as a substitute for the money you owe him'.[82]

Such a measure might be regarded as an extension of the principle which allowed a man to offer himself as a pledge for payment of a debt. But could such draconian action really have been standard policy? Nachtigal's description of King Ali continues: 'And to avoid too frequent resort to violent measures of this kind, he later reminded the merchants who came to Wadai that they should sell only for cash.'

---

[81] II, 52-3.
[82] IV, 52.

CHAPTER II

THE SIZE OF THE SLAVE POPULATION

> We raided Mokolo and captured 30 slaves and three cows. Barde died on the Mokolo expedition....We reckoned up the possessions of Barde which came to 40 slaves and ten horses.
>
> (Hamman Yaji, p. 60, 7 and 18 August 1916)

In the nature of things statistical precision is not to be expected in any estimate of the number of slaves in Africa. Nachtigal made some valiant efforts to measure the total population of several of the countries which he visited, but he did not attempt to distinguish between free and slave, and indeed, as will be shown later (see p. 54 ff.), it was often difficult to make a perfectly clearcut distinction. Clapperton did try to take account of this distinction for Kano in Hausaland, where he travelled nearly half a century before Nachtigal crossed the Sahara, but with variant results. In 1824 he judged that more than half the population of Kano, then totalling between 30,000 and 40,000, were slaves;[1] in 1827, however, he was told that there were 30 slaves in Kano to every free man.[2] According to Barth, slaves in Kano province in the 1850s were at least as numerous as free men,[3] and a modern writer has estimated the proportion of slaves to total population among the Hausa at the end of the nineteenth century as ranging from under 25 to about 50 per cent.[4]

---

[1] Bovill, *Missions*, IV, 650.

[2] H. Clapperton, *Journal of a second expedition into the interior of Africa*, London 1829, with the Journal of Richard Lander from Kano to the seacoast, 171.

[3] H. Barth, *Travels and discoveries in north and central Africa*, 3 vols, New York 1857-9, reprinted London 1965, I, 523.

[4] Irmgard Sellnow, 'Die Stellung der Sklaven in der Hausa-Gesellschaft',

Stories of individuals owning huge numbers of slaves are frequent. There may well be a touch of fantasy in some of these large round numbers, which appear here and in other parts of our story: the natural inclination to inflate numbers may have been particularly difficult to resist in the absence of such countervailing elements as a property tax. It would be tedious to attach a sceptical qualifying phrase on each occasion; and in some cases, where the reporter is a careful eye-witness such as Nachtigal, even high numbers may be accepted.

Of Awdaghast, the eleventh-century Saharan town, it was said that a wealthy man might own as many as 1,000 slaves.[5] Similar reports circulated of Timbuktu in the sixteenth century.[6] In the eighteenth century—though this is a non-Muslim example—some *prazo*, or crown estate, holders on the Zambezi boasted of slaves in tens of thousands: recent research suggests that in fact even 1,000 was a large establishment for a *prazo*, and fewer than a hundred slaves was probably normal. Even so, a total slave population there of 30,000 in the eighteenth century is possible.[7] Clapperton, in Borgu in 1824, was troubled by the matrimonial ambitions of a friend, a portly Arab widow, the richest person in town and owner of 1,000 slaves.[8]

Nachtigal's observations supply further confirmation for large slave concentrations. Kuka (or Kukawa), the capital of Borno, was Nachtigal's principal base on his travels. Dorugu, who visited there in 1855, exclaimed: 'The city of Kukawa— and I am telling you the truth—is a slave city.'[9] In February 1871, one of the most important men at the Kuka court, Lamino, died. Nachtigal had regarded him highly:

Mitt. des Instituts für Orientforschung, 1964, 88.

[5] N. Levtzion and J.F.P. Hopkins, eds, *Corpus of early Arabic sources for West African history*, Cambridge 1981, 74. Hereafter simply *Corpus*.

[6] Leo Africanus (sixteenth century), *The history and description of Africa*, tr. J. Pory, 1640, reprinted by Hakluyt Society, 3 vols, 1896 (hereafter Leo Africanus A), III, 825; *Description de l'Afrique*, tr. and ed. A. Epaulard and others, 2 vols, Paris 1956 (hereafter Leo Africanus B), II, 469.

[7] M. D. D. Newitt, 'The Portuguese on the Zambezi: an historical interpretation of the Prazo system', *Journal of African History*, 1969, 77.

[8] Clapperton, 1829, 85-6; also 81.

[9] Kirk-Greene and Newman, 80.

being what he was, he was feared by evildoers, hated by the intriguers at court, respected by people who did not get into the public eye, esteemed by the king, adored by the Shuwa, idolised by his slaves and blessed by the poor.[10]

Immediately after Lamino's death,

the eunuch-treasurer of the palace appeared in the house of mourning, to equip all the storerooms and depositories with padlocks, and left open only that part of the house where the women lived and the most distinguished slaves of the household were receiving visits of condolence.[11]

The dead man's estate included several thousand slaves. This was an exceptional case, but many other men of high rank had substantial slave establishments; Nachtigal observed such individuals, giving public audiences in the evening in the midst of their slaves, clients and servants, with whom they would also perform the sunset prayer.[12] During the rainy season of 1870, in many houses 'slaves by the dozen lay stricken by the fever, and their masters suffered no less than they did'.[13]

Another major slave-dealer—he seems to have been more actively a trader than were many of the great men among Nachtigal's acquaintance in Borno—was Hajj Ahmed Tangatanga, a Dongolan who had been persuaded by the king of Wadai to settle in that country, where he became the most important merchant,[14] having also administrative duties.[15] Hajj Ahmed always 'travelled in great comfort and had with him at least thirty to forty slaves and twenty women, wives and servants'.[16] Nachtigal was one of Hajj Ahmed's party on the road from Wadai to Darfur: merchants of the caravan would often eat together, and drink coffee and tea, in the evening. Having no slave-girl (for the cooking), Nachtigal made no contribution to the meal, but preparing the coffee fell to his

[10] II, 137. See also p. 152 below.
[11] II, 301-2.
[12] II, 160.
[13] II, 271; III, 198, evidently discussing the same situation, specifies 'the houses of the great dignitaries'.
[14] IV, 56-7.
[15] IV, 51 and 91.
[16] IV, 236.

people. Slaves kept up a great bonfire, into the cold night, while the party were entertained by an Egyptian story-teller 'with fairy tales from the *Thousand and One Nights*, or with stories of the glories of the Caliphate in Bagdad or of the celebrated conquest of North Africa in the early days of Islam'.[17] What a contrast to the exodus from Bagirmi (see 'Slaves on the march' below)! On the way, Hajj Ahmed added two more slaves, a young deaf-mute and a small girl, for whom together he exchanged one mare.[18]

Several times Nachtigal mentions slaves in conjunction with the layout of a town or a dwelling, though he nowhere focusses specifically on this combined analysiṣ. For example, after the earlier Kuka had been destroyed by King Muhammad Sherif of Wadai and his forces towards mid-century, Shaykh Umar

> rebuilt it in the form of two towns, himself and his officials and slaves occupying most of the eastern town, while the western served chiefly for the ordinary people and as a residence for foreigners.[19]

At the time of Nachtigal's visit, perhaps two-thirds of the city's population were living in the smaller dwellings of the congested western town—'despite the abundance of slaves which they conceal, the extended houses of the wealthy in the royal [eastern] town occupy a disproportionately large area'.[20]

Such extended Borno houses often covered an area sufficient in Europe for a house and flower and vegetable gardens, with outer courtyards for the male slaves, the huts of the women and the female slaves being in the inner courtyards.[21] One outer courtyard, carefully enclosed against the 'evil eye', provided stabling for the horses, ceaselessly tended by slaves and kept in great cleanliness and exemplary order.[22]

Abeshr, in Wadai, was much less tidily arranged than Kuka; Nachtigal mentions, living around the Queen Mother's extensive

[17] IV, 235-6. Ahmed was himself a story-teller (p. 232).
[18] IV, 243.
[19] II, 120.
[20] II, 162-3.
[21] Dorugu's first home, as a slave, in Zinder, was a compound divided in two, male slaves on one side, female on the other, connected only by one passage in front of the master's doorway (Kirk-Greene and Newman, 39).
[22] II, 152.

palace and the residence of the king, protégés, foreign traders, slaves, and here and there a prince.[23]

Very different are the branch and straw huts of Ngigmi, portable so that they may be withdrawn as the waters of Lake Chad rise each year: 'close to the main hut are erected, in proportion to the importance of the household, one or more smaller huts for women, children and slaves.'[24] Nachtigal stresses, in several contexts, the extent of slave-owning even amongst the poorer levels of society.

> It can be understood that in small villages where every household is on its own, and where still there is no beginning of a suitable division of labour to generate and maintain markets, the time of the inhabitants is fully occupied, and that even less well-to-do people cannot well dispense with the help of a few slaves. The domestic animals in particular are entrusted to the male slaves, who have to drive them to the pastures or cut fodder for them, while the female slaves help the mistress in all domestic duties.[25]

Slaves were naturally most in evidence wherever a significant fraction of the population enjoyed incomes which, judged by the local standards, might be regarded as comparatively comfortable. In poorer regions slaves were scarcer, but still not a negligible proportion in the population. Among the Budduma, the Kanuri nickname for the 'reed men' who lived on the islands in Lake Chad, while a poor man might be without any slaves, the average person owned two or three.[26] The Kanem desert was probably poorer still than Lake Chad, but Nachtigal's expectation that slave girls would be too few there to tempt Soliman, his unreliable Kanembu servant, to cultivate his taste for amorous adventure was certainly disappointed.[27] Even where the standard of living was desperately low for everybody, and slaves not easy to come by, their number was not negligible. Richardson, visiting the desert mountains midway between Tripoli and Ghadames in the 1840s, was told by a local shaykh that there were thirty slaves

[23] IV, 66.
[24] II, 102.
[25] III, 131-2. See also p. 211 below.
[26] MacLeod, 1912, 227.
[27] II, 320, 341.

in his district, and wondered 'how the people could keep slaves when they can scarcely keep themselves'.[28] A similar situation confronted Nachtigal when he penetrated Tibesti, a rugged poor country in the central Sahara. His negotiations for the hire of camels there once broke down because the Tubu woman who owned them would accept in return nothing less than Sa'ad, another of Nachtigal's servants, who had already been an object of great interest among the women of the country.[29] According to a census of 1949, there were in Ahaggar, in equally rough country in the west-central Sahara, 3960 fair-skinned pastoral Tuareg, and 1552 slaves, living in Tuareg camps.[30]

At one time, pioneer geographers of Africa, trying to visualize conditions in the interior, filled the Sahara with slaves. Cooley, for example, wrote:

> if the vast extent be considered of the region in which man has no riches but slaves, no enjoyment but slaves, no article of trade but slaves, and where the hearts of wandering thousands are closed against pity by the galling misery of life, it will be difficult to resist the conviction that the solid buttress on which slavery rests in Africa, is—The Desert.[31]

Eye-witness reports from travellers in the Sahara soon corrected this impression, but while there may have been proportionately fewer slaves in the Sahara than in happier regions, it remains surprising that the desert supported as many as it did.

Barth, in Kano city in 1851, while admitting a slave population possibly up to half (see p. 1), is less inclined than Nachtigal to attribute slave ownership to the ordinary people.

> The number of domestic slaves, of course, is very considerable; but I think it hardly equals, certainly does not exceed, that of free men, for, while the wealthy have many slaves, the poorer class, which is far more numerous, have few or none.[32]

[28] James Richardson, *Travels in the great desert of Sahara, in the years of 1845 and 1846,* London 1848, II, 63.
[29] I, 323-4; see also p. 144 below.
[30] Nicolaisen, 1997, II, 597.
[31] W.D. Cooley, *The Negroland of the Arabs,* London 1841, reprinted 1966, 139.
[32] Barth, 1965, I, 510.

THE SIZE OF THE SLAVE POPULATION 39

Even when full allowance is made for the difficulty of distinguishing between free and slave, the inadequate statistics, and simple boastfulness, it is clear that slavery was a highly important institution in each country through which Nachtigal passed, as in many other parts of Muslim Africa, and that slaves formed a substantial proportion of the population, in some areas perhaps even a majority. The complex and difficult problems which presented themselves when, after the slave trade had been eradicated, the colonizing European powers faced the task of getting rid of domestic slavery indicated clearly that the number of persons concerned was very large.[33] The importance of slaves, economically and in other ways, is explored in subsequent chapters.

---

[33] According to one estimate published in 1908, a quarter of the population of the French West African territories which were under civil administration were not free. In Senegal there were 200,000 '*captifs*', in Upper Senegal and Niger 600,000, in Dahomey 250,000, in the Ivory Coast 500,000, and in Guinea 450,000 (G. Deherme, *L'Afrique occidentale française*, Paris 1908, 383).

CHAPTER III

SLAVE STATUS AND RELIGION

Pagan slaving

'You will eat', they were mocked, 'of your Lords Cost, but not die with him; who excuse themselves, saying Life is sweet, and no man would willingly leave or have it taken away against his will.' (J. Ogilby, *Africa: being an accurate description....*, London 1670, mainly derived from the Dutch of O. Dapper, 396)

Nachtigal has next to nothing to say about the number of slaves held by Pagan masters; and to the slave practices of Pagan people, he made only a few incidental references. The Pagan (or near Pagan, for Islam was spreading amongst them) slavers of whom Nachtigal heard most during his travels were the Budduma, the elusive, uncontrollable island people of Lake Chad. He mentions their frequent raids upon the lakeshore Borno villages, for whose inhabitants, both free people and slaves, the risk of being captured by the Budduma was a constant concern, particularly at times of high water. In the winter

> a detachment of armoured horsemen was kept on the alert with their horses saddled, to hasten, at a signal from the drum of the shore watch, at once to the threatened spot; and the [local] governor's small company of soldiers armed with muskets, for whom the Chad islanders have a special respect, zealously endeavoured by frequent firing to scare away the dreaded enemy.[1]

Such vigilance notwithstanding, no winter passed without the most painful experiences being inflicted upon the exposed mainlanders.

[1] III, 218.

In the last days of December 1870, for example, a substantial village of Darbiggeli Shuwa was attacked, part of the male population massacred, and the remaining 142 persons, mostly women and children, dragged into slavery. During this year of abundant water, many an innocent farm worker from the lakeside ended up as a slave on the islands of the Budduma, with little prospect, despite the small distance, of ever seeing his home again.[2]

The gender distinctions are standard, men usually killed, women and children enslaved; elsewhere in his account, referring again to the kidnapping of individual field labourers, Nachtigal specifies 'slaves or women'.[3]

While travelling to Katsina, Barth once met a Borno slave who had first been enslaved by the Budduma. Later captured by the Awlad Sulayman, the turbulent Arab tribe whose varying fortunes Nachtigal described at considerable length, he was finally taken from them by the Kelowi, a Tuareg tribe, but remained throughout a fervent admirer of the independent freebooters who had initiated his career as a slave.[4] Another of Barth's friends had been a counter-raider against the Budduma, until they gave him a wife and he half-settled among them.[5]

Nachtigal also gleaned a small amount of slavery data from Bagirmi's Pagan neighbours, for example the inclusion of slaves amongst marriage-related payments, a procedure widespread also among Muslims (see below, pp. 312-15):

> According to terms previously agreed, the father of the chosen woman is paid a horse, some slaves, a certain number of fat dogs; in the event of infertility, the wife returns to her parents' house in exchange for repayment of the bride-price [*Kaufpreis*], or she is made over to another man for a specified price, or takes the status of a slave.[6]

There was also some information, again second-hand, about the power to enslave vested in kings, maybe in husbands too:

[2] III,·115.
[3] III, 218.
[4] Barth, 1965, I, 447.
[5] *ibid.*, II, 39-40.
[6] III, 390. Among the Budduma, the gifts which a bride received from her parents included two female slaves (MacLeod, 1912, 230).

That anyone should sell his wife and children in times of distress, as was reported to me concerning the Somraï, I doubt; it seems to be certain, however, that the chiefs of the centralised dominions have the power to treat their subjects in this way, and that they sometimes find reasons for actually doing so.... On the least pretext, he [the ruler of Somraï] is able to despoil one of his subjects of all that he possesses, to reduce his wife and his children to slavery, and to take away his life.... He rules the country so despotically that theft is almost unknown there: almost all offences lead to confiscation or capital punishment.[7]

Finally, among these Pagan slaving notes from the Bagirmi area, there is the theme of burial alive:

Among the Somraï and Nyillem the custom prevailed of burying alive with the dead chief a male slave of the age of a *sedasi* (12-15 years old) and a barely nubile virgin slave girl, in order, as I was told, that they might chase the flies away from their deceased master and hand him food and drink. Because of the contact with the Muhammadan Bagirmi, this barbaric custom has died out in Somraï; whether it still survives among the Nyillem, as I was assured, I must leave an open question.[8]

The above is another example of the way in which the *sedasi* slave is regarded almost as a standard term of measurement. Such sacrifice was quite common in non-Muslim Africa, and examples might be cited from both east and west.[9] In the Cape Mount area, in what is now modern Liberia, one or two slaves would accompany a nobleman to the grave, and hence it was usual for slaves to run away when their master was dying, returning only later, to face the reproof quoted at the head of this section. Centuries earlier, Ibn Battuta heard of a similar instance, when a black ruler died in west Africa, and was buried with some of his intimates and slaves (*khuddam*), and thirty sons and daughters of his chief men. A Muslim Berber

---

[7] III, 390 and notes. The second and third sentences from the French of Gourdault, *Tour*, 379-80; I suppose 'confiscation' includes enslavement.
[8] III, 392.
[9] See R. Burton, *Lake regions of central Africa*, London 1860, reprinted New York 1961, II, 25-6, for the burial alive of female slaves at the funeral of a Wanyamwezi chief.

there at the time, who had become close to the ruler, had to pay a heavy ransom to rescue his own son from being included in this number.[10]

Next, cannibalism. The reports which appeared from time to time about cannibalism often mention slaves as the victims. It should be added, however, that such reports are often secondhand. D'Ollone, in the hinterland of Liberia, contemplated reprisals against the local people, 'ces monstres qui nous offrent quelques captifs pour obtenir une paix qui leur permette de manger tranquillement les autres';[11] his report that 60,000 of Samori's followers, in the closing years of the nineteenth century, met this end seems merely hearsay. In Cameroon, German traders complained that their Hausa rivals sold slaves to cannibals, but there was no evidence for this, and the German administration thought on the contrary that the Hausa meat trade helped prevent cannibalism.[12]

Secondhand, and probably often no less ludicrous than similar beliefs which were indeed widely held among non-Europeans about Europeans themselves. Nachtigal's hopes of establishing useful contacts with some of the Pagans who thronged the war-camp of the fugitive king of Bagirmi were frustrated by their profound suspicion that white men were not only expert sorcerers, but also bought up black men as slaves, not in order to get them to work, but to satisfy their culinary tastes, or to dye cloth red with their blood, or make soap with their brains.[13] In north Arabia Doughty was asked in 1876 about the land in the Christian seas where black men were bred up for eating.[14]

Nachtigal also picked up rumours that cannibalism was still practised among several peoples in Wadai and Darfur, including

[10] *Corpus*, 281. This passage is not quoted in the recently reprinted *Ibn Battuta in black Africa*, though it is discussed in the notes on pp. 76-7, where the editors conclude (political correctness surmounting the serious difficulties of proving an absolute negative) that archaeology has shown that the custom of burial alive with a dead ruler was 'carried on without any possibility of cultural diffusion in many different parts of the world'.

[11] *Mission Hostains-d'Ollone, 1898-1900*, Paris 1901, 210.

[12] H. Rudin, *Germans in the Cameroons*, London 1938, 233-4, 299.

[13] III, 335-6 and note; see also pp. 133-4 below.

[14] C.M. Doughty, *Arabia deserta*, London 1888, reprinted 1923, I, 149.

even some nominal Muslims,[15] and that waterbags made of human skin were still sometimes brought into Darfur.[16] In one respect, however, the evidence does seem rather stronger. This is the great annual *konda* festival in Darfur, which Nachtigal describes in elaborate, exquisitely revolting detail. In his day, it involved, among many other disagreeable features, eating the putrified entrails of a specially selected wether; the wether was said to have replaced, as late as the beginning of the nineteenth century, a virgin who had scarcely reached puberty. But there is no indication here that the virgin should (or even could) be a slave. Slaves were involved, but as the alleged executioners of any of the royal family unable to stomach the meal.[17]

Other barbarities too were reported as being practised against slaves, such as sacrificial killing often in conjunction with a traditional secret society,[18] and simple cruelty. One traveller told of the first head of the Gizima clan of the Loma people in Liberia, who, among other things, kept a slave chained to a post, cutting pieces from him to feed to his dog, until the victim died and was replaced by another.[19] This, however, was said to have been at least 200 years before, and many such tales are similarly associated with a somewhat distant, and also perhaps somewhat legendary, past.

The advance of Islam indeed effectively ended some of the harsher aspects of Pagan slaving; yet it was not the case that the slave in Pagan societies had been entirely without rights. Circumstances of course varied greatly, but a survey of the position of slaves amongst various Liberian peoples reveals examples of the following benefits extended to slaves: the belief that upright slaves might hope for the same rewards in the next life as did other people;[20] the opportunity for some independent farming; the possibility of some redress in cases of injustice; an arrangement by which a slave might himself

[15] IV, 141, 151, 267, 356.
[16] IV, 267.
[17] IV, 338-41, 366.
[18] See for example G. W. Harley, *Notes on the Poro in Liberia*, Cambridge, MA 1941, reprinted New York 1968, 14.
[19] G. Schwab, *Tribes of the Liberian hinterland*, Cambridge, MA 1947, 22.
[20] *ibid.*, 329.

change his master (see below p. 81 for a parallel practice in Muslim society); the chance of freedom by purchase, gift, or on the master's death; the right of a slave in certain cases to inherit equally with his master's own sons; and permission granted in some societies to a slave to marry one of his deceased master's widows.[21] Indeed, one survey of Muslim Africa, taking account of such rights in the old societies, suggests that the liberalizing impact of Islam was probably of more importance in the case of captives and newly acquired slaves than for those who had already become established as domestic slaves or serfs.[22] Some non-Muslim peoples, such as the Kru on the West African coast, boast that they have never been slaves, nor dealt in slaves.[23]

A curious footnote to the contrast between Muslim and Pagan slave-owning arose in the British protectorate of Zanzibar and Pemba. There, in the early days, the British admitted the legality of slavery, as being sanctioned by Islamic law, to the support of which the British were then committed. But Sir John Kirk, the Consul-General, ruled that no slave could be the legal property of a Pagan, since slave-owning was recognized only by Islamic law, to which in turn only Muslims could appeal.[24] This is by no means the only context in which European colonialism, consciously or unconsciously, favoured Muslims over Pagans.

One final linguistic note, to close this section. Nachtigal includes 'slave' amongst his list of 'some very important expressions' in the language of the Musgo, a people living in the Logon area, which are entirely that language's own.[25] Though Nachtigal does not draw this conclusion, the peculiarity of the word seems to suggest that the concept it represents is indigenous, not simply imported.

---

[21] Schwab, 1947, 441-2.
[22] I.M. Lewis, ed., *Islam in tropical Africa*, London 1966, 51 The second edition, of 1980, omits five papers, and changes the sequence of the rest—all page references below are to 1966 only).
[23] Graham Greene, *Journey without maps*, London 1963, 44.
[24] F.D. Lugard, *The rise of our east African empire*, Edinburgh 1893, I, 184-5.
[25] III, 183.

Jihad *and slave-raiding*

'He set his stallion at us, crying out, "Today your beds shall lie empty!"'
(*Shaihu Umar*, p. 47)

The motives which impelled Muslim warriors in Africa to embark on slave raids against their Pagan neighbours were inevitably quite mixed. Strictly interpreted and between parties both of good standing, the *shari'ah*, or law of Islam, forbids any Muslim to enslave a co-religionist. On the other hand, *jihad*, holy war directed against non-Muslims, was approved by the *shari'ah*, and might, in some circumstances, be a positive duty. It was therefore natural that slave raiding, which in principle should be directed exclusively against non-Muslims, should acquire some of the characteristics of religious war between Muslim and Pagan.[26] The launching of a slave-raid was indeed only rarely marked by the procedures proper to a *jihad* (see the raid on Deba, p. 23 above), and Nachtigal does not so much as mention the word throughout the whole of *Sahara and Sudan*, although there is a great deal of fighting recorded there, of many kinds, in many places, at many times, by many people. This somewhat surprising silence may in part reflect Nachtigal's relative lack of interest in purely religious matters, but it does also suggest that such proprieties were generally not high priority among local participants. The conclusion of the campaign, however, whether it had been consecrated as *jihad* or not, might be much the same, and the subsequent fate of those who were captured on a slave raid had at least to some extent to be determined according to the principles of the Muslim law.

From the earliest days of Islam, enslavement had been one likely prospect for a prisoner of war. The law governing these prisoners of war was based on two Quranic injuctions, Surahs viii. 68 and xlvii. 4:

---

[26] Pagans were the chief victims of Muslim slaving in Africa, but Christians might also on occasion be liable. In 1631 a revolt in Mombasa led to almost all the Portuguese there being killed, and among the African Christians in Mombasa many, refusing to recant, died as martyrs; while 400 were sent as slaves to the market in Mecca (G. S. P. Freeman-Grenville, 'The Coast, 1498-1840', in R. Oliver and G. Mathew (eds), *History of East Africa*, Oxford 1963, I, 140).

JIHAD AND SLAVE-RAIDING

It has not been for any prophet to have captives until he slaughters in the land.

So, when ye meet *in battle* those who disbelieve, then *let there* be the striking off of heads until, when ye have slaughtered them, then make the bond strong. Then *grant* either favour afterwards, or ransom, till war lays down its burdens.[27]

While the schools of law varied somewhat in details of the correct treatment to be accorded to prisoners of war, there were six principal alternatives: execution, usually only in exceptional circumstances; ransom; exchange against Muslim prisoners; taxation—the *jizya* and *kharaj* taxes, nominally applicable only to People of the Book, that is Christians and Jews; free release; and enslavement.[28] If a *dhimmi*, or protected person (that is one who had agreed to pay the *jizya*), broke his agreement and left Muslim territory to go to an enemy land, he became, unless he had been driven to this resort by injustice suffered amongst the Muslims, liable to enslavement if he were ever again captured.[29] There was general agreement that women and children among the prisoners ought not to be killed, but rather enslaved and divided as spoil among the victors,[30] or, if their circumstances merited it, included among

---

[27] These verses are cited in Khadduri, 1955, 127. A 1964 translation, by Muhammad Asad, of the Quran offers a modernist interpretation. It translates the first verse, 'It does not behoove a prophet to keep captives unless he has battled strenuously on earth', and continues with this commentary: '*i.e.*, as an aftermath of a war in a just cause. As almost always in the Quran, an injunction addressed to the Prophet is, by implication, binding on his followers as well. Consequently, the above verse lays down that no person may be taken, or for any time retained, in captivity, unless he was taken prisoner in a *jihad*—that is, a holy war in defence of the Faith or of freedom ... and that, therefore, the acquisition of a slave by "peaceful" means, and the keeping of a slave thus acquired, is entirely prohibited: which, to all practical purposes, amounts to a prohibition of slavery as a "social institution". But even with regard to captives taken in war, the Quran ordains (in xlvii. 4) that they should be freed after the war is over.'

[28] Khadduri, 1955, 127-8; Ibn Abi Zayd, 343; Khalil ibn Ishaq, *Abrégé de la loi musulmane selon le rite de l'Imâm Mâlek*, I, 'Le rituel', tr. G.-H. Bousquet, Publications de l'Institut d'études Orientales de la Faculté des Lettres d'Alger, 1956, 209.

[29] Khalil ibn Ishaq, I, 217.

[30] Khadduri, 1955, 129.

those upon whom the *jizya* was levied.[31] A captive woman, pregnant with the child of a Muslim, might be kept enslaved; and, should she have conceived before the father's conversion to Islam, the child would be a slave like his mother. And so on. A complete survey of the relevant legal conditions is impossible here; the few examples offered will I hope suffice to give an idea of complexity of the regulations. In tropical Africa the strict application of all these rules, or of any of them, often proved impracticable.

The distribution of booty was subject to certain regulations. A horseman, for example, got one share, his horse two, while a slave, a woman or a minor, unless the minor joined actively and joined with permission in the campaign, received nothing.[32] Special restrictions applied to the distribution of enslaved prisoners: when they were given out, husbands (if such had survived) and wives should not be separated, nor parents and children.[33]

There is no sign of any such concern for the families of enslaved persons, in *Sahara and Sudan*; there are, on the contrary, many references to severed children, being sold for less than the cost of a shirt (see below, p. 376), dying, running away, being handed on as separate free-standing units, and so forth. Were husband and wife to be captured together, the husband would be vulnerable to that precautionary cull which many raiders practised (see below, p. 180). Dorugu's description of his enslavement is probably both realistic and widely applicable:

> The Hausa man captured my father and someone else captured my father's wife, although who it was I don't know. All the children in town were crying. Mothers were separated from their children and husbands were separated from their wives. And thus we were led away.[34]

Dorugu's own mother had been kidnapped into slavery in a separate, earlier incident.[35]

---

[31] Khalil ibn Ishaq, I, 209, 217.
[32] Ibn Abi Zayd, 164; Khalil ibn Ishaq, I, 212-13.
[33] Khadduri, 1955, 130-1.
[34] Kirk-Greene and Newman, 36.
[35] *ibid.*, 34.

The only booty rule which was fairly widely known, and to observe which sporadic efforts were made, was the *khums* rule, the rule that one-fifth of booty taken should go to the state. Hamman Yaji was aware of this requirement, but, it seems, only just: 'in April 1919, I raided the pagans of Rowa and captured 50 cattle and 33 slaves. We calculated my fifth share as 17 slaves and 25 cattle.'[36]

While the *khums* rule may have been imperfectly understood, there was sometimes a keen sense that booty should be reported to the leadership of the expedition, or to the authorities at home, who would decide about its distribution. The beginning of young Umar's troubles and adventures lay in the false accusation, brought against his father by jealous colleagues, that he had brought home four slaves, and had then reported only two of these to the chief.[37]

The combination of the legal position outlined above, the nature of the domestic demands to be described in Chapter V, the normal vicissitudes of warfare, and culling, may explain why female slaves figure more prominently than male in Mulim tropical Africa, and in the trans-Saharan trade, than in the Atlantic trade. The possibility that this prominence, in turn, is in part responsible for the readier absorption of black slaves in North African and Middle Eastern society, than in that of the United States, is interesting, but speculative.

The religious tension between Muslim and Pagan, coming to a climax in *jihad*, was sometimes reinforced in other respects also. The biographer of Alooma, ruler of Borno in the later part of the sixteenth century, mentioned more than once and with evident approval his master's slave-raiding during Ramadan.

> He camped with his army on the second of Ramadan (of great power) and remained making raids and capturing slaves till the end of the month.[38]

[36] Hamman Yaji, 69.

[37] *Shaihu Umar*, 24-6. For further booty references, see 'Soldiers' below, and also index entries.

[38] Ahmed ibn Fartua, *History of the first twelve years of the reign of Mai Idris Alooma of Bornu (1571-1583)*, H. R. Palmer (tr.), 1926/1970, 40, see also 51; or, Dierk Lange, *A Sudanic chronicle: the Borno expeditions of Idris Alauma (1564-1576) according to the account of Ahmad b. Furtu*, Stuttgart 1987, 84, 99-100 and n. 5. Muslim slaving during the Christian Lent is reported from

In general, however, it might be expected that the appropriate time for slave-raiding would be determined by the seasonal changes of the solar calendar rather than by the lunar calendar of the faith. With one exception, Nachtigal does not explicitly identify Ramadan as the time for any particular fighting. The exception occurred on the festival day immediately after Ramadan 1871. He was then travelling with the nomadic Awlad Sulayman, in Kanem.

> When news came in the morning that the expected Tripolitanian cousins had actually arrived in the Zommeze valley, a small raid was immediately arranged in their honour, almost as a sport, and a proposal to this effect was sent to them. Their affirmative answer arrived towards evening. Soon afterwards Abd el-Jlil's kettledrum was calling the men together, and at nightfall they all mounted for a surprise attack...upon a section, living nearby, of the Hawalla tribe... [Fortunately the intended victims had been forewarned, and escaped, leaving only straw containers, chickens and the like.] The whole enterprise would therefore have petered out rather harmlessly, if the Tripolitanian confederates on their way back...had not discovered a place of refuge of those who had been attacked, and in order that they might carry off a few head of cattle and a half-dozen children, had killed ten of the unfortunates.[39]

Further west, in the Senegal area, during the flourishing period of the Tokolor theocracies in the later nineteenth century, there was often trouble between Muslims and the adherents of traditional secret societies, such as the Komo. Once Tokolor horsemen broke up a Komo festival, capturing

---

Ethiopia at the end of the fifteenth century, when Mahfuz, ruler of Harar, began ravaging Ethiopia each year in Lent, killing the men and enslaving the women and children, some for sale and others for presentation to the Sharif of Mecca (W. Cornwallis Harris, *The highlands of Aethiopia*, London 1844/1968, II, 54-5). The purpose was to strike at the Christians when they were weakened by the severe fast of the eastern churches. As for Ramadan, Muslims on *jihad* would legally be exempt from fasting. Richardson, 1848, I, 222, heard of some central Saharan raiders postponing their activities until Ramadan was finished; he does not indicate how important slaves were in the prospective loot.

[39] III, 29.

JIHAD AND SLAVE-RAIDING

Reception by Abu Sekkin, 4 April 1872. III, 318.

two men in ceremonial costume. The Tokolor chief wondered at these strange creatures, and proposed burning them to discover their real identity, since evidently they could not be men. The unfortunate captives protested that they were in truth only men, and, stripped of their adornment, they were forthwith sold as slaves in the nearest market.[40]

Christian meddling with a quasi-religious exercise was not well received, whether it came from Europeans or from Africans, as, for example, in the banning of the slave trade by King Theodore of Ethiopia.[41] In April 1872 Nachtigal accompanied the forces of Abu Sekkin, the king of Bagirmi, who had been driven from his capital by an attack from Wadai, on a raid against the Pagan Kimre. Two of Nachtigal's servants played an active part in this expedition and, better equipped with firearms than the local forces, fired the shots which made possible such success as the raiders eventually achieved. Fortunately, as Nachtigal observed, his men did not have much ammunition, and their skill was very limited. But they vigorously rejected Nachtigal's efforts to restrain them, maintaining that harrying Pagans who refused submission to a Muslim king and rejected the law of Islam was a purely religious matter in which a Christian had no right to interfere.[42] A variation on this theme comes from East Africa in 1804, where Dallons, a French slave-trader, said that the Zanzibaris put up the prices of slaves at will, and 'end by making us fear that we shall not obtain them at any price, because their religion, as they say, forbids them...to sell to white men'.[43] In 1855 Speke found Somalis greatly discomposed about rumoured British interference with the slave trade, which they regarded as their

---

[40] L. Tauxier, *La religion bambara*, Paris 1927, 300.

[41] J. L. Krapf, *Travels, researches and missionary labours during an eighteen years' residence in eastern Africa*, London 1860, 84. Perhaps a similar annoyance is discernible amongst Pagans also. The following prayer was addressed to the Borfimor, the sacred object of the human leopard society in Sierra Leone: 'Make no trouble meet them. Make they get slaves. Make English no sabby they get slaves for get free. Make they gentry' (T.J. Alldridge, *The Sherbro and its hinterland*, London 1901, 155).

[42] III, 344; See below, p. 352.

[43] G.S.P. Freeman-Grenville, *The East African coast: select documents from the first to the earlier nineteenth century*, Oxford 1962, 2nd edn, London 1975, 99.

Quranic right.[44] Such resentment produced even livelier scenes during Ramadan in 1880, when Swahilis and Arabs from Mombasa, vowing to make soup of the livers of the Church Missionary Society missionaries, attacked the C.M.S. freed slave settlement at Freretown; the missionaries defended themselves with arms, and later admitted the possession of a white flag, bearing the word Freedom, to be unfurled as signal for all the Mombasa slaves to rise against their masters.[45]

The concentration upon Pagans, and to a much lesser extent Christians, as the most eligible candidates for enslavement may have slowed down the spread of Islam. The exclusion from Islam in sixteenth-century Songhay of the masses, has been explained as a consequence of the fact that a Muslim was *ipso facto* a free man.[46] It has been argued that later there was no consistent propagation of Islam by Arab traders in the East African interior because conversions would have restricted the supply of slaves,[47] or by the Turko-Egyptians and others advancing up the Nile, because the local people were more valuable as Pagan taxpayers or slave labour.[48] Nachtigal attributed a similar attitude to the Muslims of Bagirmi. Noting that they had made no effort to share the blessings of Islam with their Pagan neighbours, he explained this by the fact that for 300 years the Pagans had been regarded merely as a rich source of slaves.[49] One writer goes so far as to say that Muslim warriors were careful not to convert people who could be

[44] J.H. Speke, *What led to the discovery of the source of the Nile*, Edinburgh 1864, 116-17.

[45] J. Gray, 'Zanzibar and the coast belt, 1840-84', in Oliver and Mathew, 1963, I, 245; R. Oliver, *The missionary factor in East Africa*, 2nd edn, London 1965, 55-6.

[46] J. Rouch, 'Contribution à l'histoire des Songhay', *Mémoires de l'Institut français d'Afrique noire*, no. 29, 1953, 193. But see pp. 70-1 below.

[47] O. F. Raum, 'German East Africa', in V. Harlow and E.M. Chilver (eds), *History of East Africa*, Oxford 1965 II, 167; Froelich, 1962, 56; Oliver, 1965, 202.

[48] R. C. Stevenson, 'Some aspects of the spread of Islam in the Nuba mountains', in Lewis, 1966, 211. He adds that massive slave-raiding, even if undertaken with little interest in extending the faith, and leading to the eventual return home of only a very few converted slaves, might nevertheless prepare the ground for Islam by breaking up traditional patterns of life. See also p. 244 below.

[49] III, 392.

enslaved or heavily taxed; this, he maintains, was especially clear in Adamawa, the modern northern Cameroon.[50] In this respect, therefore, the suppression of slave-trading might be seen as removing one of the great obstacles to the spread of Islam;[51] with perhaps even the further corollary that, if Africa had ever become completely Muslim, slavery would inevitably have disappeared, in default of any Pagans who could legitimately be enslaved.[52]

These generalizations, in part correct, perhaps err in attributing too great a uniformity to the motives and practices of Muslims. Traders, and warriors on essentially secular campaigns, could scarcely be expected to display more than a tepid interest in evangelization. Where religious purposes were more to the fore, whether expressed militarily or peacefully, concern for the conversion of Pagans was widespread.

Slave and free status

'When my mother heard this, she said, "A'a, master, the cadi at Murzuk put me in your company for you to take me to my son, and now are you saying that I am your slave?"' (*Shaihu Umar*, p. 68)

Problems of status definition were clearly real, as the following illustrations show. In the game of population mobility, prisoners of war were a valued prize. In dealing with Muslim opponents, however, it made a great deal of difference, at least in theory and often in practice too, whether any particular prisoner had been free or slave before capture. A very visible example of this, on an unusually large scale, occurred in 1871, when King Ali of Wadai captured the capital of Bagirmi, Massenya; Abu Sekkin, the legitimate Bagirmi ruler, barely escaped with his life. A great deal of plunder fell into the hands of the victorious invaders from Wadai.

> The greatest treasure, however, consisted of the large number of slaves and prisoners of war whom King Ali carried away, giving away and selling the former, settling the latter in Wadai. Especially the free Bagirmi the intelligent prince

[50] J.-C. Froelich, 'Essai sur les causes et méthodes de l'Islamisation de l'Afrique de l'Ouest du XIe siècle au XXe siècle', in Lewis, 1966, 168-9.
[51] T.W. Arnold, *The preaching of Islam*, London 1913/1961, 362.
[52] L.G. Binger, *Esclavage, Islamisme, Christianisme*, Paris 1891, 34-6.

very deliberately directed to Wadai, preferably choosing among them people who understood architecture, weaving, tailoring, saddlery and dyeing. These he domiciled in the few large places of the country (Abeshr, Nimro etc.), and the others he settled as cultivators of the soil in scattered colonies, for in all industrial work the Bagirmi were superior to his subjects. Even if one is unwilling to take literally the reports, unquestioned in those countries, of some 30,000 people who were transported in this way to Wadai: half this number may still be near the truth.[53]

The above account is taken from Nachtigal's history of Bagirmi. He returned to the subject when he was in Abeshr, varying, or enlarging upon, various details. Nachtigal begins by mentioning that the king was away on an expedition to inspect one of his Bagirmi settlements. 'There were several of these in the country, and the king followed their development with the greatest interest.'[54] This detail about the royal concern is in itself very interesting. Nachtigal is still doubtful about 30,000, suggesting that between 12,000 and 15,000 might perhaps be an underestimate.[55] Most of the prisoners were slaves; of these a great number had been distributed among the king's officials, while others had been sold and taken abroad already. According to Nachtigal's friend, Hajj Salim (see below, pp. 136-7), and despite the king's religious convictions, the distinction between free and slave amongst the prisoners did not seem to have been properly observed.

> It would, indeed, sometimes be difficult to establish free birth; and during my visit disputes about individual slaves from Bagirmi still came before the king for his decision nearly every time I had an audience with him. He then summoned a high official from Bagirmi whom he had taken into his service, who had to determine the genealogical tree of the persons concerned, and in their presence report to the king.[56]

[53] III, 425.
[54] IV, 67. The English *Sahara and Sudan* refers here to people being moved from Wadai to Bagirmi, an error so manifest that we may hope no one has been misled by it.
[55] Oral tradition in the early twentieth century continued to use the figure 30,000, which was, however, said to be the number of Bagirmi killed or enslaved; MacLeod, 1912, 143.
[56] IV, 67.

The free young women were married to officials, the older women being employed as servants by members of the royal house. Some of the men were settled in the capital, others in the countryside as agricultural workers. Since the Bagirmi surpassed by far the Wadaians, the most barbarous of all the Sudan people, in handicrafts, all such tasks fell to the Bagirmi: building clay houses, and stronger and more elegant straw and reed houses; the manufacture of saddles for the king and his leading dignitaries; making silk cords, or cords, talisman pouches, knife-sheaths and other leather goods; producing cotton strips of a fineness hitherto unknown in Wadai—'and a respectable garment could be made only by a Bagirmi tailor.' The workers on the land were also far superior.

> In general, indeed, the success achieved by King Ali in civilising his country by the forced migration of the people of Bagirmi was to be rated more highly than the treasures, rich as they were in the circumstances of those countries, which he was said to have seized in Massenya.[57]

The device adopted to settle disputes about slave status was, however, less effective. During Nachtigal's visit, some who claimed to be free were still being treated as slaves, though the market price for these 'hot' slaves, as the current jargon called them, was depressed by the element of risk below that offered for the 'cold' variety, about whose status there was no dispute. By means not clearly explained a good many 'hot' slaves accompanied the caravan with which Nachtigal eventually travelled from Abeshr to Darfur, and, as some difficulty was apparently feared in getting them out of the country, the caravan split into two sections, the one with the 'hot' slaves proceeding to the frontier by devious routes.[58]

Travelling from Abeshr eastwards towards Darfur, Hajj Ahmed Tangatanga's caravan, with Nachtigal one of its members, passed two Bagirmi colonies settled by King Ali, each a village 'distinguished by its cleanliness and the good architecture of its huts, and by the appearance of a measure of prosperity'.[59] Nachtigal again reiterated how extremely fond

[57] IV, 67-8.
[58] IV, 231.
[59] IV, 231.

of these Bagirmi colonists the king was, valuing their superiority to his own subjects in agriculture, in handicrafts, and in artistic skill.

Uncertainty about status was well exemplified by a 17-year-old boy, Mohammedu, the son of freed parents, who had not realized that his status was that of a slave until he was suddenly transported from his home town to enter the service of Shaykh Umar, the ruler of Borno,[60] with whom Nachtigal had established very friendly relations. This boy, with a younger colleague, was later lent to Nachtigal, whom he served faithfully for nearly three years (see pp. 67-8).

False allegations of slave status might be made. Muhammad al-Qatruni, Nachtigal's principal servant and companion for the first half of his travels, was momentarily kidnapped on the dangerous journey into Tibesti, by a man claiming that Muhammad was actually a slave of his father's. This was the only occasion on his Africa journey that Nachtigal threatened to shoot in anger. Muhammad was rescued; but two other members of Nachtigal's party, who had known Muhammad from childhood and could easily have testified to his free birth, were too frightened by the kidnapper to speak out.[61]

Shaihu Umar's mother, tricked into slavery by an unscrupulous trader, failed twice, even before a *qadi*, in Murzuq and again in Tripoli, to establish her freedom, because just such false allegations of slave status were believed.[62]

Quarrels among Muslims increased the possibilities of dispute over such points. Shaykh Ahmad al-Bakkai, the distinguished Timbuktu scholar, about 1861, remonstrating with the invading champion al-Hajj Umar, cited, among other points, the complaint that al-Hajj Umar's troops had taken one of his own free wives, treating her as a slave, while the slave of a *sharif* had likewise been taken by them, but on the ground that she was actually a free woman.[63]

Of course, in many instances, very likely in most, the distinction between free persons and slaves is straightforward

[60] III, 58.

[61] I, 269.

[62] *Shaihu Umar*, 65-70. See the quotation at the head of this section.

[63] MS. Arabe 5259, Bibliothèque nationale, Paris, ff. 67-8, 69; I am indebted to J.R. Willis for this reference.

enough, and occasions no difficulty. This seems to have been the case in one of the Sokoto letters, this one from the emir of Gwandu to the Sokoto caliph:

> ...of the men of Yabo who joined the heathen in raising a rebellion, we have captured some. They went to the Jega market and on their return we caught them at Massama with their loads, twenty-nine men in all. Of these thirteen are slaves, and the rest free men. The free men we are sending to you, the slaves and loads we have retained in accordance with your orders in your letter....All the free men who have been found, you will see, if Allah wills.[64]

Nachtigal also refers, on several occasions, to half-free or half-slave people. For example,

> impecunious people and half-free slaves, who seek to earn an income at their own discretion and pay to their masters only a fixed contribution, have cut dry grass for domestic animals, collected firewood, woven *siggedi* from *sukko* straw for the repair of fences and the covering of huts, and in the woods have cut poles for fences and verandas, wood for roofing the earthen houses and branches for the framework of the straw huts. To be able to store up these articles in such quantities, they must have worked for a great part of the preceding week, for there are neither woods nor grassy meadows in the neighbourhood of the town, and anything available within reach had been sacrificed long ago to the demands of Kuka's numerous population.[65]

Other people on this rather porous boundary between the free and the slave provide the permanent, settled population of oases in Borku: a

> few slaves, descendants of slaves, or poor clients, who have gradually acquired a small property in date palms....A sparse population of slaves, half-free people, and poor immigrants....Natives who no longer had the camels demanded or warranted by a nomadic life, fugitive murderers, prisoners of war who because of religious scruples had not been enslaved, but also had not been ransomed, perhaps also slaves who had been freed, might settle, gradually acquire some small property, intermarry among

[64] Backwell, 1927/1969, no. 2, pp. 16-18.
[65] II, 204-5.

themselves and sometimes with the nomads, and thus in the course of time formed a new tribe, which was to be sure more or less despised by the pure nomads.[66]

At an altogether different social level, Nachtigal applies the term half-slave to some senior officials in the Darfur government.[67] Such half-and-half people may well have been in one of the intermediary categories, specifically provided for by religious law (see pp. 74-5).

Such status problems may have been further complicated by the fact that in certain respects slaves and freemen were outwardly much alike. A slave often had, like a free man, the right to earn something for himself, and to own property, even to own other slaves. The master might ultimately be responsible for all his slave's possessions; the Maliki law provided, for example, that a man who had sworn an oath not to ride any beast of his own, and then rode his slave's, would be guilty of perjury.[68] The right of a slave to purchase his freedom would, however, have been purely nominal if he had been unable *de facto* to accumulate the means for this purpose. Clapperton said of the Sokoto empire that property-owning slaves were common, though on their death their property was inherited by their owners.[69] He qualified this by adding that masters inherited only if their slaves died childless; if this is correct it is a deviation from strict religious law, according to which, as we have already seen (see above pp. 16 and 17), slaves, even if partially free, do not inherit. Clapperton's description of the combination of free enterprise and slave labour in agriculture is given below (see p. 216).

The contribution of slaves to religious activity

'....my son Yaya finished the Quran, and I gave him a slave girl and a cow.' (Hamman Yaji, p. 54, 20 December 1913)

The acquisition and possession of slaves facilitated religious study, and other pious exercises, in various ways. Slaves might form part of the alms which clerics received. Nachtigal gives

[66] II, 415-16.
[67] IV, 333.
[68] Khalil ibn Ishaq, I, 192.
[69] Clapperton, 1829, 249, see also 214.

a vivid sketch of the upward mobility (including slave ownership) within the reach of any aspiring holy man fortunate enough to gain the favourable attention of Shaykh Umar, the devout ruler of Borno.

> A poor *faqih*, in filth and extreme poverty, is seen for weeks together making a daily pilgrimage to the royal residence until he has won over one of the great men who introduces him to the generous Shaykh. Soon after one meets him in a new Bornu or Hausa dress, or with a burnus decorating his shoulders, and after some months he is seen perhaps, on horseback, accompanied by some slaves, and without a trace of the humility which seemed to characterise him only a short time before.[70]

Some stories of the largesse practised by pious rulers in the past should perhaps be regarded as moral anecdotes, setting an example for subsequent rulers to follow, rather than as sober historical record, but they no doubt do indicate widespread approval of slaves as appropriate alms.

A clerical chronicler of the sixteenth century somewhat disingenuously praised Askiya Muhammad I because, 'full of regard for the *ulama*, he distributed slaves and riches generously to them to assure the interests of the Muslims and to aid them in their submission to God and in the practice of the faith'.[71] On the Prophet Muhammad's birthday the poets of Fez gathered before the governor, and the best performer was proclaimed the prince of poets; a little wistfully, recalling perhaps the bounty which had once rewarded his own youthful verses (see below p. 309), Leo Africanus looked back to the good old days when every poet received 50 ducats, and the winner 100 ducats, an excellent horse, a woman slave and the king's own robe—130 years had passed '...since this custome, together with the maiestie of the Fessan kingdome, decaied'.[72] Askiya Daud of Songhay, in the mid-sixteenth century, had at his disposal a large property, including slaves, unexpectedly inherited from one of his slaves. From this were given 100 cows to the muezzins of the capital, and to the sister of a *qadi* 1000

---

[70] II, 174.
[71] Kati, 115.
[72] Leo Africanus, A, II, 455; B, I, 214-15.

sheep and goats. The numerous slaves which had thus fallen into Daud's hands he divided, one hundred for the Timbuktu *qadi*, the rest in batches of twenty-seven. One batch went to the *imam*, and one to the main mosque, the women to make mats and carpets for the mosque, and the men to carry the clay and work the wood needed for its maintenance. Two batches were sent to the *qadi* of the capital, one for his own use, the other, or the proceeds from its sale, to be redistributed among those who had a legal right to alms; and one to a *sharif*, charged to share the bounty with all the other *sharifs* and their families. The members of this last batch, later freed, subsequently gave themselves out as also being genuine *sharifs*.[73] One high Songhay official, who murdered a rival in 1588, gave ten slaves and 100,000 cowries to students for a penitential recitation of the Quran on his behalf.[74]

In the last of the foregoing examples, a specified religious task is, in economic terms, being bought and paid for: ten slaves and 100,000 cowries for a penitential Quran recitation. The sources abound in such instances. On 6 May 1926, Hamman Yaji noted in his diary: 'I said goodbye to Malam Ibrahim and Malam Hamman Sa'id. Their fee for reading the Quran was 15 s[hillings].'[75] Often a more mechanical, utilitarian transaction is involved. Hamman Yaji again, his spirit evidently failing him at the imminent prospect of a European colonial officer, records this for 1 March 1919:

> The same day I made arrangement with my scribe Amin by which if I do a certain thing the Christian will not stop at Madagali [Hamman Yaji's capital]. I gave him [the scribe] a slave for this, and if God does prevent him [the officer] from staying here I will give him [the scribe] two slaves.[76]

The diary's editors surmise that this probably refers to a charm, but the requirement that Hamman Yaji himself should actually do something suggests more activity, a special prayer, some ritual action, or whatever. On 2 March, the diary laconically continues, the officer 'arrived at Madagali and stayed for

---

[73] Kati, 189-99; gifts mainly to assure Daud's place in paradise.
[74] *ibid.*, 237.
[75] p. 127.
[76] p. 68.

two nights. He paid 50 shillings.' What Amin the scribe was eventually paid is not mentioned. Interestingly, and typically, on the very same day that he was arranging matters spiritually with the scribe Amin, Hamman Yaji was embarking on direct secular negotiation with the approaching official: 'I sent off Jarma and Barade to the Commandant regarding my pagans in Gwoza and others.' Payment for this activity also was in slaves: 'I promised them that if they got what I wanted from him I would give them a slave-girl each.'[77]

Another religious engagement, though for what specific purpose is not stated, occurs for 16 September 1922: '... I rewarded Malam Gaji for all his work by giving him a small slave. That is in full settlement of his work.'[78] The sort of work done for payment by a *malam* or religious specialist would certainly be religious, albeit of a manipulative kind. We are here very much on the shadowy borderland between Muslim and indigenous African practice. Among the grammatical examples cited by Koelle, the pioneering Africanist linguist, for the Vai language is one which aptly illustrates this overlapping: 'We will give you eight slaves, four for the diviners and four for the Muslims'.[79] Although slaves were clearly a very acceptable payment in such cases, they were not the only one, as illustrated by another journal entry, 26 February 1925: '...I gave the Kadi's son, Biyeri, a horse, and he promised me that when he returned home he would send me a spell.'[80] Or again, in July 1925,

> ... I finally dismissed the Imam of Nyiburi. I had kept him 45 days and his pay was three cows. I gave him 4 s[hillings] and will give him the whole amount if God in His power grants us the fulfilment of our desire.[81]

Notice again the payment by results. There is also one apparent payment in advance, in May 1920: 'I gave Malam Muhammad two slaves as a deposit.'[82]

---

[77] Hamman Yaji, 68.
[78] *ibid.*, 80.
[79] S. Koelle, *Outlines of a grammar of the Vei language*, London 1854/1968, 95, see also 108.
[80] Hamman Yaji, 110; see also 20 January 1923, on p. 82.
[81] *ibid.*, 115.
[82] *ibid.*, 72.

The exchange of slaves often occurred in an educational context, as illustrated in the quotation at the head of this section. Among the Fulani of nineteenth-century Masina, it was not rare for well-to-do families to give milch cows, or slaves, to the clerics who were teaching their children.[83] Another cleric, much impressed by the youthful learning of Shehu Ahmadu, the later founder of the Masina theocracy, gave him a slave, asking in return for his prayers; the slave subsequently rose to be a general of captives and freed captives in Masina.[84] In the Timbuktu area when a pupil finished the memorization of the Quran, his teacher would receive five cattle, or a camel or a slave, or the equivalent.[85] Even in poverty-stricken Mauritania, where students had to take turns to go out and care for the animals carrying their books or slates with them, a student might occasionally have a slave to relieve him of this work.[86] Even a teacher who had fallen into disfavour might yet hope for something: Samori, the nineteenth-century Mandingo leader in West Africa, after quarrelling with his former master, defeated and captured him, and then offered him, as one deeply versed in the Quran, wives and slaves if he would freely remain with him.[87]

Beyond this direct involvement of slaves in education lay the general contribution of slave labour, on the farms and elsewhere, releasing slave-owners from such menial tasks and leaving them free for study. In this respect, the abolition of slavery imposed by the European colonial authorities had, quite unintentionally, the effect of checking Islam, as both teachers and students found that they now had less time for academic and religious work.[88] The decline of Touba, founded by the Jahanka in 1815 and one of the three main centres of Islam in the area which is now the modern state of Guinea,

---

[83] A.H. Ba and J. Daget, *L'empire peul du Macina*, I, The Hague 1962, 64.
[84] *ibid.*, 52, 105.
[85] P. Marty, *Etudes sur l'Islam et les tribus du Soudan*, Paris 1920, II, 83.
[86] Ahmad bin al-Amin al-Shinqiti, *Al-wasit fi tarajim udaba Shinqit*, Cairo 1911, 493; partly translated by M. Teffahi, as Ahmed Lamine ech Chenguiti, *El Wasit*, Saint-Louis (Senegal) 1953, 115.
[87] A. Kouroubari, 'Histoire de l'Iman [*sic*] Samori', *Bulletin de l'Institut français d'Afrique noire*, series B, 1959, 547.
[88] V. Thompson and R. Adloff, *French West Africa*, London 1958, 149.

was attributed to the liberation of the slaves, which obliged masters and disciples to farm for food.[89] On the other hand, in the case of slaves of non-Muslim masters, the abolition of slavery has sometimes led to the ex-slaves becoming Muslim; this is reported in parts of Mossi country.[90]

In some instances modern education reverses the old pattern, and the despised black man, son or grandson of a slave, becomes a teacher. This has happened sometimes in Mauritania, where the blacks have been much readier to take advantage of French western education than have the nomads. But racial antagonism in the country, rooted in past slavery, continues, and modern schools among the nomads are handicapped by being staffed often by blacks, whom the nomads still regard as of slave status. One black teacher was stoned by his pupils for asking them to carry their own food sacks.[91]

Religious conversion and commitment

'On Friday the 1st of Muharram my wife Umm Asta Belel said that in respect of her being a Muslim she was tired of it, and in respect of her being a pagan it would be better for her.' (Hamman Yaji, p. 80, 25 August 1922)

The tendency for slaves to adopt the religion of their masters has been widespread, in Africa and outside. The Portuguese crown, for example, towards the end of the seventeenth century, was concerned about heretical (that is to say, Protestant) foreigners in Brazil, who might own slaves and teach them heresy. It was suggested that heretics be forbidden to own slaves, or even that they be expelled from the country.[92]

Within tropical Africa, the adoption of Islam by the slaves of Muslim masters was, by and large, normal procedure, often deliberately fostered by the slave-owners. In 1606 a Portuguese Franciscan friar at Pate, on the east coast, heard of traders who came from Arabia to barter for African boys, who were then taken to Arabia, made Muslim, and kept as slaves.[93] Krapf, an

---

[89] M. Houis, *La Guinée française*, Paris 1953, 40.
[90] E.P. Skinner, 'Islam in Mossi society' in Lewis, 1966, 362; almost all liberated slaves and serfs in Nobéré, a Mossi district, became Muslim.
[91] Thompson and Adloff, 1958, 162, 532.
[92] Verger, 1976, 50-1.
[93] Freeman-Grenville, 1962/1975, 162.

early Anglican missionary, on a Persian ship in the Red Sea in 1838, witnessed some Galla slave boys being taught the Muslim prayer.[94] Later in the nineteenth century, Speke told how slaves bought in Zanzibar were circumcised, and taught to distinguish between clean and unclean animals. They also learnt some Arabic words and some even went on pilgrimage.[95] On his way from the West African coast to Futa Jallon in 1873, Blyden visited a slave town called Fansiggah. Here the king had built a mosque among the Pagan slaves; it was compulsory for children to learn the Quran, and optional for their parents to attend prayers. Blyden thought this a widespread practice among Muslim chiefs.[96]

Such attention by the master to the conversion of his slaves had in part a practical purpose. Speke remarked that until the slaves in Zanzibar had been circumcised, and had learnt which meats were legally clean, they could not slaughter and prepare food for their masters. Such practical points applied throughout Muslim Africa. But they do not provide a full explanation, for there was also, among some masters at least, concern for the eternal salvation of their slaves. Krapf commented that Muslim traders thought they were behaving mercifully in selling as slaves Pagans, who must in this way become Muslim,[97] a view reminiscent of some earlier Christian argument about the trans-Atlantic trade.[98] The feeling was sometimes ultimately reciprocated, as is suggested in the story of the enslaved Zanj king (see pp. 85-6). Doughty found that the African slaves in Arabia apparently bore no resentment over their condition, and were even grateful for the opportunity of salvation.[99]

There is some evidence that the attempts of slaves to better their understanding of Islam did not always meet with a sympathetic reception. Among the Fulani of Adamawa, for

[94] Krapf, 1860, 20.
[95] J.H. Speke, *Journal of the discovery of the source of the Nile*, London 1863, xxv-vi, xxviii.
[96] H.R. Lynch, *Edward Wilmot Blyden: pan-Negro patriot*, London 1967, 97.
[97] Krapf, 1860, 121.
[98] D.P. Mannix and M. Cowley, *Black cargoes: a history of the Atlantic slave trade (1518-1865)*, New York 1962, xii, 8, 26, 44, 58-60.
[99] Doughty, I, 554-5.

example, such an effort was more likely to be received with irony than with approval by the master.[100] The dances of the free pastoral Fulani included prayers and the participation of the *imam*, while the dances of their slaves lacked such religious embellishment, though the slaves were Muslim and would on other occasions pray with their masters.[101]

It was not uncommon for slaves to join with their masters in joint fulfilment of standard religious obligations. Nachtigal, at almost the same time that Blyden was in Fansiggah, watching the Muslim instruction of slaves there, saw slaves and masters praying together in Borno, in the streets at evening (see p. 35 above).[102]

In fact, to refuse to join in this way might have striking symbolic impact, as in 1926 in Sierra Leone, when slaves claiming freedom underlined their demand by praying separately from their masters in Ramadan.[103]

The religious obligations of a Muslim slave were somewhat laxer than those of his free colleague. The congregational prayer on Friday is required of all free Muslims, with certain exemptions as for disability. It was not required for a slave, though if he should happen to be present then he should join in.[104] It was recommended for a partially free slave, in the *mukatib* category (see p. 75), even without his master's permission: but for an ordinary slave, or even a *mudabbar* slave (see pp. 74-5), only with such permission.[105]

Al-Hajj Umar, arguing in favour of the superiority of the internal *jihad*, the struggle to control one's own evil inclinations, over the external, or military, *jihad*, said that the former was incumbent upon all, free and slave, male and female, while the latter was required only of free men, although participation was permitted to a slave who had his master's permission.[106]

---

[100] P.F. Lacroix, 'L'Islam peul de l'Adamawa', in Lewis, 1966, 402.

[101] D.J. Stenning, 'Cattle values and Islamic values in a pastoral population', in Lewis, 1966, 394.

[102] II, 160.

[103] Paper N.A. 13/1926, 5 May 1926, at Kabala District Office, Sierra Leone.

[104] Ibn Abi Zayd, 95.

[105] Khalil bin Ishaq, I, 87.

[106] J.R. Willis, 'Al-Hajj Umar...the doctrinal basis of his Islamic reformist

Similarly a slave was not required to make the pilgrimage; indeed, should he do so, but without his master's permission, his pilgrimage would be invalid.[107] With such permission, however, it was a valid act of worship, and indeed some schools of law allowed a slave to deputize as pilgrim for a free man.[108] Impressive legal complications may arise from these complex provisions: what is the position, for instance, of a slave whose master authorizes him to go on pilgrimage, but who is then bought by a new owner who is unaware of this authorization? or of a slave thus authorized who somehow vitiates, say by some ritual irregularity, his pilgrimage?[109]

These special exceptions and disabilities for slave Muslims did not mean that the slaves were necessarily any the less devout. Many authors, though some added that the Muslim education of slaves was often rudimentary, comment on the devotion, even fanaticism, of slaves.[110] The tale of the pious black slave, the 468th of the *Arabian Nights*, illustrates one popular Middle Eastern image of such a slave: whose prayer was powerful enough to bring rain in time of drought, or to encompass the slave's own suicide, though his commercial value was low. The elder of the two slaves whose services were transferred to Nachtigal by Shaykh Umar was not merely a nominal but a deeply committed Muslim; the younger one was a Muslim too, though less strict. Nachtigal's comments on his relationship with Billama, the younger, and Mohammedu are interesting:

> On his transfer to my service, Billama felt only a confused fear, and the antipathy towards me which the popular opinion of Christians had created in him; Mohammedu, however, was full of conscious hostility to his infidel master (see above, p. 57, and below, p. 287). I explained to him in a friendly way that, while the Shaykh had allotted him to my service, he did not on that account have to consider himself as a slave, for we Christians regarded slavery as unlawful, and that he could therefore run away whenever he wanted.

---

movement...', University of London thesis, 1970, 107 & note.
[107] el-Nager, 1969, 13.
[108] *ibid.*, 13; see also p. 230 below.
[109] Khalil ibn Ishaq, I, 175-6.
[110] See for example C. Snouck Hurgronje, *Mekka in the latter part of the 19th century*, Leiden and London 1931, 11; Richardson, 1848, I, 195.

I then put to him the consideration that it would be to his advantage to serve me faithfully: firstly because I would never sell him; secondly because I would probably clothe and feed him better than anyone else under whose control he might come; thirdly because I should leave him undisturbed in the religion to which he was devoted; and fourthly that I would never take him to my own home country, but would rather provide him with the means to return to Bornu after we had arrived on the coast or in Egypt, and draw up a letter of emancipation, which I would ask the Shaykh to validate in a special document. He was intelligent enough to take these reasons into account and to submit willingly to his situation. But if it was not easy for such impressionable young men, resisting the prejudices of the crowd and exposed as 'the slaves of a Christian' ['*Christensclaven*'] to the ridicule and derision of neighbours and other slaves, to remain faithfully and willingly in their employment, so still less might I hope soon to gain their genuine affection and loyalty. However good the service that the boys, especially Mohammedu, gave me in the years which followed, their feelings towards me in fact became more friendly only in Egypt, where the hatred which attached to me as a Christian disappeared, and where they had an opportunity to observe the great kindness and generosity of the Khedive towards me.[111]

Slave status was not incompatible, in certain cases, with considerable religious learning—although in many of the available examples such learning may have been acquired before the individual's enslavement. Among black slaves in Bahia, Quran schools flourished; the police tried, during the disturbances and slave rebellion of 1835, to arrest the teachers of these schools, on the grounds that they were dangerous agitators.[112] It was possible for education so far to outweigh distinctions of slave and free status that a slave might teach freedmen in such a school.[113] Such literacy was not always a cause of concern to the authorities, even in the New World: a slave sold in Jamaica about 1805 was employed later as a

[111] III, 58-9.
[112] Verger, 1976, 297ff.
[113] *ibid.*, 461.

storeman, keeping his accounts in Arabic since he could not read or write English.[114]

Another story, concerning King Ali of Wadai and the Sanusiya, would, if true, provide an example of unusually advanced Muslim qualifications and activity amongst slaves. According to this, King Ali was eager to reverse the xenophobic excesses of his father, and to re-open intercourse between Wadai and the outside world. A caravan of slaves, despatched by a party of Wadai merchants, was captured by nomads on the frontier between Egypt and Tripolitania. However, Muhammad bin Ali el-Senusi intervened, and arranged for the slaves to be bought, instructed in Islam, freed, and finally returned to Wadai as missionaries.[115]

Though in the following instance the letters are mundane rather than religious, the story of Abd Masuma, a nineteenth-century slave poet in Mauritania, warrants retelling. Abd Masuma was deeply in love with his master's wife. His master, aware of this, tied him to a stake and left him to perish. There, another poet, who was himself in love and who had wandered for days seeking someone to complete a love poem for him, found him. Abd Masuma was unwilling to be released, and by that the wanderer knew that the captive was also in love. The wanderer recited some lines, and Abd Masuma did likewise, revealing that he was also a poet. The wanderer asked him to complete the unfinished poem for him. Abd Masuma agreed, if it should be a love poem. And so it was done.[116]

It has been said that slaves 'were readily accepted into the clergy',[117] but it would seem that instances of this were rare. The law allows a high-ranking slave to act as *imam* for free men.[118] For freedmen, the opportunities for clerical appointment were better. A curious episode, in Darfur in the 1780s, illustrates this. The sultan of Darfur at that time, Tirab, marched out with all his troops to confront a threatened attack from

[114] P. D. Curtin, *Africa remembered: narratives by west Africans from the era of the slave trade*, Madison, Milwaukee and London, 1968, 155.

[115] H. Duveyrier, *La confrérie musulmane de Sidi Muhammad ben Ali es-Senousi*, Rome 1918, 17; cited in *Sahara and Sudan*, IV, 43 n.

[116] H.T. Norris, *Shinqiti folk literature and song*, Oxford 1968, 57-8.

[117] Lewis, 1966, 51.

[118] Khalil ibn Ishaq, I, 77.

Kordofan; but, not wishing to leave his capital empty, the sultan freed 100 of his slaves, making the greatest of them *hakim*, or chief official, for the town. The sultan also instructed each of his men to free one or more slaves, and one slave of the *imam*, thus freed, was himself appointed an *imam*.[119]

Nachtigal twice sketches the various Pagan peoples with whom the Bagirmi had relations, sometimes quite friendly but often hostile. Within this shifting pattern, there was certainly some Muslim influence at work, from the Bagirmi side; though Nachtigal almost never directed his attention to this theme, and says very little about it. That some Muslim religious penetration is possible, even amid the clamour of violence, is shown by a tiny (and admittedly unusual) entry in Hamman Yaji's diary: 'Two pagans came to me from Duhu and asked me to admit them to Islam.'[120] The forthright comment by Hamman Yaji's wife, quoted at the head of this section, shows the potential for some movement also in the opposite direction. However, because neither she nor the two Pagans seem to have been slaves, they stand outside the slavery theme.

Emancipation

'I arrested Galwa and Buba Maradi for their offence in not obeying my summons and I had them flogged and imprisoned. Galwa, however, I will free from slavery when he comes out of prison in three days' time, if there is a reason for his being freed.' (Hamman Yaji, p. 115, 31 July 1925)

Slaves belonging to a real Muslim would, it has been said, be keen to give unmistakable witness of their new faith, in order thus to win their freedom.[121] But while the conversion of slaves to Islam was very general, converted slaves could not count on emancipation. The ecstatic cry of Blyden, nineteenth-century West Indian champion of African Islam, that 'the slave who embraces Islam is free',[122] may be true in an apocalyptic or spiritual, or perhaps a Pickwickian, sense; as a generalization about ordinary affairs it is unfounded. It is difficult to find

[119] Na'um Shuqair, *Tarikh al-sudan*, Cairo 1903, I, 118.
[120] p. 83, 15 June 1922.
[121] C. Monteil, *Les Bambara du Ségou et du Kaarta*, Paris 1924, 337.
[122] E.W. Blyden, *Christianity, Islam and the Negro race*, London 1887, reprinted 1967, 175-6.

anything in the historical record to justify Blyden's confident assertion of 1871 that

> the introduction of Islam into Central and West Africa has been the most important, if not the sole, preservative against the desolations of the slave-trade. Mohammedanism furnished a protection to the tribes who embraced it by effectually binding them together in one strong religious fraternity, and enabling them by their united effort to baffle the attempt of the powerful Pagan slave-hunters.[123]

Blyden later commended the British occupation of Egypt, in 1882, as tending to supply a like preservative against the slave trade, but in this case against the Arab trade in blacks.[124]

Freeing a slave was widely regarded as a meritorious act, but conversion and emancipation were only occasionally linked by deliberate policy. This appears to have been the case, for example, in the Masina theocracy of the early nineteenth century. There the slaves of the state, i.e. prisoners of war not voluntarily practising Islam, were settled in cultivable areas, under clerical overseers who both organized the farm work and without constraint initiated the captives in Islam. When such a slave could justify his faith, and pray without help, he was freed.[125] This may, however, have been more an ideal than what actually happened. The same account of Masina says, a little later, that a prisoner was kept for three days with the clerics, who tried to convert him; if he refused, he was executed on the third day, his body remaining unburied and his heirs having no rights of succession.[126] A somewhat comparable situation may have existed in Adamawa, where Usuman dan Fodio, in his initial instructions to the Emir Adama, said that slaves who had become true Muslims might be liberated;[127] but despite this Adamawa became the major slave reservoir of the Sokoto empire.

In the vast majority of cases, a slave had to look elsewhere for hopes of emancipation. Piety was one possibility. Both the

[123] Blyden, 1887/1967, 186.
[124] Lynch, 1967, 193.
[125] Ba and Daget, 1962, I, 66-7.
[126] *ibid.*, 1962, I, 119 n.
[127] M.Z. Njeuma, *Fulani hegemony in Yola (Old Adamawa): 1809-1901*, n.p. 1978, 75.

Quran (Surah xxiv.33) and the traditions of the Prophet urge the freeing of slaves, whether for heavenly or secular recompense. Maliki law cites the tradition: 'whosoever frees a slave who is a Muslim, God will redeem every member of his body, limb for limb, from hell-fire'.[128] However, such an act was only one of many virtuous observances open to the pious, and by no means the most prominent one. Bello, sultan of Sokoto, cited not only the tradition just quoted, but also the further commentary of the lawyers, to the effect that giving alms (*sadaqah*) was preferable to freeing a slave (*'itq*); freeing a slave was rewarded by freedom from damnation, but so was affirming the unity of God, while to repeat this ten times was equivalent to freeing four Arabs, or one hundred times, to freeing ten slaves.[129]

While such qualifications need to be mentioned, there are still many examples of slaves being freed as an act of individual piety. Mansa Musa, the celebrated fourteenth-century ruler of Mali, it is said won added renown by emancipating a slave every day.[130] Of a certain cleric in Timbuktu it is recorded that he bought a large number of slaves, and freed them for the love of God and in view of the life hereafter.[131] Oral tradition recalls of Ngolo, later in the eighteenth century to become king of Segu and perhaps the strongest ruler of his day in the western Sudan, that he had been enslaved as a youth, but had been freed by his master, a cleric, on learning half the Quran.[132] Ngolo, however, was not a very reliable Muslim. Baba of Karo recalled that the reason why her grandfather had freed his slaves 'was because he wanted to be rewarded when he died—because of religion'.[133]

Pious emancipation might appropriately occur on the occasion of some religious festival, especially at the end of Ramadan. In Sokoto in 1824, several slaves were freed at this

[128] F.H. Ruxton, *Maliki law*, London 1916, 351 n. 6.
[129] Muhammad Bello, 'Tanbih al-raqid', unpublished MS. cited in el-Nager, 1969, 367, 384-5.
[130] Kati, 55.
[131] Abd al-Rahman ibn Abdullah al-Sadi, *Tarikh al-Sudan*, tr. O. Houdas, Paris 1913-14, reprinted 1964, 84.
[132] C. Monteil, 1924, 47-8.
[133] Mary Smith, 1954/1981, 40.

time, Clapperton's landlord himself liberating fifteen.[134] Or emancipation might follow the accomplishment, by the slave, of some special religious task, such as the pilgrimage (see pp. 67, 229-30). Emancipation might itself provide the occasion for a festival. The Hausa celebrated a slave's payment of his redemption money, and receiving his freedom, in much the same way as the naming of a baby on the eighth day after birth: a cleric shaved the head of the ex-slave, giving him a Muslim name and sacrificing a ram.[135] There may be a brief echo of something similar in Hamman Yaji's fleeting diary entry for January 1925: 'I named a slave girl Tada after I had freed her.'[136]

The piety of the master might be stimulated by his own distress: in illness, for example, he might seek God's mercy through such devout acts. Usuman dan Fodio, condemning some Hausa, who were alleged to sacrifice a slave in the hope of recovery from a serious illness, added that to free a slave in such hope might be effective.[137] Similar emancipation was apparently quite well known on the east coast in more recent times.[138]

In Muslim society, a master's death may sometimes confer freedom on his slaves. Clapperton said that this was frequent among the Fulani,[139] but on the whole it seems to have been rare in Africa. Jobson spoke of slaves and their children as perpetual bondmen to their clerical Mandingo masters and their children.[140] In Adamawa, slaves were, like other property, distributed among the heirs of a deceased master.[141] Speke

[134] Bovill, *Missions*, IV, 714; see also pp. 701-2.
[135] J.S. Trimingham, *The influence of Islam on Africa*, London and Beirut 1968, 92-3.
[136] p. 108.
[137] H.R. Palmer, 'An early Fulani conception of Islam', *Journal of the African Society*, 1914, 59.
[138] M.W.H. Beech, 'Slavery on the east coast of Africa', *Journal of the African Society*, 1916, 148.
[139] Bovill, *Missions*, IV, 654; Clapperton here mentions also manumission at religious festivals.
[140] R. Jobson, *The golden trade, or, A discovery of the River Gambra, and the golden trade of the Aethiopians*, London 1623, reprinted 1932, 84-5.
[141] J.-C. Froelich, 'Le commandement et l'organisation sociale chez les Foulbé de l'Adamawa', *Études camerounaises*, 1954, 19.

contrasted the situation in Arabia, where slaves would be freed in accord with the 'Muhammadan creed', with the custom in Zanzibar of willing one's slaves to one's heirs.[142] Sometimes African slaves sold outside Africa were released when their master died. Speke's principal African guide, Bombay, taken as a slave to India, had been freed there on his master's death.[143] Almas, the man nominated by Shaykh Umar as Nachtigal's guide on a six-month expedition to Bagirmi, had been taken to Constantinople as a slave in childhood, and there freed in consequence of the death of his master.[144]

Speke is not altogether accurate in stating that Muslim law requires the freeing of slaves on the master's death. This is legally required only in the case of a slave who is *umm al-walad,* mother of the child, that is to say a slave who has borne her master a child.[145] There is however a special category of slave-to-be-freed, who is called *mudabbar.* A *mudabbar* slave has received his master's assurance that, on the master's death, the slave will be freed: a situation much like that which obtained, for example, among Christian masters in Brazil, who sometimes assuaged their consciences by making provision in their wills for freeing some of their slaves after their death.[146] In Muslim law, after such an assurance has been given, the *mudabbar* slave may not be sold, but he continues to work for his master, and his property is, at least in law, at his master's disposal. A master may still enjoy sexual relations with a female slave who is *mudabbar.* There are certain qualifications. A man may retract his last testament, if he wishes, including the provision to enfranchise a slave. A debtor whose patrimony does not cover his debts may not validly free a slave. Nor may a slave be made *mudabbar* unless he falls within that third of the estate over which the testator has powers of independent allocation. And again, if someone owns only part of a slave (i.e. the ownership is shared between two people) and he frees the slave, the slave does not become a free man until due

---

[142] Speke, 1863, xxvi.
[143] Speke, 1864, 211-12.
[144] III, 53; see below, pp. 95-6.
[145] Ibn Abi Zayd, 226.
[146] Verger, 1976, 432.

compensation has been paid to the co-owner.[147] Some slaves might gain their freedom through their master's last will and testament when he had adopted this device to frustrate the expectations of avaricious heirs.

Another type of freed slave was the *mukatib*, a slave freed by *kitaba*, or contract. Under this arrangement, a contract was made between the owner and his slave, usually for the payment of a certain sum, and, after payment had been completed, the slave was released. Should he however fall behind in his instalments, he returned to his original state of unqualified servitude, and the master kept what had already been paid.[148] The *mukatib* slave was, in some respects, in a slightly stronger position than the *mudabbar*; we have earlier mentioned that it was recommended for the *mukatib*, but not for the *mudabbar*, to attend the Friday prayer even without his master's authorization (see p. 66); similarly, if a *mukatib* slave makes a vow, his master should not prevent him from fulfilling it unless such fulfilment might interfere with the payments, while for another slave the master may forbid fulfilment of the vow, though the vow remains binding and the slave must resume it should he ever subsequently become free.[149]

I have already pointed out that the provision, in the legal texts, of the opportunity for the slave to earn the means to purchase his freedom, complements the traditional acknowledgment in many parts of Muslim Africa of the slave's right to own property (see p. 59 above). The income opportunities of slaves naturally varied greatly according to the type of employment to which they were assigned: slaves dwelling in town, and occupied in commerce or crafts, were more favourably placed than those on the farm or in the mines. This was the case also in Brazil,[150] where the *mukatib* arrangement had a close parallel, just as did the *mudabbar*. A slave in Brazil might oblige his master to free him, by offering his cost price; newborn slaves were being sold for the equivalent of £5 in 1816, and if this were offered at the baptism, the master had

[147] Ibn Abi Zayd, 220 ff.; a vow to free someone else's slave is not binding (168).
[148] *ibid.*, 222-4.
[149] Khalil ibn Ishaq, I, 139.
[150] Verger, 1976, 42-9.

to free the slave. Some slaves asked important people to stand as godparents, hoping that they would not allow their godchildren to remain in slavery.[151]

Another variety of emancipation which figures prominently in the legal texts is emancipation granted as a form of *kaffara*, or legal expiation for some wrongdoing. The necessary (i.e. *wajib*) expiation for non-intentional homicide was to free a slave. If this was beyond your resources, you should fast for two consecutive months. Even if your offence is pardoned, you were still encouraged to fulfil the expiation.[152] For breaking Ramadan intentionally, the expiation was also either to free a slave, or to fast two subsequent months, with a further alternative of giving a *mudd*, approximately a peck, of grain to each of sixty poor persons.[153] This last alternative was the one preferred by the law.[154] To atone for a broken oath, you might give ten poor free Muslims a *mudd* each, or more, or you might clothe them, or free a Muslim slave; or, if you were too poor to manage any of these alternatives, you might fast three days.[155] It was not permitted to combine the alternatives, for example freeing half a slave and feeding five poor people.[156] Whoever swore to renounce sexual relations with his wife—this was called *tazahara*—might resume them only after the expiation of freeing a believing slave, without bodily defects, whom the master owns fully and whose servitude is total.[157] The definition of the slave suitable for emancipation in a case of *tazahara* is the standard also in violations of Ramadan or in broken oaths.[158] (The contrary case, in which a wife or concubine intends a voluntary fast involving sexual abstinence, was not allowed without the master's permission.[159])

[151] .Verger, 1976, 454.
[152] Ibn Abi Zayd, 250.
[153] *ibid.*, 120-2.
[154] Khalil ibn Ishaq, I, 134.
[155] Ibn Abi Zayd, 166-8; Khalil ibn Ishaq, I, 188-9.
[156] Khalil ibn Ishaq, I, 189.
[157] Ibn Abi Zayd, 188; but p. 190 says that there is nothing wrong with freeing a one-eyed slave or an illegitimate child, but adds that among Muslims of the Maliki rite it is better to pray and fast.
[158] Khalil ibn Ishaq, I, 134, 188-9.
[159] *ibid.*, I, 137. Compare pp. 192, 205 below.

It is not easy to find many practical illustrations of these acts of compensatory emancipation in the African sources, but at least two categories—violations of Ramadan, and *tazahara*—are mentioned as of actual importance in East Africa.[160]

So deeply ingrained was the idea that to free a slave was a fitting expiation for wrongdoing, that it may be found also in heretical Muslim sects. For example, among the eccentric teachings of the Baraghwata, in eleventh-century Morocco, was a ban on killing cocks, since these birds were believed to indicate the hours of prayer; and whoever killed one was liable to the penalty of liberating a slave.[161]

Ransom is another means of procuring freedom, not unambiguously relevant for us since not all those who were ransomed, or who might theoretically have been ransomed but were not, or who refused to be ransomed, were slaves. Nachtigal encountered situations involving ransom, and comparable references occur elsewhere in the literature.

Ransom, as we have already seen in the discussion of *jihad*, is one option recommended in the Quran (see above, p. 47). The first ransom incident in Nachtigal's travels occurred when he was still on his way into Tibesti. On this occasion, despite the best efforts of Nachtigal and his immediate companions at vigilance, a local man succeeded in making off with a good double-barrelled hunting gun. The weapon was not stolen for its own sake, but to be used as a ransom for a brother of the thief, a brother then being held prisoner in Kanem by the Awlad Sulayman Arabs.[162]

Nachtigal next took up the theme of ransom when he was himself staying, and travelling, with the Awlad Sulayman. Nachtigal does not tell us whether he found the gun-thief's brother still in captivity. Nachtigal does tell us about Khamis, an expert tracker, captured as a child from the Mahamid Arabs, but later so loyal to the Awlad Sulayman that he would never run away, despite his first-class knowledge of the region.

Among the Awlad Sulayman a prisoner of war differs from a

---

[160] Beech, 1916, 148.
[161] Ibn Abi Zar al-Gharnati, *Roudh el-Kartas*, A. Beaumier (tr.), Paris 1860, 181.
[162] I, 273 and n., 395-6.

slave only in so far as, unlike a captured Negro or Ennedi man, he can scarcely ever be sold. In such a case skin colour and Arab origin are given more weight than the properly decisive question of religion....If Arab prisoners of war fall into the hands of their enemies when young, and are not exchanged or ransomed by their relations, they assimilate themselves to their new company, become freed men with a certain dependent relationship, marry a girl in a similar situation, rank above the despised status of a real slave, though of course without being full citizens, and scarcely ever return to their own tribe.[163]

Even those who had no claim to special consideration on religious or racial grounds, and who were simply slaves, were treated by the Awlad Sulayman with benevolence. Barbarously and cruelly as they may have been seized, captives were generally received humanely into the family circle. Hazaz, a particular friend of Nachtigal's, owned a thirteen-year-old slave boy, Kore, not an Arab, and whom he loved

> almost as much as his own children, and would not have sold at any price. Kore...fully returned the love of his master. He was entirely one of the family, and his father, a well-to-do man who came from time to time with a rich ransom, could in no way induce him to return home.[164]

Hamman Yaji witnessed a similar refusal to go home:

> A letter came from the Christian Mr. Wilkinson, saying that Ghamiri had made a complaint against me. He ordered me to return the girl to her mother, but she rejected her parents and said to them that she would never return to the pagans....On the next day, Friday, the Kadi of Madagali, Abba, came into my presence, and she told him the same as she had told me. I therefore wrote a letter to the Judge of the North, Mr. Wilkinson.[165]

Nachtigal observed more elaborate ransom arrangements a little later, when an Awlad Sulayman raid against the Bideyat

---

[163] II, 351. Among the sedentary population of Borku there were prisoners of war who had not been ransomed, but because of religious scruples had not been made slaves (p. 58 above).

[164] II, 352.

[165] pp. 143-4, 21-22 July 1927.

people of Ennedi went wrong, leaving several of the raiders in the hands of their intended victims.

Although there were many kinsfolk of the Bideyat among the slaves of the Arabs, no exchange, such as might have been expected, was sought for them against the recently captured prisoners of war. The feeling of solidarity was not sufficiently strong among the inhabitants of Ennedi, and only the master of an Arab prisoner who had a family member among the Awlad Sulayman or Mgharba demanded an exchange; the others claimed a ransom of ten camels per man, but were satisfied with less if the prisoner's family were not rich enough. The conditions must be described as reasonable, even as moderate, for the Arabs, it must be admitted, had they been masters of the situation, would not have shown any such leniency.[166]

A few days later, a *murabid*, a Muslim cleric or holy man, missing and presumed dead on the raid, appeared unheralded in the camp of the Awlad Sulayman: 'In view of his religious character and his poverty, he had been released on his promise to despatch later as high a price as possible for his freedom.'[167]

Hamman Yaji supplies further ransom examples:

Yokodu Koro complained against me to the Resident and said that he had an accusation against me. He claimed I had said that I intended to give him £3 on account of the ransom of his female slave named Zamanei... Yokodu Koro made some very violent remarks, and was sent to the Kadi, who sentenced him to £2 fine and gave a judgment that his female slave Zamanei was free. Further, he ordered him to pay up Zamanei's property, namely a woollen mat, two pots and four sashes.[168]

---

[166] II, 377-8. For people and cattle held for ransom against ivory, see below, p. 111.

[167] II, 378. See above, pp. 20-1.

[168] Hamman Yaji, 133, 11 October 1926. It is interesting to notice, in both this and the preceding Hamman Yaji reference, how the colonial authorities are being drawn into local slavery procedures. Another example, p. 126, 19 April 1926: 'On the same day I cleared Gabdo of guilt before the Resident, who told him not to do as he had been doing, or he would prevent himself being given his freedom.' Lovejoy and Hogendorn discuss ransom in colonial Northern Nigeria in great detail; see their index.

In October 1921, a complicated exchange is entered, which may have centred upon Hamman Yaji having held the wife of a village chief for ransom, though just what was going on behind all the detail is not quite clear:

> I sent for Arnado Muduvu, Fashakha, and took from him 3 cows and a man of his, and I returned to him one cow, his wife and all his goods.[169]

Ransom appears on the last day of Hamman Yaji's journal: 'I sent Tataraktu a slave-girl from my house, who belonged to the Webengo pagans. His wife gave me 32 s[hillings] as her ransom.'[170] At first reading, this seemed to me rather like disguised sale at a knock-down price. Perhaps I was too cynical, for I later noticed a similar entry: 'the pagans of Subala ransomed their women at 36 shillings a woman.' That was in November 1914,[171] nearly thirteen years earlier. So there may have been a fairly steady going rate for that particular job.

There are also one or two references to a straightforward exchange of hostages, in some measure comparable to ransom, but not involving slavery or emancipation.[172]

And one final, somewhat eccentric, ransom incident. This comes from another of the Sokoto letters. A raid, led by the over-exuberant Mahe Sarkin Mafara (see pp. 171-2), has misfired, and a grandson of the Sokoto caliph has fallen into the hands of the enemy, who have had French help. A letter to the caliph reports this:

> ... the Christians have put a heavy ransom on him. They have stipulated for twenty pairs of trousers...twenty black Kano cloths...forty cloths... and twenty cloths...in all a hundred, also three youths and two girls. This is the ransom which they have imposed, for your information.[173]

Emancipation might come almost instantaneously. Hamman Yaji again. 'I raided the pagans of Kara, who are between me and the Mandara people named Dhunfa, and we captured four slaves, of whom I returned two and kept two. We got a

[169] p. 77.
[170] p. 145, 25 August 1927.
[171] p. 56.
[172] For example, I, 340, between Tibesti and Fezzan.
[173] Backwell, 1927/1969, no. 16, pp. 23-4.

cow and killed four men.'[174] This sounds as though the Dhunfa Mandarans and Madagali might have had joint slaving rights in the area. Again, and still more surprisingly: 'I raided Kanikela and captured five slave girls, whom I let go, and 20 cattle.'[175]

Another possibility of change for the slave, though not equivalent to emancipation, is found in a curious custom reported in variant forms from the western Sahara and Sudan. According to one account, if a discontented slave succeeds in cutting the ear of a free man, not his master, or of a child of such a free man, then the slave passes to the wounded man and can be redeemed only at enormous cost. An unusually amiable chief, the *almami* of Dimar, was said little by little to have lost both ears in this way.[176] Another description says that the person seeking transfer must try to cut the ear of his prospective master, or to kill his horse.[177] Yet another, speaking of the Kel-Air Tuareg, says that the act sealing the transfer is to cut the ear of a child or a horse of a free man, or to kill his camel.[178] A more recent statement says that, among the Tuareg, if a slave cuts a piece from the ear of a riding-camel of another master, that other master must take him as compensation for the damage done, and the original owner has no claim or redress.

> It is an extreme loss of prestige for a Tuareg to lose his slave in this way, and is a great mark of honour for the new master, who will receive his new slave with favour and give him clothes and a camel with a saddle.[179]

---

[174] p. 71; 16 September 1919.

[175] p. 58, January/February 1916. Kanikela is not indexed.

[176] W.W. Reade, *Savage Africa*, London 1864, 582.

[177] R. Caillié, *Journal d'un voyage à Tembouctou . . .*, Paris 1830, reprinted 1965, I, 155-6; he however speaks of a tributary, rather than a slave, and adds that the fugitive takes all his livestock and possessions with him; should he be recaptured before cutting the ear, or killing the horse, he is beaten and loses all his property.

[178] P. Marty, *L'Islam et les tribus dans la colonie du Niger*, Paris 1931, 245-6.

[179] Nicolaisen, 1997, II, 602. These provisions, in a distant and curiously inverted form, perhaps echo the law of Moses on Sinai, that the master shall pierce the ear of a slave who does not wish to go free, as a sign of his perpetual bondage (Exodus xxi. 6).

Emancipation in Africa was sometimes a regulated, formal business. In Sokoto, the letter of manumission had to be signed before a *qadi*, and attested by two witnesses.[180] The Sokoto letter no.103 in Backwell's collection illustrates this very well, from Sarkin Kaya to the Sokoto caliph:

> I give thanks to you for all the kindness you have done, in that you have brought to an end the quarrel between me and my rivals. May Allah increase your days, and give you power over your enemies. Allah alone knows the extent of my thanks to you. I have sent by my messenger 2,500 cowries along with Machudo, no more and no less. Also to inform you that I have freed Shamaki [?,] Baraya and Alyara. I beg that you will write for each of them redemption papers and have them witnessed.[181]

It seems possible that these manumissions may have been penalties, or acts of atonement.

Such a letter was called '*ataqa*. Richardson, in the desert between Soqna and Murzuq in 1846, heard slaves on their way north singing of their lost homes in Borno and Mandara, and adding, 'O God, give us our Atkah, let us go to our dear home.'[182] Richardson's own servant, Said, was anxious to receive his '*ataqa*, lest he be stolen and sold again.[183] Said's circumstances were somewhat unusual. He had been a slave of Sidi Mustafa, the Consular Agent of Britain in Jerbah, near Tunis. When it was discovered that Sidi Mustafa was keeping slaves, he was dismissed as Agent. Hoping to be reinstated, he prepared documents stating that he had freed all his slaves; these papers went to the British Consul-General. He was not, however, reinstated, and subsequently tried to resume power over his slaves, or ex-slaves. Said thus had to run away—which he did—in order to secure his freedom in practice, though he remained technically a free man because of the paper with the Consul-General.[184] Richardson reassured Said about his

---

[180] Bovill, *Missions*, IV, 654.

[181] p. 63; see also notes on pp. 62 and 64.

[182] Richardson, 1848, II, 377. Whittier, the American poet, wrote a poem based on this song reported by Richardson, including these lines: 'Hear us, save us, make us free; Send our Atka down from thee!'

[183] Richardson, 1848, I, 147.

[184] *ibid.*, I, 14.

legal position; but on at least one occasion a Saharan Tuareg chief did try to confiscate Said for himself.[185]

Denham, returning to Tripoli in 1825, applied through the Consul-General for the Pasha to set his seal to the freedom of a Mandara boy whom Denham had purchased, this being the only legal way for a Christian to free a slave in a Muslim country.[186] Other explorers, such as Richard Lander, who were able to free their slaves under Christian governments, in Lander's case in 1828 at Cape Coast in modern Ghana, presumably followed a less complicated procedure.[187] For the two slaves lent to Nachtigal, he promised to have a letter of emancipation drawn up, which would be formally validated by Shaykh Umar before they left Kuka, so that there should be no question about their status on their return home.[188] Nachtigal, however, made no comment on the practical problems of legal documentation in a country where slavery was commonplace, paper rare, and clothing not normally designed as a receptacle for documents. Lugard in East Africa had feared complications arising from freedom papers, which might be lost, abandoned, or even sold—in fact, thought Lugard, a freed slave might even sell both his paper and then himself, a double profit.[189] Such problems are said to have seriously impaired the efficiency of anti-slavery decrees in Ethiopia at various times during this century.[190]

The return of the slaves

'One of them said...: "This is the boatwork of Moslems." I said, "Perhaps they do the same in the Christian countries." He said, "They're learning."' (Dorugu, talking to two Hausa slave boys bound for Istanbul, on the steamer to Malta. Kirk-Greene and Newman, p. 86).

Enfranchised slaves often made no effort to return to their native country, but continued 'to reside near their old masters, still acknowledging them as their superiors, and presenting

[185] Richardson, 1848, I, 432.
[186] Bovill, *Missions*, III, 511-2.
[187] Lander, in Clapperton, 1829, 326-7.
[188] III, 58 & note. See p. 68 above.
[189] Lugard, 1893, I, 225-6.
[190] M. Pollaud-Dulian, *Aujourd'hui l'esclavage*, Paris 1967, 38.

them yearly with a portion of their earnings.'[191] Nachtigal describes such a pattern in Tripoli, probably the easiest place in the world for a freed slave to return home from, if he or she wished to do so. Remarking that the slave trade is indeed strictly prohibited in Tripoli, and has certainly declined very much, he goes on:

> nevertheless there is still a considerable clandestine traffic in black human ware. As before, several slave caravans come to Tripoli every year; each year, however, the size of the caravans is diminishing, and instead of being taken into the town, the slaves are brought into the gardens of the Meshiya, in order that they may be sold there gradually one by one. This end having been happily achieved, the poor strangers are freed from all their worries. They are treated with the utmost humanity, provided with a letter of manumission, *ataka*, and soon stand in a relationship similar to that of the Roman freedmen to their masters. As soon as the inclination to get married grips them—and with a Negro this inevitably happens very soon—and there is no chance of setting up an independent establishment in their master's house, they are domiciled outside it; their relationship with their former master is, however, scarcely ever completely dissolved.[192]

This sort of relationship is called *wilaa*, which may perhaps be rendered patronage.[193]

This sounds almost too good to be true, and Nachtigal may here be standing a little too close to his friends in Tripoli officialdom. Dorugu was in Tripoli less than fifteen years before Nachtigal set out on his travels. His account of roughly the same situation requires a good deal more initiative, discipline and self-sacrifice on the part of the slave, and it is presumably from the slaves that his information comes.

> Outside Tripoli there is a small town of slaves who have been set free but who are unable to return to their own

---

[191] Bovill, *Missions*, IV, 701-2. *Cf.* Beech, 1916, 145, for the same sort of pattern in East Africa.
[192] I, 16-17.
[193] Ibn Abi Zayd, 220 ff.; *cf.* F.D. Lugard, 'Slavery in all its forms', *Africa*, 1933, 9-10, commenting on the Hanafi code.

countries.[194]...The Hausa people there would like to return home but they don't have enough money to get back to their country. When some of the slaves get money, they hide it away; then when they see that they can buy themselves from their owners, they go to them and do so.[195]

There are other such settlements of black African people, some even closer to their original homes than was Tripoli, some very much further away. Among the blacks in Murzuq were some freedmen who had found a new home in Fezzan.[196] In Ghadames, a considerable number of blacks, offspring of liberated slaves, were settled in the Arab suburb.[197] Bowen, a Baptist missionary who was in West Africa, closer to the coast, at the same time as Barth was moving about in the interior, met a Yoruba woman, 'wife of a Bedouin', who had returned home after having been, so she said, to Constantinople. Yoruba slaves were, he was told, to be found in Tripoli, Fezzan, and many other places.[198] We are not told whether these were still slaves or had been freed, whether settled, or trying to get home. Such African groups were found outside Africa as well: in India, for example, colonies of Africans survived long after they had ceased to be slaves, and the explorer Burton, having learnt their language, was surprised to find on his arrival in East Africa that he already knew Swahili.[199]

Many other slaves sought with varying degrees of diligence to return home. An early, picturesque, and presumably partly legendary example of such return, which nonetheless illustrates various crucial aspects (such as the religious impact and gratitude for this, and the risk of re-enslavement), is the well-known story of a king on the Zanj coast, probably southern Somalia or northern Kenya. In AD 922 a ship from Oman was driven by accident upon the coast. Ship and crew were kindly

[194] Kirk-Greene and Newman, Dorugu's editors, add that 'most of these had been brought to North Africa as slaves, although a few had come on their own and were stranded there' (p. 127, note 3).
[195] *ibid.*, 85-6.
[196] I, 91.
[197] Richardson, 1848 I, 229.
[198] T.J. Bowen, *Adventures and missionary labours in several countries in the interior of Africa from 1849 to 1856*, Charleston, SC 1857, reprinted 1968, 218.
[199] Lugard, 1893, I, 183 n.

received, but repaid this hospitality by kidnapping the local king. He was sold in Oman, and taken to Basra, where he learnt to pray, to fast, and to read parts of the Quran. Sold again, he was taken to Bagdad, where he finished learning the Quran, and prayed in the congregation of the mosque. He then ran away with a party of pilgrims from Khorasan, and with them performed the pilgrimage to Mecca. He joined a returning pilgrimage caravan to Cairo, and thence begged his way up the Nile. Twice he was seized as a slave by other blacks, but escaped, and finally returned home to resume his throne. Later, the same Oman ship was driven again on the same coast. The king again received his kidnappers well, forgiving them their offence since it had led to his own salvation. His only regret was that he had never reimbursed his owner in Bagdad for the losses suffered when he ran away. He would have liked to send him the purchase price, multiplied ten times as damages for the delay, but decided against entrusting this commission to his visitors, whom he released after guarding against a second kidnapping.[200]

Less dramatic instances abound in later times. For much of the first five centuries of Islam, there was peace between Nubia and Egypt, and many slaves were sold north down the Nile. It has been estimated that in the eleventh century AD there were 50,000 slaves in Egypt. These provided a main prop of the Fatimid regime; many became Muslim, and some may have returned home when the Fatimids fell.[201]

[200] Freeman-Grenville, 1962/1975, 9 ff. A better substantiated account of a slave of royal blood concerns Médicon, a nephew of a Borno ruler, who was enslaved in the fighting which broke out in Borno during one of his uncle's pilgrimages. Médicon, his rank unrecognized, was sold to North Africa, but his uncle later sought him out and he was redeemed. A French doctor, himself a slave, met him in Tripoli in 1669. We are not told what, if any, were the religious consequences of Médicon's temporary enslavement. C. de la Roncière, 'Une histoire du Bornou au XVIIe siècle par un chirurgien français captif à Tripoli', *Revue de l'histoire des colonies françaises*, 1919, 2me semestre 86-8.

[201] Y.F. Hasan, 'The penetration of Islam in the eastern Sudan', in Lewis, 1966, 151. An even earlier instance of the return of freed slaves, from the Yemen to the Niger bend, has been suggested (Houdas, in al-Sadi, 9.) in the case of the first za of Koukiya, original cradle of the Songhay empire. There is no proof that this man was a Muslim; his return, if such it was, may indeed have antedated Islam. However, there is no direct evidence either that he

As European travellers became more numerous, penetrating the interior of Africa, we can gather a larger number of specific instances of freed slaves homeward-bound. Specific, but rarely detailed: few of the travellers seem to have realised just how interesting the stories of the returners might have been. Denham and Clapperton, starting from Tripoli in 1822, had several freed slaves in their caravan. The pasha had freed twenty-four from the castle, sixteen of them women. An elderly notable, Muhammad D'Ghies, had freed three Bagirmi slave girls, all under twenty, sisters. Two had been his own property; when he learnt that three sisters had been brought to Tripoli, and the third had been sold to someone else, he searched for her, bought her, and freed her so that she might return with the other two.[202] On the way Denham mentions nearly thirty freed slaves leaving the caravan at Lari, to take the road to their home in Kanem.[203] The caravan with which Barth travelled from Tripoli included sixteen freed slaves.[204]

Nachtigal's own immediate party, as he travelled south across the Sahara at the beginning of his great adventure, included two individuals with slave backgrounds. Sa'ad, a black servant hired in Tripoli, identified as 'a married freedman of a respected citizen of the town'.[205] Sa'ad certainly had no intention of returning to any aboriginal southern home of his: confronted by the prospect of imminent death by thirst, on the journey from Fezzan to Tibesti, he earnestly enjoined upon Nachtigal, should Nachtigal survive and Sa'ad not, the care of his wife and children in Tripoli.[206] Sa'ad left Nachtigal's service, and departed from Kuka with a large northbound caravan including 1,400 slaves long before the end of Nachtigal's travels.[207] The parting appears to have been amicable; whether

was black; this is surmised from the fact that the chronicles do not comment on his race, which they might have done had he been in any way locally unusual.

[202] Bovill, *Missions*, II, 157-8.
[203] *ibid.*, II, 233; one was a deaf-mute woman, see above, pp. xvii-xviii.
[204] A.A. Boahen, *Britain, the Sahara, and the Western Sudan, 1788-1861*, Oxford 1964, 186; J. Richardson, *Narrative of a mission to central Africa...1850-1*, 1853, I, 8, 163.
[205] I, 22.
[206] I, 228.
[207] II, 233; see also p. 166.

Sa'ad reached his adopted home safely, and was re-united with his family, *Sahara and Sudan* does not tell us.

The other man with slave associations, hired in Tripoli, was Ali of Mandara, 'who had been born in Mandara to the south of Bornu, and had a dubious past with regard to gaining his freedom'.[208] In Murzuq, after the Tibesti expedition, Nachtigal noted that Ali from Mandara, who had often been caught thieving, had long since been released from Nachtigal's service, though 'I allowed him to return under my protection to his home only because he would otherwise certainly have relapsed into slavery'.[209] Nachtigal's compassionate concern for Ali from Mandara not only brought him to Kuka, but also allowed him accommodation in Nachtigal's dwelling, where Ali soon displayed again his skill in peculation.[210] After Nachtigal had set off for Kanem with the Awlad Sulayman, Ali changed into goods the modest proceeds from his thefts, and left for home.[211]

Alexine Tinne, the Dutch traveller who was in Murzuq at the same time as Nachtigal, and who was murdered by supposedly reliable Tuareg and Arab companions at the same time that Nachtigal was escaping, almost miraculously, an identical, and far more predictable fate at Tubu hands in Tibesti, had amongst other followers in her considerable and motley retinue 'some Negroes from the Upper Nile who belonged to her', and some 'freed Negro slaves who were hoping under her protection to get back to their homes'.[212]

Among the black Africans whom Nachtigal observed in Murzuq there were, in addition to those more or less permanently established there (and mentioned towards the beginning this section), also outgoing pilgrims, and freedmen who were trying to get back to their own countries.[213] As late as 1906 there were many freed slaves in Tripoli, from Wadai, Kanem, Borno and Bagirmi, anxious to join Hanns Vischer's

[208] I, 22.
[209] III, 25.
[210] II, 164, 166.
[211] III, 54.
[212] I, 32; see also II, 4: 'the train of freedmen, or of slaves who had been liberated by her, who hoped to get to the Sudan under her protection'.
[213] I, 91.

caravan on his journey to Borno.[214] One of these, a pilgrim, had been taken as a slave from Borno to upper Egypt sixty years earlier, and had served as a corporal in the Sudanese army, being with Gordon at Khartoum.[215] The emancipation of the slaves imposed by the colonial powers may have allowed some to return home who might not otherwise have ever done so.

Nachtigal's two freedman (or slave?) companions, Sa'ad, and Ali from Mandara, differed about the return of the native. Sa'ad had no wish to seek out his original homeland; there is no identification even of interest in visiting it. But Ali was an avid returner. The slave's return, or the freedman's was not necessarily a once-and-for-all event. Koelle, the missionary and distinguished pioneer linguist, working in Freetown in the mid-nineteenth century, met a native of Falaba, in the north-eastern interior of modern Sierra Leone. This man had been enslaved by the Fulani, and had later found his way to Freetown, whence he had visited Falaba several times.[216] Nor is the return always associated with emancipation. Another of Koelle's linguistic informants in Freetown had been one of the slaves sent in tribute to Bauchi; despite this uprooting, the slave had been able to keep up his own language, both because he found many of his countrymen in Bauchi, and also because he was able, while still a slave, to return occasionally to his own home.[217] Early British administrators in north-eastern Nigeria reported that a particular people there, the Wurubo, had been an unprofitable investment as slaves, for they quickly died in captivity; yet the Wurubo women had proved good concubines for their Fulani masters, 'if allowed to be in constant communication with their own people'.[218]

Nor was the return home always a happy one. Duncan, travelling in West Africa in 1845, met in Yoruba country a freedman who had been born in Borno. This man had been taken in the wars and sold, passing eventually to Bahia, where

[214] Hanns Vischer, *Across the Sahara*, London 1910, 18.
[215] *ibid.*, 21.
[216] Koelle, *Polyglotta Africana*, 1854/1963, 3.
[217] *ibid.*, 19.
[218] F.H. Ruxton, 'Notes on the tribes of the Muri Province', *Journal of the African Society*, April 1908, 383.

he worked for 21 years, partly as head cook for a Liverpool firm. Finally freed, as the slave of a British subject, he returned to Whydah on the African coast, and thence home.

> But now the spell was broken, and all his happy dreams of more than twenty years had vanished. His native town had twice been burnt down by the enemy, and was chiefly inhabited by strangers from a far country. He was now an obscure stranger, and looked upon with suspicion, and his long-cherished home was to him a desolate waste.

He resolved to attempt a second return, this time to Bahia.[219]

Divided about going home, Sa'ad and Ali together represented all those about whose status there might be some doubt, real or alleged. This problem is examined under 'Slave and free status' above. To give one further example here, among the very first recruits to help man the pioneer British post at Lokoja, inside the margins of the Sokoto caliphate, in the mid-nineteenth century, were 'a number of Hausa freed slaves in Sierra Leone who wanted to return to their homeland, but had not for fear of being taken by slavers while on the journey'.[220]

Even before the European colonial period, western governments might occasionally intervene, in special cases, to help safeguard returning freed slaves on their homeward journey. When it seemed that Dorugu and his African colleague were eager to leave England, where they had been helping with African language studies, and to return home, the Foreign Secretary wrote accordingly to the British Consul in Tripoli in February 1856. The letter first emphasises that the two young men are now free: they had been 'bought out of slavery and made free in Central Africa by the late Dr. Overweg, and after his death were taken by Dr. Barth into his service, as free men'. The Consul is instructed, on their arrival at Tripoli,

> and in order that their freedom may be sufficiently ensured on their return to their own country, to furnish them with an Arabic passport, such as liberated slaves generally receive in Tripoli, countersigned by the Kadhi; and to place them

---

[219] J. Duncan, *Travels in western Africa in 1845 and 1846*, London 1847, II, 175-7.

[220] Lovejoy and Hogendorn, 11.

under the protection of some trustworthy man, going either to Kano or Kuka. You will also furnish them with a camel.[221]

Another category of returners, and one which introduces the question of their religious impact: there were also Muslim slaves returning across the Atlantic to the West African coast. In Dahomey, for example, the returned slave or freedman was clearly a pioneer Muslim, for Islam was established there as much by slaves coming from Brazil as by Muslims descending from the interior.[222] Even Liberia was a little affected. In 1829 a freed slave, Abd al-Rahman, originally from Timbo in Futa Jallon, returned from America, coming to Monrovia. He claimed to be a brother to the *almami* of Futa Jallon, and the Liberians hoped that his homeward journey via Monrovia might stimulate their own links, particularly in trade, with Futa Jallon. But Abd al-Rahman died in Monrovia during the first rains.[223]

The religious impact of Muslim slaves returning is difficult to assess precisely. In the incidents listed above several have an explicitly Muslim aspect. Elsewhere (see above, p. 69), we have noted the slaves bought by the Sanusiya, freed, educated, and sent back to Wadai as missionaries.[224] Some of the slaves freed by the European colonialists may have carried the seeds of Islam with them, home to fields hitherto unsown.[225] And, while our overall knowledge about the returning Muslim slave is still fragmentary, the potential religious importance of this category of person is abundantly clear in the Christian history of West Africa. Here, the return of the freed slaves is the main early theme, first in the creation of the colony of Sierra Leone, and then in the planting of Christianity in southern Nigeria, especially Abeokuta, as freedmen passed from Freetown back to their native country.[226] The idea for the Nigerian return was

[221] Kirk-Greene and Newman, 5-6.
[222] Marty, 1926, 32-3, 51-2, 108, 145.
[223] S. Wilkeson, *A concise history of the commencement, progress and present condition of the American colonies in Liberia*, Washington 1839, 40.
[224] H. Duveyrier, 1918, 16-7; cited by E.E. Evans-Pritchard, *The Sanusi of Cyrenaica*, Oxford 1949, reprinted 1973, 16.
[225] Marty, 1920, II, 180.
[226] Subsequent expansion from Abeokuta provides further parallels: for example, when the Church Missionary Society began work in 1895 in Ado,

apparently inspired by the example of two Hausa, emancipated in Trinidad, who passed through Freetown in 1837 on their way to Badagry and inland homewards.[227] Evidently bolder than the recruits for Lokoja mentioned just above, who waited for British protection before undertaking such a venture.

The religious transference of which slaves and ex-slaves might be the agents was by no means all one way and in favour of the dissemination of Islam amongst societies where it was previously little known. Newly acquired slaves coming from non-Muslim backgrounds into Muslim society might bring with them traditional beliefs and strange powers. In Ghadames, while the slaves as a group celebrated such festivals as that at the end of Ramadan, or *lailat al-qadr*, the Night of Power, late in Ramadan, they maintained also their own observances, such as a special dance at the cemetery of the slaves.[228] Richardson thought that most of the slaves in Ghadames came from Borno;[229] but the commonest African language in the town was Hausa,[230] and when he was himself dispirited and unwell, the blacks said that he was possessed by the *bori*, the spirits of traditional Hausa belief (see p. 16).[231] On his second journey, Richardson again had opportunity to see *bori* possession among black Africans, this time the servants of his own expedition.[232] Among the ex-slaves joining Vischer's caravan in 1906 were several Bagirmi women, who had been brought to North Africa when quite young. Outstanding among these was Hawa, nearly six feet tall, who became a dominant and very valuable person in Vischer's party—in considerable measure because

---

the largest town in the Ekiti area of southern Nigeria, the first preacher was an Ekiti who had been enslaved and taken to Abeokuta, where he became a Christian (J.D.Y. Peel, *Aladura: a religious movement among the Yoruba*, London 1968, 51-2).

[227] C. Fyfe, 'Four Sierra Leone recaptives', *Journal of African History*, 1961, 82.

[228] Richardson, 1848, I, 223-4, 249-50, 279-80.

[229] *ibid.*, I, 148.

[230] *ibid.*, I, 281.

[231] *ibid.*, I, 361.

[232] Richardson, 1853, I, 286-7.

of the prestige given her by the fits of spirit possession to which she was subject.[233]

In Mauritania, such developments once took a more serious turn. There, sorcery was believed to be very widespread among the slaves of townspeople, particularly because so many slaves came from the Bambara, a Sudanese people skilled in such things. In the town the Tidjikdja, for example, a slave-owner who beat a slave would fall ill after one or two days, and soon die. A sorcerer slave always looked at the chest of a person, catching his heart and hiding it in the ashes, so that it became a ram: a man thus bewitched would not die as long as that ram was not slaughtered. This, as the chronicler recording these tales comments, is no doubt nonsense; but, he continues, it is true that if the sorcerer slave, threatened with death by the family of the bewitched, lays his hand on the breast of the bewitched person, he is loosed from the spell, and the same is true if the sorcerer dies. The people of Tidjikdja, distressed by these perils, contemplated killing their slaves, but desisted since there would then be none to care for the palm trees. So they brought instead, for a handsome fee, an expert from the Sudan, who gave the slaves something to drink. The expert departed; but the sorcery continued, until the people began killing all slaves suspected of it, and it decreased appreciably.[234]

Leaving aside the relatively limited question of religious impact, there were a good many returners about. Barth met several,[235] and he particularly recalled his astonishment at meeting in Kano a black who had lived some twenty years, from his boyhood, in Constantinople: 'He had not only learned the language perfectly, but also adopted the manners, and I might almost say the features, of the modern Greeks.'[236] Though Barth does not explicitly say so of this man, having been a slave is the most likely explanation for having had such an opportunity.

Dorugu offers this comment:

---

[233] Vischer, 1910, 52-3, 190-2.
[234] al-Shinqiti, 1911, 509-10; 1953, 137-8.
[235] For example, Barth, 1965, I, 40, 90-1.
[236] *ibid.*, I, 530.

I heard that there was a man there [at Say] who wanted to kill Abdul Karim [Barth]. A young man who spoke the Europeans' language told me. There aren't many people who speak the language of the Europeans, and there was only one in Timbuktu. He was a mallam, but he was a good-for-nothing scoundrel. He said that formerly, when he was young and went to the European regions, he was able to speak their language but now he had forgotten it all. He was a handsome man but one of bad character.[237]

Dorugu, typically, defines people primarily by language, and there is nothing here to indicate explicitly that either man, the young man in Say or the mallam in Timbuktu, had ever been a slave. Dorugu had spent time in Germany as well as England, and he once mentions the German language,[238] so his references here to 'the Europeans' language' are puzzling. Dorugu is certainly very critical of the mallam: is this an independent, African opinion, in contrast to the view of a condescending outsider, or is Dorugu echoing the attitude of his European employer, Barth? Nachtigal apparently took a poor view of the usual effects of experience of the Mediterranean Muslim world upon slaves taken there, speaking of 'the few Negroes who from a longish stay in Europe still benefit even after their return home'.[239]

Nachtigal included 'freed slaves who knew Tunis, Tripoli or Constantinople' among the many visitors who encroached upon his time in Kuka.[240] What are we to make of such references as those given, rather randomly, above, and of the returned slaves who stand behind them? Are they a dispersed group, on the margins of African society, detailed knowledge of whom is largely irrecoverable at this distance in time? Or were they significant mediators in the cultural encounter between black Africa and the wider world, helping to familiarise local people with some of the attitudes and practices of the outsiders who, with the rise of European colonialism, were beginning to intrude more and more? A possible research

---

[237] Kirk-Greene and Newman, 72.
[238] *ibid.*, 100.
[239] III, 53.
[240] II, 178.

THE RETURN OF THE SLAVES

topic, now, though not for long, for some energetic young Africanist?

Nachtigal gives us a glimpse of a possible mediating role, in the tiny kingdom of Logon, which he visited on his way to, and from, Abu Sekkin's camp.

> Master Ma'aruf [the ruler of Logon] apparently could not overcome his fear of me. This was confirmed to me by a freed Musgo slave who, after spending long years in Tripoli, had taken up his residence with the Logon people, tribally related to him, and by his knowledge of the world had attained a certain standing with the king. He told me that the king was consumed with curiosity to get to know me, but that for the time being his fear of my sorceror's arts prevailed.[241]

A public meeting was arranged, involving the whole of Nachtigal's caravan at the same time, so as to keep to a minimum the ruler's direct contact with Nachtigal. The freedman reappeared towards the end of this first Logon visit by Nachtigal, when another attempt was made to arrange a private encounter, in vain.[242] Nachtigal's halt in Logon on the return journey was briefer and lower-key. There was another public reception, at which Nachtigal presented six sheets of writing paper (his whole supply) and twenty large pack needles, all that his poverty allowed. Ma'aruf 'with the greatest firmness rebuffed' the German traveller's request for a private audience. The freedman is unmentioned in the few lines given here to Logon.[243]

A much more outstanding example than the anonymous Musgo freedman in Logon was Almas, Nachtigal's special guide on the Bagirmi journey, who appears at several points in this volume, and whose introductory description fully deserves quoting at length.

> Almas, that is jewel, pearl, came from the south of Bornu, and in his childhood had been to Constantinople as a slave. As a result of the death of his master there, he had regained his freedom, and as a young man returned to his home

[241] III, 248.
[242] III, 256.
[243] III, 440-1.

country with Eduard Vogel. When Vogel undertook his fatal journey to Wadai, Almas, who was a very useful lad, was left behind to look after his house and property, and after the death of the unfortunate explorer, he transferred to the service of Shaykh Umar. He stood now in the prime of his manhood, and was a more than ordinarily useful person, Naturally intelligent and unusually energetic and active, he was one of the few Negroes who from a longish stay in Europe still benefit even after their return home. Having lived for twenty years in the entourage of the Shaykh, keeping his eyes open, and being thus familiar with every aspect of the intrigues of court life in Kuka, he had already for a long time been a useful adviser to me in particular situations. Frequently despatched by the Shaykh and the *digma* with messages to the outlying provinces, and not seldom attached to the retinue of the princes or dignitaries on military expeditions, he had a first-rate knowledge of the country and its people, and to some extent looked at everything with the mind of a European. He was, furthermore, a very practical man and an excellent cook [see below, p. 206]. His darker sides, to be sure, were no less than his merits. In his intercourse with the great men of the Bornu court, he had embraced their evil qualities, and was fond of pleasure, vicious, arrogant, selfish to the point of unscrupulousness. Nor did he share the good nature of most of these men, but could be quite malicious and spiteful, revengeful and cruel. All in all, however, this man could be of inestimable value to me, and the essential thing was that his energetic nature had not succumbed to the luxury and pleasure-seeking of Kuka, but that he was an enterprising and courageous man.[244]

If the essential consideration, for the returning slave, is the extent to which experience gained in slavery may be turned to good account later as a returning freedman, we may mention one final relevant instance, a mirror image of all that has been discussed above. Simon Lucas was for three years a slave in Morocco. Later he became British vice-consul in Morocco, and after that Oriental interpreter for the British government. To Africa again, as a prospective explorer, failing however to reach even Fezzan. Finally, he was consul-general in Tripoli

---

[244] III, 53-4. See also note 4 here.

from 1793 to 1801. A multiple returner: a slave in Africa, he returned to government service in Britain; and on three separate occasions he returned in an official capacity to the scene of his slavery.[245]

---

[245] I, 344 note 2; see also Bovill, *Missions*, I, 4-6.

CHAPTER IV

EXPORTS AND MARKETING

Slave exports and their relation to the home market

'I asked, "Am I being sent to Bornu?" They said yes. I replied, "That's good."'
(Dorugu, in Kirk-Greene and Newman, p.40) (see p. 157 below)

The export slave trade from the Sudan region is of great antiquity. Already in the later ninth century, slave merchants were established in Zawila, east of Murzuq, dealing in black slaves.[1] Later, in the eleventh century, al-Bakri mentioned slave exports from Fezzan.[2] Ibn Battuta in the mid-fourteenth century commented that Borno was renowned for its exports of excellent slave girls, eunuchs (*fityan*), and saffron-dyed fabrics.[3] Leo Africanus gave an interesting description of trade in Borno at the beginning of the sixteenth century, Barbary merchants bringing war horses for the king, and receiving slaves in exchange. Though the king was very wealthy—his spurs and bridles, tableware, even dog chains were said to be pure gold—he preferred to pay only in slaves. And, as he went slaving only once a year, using his horses for this purpose, merchants had to wait until he returned from the annual expedition. If by chance the expedition were not sufficiently successful, the unfortunate Barbary merchant had to wait another year for payment.[4] Nachtigal commented often on

---

[1] *Corpus*, 22; al-Ya' qubi is our source here. He mentions that there were people in Zawila from as far afield as Basra, Khorasan and Kufa. Palmer (1926/1970, 5, 67) is explicit that these Asian visitors were themselves among the slave-traders, a view with which we concurred in *Slavery* 1970. However, al- Ya' qubi says only that they were there, not what they were doing there.

[2] *Corpus*, 64.

[3] Ibn Battuta, 58; *Corpus*, 302; see p. 282 below.

[4] Leo Africanus, A, III, 833-4; B, II, 480-1. See also pp. 112, 114 below.

the long periods which incoming northern merchants might have to wait in Kuka, before they were able to get away again. In his day, the problem was not the fruitfulness or otherwise of an annual royal slave hunt, but late-payers and the general chicanery of local merchants and buyers, and natural disasters such as epidemics among slaves intended for export (see below, pp. 316-17).[5] Such delays, however bad for commerce, might have a much more positive effect in terms of cultural encounter and interpenetration.

About the same time as Leo Africanus, the Borno rulers, having been driven a century before from their original bases in Kanem, east of Lake Chad, regained supremacy over their rivals there, but never found it convenient to return and settle in Kanem again. Among the reasons for staying west of Lake Chad, in Borno, may have been the proximity of slave supplies to the south, and the relatively good trade connections north to Fezzan.[6]

Denham found Borno chiefly a rendezvous for caravans, exchanging principally slaves for imports from Barbary.[7] Barth in 1851 witnessed the departure for Fezzan of a caravan of about 750 slaves, 'one of the largest slave caravans which departed during my stay in Bornu'.[8] This was the same caravan that carried northwards the effects of his dead companion Richardson.

Some slaves travelled very long distances before they were finally disposed of, and the record of a few from Borno, or even from Bagirmi, among those liberated in Sierra Leone in the first half of the nineteenth century[9] shows that the trans-Atlantic trade had some repercussions in these countries. The interest in exports which Nachtigal observed was, however, directed exclusively towards sales on the Mediterranean coast. In the trans-Saharan trade, slave exports continued to be the most important item throughout the first half of the nineteenth

---

[5] See, for example, II, 234-9 and notes, and other index entries.
[6] Palmer, 1926/1970, 4-5.
[7] Bovill, *Missions*, III, 532.
[8] Barth, 1965, II, 76-8.
[9] P.D. Curtin and Jan Vansina, 'Sources of the nineteenth-century Atlantic slave trade', *Journal of African history*, 1964, 185-208.

century and up to the time of Nachtigal's penetration into the Sahara and the Sudan.

The number exported annually along the four main routes to the Mediterranean coast, Timbuktu to Morocco, Kano to Air and Ghadames, Borno to Fezzan, and Wadai to Benghazi, Buxton had estimated in 1839 at 20,000.[10] Any figure of this kind is obviously subject to a wide margin of error; Mauny thought Buxton's estimate conservative,[11] and Nachtigal, who put the exports from Wadai alone at 15,000 (presumably per annum), seems to confirm this.[12] Boahen proposed cutting Buxton's figure by half to 10,000; still, it might be thought, too substantial to be called 'only a trickle' compared with 70,000 believed to be crossing the Atlantic at the beginning of the century.[13] In 1858 the British Consul-General at Tripoli estimated that the slave trade constituted 'more than two-thirds of the value of all the caravan trade' across the Sahara.[14] Buxton put the annual East African export of slaves at about 30,000.

By Nachtigal's time, however, this trade was definitely declining. Efforts, diplomatic and otherwise, to induce the governments of Turkey and the North African countries to outlaw the slave trade, and eventually to abolish the institution of slavery, had been, and were being, pursued with varying degrees of resolution and success. In Tunis the institution was formally abolished in 1846,[15] and in 1857 the Turkish autho-

[10] T.F. Buxton, *The African slave trade*, London, 2nd ed., 1840, reprinted 1967, 69.

[11] R. Mauny, *Tableau géographique de l'ouest africain au moyen âge*, Dakar 1961, Amsterdam 1967 379.

[12] IV, 202. Nachtigal believed that, 'particularly with King Ali's warlike spirit, which he has also endeavoured to maintain among his officials and subjects', slaves were being obtained in considerable numbers. It was to the Mejabra alone, traders from the Jalo oasis, of which Awjila was the centre, ten days south of Benghazi (IV, 412), that Nachtigal attributed the figure of 15,000; they did handle most of the Wadai/Mediterranean trade. The Tripolitanians themselves, Nachtigal stated, presumably referring to traders coming to Wadai, 'bought no slaves, and only very unwillingly accepted a few individuals, male and female, as presents for their personal needs'. This is puzzling, since slave exports were still flowing north from Kuka to Tripoli at this time.

[13] Boahen, 1964, 128.

[14] *ibid.*, 1964, 127.

[15] *ibid.*, 1964, 140.

rities issued a *firman* which declared the final abolition of the black slave trade throughout the Sultan's dominions, with the exception of the Hijaz.[16] For many years there was a good deal of evasion of such decrees, and a substantial volume of clandestine trade persisted, as Nachtigal himself witnessed. He believed that it would be a long time before humanitarian expectations that the slave trade would be suppressed could find complete satisfaction.[17] Nevertheless the eventual disappearance of the trans-Saharan traffic can now be seen to have been inevitable (see Chapter X: 'Anti-slavery measures' below).

Several observers have hazarded very high estimates of the profits to be won from the export in slaves. Harris, speaking of the Danakil on the north Somali coast in 1843, judged that the trade there yielded 300 per cent 'with the least possible risk or trouble to the merchant',[18] and Burton thought that trade in slaves who had been bought for 2 to 10 doti or tobes per head, and could be sold in Zanzibar for 14 or 15 dollars, realized nearly 500 per cent.[19] Some of these estimates were perhaps expansive, and the considerations of risk and loss to which attention is directed below (see pp. 122-37) suggest that slave-trading was not always a certain guarantee of a high-income status. Nevertheless, Nachtigal said that the trade had been very lucrative; on arrival at the Mediterranean coast, traders might count on getting for their slaves three or four times the purchase price, so substantial a margin

> that enterprising merchants do not allow themselves to be deterred even by the risk of confiscation. These goods, moreover, require no, or only insignificant, means of transport, which is an important consideration on desert journeys, but rather themselves represent such a means for lighter objects. The provisions needed for the slaves are so cheap in Bornu that they do not need to be considered in comparison with transport costs.[20]

---

[16] Boahen, 1964, 155. The slave trade was made formally illegal in Saudi Arabia in 1936, full emancipation being announced for 1962 at a cost to the government of £6.5 million as compensation.
[17] II, 233.
[18] Harris, 1844/1968, I, 345.
[19] Burton, 1860/1961, II, 61-2.
[20] II, 233. There is not, I think, much evidence of slaves carrying other

So long as the export trade continued to be profitable it provided a powerful incentive to slave-raiding. It may have made necessary the continuance of the often savage methods of slave recruitment applied in the Sudan; for the possibility of being exported, in any particular case, may have meant that people would be much less willing voluntarily to place themselves in servitude. That such voluntary action, under different circumstances, was not entirely fanciful appears from the slaves of the Portuguese crown land estates on the Zambezi. Here, while slaves were also acquired by raid, purchase or gift, it is estimated that a majority of the slave population in the eighteenth century were clients who had attached themselves to a protector. Their prime function was to serve in the private army of the estate holder, and though it was unlikely in any case that he would sell his own soldiers some volunteers first extracted a guarantee that they would not be sent abroad. Particularly in times of famine and war the slave retinues on the estates grew rapidly. The Zambezi in the nineteenth century was also a main slave-exporting region, but even when the great estate holders dominated this trade, they continued to observe the unwritten ban on selling their own people.[21]

Famine, which, as we have just seen, swelled the ranks of the volunteer slaves on the Zambesi estates, also encouraged an intermediary variety of slave, not himself a volunteer, yet surrendered voluntarily by his people: these are children, sold into slavery by their families in times of need. Krapf says that the Wanika Pagans, nominally at least dependent upon the Swahili of Mombasa, sometimes had to sell their own children to their overlords, when food was very scarce.[22] In 1904-5, in parts of northern Nigeria, there was famine, and slave-trading increased as a result. From Adamawa and the Benue region, long-standing centres of slave supply, many slaves were sold to southern Nigeria; a British official, attempting to check the traffic, intercepted and freed 200 children in less than three months. They had been sold for between 1s. 9d, (in corn) and

---

goods across the Sahara for their masters.
[21] Newitt, 1969, 76-9.
[22] Krapf, 1860, 120.

10s. (in salt); they were in lamentable condition, and 30 to 40 died in British hands.[23]

Nachtigal himself doubted the truth of reports which he had heard of Somraï men selling wives and children in time of distress, though he regarded it as certain that chiefs of the centralised dominions among Bagirmi's Pagan neighbours did have such power to sell their own subjects, and did sometimes find reasons for actually using it (see above, p. 42).[24] Reports of such practice occur in the Arabic records from the very beginning. Al-Ya'qubi, in the later ninth century, wrote: 'I have been informed that the kings of the Sudan sell their people without any pretext or war.'[25] His cautious phrasing, 'I have been informed', shows that he was not entirely persuaded himself. It may be, however, that the stark choice between starvation and slavery did, in some cases at least, lie behind the report. The truth, no doubt, includes both that choice, and the cruelty of selfish despotism.

This resort, to the sale of children, may have been widespread in cases of extreme dearth, and *jihad* and slave-raiding, by contributing to such conditions, may thus indirectly as well as directly have enlarged the supply of slaves for the export market.

However, the export trade in slaves from the Sudan countries had always possessed a sound foundation in a flourishing domestic market for slaves. Some twenty years before, Barth had estimated that slave raiding in the Sudan as a whole was stimulated much more by domestic than by export demands.[26] In 1851 he guessed that slaves exported from Kano did not exceed 5,000 a year. Of these, the greater number were carried away by small caravans to Borno and Nupe than took the direct northern road to Ghat and Fezzan, while 'a considerable number are sold into domestic slavery, either to the inhabitants of the province itself or to those of the adjoining districts'.[27]

[23] Lugard, 'Northern Nigeria', *Journal of the African Society*, July 1906, 389, 401-2.
[24] III, 390.
[25] *Corpus*, 22.
[26] Barth, 1965, I, xxix.
[27] *ibid.*, I, 515.

Barth visited Adamawa himself, but only very briefly, and under unsatisfactory and constricting circumstances. Nevertheless his summary description of slavery there points to an enormous internal demand, together with local circulation of slaves.

> Slavery exists on an immense scale in this country, and there are many private individuals who have more than a thousand slaves. In this respect the governor of the whole province is not the most powerful man, being outstripped by the governors of Chámba and Kóncha—for this reason, that Mohammed Lowel [the emir] has all his slaves settled in rûmde or slave-villages, where they cultivate grain for his use or profit, while the above-mentioned officers, who obtain all their provision in corn from subjected pagan tribes, have their whole host of slaves constantly at their disposal; and I have been assured that some of the head slaves of these men have as many as a thousand slaves each under their command, with whom they undertake occasional expeditions for their masters. I have been assured, also, that Mohammed Lowel receives every year in tribute, besides horses and cattle, about five thousand slaves, though this seems a large number.[28]

Nachtigal's observations, twenty years later, confirm Barth's judgment. Much of *Slavery* 1970, and of the present volume, is designed to show the importance, diversity and extent of domestic demand. For the moment, a single heading of the argument, stated briefly, will suffice. On the one hand, there is a quite extraordinary absence of trans-Saharan caravans, in and out of Borno. Nachtigal commented generally on 'the infrequency at that time of caravans between Tripolitania and Bornu', which resulted in funds, allocated to him in Germany, coming into his hands only years later.[29] It was from small slave caravans, going north, whom he met on his journey to Fezzan in February/March 1869, that he learnt that he would have to wait until autumn for a caravan to Borno.[30] In fact, it was over

---

[28] Barth, 1965, II, 190-1; in *Slavery* 1970 (p. 63) we quote Barth as calling Adamawa a country 'based entirely on slavery' (Barth, 1965, II, 174); see p. 240 below for his comment on colonies, free and slave, in Adamawa.

[29] I, xvi.

[30] I, 73 note. Nachtigal met first one small caravan of slaves, and soon this became an almost daily event (I, 56-7, 58—see also below, p. 135).

a year later, in April 1870, that he was at last able to move southwards.[31] As the previous caravan for Borno had left Fezzan 'a few months' before Nachtigal arrived in Fezzan, the total gap between one caravan and the next was very considerable. Having arrived in Borno, Nachtigal found an almost identical situation with respect to northbound caravans. Nachtigal entered Kuka on 6 July 1870, and left for the last time on 1 March 1873, a period of nearly three years. During this period, it seems, only two caravans left for the north. Nachtigal does not give precise dates. The first departure was probably not long after his arrival; two of his companions returned homewards with it.[32] The second caravan left while Nachtigal was visiting Abu Sekkin, the Bagirmi ruler, that is between the end of February 1872 and 24 August 1872, when Nachtigal received a letter saying that the caravan had gone. This was a gap of between 18 and 24 months,[33] comparable to that between the two southbound caravans with which he had been involved.

As for slaves for sale in Kuka, Nachtigal does not estimate numbers, but he does refer to the large market stalls of the slave dealers, the long rows of slaves of every age and price.[34] The Monday market was the great occasion, for all commodities: here the crowd of customers, surging to and fro from morning till evening, often numbered more than 10,000.[35] There were several daily markets as well, the most important of which was almost more active than the weekly market in Tripoli.[36] Rohlfs, who spent more than three months in Kuka

---

Nachtigal does not indicate just where these slaves were coming from; we may imagine that a larger caravan had arrived in Fezzan, from Borno, not long before, and that bulk was being broken there, in the hope that miniature caravanlets might more easily circumvent anti-slavery restrictions theoretically in force in Tripoli.

[31] Umar on his way home after his mother's death: 'When we halted at Murzuk we did not find any caravans going on any further, and so we remained there for some months; then we found some caravans and continued on our way.' *Shaihu Umar*, 75.

[32] II, 164, 233.
[33] II, 233 note; III, 216 note and 440.
[34] II, 215.
[35] II, 220.
[36] II, 148.

in 1866, just a few years before Nachtigal's visit, does venture to estimate numbers: sometimes thousands of slaves were brought for sale to the weekly Monday market; lots of some hundreds were available in the daily market.[37]

Numbers games are probably inherently foolish, but let us play one for a moment. The result may be quite striking. Rohlfs was not so painstaking an observer as Nachtigal, so let us cut his thousands down to one thousand, for a Monday, and his lots of some hundreds down to just 100 slaves in all for the main daily market (excluding the other daily markets altogether, as Nachtigal does not say whether slaves were for sale in them): about 1,500 slaves offered each week. Neither Nachtigal nor Rohlfs tells us how often a slave might go to market, returning unsold at evening; let us say four visits, on average, before a sale is concluded. About 1,500 slaves sold in Kuka in a month, about one northbound caravan's quota. With one caravan every eighteen months, or so, taking about 1,400 slaves (double the largest number which Barth observed; see above, p. 99) the export market absorbed about 5% of slaves sold in Kuka. If we take Nachtigal's return journey from Abu Sekkin as a model, with so many slaves disappearing into the local community as the caravan went along, with other slaves remaining in the private possession of raiders and traders, while yet others were handed on to local people (as Nachtigal passed on two girls whom he had acquired on behalf of the Sherif Ahmed el-Medeni—see below, p. 127), a great many incoming slaves were being absorbed directly into domestic use without passing through a market at all. A few of these unmarketed slaves, to be sure, might have been creamed off later for export, but I suppose only a small proportion.

Looked at in this way, the domestic demand for slaves was overwhelmingly preponderant. Slaves exported northwards loom large in the records, because observers, from al-Ya' qubi until today, have so often looked at the African interior through a Saharan lens, which obscures much of what was going on beyond the desert.

Buganda provides a more recent, non-Muslim, example,

[37] Cited in II, 215 note. G. Rohlfs, *Quer durch Afrika*, Leipzig 1874-5, I, 344; reprinted Stuttgart 1984, in a somewhat abbreviated and rearranged edition.

though the export agents there were Muslim Arabs; in 1889 Mackay, an Anglican missionary, reported that domestic demand was very great, and that it was only the surplus, perhaps 2,000 a year, which the Arabs were able to export.[38]

The decay of any traditional staple export market always creates difficult problems of economic adjustment, even if that market turns out to have been less important than it at first appeared. Slaves were important for the trade of Wadai and Borno. Still more in Bagirmi, where slaves were the only significant export item, Nachtigal thought that, unless some kind of alternative profitable production could be developed by way of the Benue, the eastern tributary of the Niger, the condition of the country was likely to deteriorate as the slave trade contracted.[39] A visitor in 1911 was told that even during the first years of French influence Bagirmi had continued exporting some 5,000 slaves a year; she remarked,

> the action of the French in checking the slave trade, together with other raids and exactions, has fallen hardly on the ruling classes. It has put an end to the only means of livelihood they have ever known.[40]

In 1905 it was estimated that of the 750 slaves liberated by the British in Bornu Province since that area had been occupied by them in 1902, well over 600 were in transit from Bagirmi.[41]

In assessing the importance of alternative trading possibilities, it is worth noting that the establishment of the slave trade in a locality seemed sometimes to choke off other trade and commercial activity. Slave-raiding was destructive. Slave recruitment through kidnapping made people wary of venturing into public places, such as markets, to trade: the British in northern Nigeria, at the very beginning of their administration, acted on complaints of this kind, and convicted kidnappers, hoping that this would encourage particularly the reticent

---

[38] J.W.H[arrison], *A.M. Mackay, pioneer missionary of the Church Missionary Society to Uganda*, London 1890, 434-5.
[39] III, 376-7, 392-3.
[40] MacLeod, 1912, 147-8, 150.
[41] Lugard, 1906, 402.

Pagan peoples to bring their produce to market.[42] Markets were traditionally places of truce, but this theory was not always effective protection: we have, for example, eye-witness accounts of Tubu raids on markets in the Lake Chad area even in the twentieth century,[43] raids which in the old days would certainly have included kidnapping.

Slaving possibilities might also affect the preferences of merchants. Among the Vai, on the west coast, the slave trade developed after the establishment there of Spanish factories, or trade posts, early in the nineteenth century. Soon all occupations save war and kidnapping were abandoned, and slave forays and hunts extended far into the interior. Civil war followed, and the European traders, refraining from interference, bought prisoners from both sides.

> Many a vessel bore across the Atlantic two inveterate enemies shackled to the same bolt, while others met on the same deck a long-lost child or brother who had been captured in the civil war.[44]

The Vai coast became one of the major centres of the Altantic slave trade.[45] In Tajura, on the coast of the horn of Africa, Harris in the 1840s found no one interested in agriculture, every man being a merchant and waxing prosperous on slave exports. Amongst the commodities of trade which he lists, salt and slaves are the two principals.[46] The Yao, east of Lake Nyasa, later to become the most notorious slavers of all the indigenous East African peoples, first began trading to the coast with tobacco, hoes and skins, buying calico, salt and beads. At that time, the Yao did not know the value of ivory or

[42] Lugard, 1906, 402.

[43] Boyd Alexander, 'Lake Chad', *Journal of the African Society*, April 1908, 231-2.

[44] Canot, 1928, 303. W.E.F. Ward, *The Royal Navy and the Slavers*, London 1969, 176, confirms this analysis, citing the views of a captain in the British West African squadron then patrolling the coast, and of a judge in Freetown. S. W. Koelle, who was there in 1850-1, says that Vai country had not extended further inland than fifteen or twenty miles until about 20 years earlier, when the chiefs were instigated by the Spaniards to expand (1854/1968, iii).

[45] P. E. H. Hair, 'Notes on the discovery of the Vai script ...', *Sierra Leone Language Review*, no.2, 1963, 41.

[46] Harris, 1844/1968, I, 61-2.

slaves.[47] Then the coast people offered them guns and powder, asking in return for ivory and slaves; and before long, the Yao were refusing to accept any other commodities from their contacts in the interior.[48] The slave trade became so much a part of the Yao national heritage that children played a game, rather like snakes-and-ladders, in which beans represented traders and slaves on their way to the coast; the loser was said 'to have died on the road'.[49] Arnot, pioneer missionary in Katanga, on his way thither in the 1870s, found many traders preferring slaves to ivory.[50] From the Oubangi area of the Congo, it was reported a little later that, although there was much ivory there, the local people would exchange it only for slaves, refusing any other trade goods.[51]

There is still some difference of opinion about the exact relationship between the slave and the ivory trades. Some authors argue that, although slavery and the slave trade had been common in East Africa before the ivory trade became prominent, the ivory trade gave further stimulus to it by increasing the demands for slave porters.[52] It has been pointed out on the other hand that most of the slaves brought to the East African coast were children and women, who, though women were indeed sometimes employed for this purpose (see p. 223 below), did not make good porters, and that the great ivory caravans consisted largely of professionals, or of slaves hired out by their masters; handling ivory, especially large tusks, was a matter for specialists.[53]

At the same time, the fact that goods given in payment for the ivory had to be headloaded into the interior also meant that people were less likely to be enslaved there simply for the

[47] Yohanna B. Abdallah, The Yaos: *Chiikala cha Wayao*, G. Meredith Sanderson (tr.), Zomba (Nyasaland) 1919, reprinted London 1973, 27-8.
[48] *ibid.*, 30-1.
[49] H. S. Stannus, 'The Wayao of Nyasaland', *Harvard African Studies*, 1922, III, 359-60.
[50] F. S. Arnot, *Garenganze: over seven years' pioneer mission work in Central Africa*, London 1889, 2nd ed. 1969, 164.
[51] H. Ward, *Five years with the Congo cannibals*, London 1890, 121.
[52] P. Ceulemans, 'Introduction de l'influence de l'Islam au Congo' in Lewis, 1966, 176-7.
[53] R. W. Beachey, 'The East African ivory trade in the nineteenth century', *Journal of African History*, 1967, 275-6.

An ivory porter. Burton, 1860/1961, I, frontispiece.

purpose of carrying ivory down to the coast, where they would themselves be sold as a subsidiary line of merchandise, and it would not be necessary to assemble a new batch of porters for each successive ivory caravan. For our purpose, however, a general analysis of the role of slaves, the part played by slave porters hired out by their owners is still significant.

Slave-raiding might on occasion be a useful lubricant for acquiring ivory, since captives could then be bartered back to their own people for ivory.[54] The Khartoum merchants, in the eastern Sudan, were particularly active in thus holding captured people, and cattle, for ransom against ivory.[55]

The arms trade

'.... I paid Sabel Surmatali a slave for 60 cartridges. In the future I shall buy them with cash.' (Hamman Yaji, p. 70, 29 August 1919. We are not told the gender of this slave: Hamman Yaji dealt overwhelmingly in female slaves.)

As slaves were one, and often the, major export item from the Sudan countries, they are frequently mentioned in conjunction with the staple imports. Slaves for salt was a widespread equation. In Mauritania it was said that a slave from the Sudan used to be bought with a bar of salt the length of his foot, but by the nineteenth century a camel load of salt was necessary to buy a slave, male or female, and even then something might be owing, to be paid in grain.[56] Salt exporters from Mauritania went to the Sudan, and returned with slaves, some of whom were used to pay debts contracted at the time of the traders' departure, some sold to neighbouring people, while a few were kept for domestic work.[57]

Similarly slaves figure largely in the arms trade, in early days especially for horses, later for guns. In fact, to give the worth, in ammunition, of a slave was sometimes much like giving his price. In Liberia, for instance, the value of a slave boy was 15

[54] Ward, 1890, 189; Oliver, 1965, 99-100.
[55] Richard Gray, *A History of the Southern Sudan, 1839-1889*, Oxford 1961, 148.
[56] al-Shinqiti, 1911, 493; 1953, 115. He reports that everything from the Sudan—cloth, horses, grain, as well as slaves—is bought with salt, and adds that it is said that some of the Sudanese sold their children for salt.
[57] *ibid.*, 1911, 493-4; 1953, 116.

kegs of powder, while a girl would fetch 10 kegs, or 100 sticks of salt.[58]

In the mid-fifteenth century, when slaves first became common in Kano, the *galadima* of Kano raided southwards, regularly sending slaves back to his ruler, who in return regularly supplied him with horses.[59] A little later in the same century, the ruler of Nupe sent 12 eunuchs to Kano in exchange for 10 horses.[60] In the early sixteenth century, Askiya Muhammad I of Songhay sold the children of slaves for horses.[61] During the same period the Berber chieftains of the southern Sahara sold horses in the Sudan at prices ranging from 10 to 15 slaves, according to quality. One Portuguese agent took horses from another Portuguese, and from a Genoese in Portugal's service, at the rate of 7 slaves each, and resold them to African dealers for 14 or 15 slaves.[62] Of Borno Leo Africanus said that the king used to give 15 or 20 slaves to the Barbary merchants for one horse;[63] he reported 6 ducats as the price of a young slave of 15 years in Gao, where horses costing 10 ducats in Europe might fetch 40 or even 50.[64] He also mentioned the usurping ruler of Gaoga (see below, p. 154-5), exchanging slaves for horses from Egypt.[65] By Barth's time the terms of trade had shifted against horses, for in Sokoto in 1853 a slave and a horse were of roughly equal value.[66] In Kuka, in 1870, a good riding-horse cost considerably more than a male slave of standard quality (see below, pp. 328-9), but the disparity was much less than that reported earlier.

The decline in the relative value of a horse may have been brought about, in part, by the increasing prominence of the gun as the most favoured weapon. Difficulties of supply also played an important part in determining prices. Farther south,

[58] Sir Harry Johnston, 1906, I, 398; the average bride-price was 6 brass kettles, 15 kegs of powder, and 5 pieces of cloth.
[59] *Kano Chronicle*, 109-10.
[60] *ibid*. III, 110-11.
[61] Kati, 106, 109.
[62] B. Davidson, *Black mother*, London 1961, 55-6.
[63] Leo Africanus, A, III, 833-4; B, II, 480.
[64] *ibid*, A, III 826-7; B, II, 471.
[65] *ibid*, A, III, 835; B, II, 482.
[66] Barth, 1965, III, 132; Lacroix, 1952, 34.

towards the forest, the prices of horses rose. At the court of Abu Sekkin, temporarily displaced ruler of Bagirmi, Nachtigal found that the best imported horses fetched eight to twelve slaves, those of medium quality five to eight, less good three to five. Prices were settled by the king himself, generally to the great satisfaction of the sellers. But the horse which the Sherif el-Medeni, Nachtigal's most trusted counsellor and friend in Kuka, had sent with Nachtigal arrived in very poor shape, having been unable to get used to the *durra* diet, and with a festering ulcer. The king gave four slaves for it; and of these, only one, a little girl, arrived safely in Kuka with Nachtigal when he returned. As Nachtigal was unable himself to feed it, he gladly accepted Abu Sekkin's offer to buy the German's own horse: as Nachtigal steadfastly refused to accept slaves for himself, the price agreed was two centners of ivory, and a 'pagan'—that is, of the inferior local breed—horse for the return journey.[67]

In northern Liberia a horse in the old days is said to have commanded as many as 100 slaves;[68] the horse was first seen in the Ganta area in Liberia late in the nineteenth century, and a chief bought one for 12 slaves.[69] While horses rose, guns fell in price nearer the Atlantic coast. Nupe became an important centre for the supply of muskets, which were traded there in exchange for slaves, as early as the middle of the eighteenth century.[70] Among the purposes of the Hausa raid, the date of which may be put approximately in the 1870s, and which is described in Sir Abubakar Tafawa Balewa's novel, *Shaihu Umar*, was the collection of slaves who could be sent to Bida, the main town of Nupe, in order procure muskets.[71] Actually on the coast, a single slave might be the price of several guns.[72]

[67] III, 365-6.
[68] Schwab, 1947, 181; the price when Schwab wrote was £5 to £10.
[69] An elderly Mano informant told Schwab (1947, 69 & n.) that the first horse had been seen when his father was about 14 years old, and that a chief bought one eight years later in what was to become French Guinea.
[70] *Kano Chronicle*, 124.
[71] p. 22.
[72] The Gio in Liberia formerly bought their guns from the Bassa, paying one slave for two guns; Schwab, 1947, 231. D'Ollone (1901, 85) in the hinterland of Liberia found a male slave worth four guns plus some other things, and a female three guns together with other goods.

Some of the nineteenth-century Muslim leaders, particularly in the second half of the century, continued to indulge in this traffic. Samori in the 1870s, for example, regularly traded slaves for horses, guns and gunpowder.[73] Hoping to obtain supplies of these commodities by trade through Kong, in the Ivory Coast, he once sent the Kong rulers 100 young men, 100 girls, and gold.[74] In Samori's time, a repeating gun cost from two to four slaves, while a horse ranged from four to twelve; horses may have been especially valued for tactical reasons, giving leaders mobility, and providing an efficient means for taking captives.[75] In 1874, a little before the conquest of Darfur by Ismail Pasha, when the southern part of the country was being harried on the one hand by the forces of Zubayr, the celebrated slaving lord, and on the other by a former subordinate of Zubayr's who had broken with his chief.

> The country was bled white by all of them, whether they were friends of the government or its enemies; the Jellaba, however, travelled secretly to both sides, exchanging manufactured articles, weapons and powder for slaves, who at that time were extraordinarily cheap there.[76]

The arms trade for slaves was sometimes done on a credit basis, the arms being advanced so that the slaves, with which the arms were to be paid for, might be captured. This was apparently the position with the horses supplied to the sixteenth-century ruler of Borno for his annual slave-raid (see above, pp. 98-9). Among the Vai, after a campaign warriors had to surrender a certain proportion of their captives, perhaps half, one-third or fewer, to the chiefs. The captives thus handed over were called war-ball, or gun-ball, and represented remuneration for the ammunition which the chiefs had provided at the beginning of the campaign.[77] The remaining

---

[73] Hargreaves, 1963, 245; Kouroubari, 1959, 549, 556; M. Legassick, 'Firearms, horses and Samorian army organization, 1870-1898', *Journal of African History*, 1966, 103, 105, 106.

[74] Kouroubari, 1959, 555.

[75] Legassick, 1966, 106 and n.

[76] IV, 362.

[77] Koelle, 1854/1968, 187; on p. 238 Koelle estimates that fewer than one-quarter of the Vai were Muslim in his time.

captives stayed with the troops as booty, on the general pattern described below (see p. 366).

The interactions between slavery and war were thus often more complicated than a simple cause and effect relationship in which the need for slaves provided a motive for slave-raids. There was also the arms trade, which we have just described; and other possible links existed, such as the chance that captives from a successful raid might be drafted into the army, becoming slave-raiders themselves.

Selection of export models

'The people of this country [Qalanbu], as well as the inhabitants of the other regions in the land of the Sudan which we have mentioned, observe the law that a person who falls victim to a thief may either sell or kill him, as he chooses.' (al-Bakri, eleventh century; *Corpus*, 78)

On the criteria which guided the selection of slaves for the export market Nachtigal offered no general comment. There is a continuing strand dating back to pre-Muslim days which links sale into slavery, and in particular into slavery in foreign parts, with punishment. It has been suggested that this arises from the customary belief in many areas in Africa that each community is responsible for the crimes of each of its members; thus an individual who repeatedly involved his community in trouble might be sold into slavery.[78]

Al-Bakri, in the eleventh century, as quoted above, said that in many Sudan countries it was the custom for a robbed man to be given the choice of either selling or killing the robber.[79] In the *History of Sudi*, on the east coast, it was said that a thief and his brothers were to be made slaves of the robbed man.[80] On the Gambia in the seventeenth century an adulterous couple would 'without redemption be sold away', the same being the penalty for other great offences, no wrongdoer being put to death; the Portuguese purchased people such as these for the West Indies.[81] Slaves exported from the Sierra

---

[78] Lugard, 1933, 13; he thought that the practice still continued, though in secret.
[79] *Corpus*, 78.
[80] Freeman-Grenville, 1962/1975, 232.
[81] Jobson, 1623, 72.

Leone area in the eighteenth century were, apart from prisoners of war, usually criminals. In the coastal areas at least, sale was rare without some preceding offence, adultery, theft, debt or witchcraft.[82] Burton reported that the Wanyamwezi, in East Africa, generally sold only criminals and prisoners, save in times of great need, when even relatives might be sold.[83] He added that the Arabs preferred to purchase men sold under suspicion of magic, as being less likely to decamp for home.[84] An attempt by a Muslim Galla governor to punish two clan chiefs for tribute default by selling them and their families led to renewed Galla civil war.[85] In Borgu, early in the nineteenth century, a woman violating the ban on intercourse during lactation would be sold; slaves in this area dreaded the seacoast, fearing that they would be eaten by the whites, and those sold there were generally prisoners of war or refractory and intractable domestic slaves.[86] In the twentieth century, in the same area, a man who found his bride not a virgin still had the right to ask of her seducer what punishment was merited, and the seducer had formally to admit that to be sold as a slave with all his family would be just.[87] In the Senegambia region Reade contrasted the Woloff, who would sell their own children, with the Mandingoes, who thought it wicked to sell a slave without just cause of complaint.[88] In Sierra Leone in the early twentieth century, heavy fines punished adultery, especially with a chief's wife, or interference with girls in Bundu, the secret society; in earlier days, failure to pay would have led to enslavement.[89]

Many of the examples cited above come from Pagan areas; and on the whole the introduction of Islam, with its prescribed system of punishments for a variety of crimes, seems to have reduced resort to sale into slavery as a penalty. Fyfe, whose

[82] C. Fyfe, *A history of Sierra Leone*, Oxford 1962, 8-9.
[83] Burton, 1860/1961, II, 33.
[84] *ibid.*, 31.
[85] E. Cerulli, 'Folk literature of the Galla of southern Abyssinia', *Harvard African Studies*, 1922, 41.
[86] Clapperton, 1829, 94-5.
[87] Marty, 1926, 220.
[88] Reade, 1864, 447-8.
[89] Alldridge, 1901, 123, 142.

comment on the eighteenth-century position in the Sierra Leone area has just been quoted, goes on to say that in some Muslim districts, where adulterers were flogged and witchcraft was less common, slaves were regularly obtained by kidnapping.[90]

It would be rash to make too sharp a distinction between Muslim and non-Muslim, for pre-Muslim survivals may continue effectual long after Islam has been formally adopted. Of the Daju in Darfur, Nachtigal says they are 'certainly Muslims', but they still have a special hut for their god, and other Pagan trappings.

> Deaths are seldom ascribed to natural causes or to the power of a supreme being, but mostly to the magic of individuals who are subject to the 'evil eye'. If such sorcerers are discovered with the help of the god and the aid of some secret arts, they are killed, their property is confiscated, and their dependents sent to Wadai as slaves.[91]

Canot reports a number of interesting instances of enslavement as punishment from Futa Jallon in the nineteenth century. When the *almami*, or ruler, there gave permission to form a caravan to trade to the coast, all roads were temporarily blocked in order to build up a party of imposing size. Debtors were arrested; if his property were insufficient to pay his debts, a delinquent Pagan was sold as a slave, but a Muslim was let off with a *bastinado*.[92] Muslims from Futa Jallon were sold into slavery only for exceptional wrong-doing. Once, a Futa Jallon caravan brought forty slaves to the coast, at the Rio Pongo, for sale; the factor there wished to refuse eight of them, as sub-standard, but the caravan leader insisted that one at least of the eight should be taken. This man had slain his own son, and judges in Futa Jallon, finding in the Quran no punishment for such a misdeed, had condemned him to be sold to

---

[90] Fyfe, 1962, 8-9.

[91] IV, 155. Nachtigal adds that the sultan, presumably of Darfur, takes many of his slaves, especially female working slaves, from the Daju tribe.

[92] Canot, 1928, 93. Maliki law does not authorize such punishment for the insolvent Muslim debtor, to whom it is rather lenient; on the other hand, a debtor may be jailed while his financial position is ascertained; Ibn Abi Zayd, p. 270. Incidentally, a slave authorized to trade on someone else's behalf is not to be sold for debts which he may then contract.

the Christians, a penalty which was regarded in that country as worse than death.[93] Even a daughter of the *almami* himself might so suffer, being sold away to the coast 'for salt'. In this particular case, the woman, whose name Canot gives us as Beeljie, had so resisted an elderly relative after having been forcibly married to him that she was sent home with an insulting message. This was regarded as behaviour grievous enough on her part to warrant her sale, even though her husband was accused of cruelty to his *harim*, and of eating unclean food. By an elaborate strategem, Canot rescued her at the coast.[94]

Closely related to the practice of enslavement as punishment is that of punishing people who are slaves already by selling them abroad. In both cases the advent of Islam may have had a restraining effect, for not only does Muslim law prescribe certain punishments other than enslavement for free offenders, but specific penalties are also spelt out for slaves (see pp. 15-16). Clapperton said of Sokoto that the children of slaves were never sold unless after repeated punishment they continued to be unmanageable; usually the slaves for sale were prisoners of war, or newly purchased duds, and in Kano he was told that it was customary to send the perpetrators of grave crimes, such as murder, to the coast to be sold to the slave-dealers.[95] In Ghadames, incorrigible thieves among the slaves were despatched to Tripoli.[96]

A profit motive may have entered in both enslavement and export. Profits in prospect from the sale of slaves may have encouraged the application of enslavement as a proper punishment. Canot, visiting the Matacan river, in north-west Sierra Leone, for slaves, describes such a result:

> My merchandise revived the memory of peccadilloes that

---

[93] Canot, 1928, 95.

[94] *ibid.*, 175-80. Such treatment of a Fulani noblewoman, for such an offence seems extreme. But while Canot's account of the reasons for Beeljie's enslavement is at second hand, and may be somewhat distorted, there is no reason to doubt his identification of her, and he was both eye-witness of her sale at the coast and deviser of her rescue.

[95] Clapperton, 1829, 171, 214.

[96] Richardson, 1848, I, 194-5, 248-9; he thought that the slaves often stole simply in order to eat.

had been long forgotten, and sentences that were forgiven. Jealous husbands, when they tasted my rum, suddenly remembered their wives' infidelities, and sold their better halves for liquor in which to forget them.... Law became profitable, and virtue had never reached so high a price.[97]

Hamman Yaji's diary includes a succinct witchcraft entry, too succinct for us to be sure what is going on, but long enough to suggest something comparable to Canot and his profitable law. On 24 November 1925,

> the pagans of Kamale accused one of their men of being a 'witch' and they caught him and brought him to me. They wanted too to reap his corn, so I sent horsemen to them.[98]

Were the horsemen despatched on an errand of mercy, to protect the unfortunate man, unjustly condemned, and his farm from predatory accusers? or, given Hamman Yaji's eye for the main chance, were the cavalry perhaps to take their share of the threatened corn?

In Senegambia, where the effects of the slave trade were not so strongly felt as in some other parts of western Africa, enslavement nevertheless replaced fines as the most common punishment, and this situation obtained until the end of the Atlantic trade.[99] A corresponding line of argument might be applied to the punishment of slaves by sale abroad. One observer, commenting on the practice of the people of Brass not to execute slaves guilty of serious offences but to sell them in distant places, clearly discerned the principle of economy,

---

[97] Canot, 1928, 219.

[98] p. 119. I do not know what the quotation marks here indicate; on p. 103 the word 'witches' occurs twice within brackets, and again I do not know exactly what these signify (but see p. 48); on p. 58 the word 'witchcraft' is used without any special indicators. See also the enigmatic but potentially very interesting witch/'witch' references, with a financial dimension, at the religious interface between Pagan subjects and Muslim rulers, on pp. 136 and 138.

[99] M. A. Klein, *Islam and imperialism in Senegal: Sine-Saloum, 1847-1914*, Edinburgh 1968, 29. He quotes a French Governor of Cayor: 'When a man has cohabited with a girl and he has had a child by her, he must pay three slaves, and if he lacks the means, he is enslaved himself. Those responsible for fights, constant theft, false accusation are condemned to considerable fines, which they are never able to pay, and then they are imprisoned and sold to the captains of ships.'

although Brass, in eastern Nigeria, was not a Muslim area. 'Two grand results,' he said,

> it will thus be seen, accrue from the transaction to the two parties immediately concerned—to the master an indemnity against loss, and to the slave rescue from a cruel death.[100]

As suggested in this quotation, enslavement or sale abroad was not in every case a harsher penalty than traditional practice might, had the export opportunity not offered, have demanded. Canot reported the arrival, amongst a caravan of unbound slave women from Futa Jallon, destined for the Atlantic crossing, of two with ropes around their necks; these, he said, would ordinarily have been burnt as witches, had not the *almami* of Futa Jallon been at that moment particularly distressed for gunpowder, which their sale might bring.[101]

Many writers have been attracted by the hypothesis which seeks to explain a large part, perhaps the great majority, of the slaves to be found in Africa, and in particular of those who crossed the Atlantic, in terms of the principle widely accepted in Africa that slavery was an appropriate punishment for certain offences. Edward Blyden, for example, believed that 'as a rule, those who were exported...belonged to the servile and criminal classes'.[102] A modern scholar has described the Atlantic slave trade as providing Africans 'with a means of getting rid of criminals and other undesirables'.[103] Another, more popular writer believes that 'until the Europeans came upon the scene, slaves were regarded inside Africa as useful and helpful people, whose ownership carried with it specific obligations—to feed, to clothe, to shelter and protect'; while properly insisting that the status of domestic slaves differed from area to area and by tribe, and not ignoring the fact of warfare and kidnapping, he has listed as the more important reasons for enslavement the custom of pledging one's self

---

[100] Adebiyi Tepowa, 'A short history of Brass and its peoples', *Journal of the African Society*, 1907, 68.

[101] Canot, 1928, 95.

[102] Blyden, 1887/1967, 126.

[103] A. E. Afigbo, 'A reassessment of the historiography of the [colonial] period' in J. F. Ade Ajayi and I. Espie (eds), *A thousand years of West African history*, Ibadan and London 1965, 442; also 'a source of easy wealth'.

when in default on a debt, and adultery, theft and certain other crimes.[104] There have even been reproaches for failing to put forward the punishment explanation even when the information available about some particular episode that is being reported has nothing whatever to say about it. Referring to eye-witness accounts of slaving expeditions returning to the market place in Kano with as many as a thousand newly captured slaves, one commentator complained of the witness, that

> it does not appear that it struck him to inquire for what reason this was done. In my humble opinion if he had done so I think he would have found it to be the punishment for some insurrectionary rising against the Sultan of Sokoto, or for resistance to the mandates of some Emir.[105]

Both in Pagan and in Muslim Africa slave status was indeed often the penalty imposed for the commission of some grave social offence, but the views just quoted imply an importance for this practice which the facts recorded in at least many parts of the continent do not justify. Even with such economic stimulus as has been outlined above, the sale as punishment principle is inadequate to account for the large masses of slaves, male and female, young and old, exported west, north or east. In Nachtigal's account of the sources from which the Kuka market drew its supplies of slaves (see p. 322) there is no hint that anyone was ever enslaved in Kuka as a result of the application of the principle of punishment. The Pagans enslaved by the Bagirmi raiders whom Nachtigal observed were collected quite indiscriminately, and there were no recognizable grades of either moral or physical quality to distinguish those who were despatched to the Kuka market and those who remained behind in Bagirmi. The picture of unscrupulous exporters dumping shoddy goods in overseas markets covers only the smaller portion of the trade: the majority of slaves for export, it seems certain, were re-exports, captives taken in war or raids.

[104] J. L. Pope-Hennessy, *Sins of the Fathers*, London 1967, 88, 176.
[105] A. E. M. Gibson, 'Slavery in western Africa', *Journal of the African Society*, 1903, 18-19. the reporter here criticised was C. H. Robinson, a pioneer Hausa linguist.

Slaves on the march

'The slaves were carried two on one camel'. (IV, 256)

Slave-hunting is by its nature a violent and brutal exercise, as Nachtigal was able himself to observe when he accompanied a raid against the Pagan Kimre in their tree houses (see above, p. 52 and below, pp. 347-56). The results on that occasion were rather disappointing, only about fifty slaves;[106] some later raids were more productive.[107] Death during the slave-raid itself was only the first mortal danger the slave had to face. He, or she, had then to pass through the marshalling yards, if the expedition were operating too far from its home base to return there the same day (as Hamman Yaji's men could almost always do). Conditions in the camp of Abu Sekkin, ruler of Bagirmi, were pretty grim for everybody, and many of the newly captured slaves who were herded together there were soon reduced to a pitiable condition. Many fell ill; all had inadequate food. As a precaution against attempts at escape to their home country which was still not very far away, and in the absence of enough chains, slaves were fastened together by strips of raw hide, even those so physically weak that movement was difficult for them.[108] Eye-witness details of both raiding and marshalling are given in Nachtigal's chapter, 'Slave raids', reproduced as an appendix to this volume.

The lot of slaves who survived raid and marshalling yard, to be then moved to an organized marketing centre, was no happier. They did not enjoy even the theoretical protection of the law, for the full slave law did not come into effect until the slaves were brought into safe Muslim territory: while still on the road they were simply booty.[109]

It had been Nachtigal's own initiative and enterprise, backed

---

[106] III, 346; or below, p. 355.
[107] For example, that against Koli, III, 358; see below, pp. 362-71.
[108] III, 363; see below, p. 338.
[109] Hurgronje, 1931, 18. According to the law, should a Muslim actually engaged on *jihad* kill someone in a category legally exempt from death, repentance, but no compensation, is necessary; if, however, the killing occurs after the booty has been assembled, then the person responsible must reimburse, to the *imam* who will add it to the booty, the value of the dead man; Khalil ibn Ishaq, I, 207.

up by the support of Shaykh Umar of Borno, which had created the southbound caravan, from Borno to Abu Sekkin; and Nachtigal had tried (with considerable success, though less than he might have wished) to keep the party as small as possible (see below, p. 323). On the return journey, there were hundreds of people, and much less unitary authority. Most of the people were slaves, and most of these had been taken in exchange for horses, another illustration of slaves in the arms trade (see above, pp. 111-15). There were also some Bagirmi wishing to return northwards. With inclement weather, the ground already sodden under foot or flooded, the slaves completely exhausted by hunger, half of them suffering from the intestinal complaint which had swept through the camp, Nachtigal wondered how such people were to survive the journey. In fact, even on the first day, with a march of only six hours, many had had to be left behind, 'despite the most pitiless thrashing with the cruel hippopotamus-hide whips'.[110] What additional measures may have been taken, Nachtigal does not mention at this point.

The whips, essential equipment for a slave caravan, are a recurrent theme. In the mid-fourteenth century, travelling south across the Sahara, Ibn Battuta met a northbound caravan, some members of which had lagged behind. Ibn Battuta and his companions later found one of them, dead, sheltering in vain beneath a tiny tree, a mile from water. And his whip still in his hand. Even at a distance of 650 years, there seems justice in that.[111]

Nachtigal paid particular attention to his own 'household'—companions and slaves—and their experience represents in individual detail the general situation in the caravan as a whole. The household had grown substantially, while in Abu Sekkin's camp. Almas, the guide, for example, had sold his Borno horse for four slaves 'and a pagan horse', delivered immediately.[112] Eventually Nachtigal found himself with about twenty persons to feed. It was impossible for him to prevent his companions from acquiring slaves, particularly since he had little or nothing to offer them instead by way of compensation.

[110] III, 428.
[111] p. 24; *Corpus*, 283.
[112] III, 348.

After some time, indeed, grain came into the market, but it was difficult to get the number of throwing-irons needed to purchase it, and the Tummok definitely refused to accept payment in any other form. For my household I needed grain daily to the value of two throwing-irons, equivalent to half a Bornu tobe, and I could calculate with some certainty the day when my property would be reduced to nothing. I had already renounced altogether the consumption of poultry, eating only soups made from the flour of cereals or of groundnuts. We were really starving.[113]

Once on the march, members of the caravan bartered throwing-irons, the popular local weapon, acquired in the war-camp, for grain. Failing to secure any grain from a Pagan chieftain, Nachtigal had to buy it, on credit and at extortionate prices, from 'more favoured but avaricious' members of the caravan.[114] Nachtigal was at first hopeful, despite the misery all around: 'I could not sufficiently regard myself as fortunate that those in my household kept up stoutly, though there were many children among them.'[115]

At Manjafa, nearly three weeks into the march, Nachtigal and two of his household, having travelled (supported by Abu Sekkin's letter of command) for a week by boat, rejoined the caravan. They found the slaves of the caravan in lamentable condition. Many had escaped—see below, pp. 163-5, in the section 'Runaway slaves'—and many had died. Most of the survivors were reduced to skeletons by their hunger and exertions. The intestinal complaint was still active, 'and in addition an eye inflammation had for some time been raging among them, which in many cases produced extensive ulcers and opacity of the cornea, and in some complete blindness'. The slaves of Almas and Hammu, two of Nachtigal's principal companions, were especially severely afflicted, but the four slaves whom Nachtigal himself was taking back to the Sherif el-Medeni, 'a young woman, a young man, and two small girls about ten years old, were still to my joy tolerably well, even though two of them had recently fallen ill likewise'.[116] And a little later:

[113] III, 361-2.
[114] III, 429.
[115] III, 430.
[116] III, 436.

Of my people's slaves, many had indeed already died, but only one had escaped, and I was especially happy that the number of those who belonged to the Sherif el-Medeni was still complete, although the condition of health of the young man and of the small girls filled me with anxiety.[117]

Soon, as the caravan approached Logon, the young man's illness became so grave that he collapsed, refusing to go further. Threats and punishment availed nothing, and Nachtigal handed him over to the chief of the nearest village, 'close though he was to the haven of refuge which the capital of Logon might be considered to be'.[118] In Kala Kafra, now near the end of the journey, Almas lost another runaway slave: having started with six slaves, of whom one had been sold 'at a derisory price because of his unfitness for the march',[119] one had died, and two had run away, he had now only two remaining.

In Afade, one day's march on from Kala Kafra, the Sherif's young woman ran away, under cover of a storm, and was never found (see below, p. 165),[120] so Nachtigal also was down to two, the ten-year-old girls. As Nachtigal and Hammu, following at some distance behind the caravan, approached the village of Otsho, the next overnight halt, after dusk, they found one of the girls.

As I have already said, the child had been ill for several days, and here, perhaps unnoticed, she had fallen behind and collapsed exhausted. The dark colour of her body differed so little from that of the marshy ground that, if she had lain there completely motionless, we should hardly have noticed the poor creature. Since every effort to induce her to move was in vain, Hammu, who still commanded more strength than I did, and in spite of his stubbornness was very good-natured, decided to place the girl astride his shoulders, and

---

[117] III, 437-8.
[118] III, 439. Compare the case of the slave who fell ill on the way out to Bagirmi: he was entrusted to a village head, payment was given for expenses, and promises made (and, it seems, kept) for his return northwards after recovery (see below, pp. 225 and 379). In the crisis-ridden circumstances of the journey back from Bagirmi, no such provision was possible.
[119] III, 441.
[120] III, 442.

to carry her to our night quarters which were apparently close at hand.[121]

In Otsho, the other little girl ran away, but was recovered (see below, p. 165).[122] Two days beyond Otsho, the lass whom Hammu had rescued, who had seemed on the way to recovery, sleeping and eating well, suddenly fell dead to the ground from the ox on which she had been riding. Next morning, one of Almas' two remaining slaves, a young boy, had disappeared, and was not found again (see below, p. 165 again).[123] So both men were down to one surviving slave each.

Commenting on such losses, Nachtigal remarked, 'one can imagine how for every one of the unfortunates who reach the great markets of the Sudan three or four must be reckoned with who die on the way or otherwise disappear.'[124] Other writers have made similar estimates. One account of the Sudanese marauder, Rabih, says that 'for each of the slaves who reached their journey's end, one must add at least five other individuals who perished either in the slave raids of the foregoing campaigns, on the journey, or through sickness following on a change of climate'.[125] Another observer, French, thought that the sale of one captive might represent a total decline of population of ten, defenders killed in attacks on villages, women and children dying of famine, old people, children and the sick who were unable to keep up with those who had captured them, or were killed on the road because a more numerous enemy was threatening, or who died of misery.[126] Nachtigal's estimate seems low; Almas had lost five out of six, and even that figure makes no allowance for casualties during the initial slave-raid, nor for losses through hunger and disease in, or escape from, Abu Sekkin's camp. For an overall, general estimate, the Frenchman quoted above —one in ten—seems closer to the actual truth than Nachtigal's

[121] III, 442-3.
[122] III, 443.
[123] III, 444-6.
[124] III, 444.
[125] J. Lippert, 'Rabah', *Mitteilungen des Seminars für orientalische Sprachen in Berlin*, 1899, *Afrikanische Studien*, 249-50.
[126] Hourst, *Mission hydrographique du Niger*, 1896, *cit.* G. Deherme, 1908, 381-2.

one in four or five. Of course, not all those who disappeared died prematurely; and a tiny proportion of the runaways may even have managed to get home again.

In fact, Almas very nearly lost his sixth and last slave as well. After a long day's march—although only one day further from Kuka itself,

> it was not to be wondered at that during the afternoon, Dalamei, Almas' young Bua slave girl, had broken down exhausted. In his violent anger at seeing the profit which he had dreamt of making from the expedition come to nothing as a result of the death or flight of nearly all his slaves, her cruel master had thrashed her in the most brutal fashion, and, with the wish that she would fall prey to the hyenas, abandoned her in the wilderness. Fortunately I found her, took her with me on my horse, and brought her safely to our night's quarters.[127]

Nachtigal, although he valued Almas as an enterprising and courageous man, had also noted that he 'could be quite malicious and spiteful, revengeful and cruel'.[128] Was Dalamei perhaps the same 'recently captured Pagan maiden of about 16', with whose beauty Abu Sekkin and sought to entice Nachtigal, but whom the king eventually gave to Almas? (see below, pp. 319, 378). On that occasion, Nachtigal wrote, 'the poor girl nearly died of fright on seeing me.'[129] It would have been a fitting closing of the circle, had Nachtigal saved her life, at the end of the day, on the outskirts of Kuka.

The Sherif el-Medeni was not in the best of humour on hearing of the slender profit from the sale of his horse, and of the fate of the slaves who had been paid for that horse. Nachtigal, ashamed that he could deliver only one of those slaves, had the day before bought, on credit, for the Sherif,

> in place of the young woman who had run away in Afade, another of about the same age, and delivered her to him with the pretty little girl who had happily overcome the manifold privations, exertions and dangers of the long journey.[130]

[127] III, 450.
[128] III, 54; see also above, p. 96.
[129] III, 365.
[130] III, 451.

Almas, at least, had not killed the faltering Dalamei. Perhaps Kuka was too close. Nachtigal had witnessed worse. Here is his account, much earlier on this trip:

> The sick were constantly being forced [by weakness] to remain behind, and their masters were seen, whip in hand, standing guard over them or with cruel blows driving them back to the caravan. When these unfortunate people, broken down and at the end of their strength, made dull and apathetic by despair, could not, even by the most barbarous punishment, be moved to get up, I was heartily inclined to congratulate them, for I believed that, a useless burden on their masters, they would simply be abandoned. Here, near their home, in the midst of luxuriant natural surroundings, in the shadow of their woods, they could perhaps recover if they were removed from the infection of their companions, and taken away from the hunger and the exertions of the journey.... When I remarked to my servant Hammu that the sick slaves who were left behind could, despite their ill-treatment, regard themselves as fortunate, he laughed at my naïveté, and invited me to observe the subsequent course of events at the next opportunity. When some time later I saw one of my Bornu companions trying in vain to compel a sick young slave-girl to continue the march, and had already ridden resignedly on my way, I recalled Hammu's remark. I turned back, and found the man, otherwise very good-natured, already occupied in cleaning his bloody knife; the young slave girl lay dead at his feet, with her throat cut and her arteries open. While I could not at first in my disgust utter a word, the man commented, as if he had been doing the most natural thing in the world: 'Yes, yes, Christian, with these damned Pagans neither good faith nor profit is to be found.' In this way I first became acquainted with the melancholy fate of those whose strength had at last failed them. When the manhunters had to give up the hope of drawing any profit from the life of their victims, they slaughtered them so that their death at least might be turned to some account. If the warning example of their butchered companions had not spurred them on to the utmost exertion of their strength, many of these poor people would indeed have had the courage to expose themselves to the most cruel punishments, sometimes

A slave caravan. Richardson, 1848, I, frontispiece.

directly endangering their lives, in order to win freedom and a stop in their home country.[131]

Most of the slaves in this caravan were young women and children. Nachtigal knew that slaves were sometimes abandoned, exhausted, in the Sahara, when there were no camels available for their transport, and that in theory a quick death by a knife seems more merciful than to perish slowly by hunger, thirst, and the sun. It was being an eye-witness—he had been spared such sights in the desert—that shocked him so profoundly.

Nachtigal's closest experience of slave casualties in the desert was at the Meshru well, in southernmost Fezzan, which he passed three times, twice on the Tibesti excursion, and again travelling south to Borno from Fezzan. The third visit was the most informative. The large caravan arrived on the evening of 9 May 1870, to find the well badly choked up. Clearing work was immediately put in hand, but the caravan did not in fact move on until the afternoon of 11 May, mainly because of the slow flow of water.[132] Had the caravan been coming from the the south, with slaves in the last stages of dehydration, such a timetable must have proved fatal for some. Denham, crossing the Sahara earlier in the century, described how slaves, belonging to an old Shuwa Arab going on pilgrimage, ran, speechless with thirst, the final miles to a well; little children, thirsty and fever-stricken, were kept moving only by the threat of the whip.[133] Vischer, who crossed the desert early in the twentieth century, remarked that it was always near a well that the greatest number of bones was seen. He attributed this to slave children falling by the wayside, and later dragging themselves to the well to find the caravan gone; and also to sick animals being abandoned there.[134] Such factors may have contributed, but the clogged well seems the most likely main cause. Choked wells attracted attention in the earliest historical records of northern Africa. 'It has been impossible,' said Pliny, 'to open the road to the Garamantes

---

[131] III, 430.
[132] II, 42.
[133] Bovill, *Missions*, III, 490, 492.
[134] Vischer, 1910, 226.

country because brigands of that race fill up the wells with sand.'[135] Rohlfs, in 1866, thought that the traveller from the Meshru well to Borno, if he followed the trail of skeletons, could not miss his way.[136]

Nachtigal did not mention the skeletons on his third visit to the well. They had, however, caught his eye nearly a year earlier, on his way to Tibesti:

> The immediate surroundings of the well were covered with bleached human bones and camel skeletons. Shuddering I observed half-buried in the sand the mummified corpses of some children, still covered with the blue cotton rags which once had formed the clothing of living beings. The poor children from the Negro countries seem in shockingly large numbers to meet their death here at this last station on a long, desperate, painful journey.[137]

Another complication of slave travel in the desert derived from the employment of contract caravaneers, handling other people's slaves for them. Richardson met such a caravan between Ghat and Ghadames, of slaves being brought to their Ghadamsi owners by Tuareg agents. Richardson thought he espied two old men labouring after the group, but discovered on closer examination that they were two small children crawling.[138] Even when being paid so much per head, the so-to-speak professionals were unlikely to have quite the same interest in the slaves' survival as the owners had. On the other hand, the professionals would have better desert skills and experience.

Cold could be another desert killer. Al-Hajj Bashir, *wazir* of Borno in 1851, and a friend of Barth, going on pilgrimage with a number of slaves for sale to defray expenses, lost 40 dead in a single night between Fezzan and Benghazi, through cold in the mountains, and swore that he would never again travel with slaves for sale. But Barth found it hard to make him

---

[135] Natural history, V, 5, *cit.* E.W Bovill, *Golden trade*, 2nd edn, 1968, 34.
[136] 1874-5, I, 223.
[137] I, 216-7; see p. 334 for the return journey from Tibesti: in the interval, Nachtigal had himself come within a whisker of dying from thirst (pp. 225-30).
[138] Richardson, 1848, I, 399-400.

sensible of the equal horrors of slave-hunting.[139] Vischer, in the mountains south of Bir Meshru, came upon a large heap of camel bones, remains of a caravan from Bilma killed by intense winter cold. One of his companions had earlier himself been halted in the same place by cold, the water freezing in the waterskins, and the camels refusing to rise, being unable to stand on their stiff legs.[140] At the other extreme, some slaves died in the fires which occasionally engulfed villages, particularly in the dry season: in western Borno, in 1853, Barth heard reports of eight female slaves, fettered together in a hut, burnt to death in such a conflagration.[141]

There was the danger, too, that a slave caravan might be attacked. In 1824 Clapperton heard at Sokoto of freedom fighters, among the Gobir Hausa, capturing a Fulani caravan, 300 slaves and six Fulani women falling to them among the spoil.[142] Barth reported of a returning slave-raiding expedition in Adamawa, that it was attacked by the irate relatives of its captives, and these were successfully freed.[143] Bu Aisha, who led the party with which Nachtigal first crossed the Sahara, was unfortunate on his return journey from Kuka to Tripoli; starting out burdened with much property and many slaves, he was plundered of his possessions before he got home, though the marauders were said to have spared the gifts which he was taking from Shaykh Umar to the Governor-General of Tripoli.[144]

There is nothing to suggest that slave-traders were careful cost accountants, and the constant possibility of losses through exhaustion and exposure, hunger and thirst, disease and desertion, and robbery, must have made the trade, if sometimes very lucrative, inevitably an exceedingly risky economic enterprise.

Epidemics were another threat. We have seen how the members of the slave caravan with which Nachtigal travelled back to Borno from Bagirmi were already much weakened,

[139] Barth, 1965, II, 44.
[140] Vischer, 1910, 230; see also Bovill, *Missions*, III, 479.
[141] Barth, 1965, III, 46.
[142] Bovill, *Missions*, IV, 698; See also pp. 691 and 697.
[143] Barth, 1965, II, 212.
[144] IV, 13-4.

even before setting out, by an 'exhausting intestinal complaint', which sounds rather like dysentery, familiar from many news reports nowadays; and how to this was added, on the way, an eye inflammation, leading in some cases to blindness. Earlier in the century, in Hausaland, Lander had met a party of thirty slaves on their way to Zaria as tax, all apparently ill with smallpox, the men bound neck to neck with twisted bullock hide.[145] An epidemic amongst slaves in transit, whether by land or sea, was much to be feared. Canot, himself an experienced slaver, who had seen smallpox break out on a slave ship, called it 'the most dreaded and unmanageable' of calamities that might befall a slaver.[146] Smallpox in a land caravan might condemn it to wander almost as a plague ship, shunned by all—as Thomson, though his was not a slave caravan, learnt with bitter cost in East Africa.[147] Nachtigal noted that while slave caravans not infrequently, over the comparatively busy road to Borno, brought smallpox into Fezzan, such epidemics seemed seldom to get as far as Tibesti, where, in the absence of enclosed villages, they died quickly away.[148] Nachtigal mentions also guinea-worm, *irq*, plural *oruq*, literally 'vein', so common in the Sudan countries, and brought thence sometimes to Fezzan, where it did not become endemic.[149] Richardson described an illness in Ghadames in mid-century, apparently guinea-worm, called *arak el-abid*, the slaves' vein, which people believed was brought back by merchants who caught it in black Africa.[150]

One further cause of distress to slaves on the march deserves mention: the imaginary fears which were current about the intrusive white men. Nachtigal described the popular reaction to his arrival at Abu Sekkin's court:

> The opinion was soon generally spread abroad that the white people were clever and experienced in all sorcery,

[145] Lander, in Clapperton, 1829, 292.
[146] Canot, 1928, 245.
[147] J. Thomson, 'To Lake Bangweolo and the unexplored regions of British Central Africa', *Geographical Journal*, 1893, 110.
[148] I, 133, 392.
[149] I, 136 and note; III, 207 and notes. The Latin name, *Filaria medinensis*, suggests a northern origin, just as guinea-worm does a southern.
[150] 1848, I, 196.

that they were buying up all the black men as slaves, but were holding them less for purposes of work than for the gratification of their culinary pleasures, or to dye cloth red with their blood and make soap out of their brains.

'Obviously,' Nachtigal concludes, 'such ideas were not at all favourable to my effort to win friends on every side'.[151]

Another source elaborates this situation a little differently:

The strangest rumours, Nachtigal there reports, circulated about him in every locality of the Pagan region. It was said that Abu Sekkin had seen coming to his aid a bizarre creature, who belonged to a nation possessing irresistible arms and sorcery, a nation among whom there are no slaves, and whose favourite dish is roast child.[152]

No consideration of Nachtigal's slavery material would be complete without mention of these details. At the same time, however, it is not clear how relevant such fears were in the Muslim context: did local people feel this way about Arabs also, or about Europeans only?[153] There is an echo of such thoughts, very much European-focussed, in Dorugu's autobiography. A Hausa child, enslaved by a Kanuri, Dorugu passed to an Arab with some, but not overwhelming, anxiety; but when Adolph Overweg, Barth's colleague, examined him, 'I was as afraid as if he were about to eat me.'[154]

Looking back over all the preceding crisis and cruelty, it would be easy to find in the writings of other early travellers, Arabs included, parallel instances of calamitous slave caravans.

[151] III, 335-6. See also p. 43 above.
[152] Gourdault, *Tour*, 390.
[153] The Africanist George Shepperson remarked, though in another context: 'This "white men are cannibals" rumor was widespread during the four centuries of the European slave trade and it continues into the period of the European Partition of Africa and well into the colonial period. It was a widely held folk belief which, in my opinion, deserves serious and detailed investigation throughout Africa and the areas of the African diaspora.' In S.L. Engerman and E.D. Genovese, eds., *Race and slavery in the western hemisphere*, Princeton 1975, 105. See also D. Grant, *The fortunate slave*, London 1968, 53-4, 113-14.
[154] Kirk-Greene and Newman, 43-4.—I remember a story, somewhere in Hausa folk-literature, about dog-men waiting in the Sahara to marry slave-girls coming from south of the desert, but have not been able to rediscover the passage.

To cite one example, not long after Nachtigal's return home: Joseph Thomson found a caravan, originally 3000 strong, living on grass and roots as they waited on the west side of Lake Tanganyika to be ferried across. Already on the trip from Manyuema two-thirds of them had died of famine, murder or disease.[155] But it would be unrealistic to suggest that such disasters were standard: just as with so many other aspects of slavery within Muslim black Africa, there was a very wide range of practice.

Nachtigal had two opportunities to see at close hand the optimum condition of slaves on the march, near the very beginning of his odyssey, travelling south from Tripoli towards Murzuq, and again approaching el-Fasher, capital of Darfur, near the end.

> In the Wadi Ghanen [about half-way, or a little further, from Tripoli to Murzuq] we met a small caravan of cheerful well-cared-for slaves, with whom we exchanged greetings with innumerable *lales* and *afias*, and with whose masters we exchanged the customary courtesies and questions and answers.[156]

And again,

> We now met small slave caravans almost daily, and the appearance and bearing of the poor creatures were on the whole quite satisfactory. Well clothed and fed, apparently cheerful and contented, they were approaching the end of their toilsome and painful wanderings. Obviously the slave trade was still flourishing [these encounters occurred in March 1869], and enquiries about the prices of slaves were taken as much as a matter of course as those about the prices of corn, oil and butter.[157]

The company of seventy women slaves, whom Denham met on his way to Murzuq in 1822, were, he said, 'much better looking, and more healthy' than any he had seen near the Mediterranean coast.[158] Other travellers' reports of caravans,

[155] J. Thomson, *To the central African lakes and back*, London, 1881, reprinted 1968, II, 73-4.

[156] I, 56-7; *lale* is Kanuri for 'welcome' (II, 40), *afia* means hail, peace (II, 241).

[157] I, 58.

[158] Bovill, *Missions*, II, 142.

often wholly or largely of women slaves, coming into North Africa were, however, not quite so reassuring,[159] and Denham described how only the most robust reached the Fezzan—he saw over 100 skeletons from one slave caravan which had left Borno with inadequate food—and how these survivors were fattened before going on to the Tripoli market.[160]

The second such vision for Nachtigal occurred exactly five years later, almost to the day, as the caravan with which he was travelling entered El-Fasher. The leader of the caravan, Hajj Ahmed Tangatanga, originally from Dongola, had left the trade articles which he intended for Egypt in Kobe, the last main halt before el-Fasher. He took with him

> only horses and slaves which he intended to turn into money in Darfur. The slaves had new clothes, and their hair was arranged in the favourite Darfur style, in small short plaits, joined together at both sides as well as at the back of the head, so that they formed a coil, and had red clay, butter, cloves, mahaleb and the like thoroughly rubbed into them. The slaves were carried two on one camel.[161]

With so many difficulties in handling slaves, it is surprising that not more traders deliberately opted out of this branch of commerce. Nachtigal met one in Wadai, Hajj Salim from Qairawan, a *sharif*, who was considered an able, enterprising and prosperous merchant.[162] He bought chiefly ivory,

> for it was his intention to return by the more convenient route via Darfur, and in view of the length of his stay [he had already been about two years in Wadai] he was afraid that ostrich feathers would be destroyed by moths, while the irritable temperament of slaves caused him too much anxiety and annoyance.[163]

Possibly 'the judicious Hajj Salim' had conscientious scruples about dealing in goods which might not be entirely legitimate: he reported to Nachtigal that King Ali of Wadai, despite his religious convictions, had not always properly observed the

---

[159] Barth, 1965, I, 95, 99-100, 166-7, 221.
[160] Bovill, *Missions*, II, 202.
[161] IV, 256.
[162] IV, 56.
[163] IV, 202.

distinction between slave and free, in respect to the captives brought to Wadai from Bagirmi.[164] Hajj Salim died in Abeshr in the summer of 1873, while Nachtigal was travelling in the south of the country.[165]

An Arabic text shares Hajj Salim's reservations about 'the irritable temperament of slaves', though favouring gold rather than ivory as an alternative.

> My uncle [Abu Muhammad] travelled to the south to trade for gold and bought a camel to ride on. He had with him a townsman, who came to my uncle asking: 'What shall I trade for?' He replied: 'I don't know.' So the townsman traded for slaves. Then they set off to return to their people. Abu Muhammad never suffered from fatigue. When the caravan set off he would ride his camel and when it encamped he would pitch his tent and rest. But the townsman was exhausted with his slave women and men—this woman had grown thin, this one was hungry, this one was sick, this one had run away, this one was afflicted by the guinea-worm —and when they encamped they had much to occupy them. Meanwhile the townsman, tired and anxious, would see Abu Muhammad sitting in the shade with his wealth bag upon bag, not at all tired. The townsman would say: 'Glory be to God who has spared Abu Muhammad these trials.'[166]

Similar sentiments, separated by a span of 700 years: Hajj Salim died in 1873, the Arabic author, al-Wisyani, a famous Ibadi writer, in the second half of the twelfth century.

---

[164] IV, 67. To my immense chagrin, the English *Sahara and Sudan*, not the German, says 'from Wadai to Bagirmi', a nonsense. See p. 55 above.

[165] IV, 120; see also 56.

[166] *Corpus*, 88-90. I have omitted the Arabic equivalents.

CHAPTER V

THE DOMESTIC SCENE, I: GENERAL TREATMENT

General treatment

'I saw a friend of mine riding on the back of his master's horse, and I called to him, "Do you see? We have become slaves." He replied, "There is nothing we can do except put our trust in God's works."' (Dorugu's narrative, Kirk-Greene and Newman, p. 37)

The fate of a slave who survived a raid upon his (or her) home, and the rigours of the journeys which then had to be made, naturally varied very widely. Some peoples accepted enslavement more easily than others: the eastern Arabs said that slaves from Ulungu quickly became unmanageable, dull and morose, and many committed suicide, a measure rarely adopted by other peoples in that area;[1] again, most slaves from Okrika in eastern Nigeria

> have always proved refractory and incorrigible, and have often died broken-hearted, offering little or no encouragement to buyers to recruit their ranks with substitutes from that place.[2]

Some areas were more dispiriting than others: slaves isolated on the island of São Tomé sometimes ate earth in order

---

[1] Thomson, 1881/1968, I, 319-20; he adds, 'And yet as slaves in Unyanyembe [modern Tabora], they are vastly better off both in food and clothing than if they were free, besides having next to no work. It must therefore arise simply from grief at being separated from their country and kindred, and from a certain sense of the degradation attending slavery.'

[2] Tepowa, 1907, 67.

to kill themselves.³ Nachtigal heard of similar despair in Tibesti (see p. 142 below).

Nachtigal's own personal exposure to Muslim slavery in Africa, on his travels, began very gently, in Tripoli and the Fezzan. We have already noticed his description of slaves and freed people resident in Tripoli (see above, pp. 84-5), under the heading 'The return of the slaves', to which title many of the freed slaves in Tripoli seem to have been exceptions, continuing to live contentedly there even though the journey home, for some, would not have been too difficult. Much the same situation prevailed in the Fezzan.

> If indeed Islam generally brings with it a mild administration of the institution of slavery, still more so does the gentle good-natured character of the Fezzaners. Slaves are treated quite as members of the family and have nothing to complain of. They rarely seek to return to their native country and their masters without hesitation employ them on trading journeys to those countries.⁴

Just as the settlers in Tripoli and Fezzan figure under 'The return of the slaves' as exceptions, so some of the captives held by the Awlad Sulayman are exceptions under 'Emancipation', for Nachtigal encountered some who resolutely refused to surrender their imposed status—Khamis, the expert tracker who never made use of his skill to escape, or the young slave boy, Kore, rejecting his father's repeated ransom attempts (see above, pp. 78).⁵ It was usually Arab captives who might make a place for themselves in the host society,'above the despised status of a real slave'—but Kore was not an Arab, yet was loved almost as a son.

Kore's case is unambiguous: he was offered the choice between remaining with his captors, and returning to his original family. He chose the former. The case of Dorugu is less straightforward, but he too seems to have had the chance of home and freedom, and to have failed to exert himself to seize this opportunity. Once for freedom, twice for home. In

---

³ D. Crawford, *Thinking black: 22 years without a break in the long grass of central Africa*, London 1914, 2nd edn, 75.
⁴ I, 122.
⁵ II, 351-2.

Zinder, his first major stopping point after capture, Dorugu learnt that his father had been freed by the chief of Zinder. Father and son both been taken in the same surprise raid, but had not been re-united amongst the captives. The chief said to Dorugu's father: 'Go look for your son. When you find him, take him back to your town with you.'

> My father took his drum and went around drumming, because he knew that if I heard the sound of his drum I would come to him. From inside the house, I heard drumming that sounded like his, but I was not allowed to leave the house except when I went to get water for the horses. While I was in the house, other slaves belonging to my master went to fetch water and on the way met my father resting against a rock. He was waiting for me to come, but I had not gone to fetch water. He asked them, 'Where is Dorugu?' They said, 'He's in the house. We called him but he didn't hear us.' They went on to get the water and then returned and informed me, 'Dorugu, we just saw your father sitting there on the way to the water. He was waiting for you.' I asked them, 'Why didn't you call me?' They said, 'We called you but you didn't hear us.'[6]

That is all that is said in Dorugu's narrative, a strangely inconclusive episode. The next narrative item is the encounter with the hospitable concubine, about which Dorugu has rather more to tell us (see below, pp. 190-1). A good deal later, after having been given his freedom, Dorugu returned to Zinder, with Barth.

> While we were in Zinder I saw some people from towns near my grandmother's. On one occasion, I found a boy, a friend of mine, and told him to go tell my grandmother that I was in Zinder and that she should tell my father to come and get me. However, I don't think he went, because if you leave Zinder in the morning, you can be in my grandmother's town by afternoon. When I failed to hear any news from him, I met some Hausa men who said they would take me to my father. I didn't agree to it because I was afraid that they would sell me, since they were traders who had come to Zinder to attend the market.[7]

[6] Kirk-Greene and Newman, 38-9. See below, p. 211.
[7] *ibid.*, 54.

The fear of re-enslavement is significant, even though Dorugu had been given a formal document of emancipation,[8] and was in Zinder with Barth. That one request, to a friend to carry a message to Dorugu's grandmother, seems to have been all the effort Dorugu made to re-establish contact, despite staying in Zinder about a month.

As the party left Zinder, they passed the road leading to the grandmother's home, and seem to have been even in sight of the village. The next night they camped on the road to Kanche.

> I asked some men there if they knew my father. They asked me, 'What is his name?' I told them, 'Kwage.' They replied, 'Are you the son of Kwage the drummer?' I said, 'Yes.' They said, 'Your father passed by here yesterday on the way to Kanche.' When I heard that, I felt very sad. But it was God who was leading me.[9]

Enslavement could sometimes open up new opportunities. For many slaves it was a matter of making the best of an, initially, bad job. Kore and Dorugu suggest that, at least for some, enslavement could be a chosen career, chosen in the sense that the opportunity to depart from it was refused (see also the dwarf on p. 328 below). Dorugu was surprisingly lethargic about linking up with his father even when this would have meant home and freedom. Later, after emancipation, he seems to have remained desultory about home.

A great deal depended upon the extent to which the host society facilitated incorporation. A particularly interesting illustration of the possible absorption of incoming slave elements concerns the Tubu or Teda people of Tibesti. It is a miniature example, both in terms of the small size of the host society, and the smaller still numbers of incoming slaves. It has, nevertheless, a special interest, in two respects. First, the Tibesti homeland is one of the least welcoming, and most deeply poverty-stricken, areas in Africa. If the social assimilation of slaves can, even so, happen here, then it can happen anywhere in Muslim black Africa. And second, although all

---

[8] Kirk-Greene and Newman, 49.

[9] *ibid.*, 55. Barth had already told Dorugu that he would give him back to his father if opportunity arose (p. 54).

the material which I shall use in this miniscule exegetical exercise is imbedded in Nachtigal's account, yet he is himself not at all consciously concerned with any element of incorporation; quite the contrary, he concentrates only on the negative aspects of the slave condition in Tibesti, destitution, despair, death.

Let us look first at the negative side, postponing for the moment any more positive considerations which Nachtigal, almost unwittingly, offers. 'Any thinking slave in Tibesti,' Nachtigal observed,

> must be driven to despair. If in other countries he has a bad master, he is sustained by the hope of passing into the hands of a more benevolent one, or, if necessary, of running away. From Tibesti, however, there is no escape; there his hopes and his life come to an end. To run away means certain and speedy death in the pathless wilderness, to remain means an unending series of misfortunes, often nothing but a slow death. Cases are known where slaves coming from Bornu have taken their own lives when they were bought in exchange for camels[10] by the Tubu Reshade in Kawar, although as a rule they adapt themselves to every turn of fate with a resignation and an ease which we cannot comprehend. So general is fear of becoming a slave among the Tubu, and anyone who has seen them close at hand understands why the pitiable victims prefer death.[11]

This was not simply hearsay, or a general overview. Nachtigal himself spent a considerable time in Tibesti; he had been close at hand. Many slave-owners brought their slaves, apparently ill, to him for his medical attention. The slaves seemed to Nachtigal to be in fact 'on the road to slow starvation only because of insufficient and unsuitable food'.

> The slaves of the Tubu Reshade were really in a heart-rending condition of degradation. In general people in Tibesti had the barest living, and slaves were accordingly subjected to nothing short of a continuous starvation diet, which must have been all the more grievous for those who came from

---

[10] The English *Sahara and Sudan* reads 'bartered for camels', which might be ambiguous, hence the change above; the German is '*gegen Kameele eingetauscht wurden*'.
[11] I, 324.

the fertile productive countries of the Sudan. The luxury of clothing was likewise rarely permitted to them. A little piece of cotton cloth or of leather had to suffice for them, with the function of the fig-leaf of paradise, and not much larger, and this, together with hunger, often brought a speedy death to the Negroes, their constitutions so sensitive to cold.[12]

Rather bleak. What of the positive considerations to which I alluded a little earlier? Some of these are precise, based on Nachtigal's own personal experience and observation. Others are more general. The precise first.

In the midst of the sombre account which Nachtigal gives, and from which we have just quoted, about the terrible conditions for slaves in Tibesti, slave-owners cared enough about their slaves to bring them to Nachtigal for help. To be sure, slaves were property, and a dead slave meant a financial loss, but for slave-owners to bring their slaves to Nachtigal may suggest a relationship at least slightly more than that between owner and chattel. Again, when a Tibesti man, veiled as usual and unrecognised, was passing with a well-laden camel through the valley in which Nachtigal was effectively being held prisoner, the rumour spread that one of Nachtigal's people was trying to leave, carrying Nachtigal's baggage (already drastically eroded) to safety. 'A mob of women, children and slaves at once collected, insulted and threatened him, and then started to stone him'[13]—another hint of active slave participation in local society. Another tiny vignette, a description of the early morning routine of Arami, Nachtigal's principal protector, and indeed the most respected man in Tibesti:

> In the morning he went off very early to his dates, which had just ripened, cut some of them, carried them home on his shoulders, arranged the work of the day for his sister and a slave, and worked on his hut.[14]

We may assume (Nachtigal does not himself say) that the arrangement made each day for the sister, and that for the slave, differed: nevertheless, there is an inkling here of a

[12] I, 324.
[13] I, 317.
[14] I, 313.

functioning domestic unit bridging, to however limited an extent, the divide between free and slave.

These are all tiny details, though, taken together, they do suggest more social interaction between free and slave in Tibesti than Nachtigal's gloomy generalisations leave room for. At the opposite end of the scale of size, Nachtigal comments several times on the diversity of skin colour amongst the Tubu, and attributes much of this to the intimate incorporation of black slaves within the Tubu population. This, however, occurred much more amongst the Tubu who had migrated, whether permanently or as visitors, westward to Fezzan, than amongst those staying at home in Tibesti.[15] One of Nachtigal's less effectual companions, the Tubu, Kolokomi,

> indeed claimed to have some Tuareg blood in his veins, rare as admixtures between the two tribes are said to be, except when female prisoners of war have passed into the enemy tribe.[16]

Sa'ad, the freedman settled in Tripoli who was one of Nachtigal's original servants (see above, p. 87-8), provides a final snippet of evidence about slave incorporation in Tibesti.

> Ugly, surly and unreliable as Sa'ad was, he had...frequently been an object ardently coveted by the housewives of Bardai, and from this had sprung many an hour of anxious concern for him about his future.

Nachtigal's negotiations for the hire of two camels belonging to a local woman broke down when she caught sight of Sa'ad, and decided forthwith that he was the only payment she would accept.[17] It seems likely that domestic labour was the key factor here, rather than any sexual agenda, though ardent covetousness (*lebhafte Begehrlichkeit*) does sound a little strong.

An anthropological study of slaves among the Tuareg, another people living often in harsh desert conditions, describes how, through the classificatory kinship system and in particular through avoidance and joking relations, slaves are

---

[15] See, for example, I, 99, 170-3, 179-80, 204, 206, 241, 291, 313, 384-9, 397 and elsewhere.

[16] I, 191.

[17] I, 323-4; see also p. 38 above.

incorporated into the same social pattern as their master, and made an integral part not only of the society but also of the actual family. While it is rare for a slave to eat with his master, and slaves live with wind and sun screens rather than in tents, there is otherwise little difference, and clothing and ornaments of free and slave are much the same.[18]

This sort of incorporation, of slaves into the slave-owning society, was quite common in Africa. In Hausaland, a slave, if acquired young enough, might be given the tattoo marks of his master's people.[19] In Arabia, some people claiming descent from local Arab tribes, or from Arabic-speaking North Africans, might well derive in fact from Sudanese slaves of these groups, 'since the name of an Arabic tribe or nation is of both free and bond'.[20]

In some places, the incorporation of slaves within the slave-owning society was furthered by special organizations amongst the slaves themselves. In Mecca, each community of black slaves had its own shaykh, who settled disputes by his judicial sentences which were carried out by a supporting official, the *naqib*.[21] In Ghadames, there was but a single shaykh of the slaves,[22] who thus described his own functions to Richardson:

> Be it known, Oh Christian! I am the Sheikh of the slaves, my name is Ahmed. I am from Timbuctoo. The people of Bambara are the finest in the world. They are brave—they fear none. Now, hear me: I know all the names of the slaves in Ghadames: I watch over all their conduct, to punish them when they behave badly, to praise them when they do well. They all fear me. For my trouble I receive nothing. I am a slave myself. I rarely punish the slaves. We have always here

---

[18] Nicolaisen, 1997, II, 603 ff.

[19] Tremearne, 1913, 102.

[20] Doughty (1888/1923, I, 140) suspected this of the people of el-Ally, a town in northern Arabia founded by Berber pilgrims, although the people themselves denied such admixture.

[21] Hurgronje, 1931, 11.

[22] Here also called the *qa'id al-wasfan*, head of slaves; Richardson, 1848, I, 304.

more than two hundred. If you wait, plenty of slaves will soon come from Soudan!²³

There was also a street of the slaves in Ghadames, where the slaves used to gather and talk.²⁴

Evidence of the sometimes comfortable circumstances of slaves comes from various quarters. Here is an East African description:

> No starved and ill-used slaves are to be seen, for on cases of inhumanity being reported to the Sultan [of Zanzibar], the sufferers are at once set free, and made safe from the brutality of their masters. Indeed, this class seem to have a remarkably easy time of it, and have ten times more real liberty than thousands of our [British] clerks and shop-girls. They are commonly allowed to engage themselves out to work; and no caravan ever goes up the country without a number of slaves among the porters. A jolly hearted crew they are, whose motto in life is, 'beer, women, and ease'.²⁵

Parallel instances of the possibility of intervention, should a slave be ill-treated, might be cited. Among the Ahaggar Tuareg a runaway slave is always reclaimed by his owner, but the senior chief may intervene if the slave has been misused or inadequately clothed.²⁶ According to Muslim law the judicial authority might decree the enfranchisement of a slave whose master had intentionally done anything to him which appreciably diminished his value, or would in the eyes of the world be considered degrading or humiliating, e.g. the

---

[23] Richardson, 1848, I, 101-2; *cf.* 141-2.
[24] *ibid.*, I, 147.
[25] Thomson, 1881/1968, I, 17. Doughty (1888/1923, I, 553-4) says of slaves in Arabia, that their condition was always tolerable and often happy (though somewhat harder actually within the holy cities), slave-owners often freeing slaves, marrying them out, and endowing them somewhat with camels or palms. Freedmen growing prosperous might marry into the free class, though only among members of the somewhat despised smiths' caste.—It was the Thomson quotation which the American editors chose to put on the outside back cover of their volume of *Slavery* 1970; readers who have come thus far will be able to judge for themselves how representative it is of the data as a whole.
[26] Nicolaisen, 1997, II, 603.

amputation of a part of the body or cutting off the hair of a beautiful female.[27]

A poem from Mauritania begins: This world is topsy-turvy but the world to come is sure. And, as an example of topsy-turviness, the poem laments the quite inappropriately comfortable circumstances of slaves:

> The slave is owner of two flowing shifts, while the slave girl keeps her weight through drinking milk.[28]

Many slaves, perhaps, lacking a change of garment and milk to drink, voted with their feet and ran away. The fact that 'runaway slaves', not even considered as a separate heading in *Slavery* 1970, have now exceeded almost every other section in length, shows how widespread a practice it was, and how much attention it attracted. Baba of Karo's comment on the result of British interference with slavery in Nigeria, early in this century and early in Baba's life, cites both the stay-at-homes and the runaways. 'Some slaves,' she said, 'have been with your family so long that they become like your grandmothers,' and when slavery was stopped in Hausaland, nothing much happened, so she reported some sixty years later, in her father's slave compound. The fact, however, that at that time 'some slaves whom we had bought in the market ran away' suggests that not all of them had been perfectly contented with their lot, or even resigned to it.[29]

Incorporation needed time. Even when the ordinary day-to-day life of a slave was tolerable, insecurity continued to be a normal characteristic of the slave condition, for a variety of different, and unpredictable, circumstances might lead suddenly to his or her sale or transfer. For example, a Kanuri, whom market shortages had cut off from his kola nuts, the favourite luxury of Borno, might suffer from what would be called today withdrawal symptoms:

> When one has been deprived of this luxury for a long time, the greatest sacrifices are made to get hold of it, and a Kanuri does not hesitate, for example, for this purpose to

[27] Ruxton, 1916, 352-3; Ibn Abi Zayd, 227.
[28] Norris, 1968, 30.
[29] Mary Smith, 1954/1981, 78, 67.

sell his horse or his concubine, the most valuable earthly possessions that he has.[30]

Even slaves themselves might lament the lack of kola. One of the many disadvantages of being sold as a slave across the Sahara was, according to a Borno song, to be deprived of this particular indulgence.[31]

A slave who accompanied his master on a journey might find himself left behind in some strange place as payment of some toll-obligation which his master had to meet, or as a contribution to a present to some magnate along the road. Nachtigal describes a delay, in setting out on the final leg of his Sahara and Sudan journey, from Wadai to Darfur, in February 1874:

> At last the king's camels arrived, the negotiations with the acting *shertaya* about his greeting gift, which consisted of a few slaves, were concluded, and...we were able to continue our journey.[32]

Or a slave-owner who fell on hard times might feel that in order to improve his liquidity position he had no alternative to selling some of his slaves. Or all of them, though Hajj Ahmed Tangatanga may have over-dramatised his difficulties, living at Tineat on this same Wadai to Darfur road, and overwhelmed by the obligations of hospitality:

> Ahmed assured me that sometimes on one day he had to provide up to fifty or even sixty dishes for his guests; he had seen no way out but one day after selling his last slave, to wind up his household, and it was therefore very welcome that just at that time King Ali should have him invited to Wadai.[33]

Slaves might be requisitioned as compensation, or as fines. In Vai country, in the seventeenth century, the compensation for adultery with a wife of the king was gifts or slaves.[34] Among

---
[30] II, 202.
[31] R. Prietze, 'Bornulieder', *Mitteilungen des Seminars für Orientalische Sprachen zu Berlin, Afrikanische Studien*, 1914, 221-2, 224.
[32] IV, 247.
[33] IV, 245; it was, however, some years before Ahmed finally decided upon settling in Abeshr with his family.
[34] Ogilby, 1670, 411.

one people in the Nassarawa Province of northern Nigeria, if a murderer was caught he was handed over to the family of the victim to be killed; but if the murderer escaped, a male or female slave, depending on the sex of the murdered person, was presented to the bereaved family.[35] In Mauritania, blood-money might include slaves: the loss of an ear was compensated by the gift of a woman slave, while lesser wounds received varying numbers of camels.[36] Slaves forming part of the marriage gift of a fiancé to his intended bride would normally return to his home; but the law allowed the bride's father to sell such slaves, if more money were needed for the trousseau.[37] Denham said that corporal punishment for slaves was rare in Borno, but the fact that Borno slave-owners were more than once seen by him in tears at having had to sell a slave[38] was a poor consolation perhaps for the slave thus uprooted again from his or her home.

Nor did the emancipation of a slave necessarily assure to his descendants unquestioned social acceptance; the taint of slavery in the family genealogical tree sometimes continued to be a liability. Some illustrations of the disabilities from which a member of a distinguished family might suffer if he happened to have a slave as a mother are noted below (pp. 194-5), and the tension which has continued in Mauritania between the blacks whose ancestors were once slaves and other sections of the population has also been mentioned (p. 64). In Liberia in 1874 the black American traveller, Benjamin Anderson, was told that the Mandingoes of Musadu had such 'a hard-hearted and unalterable opinion respecting the freest man if he has once been a slave' that he thought it prudent to cut out from a Monrovia newspaper which he had been given for distribution in the interior of the country a passage which 'contained an unsavoury revelation about our once being slaves'.[39] In quite recent times a social distinction is said sometimes to

[35] F.F.W. Byng-Hall, 'Notes on the Bassa Komo tribe', *Journal of the African Society*, October 1908, 20.
[36] Norris, 1968, 19.
[37] Khalil ibn Ishaq, II, 55.
[38] Bovill, *Missions*, III, 535.
[39] Benjamin Anderson, *Narrative of the expedition despatched to Musahdu . . . in 1874*, Monrovia 1912, 29. See p. 157 below for 1971 reprint.

remain in marriage alliances,[40] and cases are known of West Africans who had planned a marriage with a black American going to the United States for the wedding ceremony to avoid any risk of unpleasantness with their family.

The extent to which the slave population reproduced itself is a disputed question on which our authorities have little to say. Lugard once asserted that 'it is a known fact that slaves do not increase naturally to any appreciable extent',[41] but this so-called demographic law has been categorically rejected by other writers as a 'myth'.[42]

Jobson in the seventeenth century spoke of Gambian Mandingo Muslims and their slaves, 'which slaves they suffer to marry and cherish the race that comes of them'.[43] According to Clapperton, male slaves in Sokoto were given wives on reaching the age of eighteen or nineteen, and their children were also slaves.[44] Barth was surprised to see so few home-born slaves in the Sudan, except among the Tuareg who deliberately encouraged this. He concluded that a domestic slave was rarely allowed to marry and that this absence of reproduction was a main factor in maintaining slave-raiding.[45] Referring particularly to Tripoli, Nachtigal noted that blacks were always eager to marry with as little delay as possible. But the climate of Tripoli did not suit them, and their descendants were neither numerous nor very vigorous.[46]

Nachtigal had himself one close encounter with slave reproduction. On 11 November 1871, on his way back from his excursion into the central Sahara with the Awlad Sulayman, he was drawing near home, near enough that the danger of losing his way no longer deterred him from giving way to his exhaustion. More dragging his horse than leading him, Nachtigal crept after the Awlad Sulayman caravan.

> Only a glance at our few slaves, whose patience and bodily strength were being subjected to much more severe tests,

[40] Trimingham, 1968, 93.
[41] Lugard, 1893, I, 169.
[42] M.I. Finley, *Slavery in classical antiquity*, Cambridge 1960, 60.
[43] Jobson, 1623/1932, 84-5.
[44] Clapperton, 1829, 213-14.
[45] Barth, 1965, I, 527-8.
[46] I, 16-17; see also pp. 83-5 above.

was capable of sustaining me a little along the way. The Arabs are not cruel or hard-hearted to their slaves, but in the desert climate to which they are not accustomed the children of the tropics further to the south do not easily endure the deprivation of food. How immeasurably fortunate were we in comparison with the poor Lafia, a half-witted slave girl of Hazaz, whom I found towards the end of the day's march; she had collapsed under a *serrah* tree, in labour pains! After an exhausting journey she had still to endure the miseries of childbirth, and bore them in fact with an ease worthy of admiration. Despite my compassion at the sight of this poor creature, almost completely naked and dead-tired, I had to laugh over this opportunity to practise my expertise as a midwife. When everything ended without mishap and the little citizen of the world, destined to misery and want, had been a little cleaned up with his mother's rags, I rolled him up in a piece torn from my own garment, which was in tatters anyway, waited until his mother had recovered a little, and then, with the infant in my arms, went on to the camp with the maternity case. Our arrival here caused a considerably stir, for Lafia was not exactly distinguished for her physical attractions, and no one was willing to admit having been on terms of intimacy with her. The poor girl herself, in view of the great number of her transient admirers, and with her dull wits, could identify none of the slaves around even with some measure of probability as the progenitor of her child.[47]

This section has been the most difficult in the whole volume to bring together into some kind of internal unity, since the theme of 'general treatment' covers an enormous variety of circumstances, from callousness to comfort, from cruelty to kindness. One of the most vivid scenarios, bringing the two extremes almost face to face, comes from Barth. At the end of 1851, accompanying a military expedition by the Borno army, he had camped with the column just inside the Borno border.

I had scarcely pitched my tent when that cruel minister of police, Lamíno...brought into my presence a famous cut-throat of the name of Barka-ngólo, whose neck was secured in a large machine called 'bégo', consisting of two pieces of wood from four to five feet in length, and very heavy, so

[47] II, 494-5.

that every movement was accompanied with the greatest pain. Nevertheless, my mischievous friend persuaded himself that it would gratify me to see this miserable wretch fight with another culprit secured in the same manner, by giving to each of them a long whip of hippopotamus hide, and forcing them by threats to flog each other. It was a horrible sight, and I had great difficulty in convincing my cruel friend that such a scene was far from being agreeable to me. In order to get rid of him, I presented him with a quantity of cloves to give to his beloved 'Aáisha, of whose culinary powers we had already had several proofs (see below, p. 203). He was greatly pleased with my present, and with an amorous smile he described to me how deeply he was in love with his darling, saying that he loved her and she loved him also; 'and,' added he, in a very sentimental way, 'such a mutual love is the greatest bliss on earth.'[48]

Nachtigal knew Lamino too, and esteemed him much more highly than had Barth. After Lamino's death in February 1871, Nachtigal described him as, among other things, 'feared by evildoers...idolised by his slaves' (see above, p. 35). Ironically, in the drama and discourse which Barth here confronted, it was apparently free persons who suffered the most grievous harm, whilst upon the slave was lavished every praise.

Slave revolts

'The enemies who carried on these wars were principally the Oyo Mahomedans, with whom my country abounds—with the Foulahs, and such foreign slaves as had escaped from their owners, joined together, making a formidable force of about 20,000, who annoyed the whole country.' (Samuel Ajayi Crowther, in Curtin, ed. 1968, 299)

The outbreak of revolts such as have been noted in various parts of the world from time to time is one channel through which slave discontent might find expression. Revolt, however, required organization and courage and persistence, so that the absence of slave revolt at any time cannot be regarded as conclusive proof that slaves were not discontented.

Revolts by black slaves in Mesopotamia are reported as early as 696,[49] and in the late ninth-century Basra was for a time

---

[48] Barth, 1965, II, 338.
[49] G. Mathew, 'The East African coast until the coming of the Portu-

held by slaves from East Africa who had been employed in the saltpetre mines of the lower Euphrates.[50] The history of Brazil, another overseas export market, was also for a long time, up to the early nineteenth century, marked by slave insurrections of one kind or another.[51] Within Africa, it has been suggested that slave revolts were a threat to sixteenth-century Songhay.[52]

Nachtigal had nothing to say on this subject, unless his account of the Qairawan merchant who preferred to trade with Wadai in ivory rather than in slaves, whose irritable temperament was likely to make them troublesome,[53] is relevant, and presumably no specific incident of this kind came to his notice. Some European travellers thought that slave-owners in Africa were sometimes inclined to underestimate the risks of slave retaliation. Clapperton, noting the preponderance of slaves in the population of Kano in 1827, warned his Arab friends to 'keep a good lookout', quoting the precedent of slave revolt in San Domingo (now Haiti).[54] Speke found the slaves in Zanzibar 'spellbound', not realizing that 'if they chose to rebel, they might send the Arabs flying out of the land'[55]—the spell was not broken until a little more than a century later.

The apprehensions expressed by these travellers were, however, perhaps themselves exaggerated. The contrasts between

---

guese', in Oliver and Mathew, 1963, 101.

[50] Ibn Khaldoun, *Histoire des Berbères et des dynasties musulmanes de l'Afrique septentrionale*, tr. Baron de Slane, Algiers 1854, II 106; Freeman-Grenville, *The mediaeval history of the coast of Tanganyika*, Berlin 1962, 29, 34 (hereafter Freeman-Grenville, 1962 B). Some who escaped when this rebellion was finally crushed are said to be among the ancestors of the Ma'dan, the marshmen of southern Iraq, who have attracted considerable attention recently (G. Maxwell, *A reed shaken by the wind*, London 1957/1994, 17-20).

[51] Kent, 1965, 162. See also, J.E. Flint and I. Geiss, 'Africans overseas, 1790-1870', in *The Cambridge history of Africa*, vol. 5, 1976, ed. J.E. Flint, 427-8; interestingly, although slavery figures very prominently in the index to this *C.H.A.* volume, every single entry under 'revolts, rebellions' comes from this overseas chapter.

[52] D.A. Olderogge, 'Feudalism in the western Sudan in the sixteenth-nineteenth centuries', *Sovietskaya Etnografia*, 1957, summarized in *African Abstracts*, 1959, 11-12.

[53] IV, 202; see above, p. 136.

[54] Clapperton, 1829, 171-2.

[55] Speke, 1863, xxvi.

Haiti and Kano may well have been more important than the similarities. According to a modern historian, although there was sometimes considerable turmoil among the free population of Hausaland, there were no slave rebellions there throughout the last century.[56] This has been explained in terms of the comparative ease with which slaves there were able to work and accumulate property for themselves, and the fact that the claims which masters could make on them were fairly precisely defined, so that in some respects they enjoyed more *de facto* freedom than some of those who were technically free men[57] (compare Thomson's like comments on East African slaves, pp. 138 and 146 above). A similar psychology may be reflected in the employment of slaves rather than free men as soldiers.

There were evidently some real dangers from slave unrest. Individual murder was one. A North African merchant told Clapperton, in Hausaland in 1824, that his slaves never knew in which room he would sleep, and that he always kept a dagger and loaded pistols under his pillow. The merchant said that all the Arabs did the same, fearing to be murdered by their female slaves, as, he added, often happened.[58] That this was no foolish fear seemed to be established when Clapperton learnt in Kano in 1826 that a Ghadames merchant had been found strangled in his bed, one of a succession of such episodes.[59] A cleric from Sennar, teaching in Wadai, was murdered there by his concubines.[60] We have already described the fears in Mauritania, lest slaves exercise their supernatural powers to the same end of assassination (see above p. 93). For a much earlier parallel, Leo Africanus said that the people of Gaoga, the Bulala branch of Borno, formerly free, came under the domination of a self-established king who got his start in life when, as slave, he murdered his master and sold his goods for horses. With the mounted force thus acquired, the ex-slave himself captured more slaves, whom he traded to Egypt for

---

[56] M.G. Smith, 'The Hausa system of social status', *Africa*, 1959, 242.
[57] Sellnow, 1964, 97.
[58] Bovill, *Missions*, IV, 717.
[59] Clapperton, 1829, 171.
[60] J.S. Trimingham, A history of Islam in West Africa, O.U.P., 1962, 140.

more horses, until he was strong enough to rule the whole of Gaoga (see above p. 112).[61]

There were also larger-scale risings. These were frequently associated with runaway slaves, and may have been as often attempts at self-defence against recapture as outright revolt; where the threat of recapture did not exist the escaped slaves sometimes settled down quite peaceably in their own new homes. Such developments seem to have been particularly a feature of East Africa. In 1506 a Portuguese visitor to the north-west coast of Madagascar found there a dense population of refugee slaves from Malindi, Mombasa and even Mogadishu.[62] In the nineteenth century a town, Barder, was reported on the Juba river in present-day Somalia, where a crafty Arab had taken advantage of 'a sudden spirit of discontent shewing itself by the slave portion of the community of small tribes surrounding', and had established a local kingdom.[63] In 1867 it was estimated that more than 10,000 slaves had fled to the river Ozi, on the mainland opposite Pate island, whither a chief, Fumo Lotti, proscribed by the sultan of Zanzibar, had earlier withdrawn. The chief established a new state there, with two strong towns, Vittou and Mogogoni. The first rule of the state was to give liberty to all who crossed its borders. New arrivals were encouraged to build homes and clear farms, and were enrolled in armed defence companies.[64] These towns appear to be in the same area and of the same sort—if they are not in fact exactly the same towns—which Lugard visited in 1890. He mentions three names, Fuladoyo, Makongeni (=Mogogoni?) and Mwaiba, putting them on his map in the immediate hinterland of Malindi. He describes them as large stockaded villages, colonies of runaway slaves, and adds that he understood that they had beaten the Arabs in battle some years before. Now, the Arabs were talking of

[61] Leo Africanus, A, III, 835; B, II, 482.

[62] R.K. Kent, 'Madagascar and Africa: II. the Sakalava, Maroserana, Dady and Tromba before 1700', *Journal of African History*, 1968, 526.

[63] Harris, 1844/1968, I, notes by Lieut. Wilmot Christopher attached to frontispiece map.

[64] E.F. Berlioux, *The slave trade in Africa in 1872*, translated, London 1872, 47-8; some of the escaped slaves had come overland several hundred miles, from Somali territory.

carrying war against Fuladoyo. Lugard devised a compromise, according to which the fugitives should be given an opportunity to earn sufficient money with which to compensate their former owners.[65] He was, however, unable to see this scheme through.[66] The struggles between the Arab traders and the local chief Mirambo, in the later nineteenth century, for control of the Tabora area in Tanganyika were complicated by slaves who, armed by their Arab masters to fight against Mirambo, ran away and, joining other runaways, instead fought against the Arabs.[67]

There are West African instances too. About 1756 slaves in Futa Jallon revolted and built for themselves a fortified town, Kondeeah, which successfully resisted repeated assaults by the disgruntled ex-owners and their allies.[68] In 1838 the Koranko slaves in Kukuna rose against their Susu masters and established a fortified town in which runaway slaves were encouraged to settle.[69] Another fugitive slave fortress, the village of Gamon between the upper Senegal and upper Gambia rivers, had indirectly considerable impact on the course of events in upper Senegambia at the beginning of European colonial control there. As a young man, the Muslim cleric Momodu Lamine had been mistreated by the people of Gamon; and in later life his attempts at revenge led to widespread fighting, much of which had nothing to do with Gamon, and to Momodu Lamine's appearance in 1885-7 as a major political and military leader.[70] One revolt was recorded near Boporo in Liberia in 1866, when latent discontent was brought to a head by the decision to sell some of the slaves of a local magnate who had died leaving an estate encumbered with a heavy load of debt. In this case the slaves took possession of the town where they lived, counting on support from a neighbouring free tribe which was at variance with their masters.

[65] Lugard, 1893, I, 224 ff.
[66] *ibid.*, I, 298-9.
[67] V.L. Cameron, *Across Africa*, London 1885, 157.
[68] A.G. Laing, *Travels . . . in Western Africa*, London 1825, 126-8, 405.
[69] Fyfe, 1962, 283.
[70] H.J. Fisher, 'The early life and pilgrimage of al-Hajj Muhammad al-Amin the Soninke (d. 1887)', *Journal of African History*, 1970, 55-6.

Their ostensible allies, however, betrayed them, and the revolt was eventually crushed with barbaric severity.[71]

Another category of slave revolt was that undertaken by Muslim slaves against non-Muslim masters. The risings in Brazil, early in the nineteenth century, were of this kind. Muslim slaves and freedmen have been identified as the main instigators of these; at the time of the main rebellion, in Bahia in 1835, the police believed that there was an *imam* exercising some authority, but they never discovered him;[72] Arabic amulets were much suspected as tokens of revolt, and to be found carrying such an amulet might earn a freedman deportation, or a slave several hundred lashes.[73] The revolts have been described as 'religious wars',[74] a direct repercussion of the Fulani *jihads* of the early nineteenth century, and of the drive of Islam into the northern part of the Yoruba country, from which had emerged a considerable number of Hausa and Yoruba prisoners of war. A little ironically, many Yoruba regarded that particular phase of the Fulani *jihad* in Yorubaland which led to the establishment of the Ilorin emirate, as primarily a revolt of Muslim slaves against their Yoruba masters.[75] Samuel Crowther, enslaved as a youth during these wars, and later to become a bishop in the Anglican church, attributed the troubles of the time in Yorubaland to some Yoruba Muslims, some Fulani immigrants, 'and such foreign slaves as had escaped from their owners'.[76] Although the first prominent trouble-maker in Ilorin, Afonja, who sought to break away from his traditional Yoruba loyalties, was later himself overthrown and killed by his erstwhile Muslim colleagues, yet his connections with Islam had strengthened his appeal to Hausa slaves, whose defection in turn further weakened the loyalist Yoruba forces.[77] There were also revolts by Muslim slave officials against Muslim rulers (see below pp. 273-4).

[71] Benjamin Anderson, *Narrative of a journey to Musardu*, New York 1870, 41-4. Reprinted by Cass, London 1971, in *Journeys to Musadu*.
[72] Verger, 1976, 300, 307.
[73] *ibid.*, 317.
[74] *ibid.*, 308.
[75] Clapperton, 1829, 25, 28, 39, 172, 204.
[76] Quoted in Curtin, 1968, 294, 299.
[77] *ibid.*, 295-6.

Runaway slaves

'...I heard that my slave Burti had said that he would run away, and then I found that he had run away.' (Hamman Yaji, p. 106, 24 December 1924)

Runaway slaves appear several times in the index to *Slavery 1970*, but are not a separate heading in its main text. This omission is now to be regretted, for several reasons. First of all, running away, escape, flight, has always been a very significant, albeit non-violent, expression of slave resistance, particularly important in a Nachtigal-centred discussion since violent resistance among the enslaved seldom if ever came to the attention of the German traveller. (The case of those about to be enslaved was, of course, quite different.) Surely no non-Muslim escaper thought in these terms, and perhaps not many Muslims did so (no explicit examples have been found by the present writer in the historical record), but there is an inherent affinity between the concept of *hijrah*, withdrawal, emigration, so central in the Islamic experience, and the runaway slave's flight towards freedom. Secondly, runaway slaves constitute a notable sub-heading within the general theme of population mobility. A third reason for surprise at the previous omission of runaway slaves as a distinct topic is the abundance of relevant evidence, both on the wider historical stage, and also in the specific case of Nachtigal, who frequently himself encountered, at very close quarters, slave escape.

Slavery law is less a separate, free-standing body of the relevant provisions within the Islamic *shari'ah*, but rather a theme or thread running through many of the major headings of the law (see above, p. 14-16.). The runaway slave illustrates this: under the law of sale, for example, it is illegal to sell certain items, such as a runaway slave or a runaway camel (Ibn Abi Zayd, 208). In tax assessment, a runaway slave was counted for some taxation purposes (*zakat al-fitr*), but not—even if the owner hoped to regain him—for others (ordinary *zakat*).[78] Again, a marriage involving a runaway slave as dowry was invalid.[79]

---

[78] Khalil bin Ishaq, I, 121, 127.
[79] *ibid.*, II, 47.

At the opposite end of the spectrum, far away from these legal niceties, Hamman Yaji's diary provides some examples of grass-roots, day-to-day experience. In April 1921, a female slave belonging to one of Hamman Yaji's sons ran away to a neighbouring chief; Hamman Yaji sent a messenger and a letter after her, and she was returned.[80] In June 1922, a female slave ran away from one of Hamman Yaji's own homes.[81] In November 1923, a female slave of his who had run away returned (probably not the same one, the time gap seems too long). In this case, Hamman Yaji had sent instructions to the pagans of Chuka to capture the runaway slave; they did not do this, claiming that the message had never reached them, but he fined them one shilling each nonetheless. A man who had actually met the escaper, and sent her to her own home, was fined a gown by Hamman Yaji.[82] There may be just a hint of some sort of negotiation in this incident. A little later, negotiation is much clearer. In April 1924, a male slave of Hamman Yaji, Jauro, ran away to Gwoza, a nearby village. Hamman Yaji sent Malam Garga to bring him back. We may speculate that a malam was chosen for this task, as a natural arbitrator. The slave, however, remained unpersuaded. He would, he said, return only if Hamman Bindu were sent for him. Hamman Yaji refused to send Hamman Bindu, but did send Fadhl al Nar, principal military commander of the emirate (I do not know who Hamman Bindu was). On the fourth day after running away, Jauro Soja 'returned...after Fadhl al Nar had got to him'.[83] This seems to me to fall short of being

[80] Hamman Yaji, 76.
[81] *ibid.*, 79.
[82] *ibid.* 85.
[83] *ibid.*, 93. This case has some peculiarities, perhaps relevant to our enquiry. A year and ten days after Jauro's first exit, the diary records that Jauro Soji and eight of his family ran away (p. 112). Assuming that Jauro/Jauro Soja (both designations are used) in the first episode, and Jauro Soji in the second, are one and the same person, he seems to have been an inveterate escaper; the fact that he took his family with him the second time suggests that he was going for good. In July 1922, getting on for two years before the bout of escaping, Hamman Yaji (p. 80) notes that 'Jauro returned' from visiting the local British colonial officer, who had given Jauro 'the land which I had promised him. The people of Duhu have made their excuses now that there is no use for excuses.' Two days after Jauro's

brought back under duress. In September 1924 someone else's female slave fled to, not from, Hamman Yaji.[84]

In April 1925, one of Hamman Yaji's men, afraid after some of his own slaves had run away, gave one of those remaining to Hamman Yaji.[85] In August 1926, another female slave has fled into Hamman Yaji's territory, and Hamman Yaji intended some corrective action (not drastic, but exactly what is not clear from the rather opaque diary entry).[86] In September 1926, '...Ajia's female slave ran away.'[87] January 1927: two of Hamman Yaji's slave girls 'very nearly managed to run away. They were, however, unable to do so.'[88] July 1927: 'my concubine Awu ran away.'[89]

There are also entries about slaves, where it is not clear

---

return, Hamman Yaji received a letter from the same officer, 'saying that the Jauro's status of slavery displeased the prople of Duhu. However, [Hamman Yaji added,] I am satisfied with him.' Three days later again, '...my messenger Barade Umaru and Jauro returned with the joyful news that the officer 'had returned to me my Duhu people for me to appoint a chief of Duhu (p. 80). *Jauro* is the Fulfulde term for village head (p. 153), and the official letter speaks of 'the Jauro', but Hamman Yaji seems to use the word more as a personal name. If all these Jauro's are the same, we may imagine Hamman Yaji appointing one of his 'government slaves' as head of a subordinate group of people, who objected to having a slave in authority over them. Relations between Hamman Yaji and the Duhu pagans remained tense; at the end of 1923, the British arrested the pagan Duhu chief and two other men, sending them all to Hamman Yaji; and the British burnt the house of another local chief, treating the people harshly. The arrested chief brought Hamman Yaji a pot of honey (pp. 86-7). The British are evidently being drawn more and more actively into local politics; but their abrupt intervention at the end of 1923 does not stabilise the situation, and in April 1924 Jauro decides to cut his losses and run. He is persuaded to reconsider, but a year later he departs again, this time finally, with his family. 'Jauro Duhu', who with his pagans paid their General Tax to Hamman Yaji and the British in August 1925 (p. 116), is presumably a successor to the Jauro who had run off for a second time the previous April. Relations between Hamman Yaji and Duhu were customarily tense (see p. 12, and index references).

[84] *ibid.*, 101.
[85] *ibid.*, 111.
[86] *ibid.*, 131.
[87] *ibid.*, 131; Ajia was Hamman Yaji's head slave (p. 35).
[88] *ibid.*, 135.
[89] *ibid.*, 142; *cf.* p. 202 below.

whether these are runaways,[90] and about runaways where it is not clear whether these are slaves.[91] In some instances, the fugitives are clearly not slaves, as when Hamman Yaji received news 'that Malam Hamidu had fled with his family'.[92] There is even a runaway schoolboy, about whom the British wrote to Hamman Yaji in September 1926.[93]

There has been a good deal of discussion, in the secondary sources, about the divisive impact of territorial boundaries imposed by the European colonial powers. Hamman Yaji was acutely aware of the boundary between British Nigeria, and first German, then French, Cameroon, living as he did exactly on that boundary—though he could not have known that, one day, his emirate would be switched from Cameroon, to Nigeria. His diary notes inter-territorial movement, for example, in June 1927: 'it appeared that Wakaltu had fled to French Territory with all his goods: five men, seven women, three boys, three girls, 20 sheep and goats and his horse.'[94] In August the same year, a letter came to Hamman Yaji from the Emir al Yemen of Adamawa, asking 'for information as to the number of people who had emigrated to French Territory and the number who had immigrated from French Territory to my land'.[95] The British were also interested in the border, and movement across it.[96]

On the whole, however, on the evidence of comments in the diary, the territorial boundary does not seem to have been a hardship; its main significance for local people may have been that it increased their options, as far as responding to colonial rule was concerned. It does not seem that fugitive slaves at all made the border a target.

Before we leave Hamman Yaji, in this context at least, there

[90] For example, three slaves were returned to Hamman Yaji by the Emir of Borno; presumably these were runaways, though it is not explicitly stated (*ibid.*, 74; see also 61, 83, 94, 103, 115).

[91] 89, 103, 109, 142. On p. 101 a man accused of murder runs away.

[92] *ibid.*, 114; is it the same Hamidu, whose slave-girl ran away again a year later, this time back to Hamman Yaji's land (131)?

[93] *ibid.*, 132.

[94] *ibid.*, 142.

[95] *ibid.*, 145.

[96] *ibid.*, 102, 104, 113.

is one further passage concerning slave mobility which demands our attention, for 26 August 1917. 'I fixed the penalty for every slave who leaves me without cause at four slave girls and if he is a poor man 200 lashes.'[97] This is a surprising entry indeed, with the apparent implication that a slave with cause might leave, apparently unhindered. This is all the more enigmatic, inasmuch as the early date, August 1917, was well before any colonial influence had been exerted on local slavery patterns. And how many slaves were wealthy enough to own four slave girls, or had the means to acquire so many? Would a delinquent poor slave survive 200 lashes?[98]

Many runaway slaves simply ended up as the slaves of some other master. The Hausa novel, *Shaihu Umar*, sketches such a scenario. A friendly hunter advises Umar's father, Makau, who is entering unfamiliar territory, on the road he should follow:

> You see this little village in front of us, that's the way you should go, but do not allow yourself to go inside because, very probably, if you do go in, you will never come out again. The best thing to do is to skirt the edge of the village, and so pass it by. And when you are going to pass it, be careful not to go to the north of it, because to the north of the village there is the farm of a certain man who is a very powerful sorcerer. Any man, whether he is a stranger *or a slave fleeing back from some other country*, when he reaches this farm, he will usually stop there, not knowing what road he should take, and inevitably he will go into the farm. Now this man never leaves his farm and thus, when he sees

---

[97] Hamman Yaji, 63.

[98] There was evidently a good deal of flogging about, as for example on pp. 78, 115 and 133 of Hamman Yaji's journal. Hamman Yaji (p. 75) once claims to have had three of his female slaves flogged for adultery, 15 lashes each. My first thought here was that such occasions, involving women offenders, might have been symbolic, causing more shame than pain. However, in the introductory material of the published diary is this description, of the same incident, or something similar, given by Abba, one of Hamman Yaji's sons: '...When four female slaves of his father's favorite son, Bello, attempted to run away, Hamman Yaji ordered each to receive one hundred lashes administered by three slaves, with a fourth holding them down....They were then deprived of food for three days. One of the women, Asta Jumba, died from this treatment, while according to Abba, Dudu and Muradu retained marks of the whipping for the rest of their lives.' (p. 28)

someone stop close by it, wandering around as if lost, he comes and captures him and enslaves him.[99]

Makau was not a runaway slave himself, but certainly a stranger, forced into exile on a trumped-up charge of misappropriation of slave booty; the quotation makes clear that both stranger, and fugitive slave, would confront identical dangers in this particular context.

Letters from archives in Sokoto, dating from the period just before the British conquest in 1902, confirm the fact of re-enslavement (though without indicating just how it came about), and also make clear how complications over disputed ownership might arise:

> ...the one who is carrying this letter found his slave who fled from him last year, at Goronyo. The man in whose hands he [the slave] was found said that he had bought him from our son Muhammadu Maiturare. I beg that you [the letter is addressed to the ruler of Sokoto] will assist him to find [i.e. recover?] his slave according to the law of justice.[100]

And again:

> ...I inform you [this letter is to the Waziri, the principal government official of the Sokoto caliphate] that the bearer of this letter found his runaway slave with you. He was told that he was the slave of the Sarkin Musulmi [the ruler of the Muslims] and that he must refer to the seller. We have sought for the seller, until, we found the original one, the Sarkin Bodinga Aliyu. He it was who sold him to a Sifawa man called Abubakr. The result of my investigations I have sent to you, for I have no power in the matter, you alone have the authority. Hence we have left the decision to you and what you decide that is right.[101]

Slaves escaping from a caravan on the march, often at night when lodged in a village, or camped near one, were among the most likely simply to change hands, sometimes very quickly and with a minimum of fuss. Nachtigal's journey back to Borno, from Abu Sekkin the displaced ruler of Bagirmi, in the late summer of 1872, taught him a good deal about this

---

[99] *Shaihu Umar*, 33, italics added.
[100] Backwell, 1927/1969, letter no. 5, p. 17; see notes also on pp. 16 & 18.
[101] *ibid.*, letter no. 44, pp. 36-7, see also pp. 38-9.

particular pattern of flight. When Nachtigal called a rest day, many of his companions continued their journey regardless,

> for so many slaves were lost to them in Manjafa and Bugoman that they sought to reach the more secure conditions of Bornu as speedily as possible. In fact the slaves' attempts to escape had increased daily throughout the journey. The reason for this phenomenon was not difficult to discover. People who had been torn from their very restricted homeland, for the most part children, without any ideas of the 'wide world' or of travel, began, as day after day and week after week the exhausting marches went on with corporal punishment and insufficient food, to abandon hope that this mode of life would ever come to an end. They did not know how long their painful wanderings would continue, and they could not credit the assertions of their masters. Despairing of the future, these unhappy people accordingly seized every opportunity for flight, less in the hope of being able to return to their homes and their own people than with the desire to find rest. If they did succeed in getting away unobserved, they did not, in their weakness and despondency, get very far, but entered the first good hut, and sat quietly down. The owner of the hut did not in truth drive them away. If the caravan had already moved on, he might hope to be left in undisturbed possession of the slave bestowed upon him by heaven, and if he had to fear enquiries, he sought to bring the slave to safety somewhere. The inhabitants of the villages through which we passed frequently actually incited the slave children to run away.[102]

The hoped-for greater security of conditions in Borno was very imperfectly realised. In Kala Kafra, only a few days' journey from Kuka, the capital, the caravan was hospitably received. However, Nachtigal thought that the local people had arranged to be well reimbursed for their offerings, as next morning a large number of the remaining slaves had gone missing. Almas, Nachtigal's chief guide, had already lost three of his original six slaves, one by running away, and in Kala Kafra yet another vanished. Almas did not succeed in finding him again.[103] Two Saharan traders[104] stayed behind in Kala

[102] III, 437.
[103] III, 441.
[104] See also III, 350.

Kafra, hoping to retrieve the four slaves whom they had lost there during that first night. By the time they caught up with Nachtigal, three or four days later, eight more of their slaves had disappeared, and a pack-ox laden with ivory.[105]

The usual practice in such cases, when slaves had decamped, was for public officials to take the Quran from house to house, having the local people swear that they do not themselves have any of the missing slaves, nor do they know where such slaves might be. 'Since for them it is always only a question of being satisfied with appearances, it is easy to evade the truth.'[106]

Nachtigal himself, content though he had been at the escape of the two housekeepers-in-chains assigned to him in Abu Sekkin's war-camp (see below, p. 204), was greatly annoyed when, one day beyond Kala Kafra, a young woman absconded under cover of a violent storm during the night. She was one of four slaves, paid for a horse belonging to a friend of Nachtigal's in Kuka, and whom Nachtigal was trying to bring safely to Kuka. One had already been left behind, handed over gravely ill to the chief of a village along the way.[107] Now a second was gone. Next morning, neither the Quran, nor Nachtigal's forceful representations to the local governor, whom Nachtigal threatened with intervention by Shaykh Umar, ruler of Borno, recovered the fugitive.[108] Indeed, the very next night one of the two remaining slaves, both small girls, went off, though on this occasion enquiries by the local governor led to her discovery in a distant hut, and she was returned to Nachtigal. He attributed her bid for freedom, freedom at least from the caravan, to the particularly bad travelling conditions, and also to the serious illness of the other child.[109] Perhaps she had been encouraged also by the successful departure of the young woman the night before.

Such difficulties were widespread. Richard Burton, for example, in 1858, at Ujiji on the east shore of Lake Tanganyika, complained that the local people had a bad name for selling

[105] III, 443.
[106] III, 441.
[107] III, 439; see above, p. 125.
[108] III, 442.
[109] III, 443.

slaves cheap, and then recouping themselves by aiding and abetting desertion.[110] In more dangerous regions, escape from a caravan or expedition might lead to a tragic dénouement. Barth, in 1851, witnessed one instance of this. He had accompanied a slave-raid into Kanem, carried out by the Awlad Sulayman Arabs on behalf of the Borno authorities. An officer of al-Hajj Bashir, the leading Borno dignitary, also accompanied the expedition, in order to take back his master's share of the spoil. The most handsome of the women slaves was particularly destined for al-Hajj Bashir himself, in view of his special interests (see below, pp. 199-200). But this woman, even before she had been handed over to the Borno officer, escaped, and was eaten by wild beasts, only her clothes, ornaments, and some bones being found. The affair occasioned, said Barth, a great deal of unpleasant conversation.[111]

Returning to Bagirmi, a traditional office-holder there, from time immemorial a very distinguished person, was the *alifa ba*, the governor of the river.

> He rules in the region of the lower course of the Shari, from Bugoman downstream, draws a considerable income from the produce of the river, and all fugitive slaves who cannot be reclaimed by their masters belong to him.[112]

At first reading, this seems to imply that the number of unclaimed runaways was so great that the right to them constituted a significant proportion of the *alifa ba*'s income— a valuable perquisite, *Slavery* 1970 called it (p. 87). Now, however, on reflection, and recalling in particular just how quickly many escapers were absorbed, almost unnoticed, into local society, I wonder how many were left at a loose end, to the advantage of the governor of the river.

It is clear from the immediately foregoing discussion that the line between, on the one hand, encouraging slaves to desert, aiding and abetting them in that endeavour even if only by providing some out-of-the-way shelter, and, on the other, stealing slaves, could sometimes be delicate to trace precisely. A similar ambivalence exits in our academic assess-

---

[110] Burton, 1860/1961, II, 61. See also p. 226 below.
[111] Barth, 1965, II, 280.
[112] III, 328.

ment of the slave's own attitude: a defiant freedom-seeker from one perspective, from another a rather gullible or exhausted (or both) kidnap victim. The following entry in Hamman Yaji's diary, for August 1927, shows how the theft of slaves continued to concern even the very apex of the Sokoto caliphate, even at so late a date as 1927, even reaching out to such remote peripheries as Madagali emirate:

> ...A letter came from Sardauna [the sultan of Sokoto] to say that two men had stolen two slave girls, Habibu and Basaitu, and he does not know who they are. One of them is called Bakari.[113]

The risk of slaves running away led, naturally enough, to a variety of generally disagreeable devices to prevent such loss. Dorugu, the young Hausa slave who presents us with such an invaluable picture of western African slavery, from the inside, in the mid-19th century, describes how he very nearly had to suffer such constraints. Dorugu, captured in the border territories between the Sokoto caliphate and the kingdom of Borno, had been sent to Kukawa, the Borno capital. Here he had settled down contentedly, providing sterling service by helping to nurse the young daughter of the household through smallpox.[114] Let him continue the story in his own words:

> Once I went to a compound where there was a [slave] woman from my town. There was also a Hausa boy at her place. Both of them knew Hausa, but since they had come to Bornu they had almost forgotten how to speak it. I used to go and see them. Once when I had gone, my [surely this should be 'her'?] mistress came and saw me talking with her. She caught hold of me, took off my robe, and tied me up with her cloth. I cried and trembled with fear. She said to her son in Kanuri, 'Kalur kude shiga jer,' which means 'Bring chains and put him in them.' I could understand very little of Kanuri [the principal language of Borno], but that much I understood. Then her son went into the room to look for the chains. When I heard him grab the chains, I started to tremble. I carefully loosened the knot, and while she was chatting in Kanuri I ran away.
> I sped to my master's wife and threw myself at her feet.

---

[113] Hamman Yaji, 144. See pp. 191-2 below.
[114] Kirk-Greene and Newman, 1971, 41.

> She said to me, 'Be still!' I was speaking in Hausa, so she couldn't understand anything I was saying. She called a slave who understood Hausa, whereupon I told her everything that had happened. Shortly thereafter, I saw that other woman enter the house. She told my master's wife what she had thought. A girl who understood [Kanuri and] Hausa overheard them and related their conversation to me in Hausa. She said, 'That woman thought that, because you were talking with a slave from your town, you were planning to run away with her.' I think I didn't even reply. I just went out and sat down, and then she finally left.[115]

Even in the Sahara, where fugitive slaves would almost certainly perish, some did try to escape. Slave caravans coming to Ghadames did occasionally lose runaway slaves, and slave dealers in the town had iron manacles and leg fetters—made, ironically, in the Sudan lands—ready, though these were apparently not very much used.[116]

Nachtigal had close experience of slaves in chains. Here it is he who speaks, not the slave herself: but the tale is worth quoting, for the sake of the courageous, determined—and nameless—woman it honours. Nachtigal was at the time marooned, under conditions of deadening monotony, in Borku, in the central Sahara, with a band of nomadic Arab slave raiders from the Awlad Sulayman.

> A kindly fate gave me some occupation. Since all my efforts to get to Ennedi had been frustrated, I sought at least to collect the most abundant information possible about that country, and in this I came across the female slave of a certain Abdallah Ben Salim. She was a young Bideyat woman, who, although she had borne her master a child, was usually kept in chains because of her initial frequent attempts to escape. Since she appeared later to have become reconciled to her fate, and showed great affection for her child, she was sometimes as an experiment freed from her fetters. When the news arrived that a son of her master, scarcely more than a child, had also been taken prisoner by her compatriots in the ghazzia that had miscarried, she feigned such sincere grief that Abdallah Ben Salim seemed

---

[115] Kirk-Greene and Newman, 41-2. The first three pairs of brackets have been added.
[116] Richardson, 1848, I, 266-8, 354 and 369.

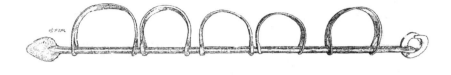
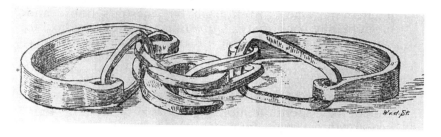

Above, foot irons and, below, manacles for slaves, from the Fulani of Ngaundere in Adamawa. S. Passarge, *Adamaua*, Berlin 1895, 261 and 262.

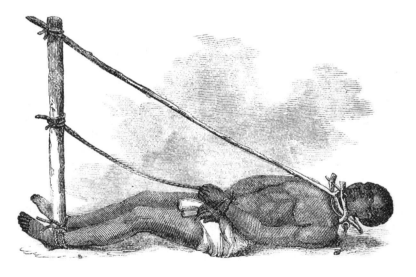

The taming stick, used by eastern Arab slavers. F.S. Arnot, 1889/1969, 205

disposed to make use of her proffered willingness personally to free the young man and to fetch him, and in the meantime permitted her to move about freely. Immediately afterwards she absconded with her infant, but was recaptured at Elleboë and from that moment was kept permanently in chains.

This woman I borrowed as an informant about her fatherland and the Ennedi language, on condition that I fetched her daily myself from her master's house and brought her back there. Unfortunately these studies, to which I owed much valuable information, came to a premature end. My teacher was a tall powerful woman, her dark skin colouring tending towards reddish, full of pride and the love of her homeland, who had never for an instant abandoned the thought of regaining her freedom by flight. One day she spent the morning hours as usual in my tent, joked with a certain bitterness about her small son, 'the little slave', to whom she had given the consoling name Allahfi (that is, God lives), and bade me farewell since she was being sent by her master to one of his friends in another *dawar* for a short while, because of a quarrel between her and his legitimate wife. I gave her a present and let her go without suspecting anything; towards evening she had run away after shattering her iron fetters, this time leaving her child behind. Her tracks again led to Elleboë, but no one caught up with her. My best wishes went with the courageous and vigorous woman, and I had regrets only for poor little Allahfi, so suddenly deprived of his mother's milk.[117]

Later, visiting the Bagirmi court in exile, with newly-captured slaves pouring in on every side, Nachtigal found that his people regarded it as beneath their dignity to prepare food themselves, or to perform other domestic duties. Accordingly, he asked the king for the loan of two working slave women. These were supplied, with their feet fastened together with short heavy chains. Despite the chains, and to Nachtigal's own sincere satisfaction, they had soon run away.[118] What alternative housekeeping arrangements were made subsequently is not specified. On the way back from Bagirmi, Nachtigal's caravan had swollen to some hundreds of people, many of

[117] II, 380.
[118] III, 334-5.

them slaves.[119] Few people in the caravan had chains with which to control their slaves, and had instead to be content with tying the slaves' feet together in camp with cords, which could easily be cut through or burnt.[120] Hamman Yaji's journal refers to people in chains, in the autumn of 1925.[121] An official report at the time tells 'of how a gang of thirteen chained men had been found working on his private farms, eleven of whom had been sentenced to periods of imprisonment ranging from 25 to 45 days, all without trial'.[122]

Thus far, almost our entire discussion of runaway slaves has focussed upon slaves running away from something: the push factor has predominated. There was also a pull factor. The hope of returning home was surely the most powerful and widespread pull of all. For many slaves, however, home was too long ago, or had been too much destroyed, or, most commonly, was too far away, to be a viable option. There might, however, be attractive sanctuaries nearer at hand, drawing in slaves on the run.

The Sokoto correspondence, already referred to earlier in this section, provides relevant evidence of pull operating within reasonable reach. Several letters refer, in one way or another, to Mahe, one of the sons of the caliph Abd al-Rahman. Mahe had been given a fief by his father, together with the title Sarkin Mafara.[123] During his father's reign, he gathered numbers of horsemen,[124] and evidently welcomed other immigrants including runaway slaves. One letter to the Sokoto caliph, replying to a question about a slave-girl and three horses (all of which have apparently gone missing: the writer has no news about the girl, neither about two of the horses), complains that Mahe has two slaves belonging to the writer, plus a horse belonging to a slave in the plaintiff's town, and four donkeys. Repeated appeals to Mahe having been in vain, the writer now begs the caliph, 'O helper of the weak', to get the people and

[119] III, 428.
[120] III, 437.
[121] Hamman Yaji, 116-17.
[122] *ibid.*, 28. See also p. 215 below.
[123] Backwell, 1927/1969, 23, says it was the fief of Dendi, and adds that the title Sarkin Mafara was honorary.
[124] *ibid.*, p. 39.

property restored, or paid for.[125] Other letters, in varying degrees of enigmatic complexity, refer to Mahe, runaway slaves, and other such problems.[126] Backwell's own commentary states that, when the next caliph assumed rule in Sokoto, he deposed Mahe, and ordered him to disband his horsemen.[127]

Murray Last also discusses the events centred upon Mafara in his still excellent, although a little older even than *Slavery* 1970, *The Sokoto caliphate*. While it is not easy to marry the two accounts, Backwell and Last, in detail, Last's summary of the settlement finally imposed by Sokoto upon Mafara includes stiff terms which seem quite pertinent to our theme: all captives to be released, a thousand slaves to be given up, and 'all (escaped) slaves taken by them...to be returned.'[128]

Such a refuge for slaves on the run might even be found in the very centre of the state. Under Pasha Mansur of Timbuktu, in the early eighteenth century, the pasha's black slaves, or *lagha*, became excessively insolent, and so abused the people that it became unsafe even to venture to the mosque for prayers. Runaway slaves took refuge with the *lagha* and were never returned. Kabara, the Niger port of Timbuktu, was entirely in the hands of the *lagha*; the traditional governorship stood vacant. Trouble came to a head when the *lagha* murdered a prominent *sharif*. The pasha was then deposed, and all *lagha* who could be caught—one was dragged from sanctuary in the *imam's* house—were executed.[129]

Two of the greatest pull factors, challenging slaves to break out of the constraining circumstances of their enslavement, have been the Islamic theocracies, and the European colonial authorities. A strange pairing, but one which might well, in the study of slavery within Africa, provide opportunity for very rewarding comparative analysis. The greatest of the Islamic revolutionaries in sub-Saharan Africa, Usuman dan Fodio, founding father of the Sokoto caliphate in what later became (approximately) northern Nigeria, included amongst his

[125] Backwell, 1927/1969, Letter no. 8, pp. 19-20, see also p. 21.
[126] *ibid.*, Letters nos. 9 (maybe), 10, 11, 45, 46.
[127] *ibid.*, p. 39.
[128] London: Longmans, 1967, 130-4. The parenthesis is Last's own.
[129] *Tedzkiret*, 27-31, 43-52, 227-8.

voluminous and wide-ranging writings specific provisions, all drawn from earlier legal authorities, relating to slaves belonging to unbelievers with whom the Muslims are at war. The law seems positively to encourage slaves to run away. The basic ruling is this: any such slave 'is free if he flees [the triliteral root of the word used here is *f.r.r*, not *h.j.r.* from which *hijrah* derives] to us or stays on till he is captured as booty'. Not only is the fugitive slave free: 'if he comes over bringing any property, it belongs to him and he does not have to give up the *khums* [the state's fifth share of all booty taken by the Muslims].' Nay, further, 'it makes no difference whether he comes over already a Muslim or not'. This unexpectedly relaxed provision has evidently surprised Usuman dan Fodio's modern commentator and translator, who adds a footnote of his own: 'Provided, it seems, he becomes a Muslim as soon as he has crossed over.' As for the stay-at-home option, 'or stays on till he is captured', this seems undermined by another quotation which Usuman dan Fodio includes: 'but when the slave remains there until he is captured as booty and then alleges that he became a Muslim before that, then he will not be believed.'[130]

All in all, an escaper's charter, a freedom manifesto. All the more straightforward, being untrammelled by any concern for the original owners' property rights in the fleeing slaves, a consideration which did often complicate European colonial reactions to such immigrants.

Al-Hajj Umar, the Senegambian revolutionary theocrat active in the mid-nineteenth century, came to much the same conclusions as had Usuman dan Fodio at the beginning of the century. Umar, as Usuman, recommended that a slave who fled to *dar al-Islam* from a Pagan master should become a free man, even if the slave were not a Muslim. Here population mobility, the welcoming of immigrant manpower, seems momentarily to have superseded religious conversion as the prime requirement. As for the slave who reversed these priorities, putting religion first by becoming a Muslim, but not running away to *dar al-Islam*, about whom Usuman seems to have been uncertain, Umar says there are differing opinions. Some held that such converts, according to Muslim law, became theoretically

[130] Usuman dan Fodio, 1978, 117.

free immediately upon conversion, and that this freedom should be extended to them in practical reality should a Muslim army ever invade the Pagan territory in which they lived; but others thought that perhaps the army should take possession of such slaves. In one respect Umar seems to have gone beyond Usuman: Umar cites some lawyers who argued that a Muslim slave, fleeing from a Muslim master (Usuman confines himself to Pagan masters) who lived outside *dar al-Islam*, became free on entering *dar al-Islam*.[131] This point of view may have had something to do with there being many more serious Muslims amongst Umar's opponents than amongst Usuman's, and any incentive to the slaves of enemy Muslims to decamp would be a useful contribution to the war effort.

What practical effect did such legal arguments have, in black Africa? First, as far as ordinary people on the ground were concerned, there was very little effect, practically nil. There is not a shred of evidence that the Bagirmi warriors, for example, with whom Nachtigal lived cheek by jowl for an extended period, knew of, or cared about, such regulations. Still less would the individuals at the heart of the matter, that is to say non-Muslim slaves, owned by non-Muslims, have the least notion of their legal rights: quite the contrary, the very idea of running away to *dar al-Islam* would have seemed ludicrous: that would be to put one's head into the very jaws of slavery. Secondly, amongst well-informed, scholarly Muslims these issues were of course understood and argued about, and may

[131] For the information about Umar, see Willis, 1970, 150-1. In his much later book (*In the path of Allah: the passion of al-Hajj 'Umar*, London 1989, 129), Willis, in characteristically allusive style, speak of slaves

> who fled the subservience of pagan lands and found freedom in the embrace of Islam. Indeed it had become an inalienable aspect of Islamic law that the loyalty of the fleeing slave should accompany his flight. Prophetic example had set the tone—Muhammad himself unfettered slaves who had come to him from Ta'if as their status was affirmed before they entered dar al-Islam. Thus for Muslims of a subsequent age conversion to Islam became a sure passport to the emancipated state.

The Ta'if incident is mentioned also by Usuman (1978, 117), whose editor believes that emancipation of these slaves derived from their running away. For the overwhelming majority of slaves, in Muslim hands, who became Muslim themselves, conversion did not lead to emancipation (see above, pp. 70-83).

have influenced actual policy in some instances. And such awareness may have filtered down, at least to Muslim slaves, particularly when these were congregated in considerable numbers, as in Yorubaland in the late eighteenth century. Thirdly, there is the purely practical point that quite apart from any knowledge of the rules, the report of slaves running away and being well received in *dar al-Islam* might easily spread. All that would be needed would be a few examples, particularly high profile ones: among the first non-Muslim slaves to defect to al-Hajj Umar was Dyeli Musa, effectively an ambassador from the neighbouring non-Muslim kingdom of Tamba.

Turning to the European colonial aspect of the fugitive slave question, as far as Nigeria is concerned, very much the most important example in Africa, the whole subject has been meticulously examined, and carefully analysed, in the painstaking work of Lovejoy and Hogendorn, *Slow death for slavery: the course of abolition in Northern Nigeria, 1897-1936*. From the beginning of a British presence, whether official, commercial or religious, in the mid-nineteenth century, on the margins of the Sokoto caliphate, runaway slaves seeking sanctuary with the newcomers led to friction between the British and the traditional Muslim authorities. Soon slaves in increasing numbers were running away, not only to British outposts, but to their own homes or elsewhere, and non-Muslim groups which had previously paid tribute, including slaves, were in open revolt.[132]

Returning to the comparison suggested earlier, between the Islamic theocracies and the European colonial regimes, as centres of attraction for runaway slaves, the fundamental principle, deep down, is the same, that slaves have a right to run away to freedom. The elaboration of this basic premise, however, is very different. For the theocracies, it applies for the most part only to slaves in non-Muslim hands, and non-Muslim slave-owners have no rights to such property, or to compensation for its loss. But the slaves themselves, whose running away to Muslim sanctuary is approved, are more universally defined, including non-Muslims as well as Muslims, though the assumption must be that the non-Muslim will convert on reaching safety and freedom. The elaborated

---

[132] Lovejoy and Hogendorn, chapters 1 and 2.

policy on the European colonial side was in one respect less radical, in another much more so. Less radical, inasmuch as the property rights of most slave-owners were recognised, so that some form of compensation was regarded as a proper part of the emancipation process. Much more radical, inasmuch as the right to freedom was universal, including slaves in Muslim hands as well as in non-Muslim.

The practical problems involved in mass slave exodus quickly became urgent for the British in Northern Nigeria, 'with desertions probably numbering in the hundreds of thousands by 1906',[133] only four years after the occupation of Sokoto.

The British needed the cooperation of the traditional local authorities. Also an uninterrupted and productive economy. And they could not cope with large numbers of people on the move. Hence, the death of slavery in Northern Nigeria was indeed slow. Population mobility had to be controlled. Ironically, this leads to another shared concern, of African theocrats and European colonialists alike. Throughout the nineteenth century, the Sokoto authorities had lived in fear of just such a mass exodus: but their runaways would not have been fleeing slaves. Instead, and worse, every Muslim, slave and free, might have gone, eastwards, had the Mahdist conviction seized the whole community of the faithful. As an indicator of how seriously this danger was taken, there is the fact that no caliph of Sokoto, this so devout, so secure, so wealthy Muslim state, from its establishment in 1804 until the present, has gone on pilgrimage. His departure might loose just such a human flood. Population mobility had to be controlled. But this takes us too far from our present slavery concerns.

A final note about the runaway slave. Occasionally, the fugitive Muslim slave found himself as far outside *dar al-Islam* after his flight as before; but in such case, if he held fast to his religious convictions, he might become the pioneer of Islam in a new area. For example, the first Muslims to establish themselves in the Eastern Cape in South Africa were runaways from Cape Town, who settled at Uitenhage about 1809.[134]

[133] Lovejoy and Hogendorn, 98. Is 'desertion', intentionally or unintentionally, a loaded word? Would it sit easily in discussions of North American slavery?

[134] S.A. Rochlin, 'Origins of Islam in the Eastern Cape', *Africana Notes and News*, 1956, 22.

CHAPTER VI

THE DOMESTIC SCENE II: SLAVES IN THE FAMILY

Domestic demand for slaves

This and the succeeding chapters examine the various kinds of demand which provided an assured foundation for the domestic slave trade in Muslim tropical Africa. The list is certainly not exhaustive, and the categories are not mutually exclusive. A slave might be in more than one category at the same time: a Circassian woman, for example, would be at the same time a concubine and a luxury slave, or a senior officer might be at once a eunuch, a soldier, and a royal slave. Equally a slave might pass successively through several categories: a girl might embark as prize money allotted to a fortunate soldier, be passed on as tribute to an overlord, serve him as concubine, and perhaps end her days as an elderly spinner artisan. Nor, of course, are these categories confined to the domestic market; as early as the seventh and eighth centuries, for instance, East African women turned up in China as part of the tribute paid to the Chinese emperor by vassals in Java and Sumatra.[1]

Concubines

'I exchanged female slaves with my man Ajia, I receiving Kutara and he Fanta.' (Hamman Yaji, p. 81, 15 October 1922)

In *Slavery* 1970 concubines constitute the largest single heading of discussion, correctly reflecting the great importance of these women. However, looking back now to that edition, it is

---

[1] Mathew, in Oliver and Mathew, 1963, 107-8.

A black African woman in Morocco. O. Lenz, *Timbouctou*, Paris 1886, 395.

clear that too much attention was paid there to the formally defined, and often humanely implemented, concubine status, neglecting other dimensions, such as the initial slave-raiding for women and girls and the concomitant slaughter of many male captives; the acute suffering, very often, of women and children on the march; the exposure to violent punishment, on the march and in the home; the extreme insecurity of many slave women, who could be passed from hand to hand most unpredictably; the extent of casual sexual encounter, almost always at male choice; and the undoubted, albeit largely undocumented, scope for abuse, including child abuse. The present book tries to redress the balance, in this section, and also at other relevant points.

Hamman Yaji's diary—engagingly frank at first glance, though if we add to it the corresponding evidence from oral tradition, from the other side, from the vanquished voice, we can see how much he indulges in 'antiseptic descriptions'[2]— chronicles such raiding. Here are some entries for 1913, more than a decade after German colonial rule was introduced. Hamman Yaji had himself been appointed chief by the Germans.

17 March: 'I sent Mahawonga to hunt out slaves for me from the pagans called Dugupchi and they found 11 slave girls and one cow.'

12 May: 'I sent my soldiers to Sukur and they destroyed the house of the Arnado [village head] and took a horse and seven slave girls and burnt their houses.'

21 May: 'I sent soldiers to Hudgudur and they captured 20 slave girls.'

11 June: 'I sent Barde [see also above, p. 33] to Wula, and they captured six slave girls and ten cattle, and killed three men.'

21 June:'I sent Barde to Mokolo and he captured 31 slave girls and eight cattle.'

25 June: 'I sent my people to the pagans of Midiri and Bula and they captured 48 slave girls and 26 cattle and we killed five persons.'

---

[2] J. H. Vaughan, in Hamman Yaji, 13-4.

6 July: 'I sent my people to Sina and they captured 30 cattle and six slave girls.'[3]

All these, and more, on a single page of the published book: in under four months, eleven raids are recorded, yielding a total of 183 captives. Most of these are specified as girls; where a figure is given without gender specification ('7 pagans', '13 slaves', 'captured 23'), it seems certain that here too, many if not all were girls and women. The casualties were surely men. This procedure was not the eccentricity of a wildcat operator on the fringes of the Sokoto caliphate; it was often repeated in slave-raiding in the interior, without access to Atlantic outlets. At the very end of 1851, Barth witnessed the main armed force of Borno raiding for slaves:

> altogether they were said to have taken one thousand, and there were certainly not less than five hundred. To our utmost horror, not less than one hundred and seventy full-grown men were mercilessly slaughtered in cold blood, the greater part of them being allowed to bleed to death, a leg having been severed from the body.[4]

One incident stands out in Hamman Yaji's sequence of raids, as an exception: 'I sent Fadhl al Nar with his men to raid Sukur and they captured 80 slaves, of whom I gave away 40. We killed 27 men and women and 17 children.'[5] Women and children were too valuable to be squandered in this way. Four days earlier, 'two rifles arrived'. Maybe that helps to explain the aberration. But why did Hamman Yaji then give away 40 slaves? There is an enigma here (see below, p. 311).

A lively interest in concubines has been manifest in African Islamic history from the very beginning. Al-Bakri recorded how one of the conquerors of North Africa, Abd al-Malik bin Marwan, received as his share of the booty from the conquest of Jalula, near Qairawan, 600 dirhems, which he invested in buying a young girl.[6] The slave girls of Awdaghast were renowned in the eleventh century:

---

[3] Hamman Yaji, 53.
[4] Barth, 1965, II, 369.
[5] Hamman Yaji, 63.
[6] Abou Obeid el-Bekri (11th century), *Description de l'Afrique septentrionale*, tr. Mac Guckin de Slane, Algiers, 1911-13, Paris 1965, 71-2.

pretty slave girls with white complexions, good figures, firm breasts, slim waists, fat buttocks, wide shoulders and sexual organs so narrow that one of them may be enjoyed as though she were a virgin indefinitely.

A merchant of Awdaghast is reported as saying

that he saw one of these women reclining on her side...and her child, an infant, played with her, passing under her waist from side to side without her having to draw away from him at all on account of the ampleness of the lower part of her body and the gracefulness of her waist.[7]

Al-Sharishi, who died in 1222, included these details in his commentary on a poem which mentions Ghana:

Many merchants from the Maghrib are to be found there. They come there for trade and find the comforts of life and security and plenty of articles of trade. They buy there slaves for concubinage and stay with the emir, who receives them most hospitably. God has endowed the slave girls there with laudable characteristics, both physical and moral, more than can be desired: their bodies are smooth, their black skins are lustrous,[8] their eyes are beautiful, their noses well shaped, their teeth white, and they smell fragrant.[9]

The pilgrimage of Mansa Musa, ruler of Mali in the fourteenth century, provided further evidence of this interest. He is said to have taken with him 14,000 slave girls for his personal service; and, in Egypt, his entourage so avidly bought 'Turkish and Ethiopian slave girls, singing girls, and garments...that the rate of the gold dinar fell by six dirhams.'[10] On this occasion the demand for slaves may have been stimulated by Mansa Musa's indoctrination in orthodoxy, for he had previously been in the habit of using the daughters of his free subjects as only slave women should be used. He was reproached in

[7] *Corpus*, 68. In East Africa, inland from Mogadishu and Brava on the Somali coast, a people called the Maracat were reported around 1600 to practise the infibulation of women, especially women slaves, who thus fetched better prices. The Maracatos also made eunuchs (Freeman-Grenville, 1962/1987, 150). There is no suggestion that infibulation was practised in eleventh-century Awdaghast.

[8] The translation of this phrase is conjectural (*Corpus*, 396).

[9] *ibid.*, 153.

[10] *ibid.*, 351.

Cairo for his licence. Is it not permitted even for kings? he asked. Not even for kings, was the reply, and he gave it up.[11] Ibn Battuta, visiting Mali in the 1350s, found a black town governor, a pilgrim, who surprised him by understanding some Arabic; he discovered that the governor had in his household a young slave girl, a Damascus Arab.[12]

The demand for slave girls as concubines was an important continuing element in the African slave-trade, domestic and for export, providing at the same time one of the reasons for insisting often that slaves should form a substantial part of any tribute. It was this slave calling in particular which sometimes led, quite naturally, to the fullest incorporation of the slave within the master's family. Even female slaves who had crossed the Atlantic might become concubines; visitors to Bahia, early in the eighteenth century, alluded to the ease with which some slave women became the mistresses, even the wives, of the Portuguese.[13] But the domestic trade within Africa, and exports to the Muslim world, were both distinct from the Atlantic trade in the degree to which the need to supply concubines was a conscious, even a dominant motive.[14]

Very early in his travels, in Fezzan, even before the Tibesti detour, Nachtigal learnt from one of his servants, Ali the Fezzaner, about the advantages of a concubine. Ali explained

> that he would never take a legitimate wife, but hoped only to save so much from his expedition with me that he could buy a slave girl for himself. Then he explained his plan in

---

[11] *Corpus*, 268.

[12] Ibn Battuta, 54; *Corpus*, 300. The governor gave Ibn Battuta a male *khumasi* slave; the editors Hamdun and King, perhaps unaware that this is a standard denomination for slaves, translate it 'a growing boy', with a footnote to give the literal meaning.

[13] Verger, 1976, 50.

[14] The special position of concubines in Muslim African society was again recognized during the progress of the abolition of slavery during European colonialism. In British East Africa, for example, a decree in 1897 allowed slaves to claim freedom if they wished, but this right was denied to concubines except in unusual circumstances, on the ground that family life should not be disturbed; see B. S. Cave, 'The end of slavery in Zanzibar and British East Africa', *Journal of the African Society*, 1909, 26, 29. In Lovejoy and Hogendorn, examining Nigeria in the colonial period, the (sub-divided) index entry for concubinage/concubines is one of the largest.

the following way: 'If I marry, I am certain that my wife will be unfaithful to me. If I buy a slave girl, she will of course perhaps be fickle too, but I am then free to sell her again as soon as I see that she is unfaithful.'[15]

Nachtigal found this reasoning, which was not uncommon, also not without justification. Not only would a slave-girl exert herself to avoid being re-sold, she 'is also by nature more industrious, more obedient and less demanding'—a chivalrous but somewhat optimistic generalisation, I think. Many people preferred lawful concubinage, and even in houses were there were also legitimate wives, the master's preference might go to the slave- girl.[16]

Nachtigal reflected again on the concubinage question later, in the context of the Kuka slave market. He suggested that the institution could be a real blessing for poor people, and for men who had to undertake long journeys. Free wives were seldom inclined to leave their homes and relations, and, according to the religious law, could not be compelled to do so.[17] If a child were born to a slave, her position was nearly as secure as[18] that of a legitimate wife, for only the most compelling reasons could induce a Muslim, however lax in his religious observances, to separate himself from the mother of his children by selling her. She had to exert herself more to ensure that by her industry and amiability she retained the goodwill of her master; there was a risk that she might gain excessive influence over him and become arrogant and extravagant, but in general a concubine involved smaller maintenance and housekeeping costs than did a free wife. The hopeful appearance of the more attractive young women in

[15] I, 95.

[16] I, 95; see also pp. 93, 179.

[17] Ibn Battuta noted that Massufa Berber wives living in Walata do not travel with the husband, and if one wished to do so her family would forbid it. He seems, however, to regard this more as a local custom, than a legal requirement (Ibn Battuta, 29; *Corpus*, 285). One reason why al-Kanemi was available to lead Borno resistance to the Fulani was that his father-in-law had refused his request to be allowed to withdraw with wife and daughter to Fezzan, to escape the Fulani menace (Barth, 1965, II, 599-600). See also *Sahara and Sudan*, II, 330 note.

[18] *Slavery* 1970, p. 109, reads 'even more secure than', a mistranslation on our part. II, 217 is correct.

the Kuka slave market contrasted with the misery and depression of their seniors.[19]

There are many examples of the concubine option working out satisfactorily. Nachtigal's friend Abd el-Ati, a cleric, who claimed also to be a *sharif* and a pilgrim—both titles widely regarded as dubious in his case—earned a precarious livelihood by teaching and secretarial work for the Awlad Sulayman, and went back to Kuka each year with some hundredweights of dates and one or two camels to live frugally with a slave woman there until the teaching season came round again.[20] Or, a somewhat ironical instance: one of the first things that Job ben Solomon, the liberated Muslim slave who created a considerable stir in London in 1733-4, did on his return home to Gambia was to buy a female slave and two horses.[21]

Just as Islamic law, at least in theory (for black African practice often fell far short of the ideal), provided a framework for the whole institution of slavery, so did it also for concubinage. By the introduction of a clear and carefully defined distinction between wives and concubines, Islamic law considerably alters the common African pattern of polygamy. This distinction is expressed in various ways; for example, although a husband must share his nights equally amongst his wives, a concubine of his is not necessarily entitled to this favour, even if she is *umm al-walad*, mother of the child.[22] (However, just as a slave-girl might receive less than a fair share, she might equally well, at her master's discretion, receive more.) A few restrictions do hedge the owner's right to his slave women as concubines. For instance, he should not

[19] II, 216-17. For further aspects of the superiority of concubines to wives, this time in Futa Jallon, see Mamadou Saliou Baldé in C. Meillassoux, ed., *L'esclavage en Afrique précoloniale*, 1975, 205-6.

[20] II, 344-6. Nachtigal mentioned also Uncle Salih, aged brother of the chief's wife in the extended Awlad Sulayman household with whom Nachtigal travelled; long a widower, he was now completely under the thumb of a young slave-girl who kept house for him (II, 334).

[21] Grant, 1968, 114; Curtin, 1968, 57.

[22] Ibn Abi Zayd, 178. The *diya*, or blood-money, for the abortive foetus of a free wife and of a concubine are the same, but only if the concubine was carrying her master's child. If she was pregnant by someone else, then the *diya* of the foetus was one-tenth the estimated value of the mother (Ibn Abi Zayd, 248).

have sexual relations with two slave sisters; if he feels drawn to this, he should sell one of the sisters, or arrange for some form of liberation to get rid of her.[23] Again, in the case of a female slave who has been made *al-muʿtaqah ila ajl*, that is, she has been promised freedom at the expiry of a certain time, although her master may require her to work, and may, provided that the time is not just nearly over, take her property, he may no longer sleep with her.[24] In some parts of Africa, the seclusion of slave women is somewhat less than that of free: in Ghadames, only half-caste and slave women—apart from the splendidly independent Tuareg women, who would even make up their own desert caravans with no men other than their small sons[25]—moved freely about the town.[26]

The distinction between wives and concubines is sometimes rephrased as between free wives and slave wives. This is misleading. The number of wives is legally limited to four, but these may be either free or slave; the number of concubines is unlimited, but these must be slave. Since a free woman may not be taken as a concubine, some jurists have argued that the prohibition of the sale, gift or transfer of any person as a slave must end the Muslim system of concubinage.[27]

The legal marriage of slave women is in some respects identical with that of free women: in the division of the husband's nights, for example, the slave-wife has equal rights with the free.[28] In other respects it is subject to certain limitations: only slave women who are Muslim are eligible to be taken in marriage by a Muslim, though he may marry free women who are Muslim, Christian or Jewish;[29] and, while a free Muslim may marry as many as four slave Muslim women—if he fears temptation and is without the means to marry free women—the slaves in this case would not be his own but the

[23] Ibn Abi Zayd, 186-8.
[24] *ibid.*, 222.
[25] Richardson, 1848, I, 332.
[26] *ibid.*, I, 119, 226.
[27] Lugard, 1933, 10.
[28] Khalil ibn Ishaq, II, 63.
[29] Theoretically, any sexual relations with women, whether free or slave, who are not of one of these religions are forbidden, but this is scarcely observed in tropical Africa.

slaves of another, his own being available as his concubines if needed.[30] The divorce formula for a slave wife differed somewhat from that for a free.[31]

For the marriage of slave men, the law again makes some distinctions. In some schools of law, the slave man can marry only two wives; but the Maliki school, which is our chief concern in tropical Africa, allows him four.[32] These wives may be slave or free; but a Muslim woman may not marry her own slave, nor the slave of her son.[33] Lesser points of legal detail might be multiplied: the oath of continence, if taken by a free husband, must bind him for a least four months, but for a slave only half that period is required.[34]

A slave, man or woman, may marry only with the master's consent.[35] But a slave in certain categories—a *mukatib* slave, and a slave authorized to take part in trade—might buy a concubine, even without his master's permission.[36]

The distinction between slave and free appears also in the penalties attached to fornication, adultery and calumny (see also above pp. 15-16). For fornication, a slave, man or woman, receives fifty strokes; a free person, if not *muhsan*, i.e. not fully legally responsible for his or her acts, receives 100 strokes, and may be banished or jailed—but slaves, and free Muslim women, are not banished; the free and *muhsan* fornicator is stoned to death.[37]

For anyone to decline to participate in a system which had so much to recommend it in practice, and which was so

---

[30] Ibn Abi Zayd, 178.

[31] *ibid.*, 182.

[32] *ibid.*, 178; Khalil ibn Ishaq, I, 30. Barth (1965, III, 183) records that the Fulani theocracy of Masina, in the first half of the nineteenth century, challenged that of Sokoto to reduce the number of allowed wives to two. Barth attributed this to the extreme orthodoxy of Masina; but it may perhaps have been a slightly guarded way of saying that the Sokoto Fulani were no better than slaves. Richardson (1848, I, 390) was told by a trader in Ghadames that it was the custom to marry two wives when visiting the Sudan lands.

[33] Ibn Abi Zayd, 178.

[34] Khalil ibn Ishaq, II, 98.

[35] Ibn Abi Zayd, 180.

[36] Khalil ibn Ishaq, II, 27.

[37] Ibn Abi Zayd, 252; see also 190.

acknowledged in principle, seemed strange indeed. Early in the seventeenth century the English trader Jobson met Buckor Sano, an African merchant on the upper Gambia. '...Hee shewed unto mee,' wrote Jobson,

> certaine young blacke women, who were standing by themselves, and had white strings crosse their bodies, which hee told me were slaves, brought for me to buy. I made answer, We were a people, who did not deale in any such commodities, neither did wee buy or sell one another, or any that had our owne shapes; he seemed to marvell much at it, and told us, it was the only merchandize, they carried down into the countrey, where they fetch all their salt, and that they were solde there to white men, who earnestly desired them, especially such young women, as hee had brought for us.[38]

The way in which women slaves and particularly concubines or concubines-to-be moved about is discussed at various points in this volume, for example under 'tribute' and 'alms and presents'. A few more examples here may help to fill out the picture specifically of concubines which it is the endeavour of this section to sketch. For example, in the seventeenth century, a Moroccan cleric, driven out by the Sultan, fled to Timbuktu. He sought the protection of the king of Segu, Mamari Biton, whose authority then extended over Timbuktu, and supported his case with a gift of two Andalusian slave girls. (Even in the ninth century, Ibn Hawqal had spoken of white slave damsels from Andalus, selling for 1000 dinars or more.)[39] Mamari Biton refused to surrender the cleric to emissaries sent from Morocco, and even allowed him to levy troops in Timbuktu.[40]

In the early nineteenth century, the chief of Mandara, threatened by Adama of Adamawa, a principality in the Sokoto empire, returned a soft answer with a concubine and other presents; Adama, undeterred and undistracted, seized the Mandara capital, though he was able to hold it for only one

---

[38] Jobson, 1623/1932, 120-1.

[39] Sir William Ouseley (tr.), *The oriental geography of Ebn Haukal, and Arabian traveller of the tenth century*, London 1800, 16.

[40] C. Monteil, 1924, 325 & n; M. Delafosse, 'Les rélations du Maroc avec le Soudan à travers les âges', *Hespéris*, 1924, 169-70.

day.[41] In 1827 Richard Lander, sole survivor of Clapperton's second expedition, accepted with gratitude the emir of Zaria's gift of a slave wife.[42] In August 1873, Nachtigal's departure from Abeshr, for Runga, was delayed while awaiting the investiture gifts for the new Runga prince, which in accordance with custom consisted of a horse, a robe of honour, and a concubine.[43]

The story of Samori illustrates the interweaving of divers slavery and concubinage themes. The mother of Samori was said to have been captured in a slave raid and reserved for the chief because of her especial beauty; Samori then joined the chief and served him for seven years in return for his mother's release. He and his mother were eventually sent home with a present of slaves and gold. Soon after, early in his independent career, Samori besieged the town of Sanankoro; the townspeople were at last forced to capitulate, and sent him twelve lovely slave girls and gold as token of their submission.[44] Momodu Lamine, returning from pilgrimage about 1880, and visiting Masina and Segu—in his time both parts of the Islamic empire which derived from al-Hajj Umar—received gifts of concubines at both places, though one story says the ruler of Segu forced him to surrender a girl he had received in Masina.[45] The Mahdist conqueror of Darfur occasionally sent gifts of slave girls, horses, or camels to Khartoum, but was nevertheless finally exiled.[46] The cleric-magician employed by Abushiri in his rebellion against the Germans in East Africa in 1890 asked for 1000 rupees, two handsome boy slaves, and two girl slaves 'with necks slim as bamboos'.[47]

The inexhaustible detail of Hamman Yaji's short diary provides some sample twentieth-century references to the

[41] R. M. East, *Stories of old Adamawa*, Zaria 1934, reprinted 1967, 23-5.
[42] Lander, in Clapperton, 1829, 304-5. A misnomer, see p. 185 above.
[43] IV, 84.
[44] Kouroubari, 1959, 545- 6.
[45] Fisher, 1970, 61-2.
[46] R. C. Slatin, *Fire and sword in the Sudan*, London and New York 1896, 274; see Zoga Bey in index.
[47] J. W. T. Allen (tr.), *The German conquest of the Swahili coast: Utanzi wa vita wadeshi kutamalaki mrima*, Dar-es-Salaam 1960, 59.

circulation of slave-girls, taken so-to-speak from the daily round:

> 'I gave my man Sa'id a female slave.' (26 September 1922) 'I exchanged a female slave with my son Yusuf by giving him a young one and taking Suikado. But he said he did not want a girl, he wanted a boy slave.' (24 November 1922) 'Arnado Sukur gave me two small slaves, one a boy and the other a girl.' (5 February 1923) 'The cause of the trouble was that I had ordered them to bring me some slave girls but Samaki refused as did also his brother. However, they now asked pardon.' (28 May 1923) 'I returned to Ahmadu Kuja his female slave by the hand of his brother Bukhari.' (8 November 1924; is this another runaway incident?)[48]

There is a tiny vignette of Hamman Yaji with one of his female slaves, Kujji, which deserves inclusion, even though Kujji seems to be well established, and unlikely soon to circulate. On 27 May 1924,

> my young slave Samaki and Jauro quarrelled in front of me. Samaki shouted at me and made me angry. So I took some things away from him, namely my horses and my pagans and gave them to Jauro Bamgel. Then I sent him before the Court, but nothing was proved against him....[Two days later,] while I was sitting with my female slave Kujji talking to her, she said: 'Poverty has oppressed him,' as though she said: 'His property is destroyed.' So the same day I returned to Samaki his property.'[49]

A final, eccentric illustration of slave-girl mobility: a Tuareg in Ghadames told Richardson, perhaps vaingloriously, that he had taken an unusual lizard to the Sudan, and had given it to a black prince in exchange for a young female slave.[50]

While the concubine was surely the key figure in securing the eventual integration of the immigrant slaves into the host society, and thus maximising the positive contribution of population mobility, other individuals might also succeed to quite a remarkable degree, and in quite a remarkably short time, in establishing themselves in their new surroundings. In the novelette *Shaihu Umar*, the young hero was captured, not

[48] Hamman Yaji, 81-2, 103.
[49] *ibid.*, 94.
[50] Richardson, 1848, I, 204-5.

quite as a tiny child, but still small enough to be carried on his mother's back. After two years as his captor's slave in Kano, he was transferred to an Egyptian. The chapter heading in the book is 'I am sold to an Arab', but Umar's first owner gives this explanation:

> Umar, here is Abdulkarim asking a favour of me: he's wanting you. Now of course this does not mean that he wants you to become his slave. What he wants is, if you are agreeable and you think you will be able to live with him, that you should become his son, for he has no son, not even a kinsman's son living with him. I for my part have agreed that you should go with him, and now it's just your consent that we are waiting for.[51]

Umar travels to Egypt with Abdulkarim; 25 of the 80 slaves with whom Abdulkarim set out died on the way, and Umar was well aware of the preferential treatment he received. Umar is sent to the local Quran school, does very well, is very generously supported by his adopted parents, and eventually becomes teacher and *imam* himself.[52]

That is a story; Dorugu's report is autobiography. In his first household as a slave, in Zinder, he went every day to the female slaves' quarters, to chat and laugh and play. 'No one else went except me, for I was very innocent.' Each time he had to pass his master's doorway; his master called out a friendly greeting, and Dorugu laughed in reply. I quote the following passage in full, for it is a woman speaking to us, from within the heart of the slave structure. We have a slave-raiding witness, in the only partly varnished voice of Hamman Yaji. We have a uniquely detailed eyewitness account from Nachtigal. We hear the voices of male slaves, in Dorugu and a number of others. And here is also a woman, mistress in her own space, setting her own agenda, seeking her own fulfilment, exercising her own authority.

> Our master had one slave, a concubine, who was the head of all the female slaves. Once when I went to them in the evening, my master's concubine was in her room. When she called me I thought she had something good to tell me. She

---
[51] *Shaihu Umar*, 56.
[52] *ibid.*, 61-4.

climbed on her bed and said to me, 'Barka Gana [his Kanuri name, given him by his new people], get up on the bed.'
I asked, 'What am I supposed to do?'
'Come lie with me.'
'I can't.'
When she called me my body began to tremble. I was sitting close to the fire. The room was dark.
She called to me, 'Come here!'
'I won't.'
'Why not?'
'I don't know.'
'Are you afraid?'
'Yes.'
'What are you afraid of?'
'I don't want to sleep with you.'
'I insist that you sleep with me.'
I wanted to run away but she stopped me. I repeated, 'I refuse!'
She said, 'All right, but when you leave don't say anything to anyone. If I hear that you've told anyone, I'll beat you.'
I said, 'I understand. I won't tell anyone.'

A little later, Dorugu reflects: 'I think the woman behaved that way toward me on purpose because she thought I was accustomed to sleeping with female slaves in our town.'[53] This seems a misjudgment. It was because Dorugu was 'very innocent' that he was allowed into the women's quarters at all; and it was, presumably, just because of this innocence that he was sexually attractive to the concubine.[54] Dorugu, to his satisfaction, was quickly sent to his master's home in Kuka. Dorugu got on well with the master's wife and their four-year-old daughter. When the daughter fell ill with smallpox, the mother,

---

[53] Kirk-Greene and Newman, 39-40.

[54] Is there, perhaps, a sexual agenda also to Umar's childhood record? In Kano, before Abdulkarim adopted (or bought) Umar, Umar was sent to him with food every day. 'Sometimes, when I brought it to him, he would ask me whether I liked him. When I went away he would take hold of me and stroke my head, blessing me. Sometimes, when I was about to return home, he would fetch some dates, and some other kind of food, and give them to me.' (*Shaihu Umar*, 54) And, the evening before they set out for Egypt, 'he made me go into the hut with him, and we slept together on one rug until first light' (p. 58).

an old slave woman in charge of the other slaves, and Dorugu, cared for her.[55]

Umar and Dorugu, two facilitators, male, of that assimilation which must follow population mobility, enforced or encouraged, if the system is to work.

Of course, the concubine arrangement did not always function smoothly. There might, for instance, be ructions between one concubine and another, or between concubine and master. One night on the road to Wadai, Nachtigal's rest was disturbed

> by a domestic scene of Otman [Nachtigal's guide on this journey] with his favourite slave Falmata, whom he cruelly whipped; she fled to me looking for protection, with the blood from a wound on her head streaming over me and my bed. It appeared that the jealousy of one slave girl for another had been the cause of this unpleasant contretemps.[56]

The party was travelling through a district made unsafe by lions, rhinoceroses and thieves, and had had to camp close together, within a thorn fence. This circumstance may have given Nachtigal this unusually intimate insight into domestic relationships.

Early in the twentieth century the story was current, concerning one of the towns of the North African coast, of an Arab who killed a black slave who would not respond to his advances. He buried her in the house, but her spirit returned each night, in the form of a blue light, frightening away lodgers and doing her former master much harm.[57] Occasionally concubines murdered owners (see above, p. 154).

Trouble might also arise over the buying and selling of high-quality concubines. Ibn Battuta experienced this in Takadda, just before he set off for home:

> When I came to Takadda I wished to buy an educated slave girl but could not find one. Then the qadi Abu Ibrahim sent me a slave girl belonging to one of his friends so I bought her for 25 mithqals. Then her owner repented and wished

---

[55] Kirk-Greene and Newman, 40-1.
[56] IV, 39.
[57] Vischer, 1910, 74.

to revoke the bargain, so I said to him: 'If you will indicate another one to me I will release you.' So he indicated to me a slave belonging to 'Ali Aghyul, who was the Moroccan from Tadla who had refused to take up any of my belongings when my camel...collapsed and refused to give my boy a drink of water when he was thirsty. So I bought her from him, she being better than the first one, and released my first friend [from the bargain]. Then this Moroccan regretted having sold the slave and wished to revoke the bargain. He importuned me to do so but I declined to do anything but reward him for his evil acts. He almost went mad and died from grief. But I let him off afterwards.[58]

In such a case, should the disappointed prospective purchaser be in a position to express his anger, extensive disruption might follow: one Mauritanian war arose from the refusal of the owner of a slave girl to sell her to a chief who desired her.[59]

Of course, if no legal arrangement could be arrived at, there was always the possibility of illicit liaison. In Wadai, Nachtigal heard this story about Aqid Jerma, a close confidant of King Ali—both men had been involved in the murder of Eduard Vogel in 1856, in or near Abeshr. While Aqid Jerma was still alive, his eldest son

> had allowed himself to embark on an intrigue with a slave girl from the royal household, the consequences of which could not remain concealed from the king. When the king had learnt about the state of affairs, he summoned the father [Aqid Jerma] of the delinquent, reported the affair to him, and asked what in his view should be done to the guilty party. Fear of the king went so far in Wadai, and the conviction of his inexorable severity was so profound, that without hesitation the father replied: This crime, my master, can be expiated only by death. The king then on this occasion, as very rarely happened, tempered justice with

[58] Ibn Battuta, 57-8; *Corpus*, 302; the translation is from the *Corpus*, and the brackets are the editors'.

[59] al-Shinqiti, 1911, 479; 1953, 95. A variant instance of the same theme occurs in the Hausa tale of a chief who wished the wife of one of his slaves. He sent the husband on a journey. But the wife shamed the chief, saying that the master does not sup of the same vessel as his dog (Tremearne, 1913, 26-7).

mercy and contented himself with depriving the guilty man of his office. Only later, many years after, was he in some measure restored to favour and appointed Aqid of the Khozzam.[60]

Another sometimes important complication, arising from concubinage and with the potential of leading to conflict, was rivalry among children. In strict law the child of a free wife and the child of a concubine were exactly equal in status and privileges.[61] But respect for the law was not always effective in eradicating the feeling that it was only right and proper to prefer the son of a free woman to the son of a bondwoman. The Shirazi, or Persian, emigration to East Africa was said to have been led by Ali, son of the sultan by an Ethiopian slave, held in little esteem by his half-brothers, offspring of a Persian noblewoman.[62] When the sultan Yusuf of Wadai died in 1898, his eldest son was passed over in the succession because his mother had been a slave.[63] The distinction was sometimes on the father's side, not the mother's. Fulani origins, traditionally derived from a single royal mother, distinguish between her children by her first husband, a free Arab, and those by her second, a freed slave. The two main Fulani groups, settled and nomad, dispute which has the former, more honoured, descent.[64]

Powerful individuals might rise from concubine birth to great eminence, even despite prejudice, and several folk-tales tell of such triumphs by the despised mother or her child.[65] Abu Yazid, who revolted in 928-9 against the Fatimids of North Africa, was the son of a black concubine, born on the banks of the Niger.[66] One story traces the origin of the title *galadima*, a very senior official in Borno, to the appointment of a *mai's* son, born to him by a concubine, to some high position.[67] The

[60] IV, 84-5.
[61] M. Gaudefroy-Demombynes, *Muslim institutions*, London 1950, 136-7.
[62] Freeman-Grenville, 1962/1975, 89-90.
[63] Theobald, 1965, 60.
[64] Lacroix, 1952, 5-6; E. A. Brackenbury, 'Notes on the "Bororo Fulbe" or nomad "Cattle Fulani"', *Journal of the African Society*, 1924, 211.
[65] Tremearne 1913, 283, 317.
[66] Ibn Khaldun, II, 530, III 201.
[67] P. A. Benton, *Kanuri Readings*, London 1911, 25-6. See also II, 251

founder of the first independent dynasty of Nupe, in West Africa, was not born of a concubine, but was none the less partly tainted by slave status. He came of a chiefly mother in Nupe, while his father was a member of the ruling family in Igala, then overlords to Nupe. But the father returned to Igala, whither the son himself, Tsoede, was later sent as part of the annual slave tribute owed by Nupe to Igala. In Igala, his father recognized him, and took him into his family. Later Tsoede escaped the machinations of his half-brothers, returned to Nupe, and set up his own kingdom.[68] Muhammad al-Fadl, a renowned nineteenth-century ruler of Darfur, was the son of a Begu concubine, paid in tribute to the Darfur king by immigrants from the Bahr al-Ghazal. On his succession, Muhammad decreed the Begus free for ever, ended the tribute, and made the buying or selling of Begus a crime punishable by death.[69] Mutesa, later *kabaka* of Buganda, was said to be the son of a woman sold into slavery soon after his birth, but this was disputed.[70]

In some cases, such an origin might not prove a serious obstacle: Aliyu Babba, the son of Sultan Bello, though his mother was a Hausa concubine, preceded three of his brothers and one uncle as sultan of Sokoto. His easy-going amiability has been attributed to his Hausa inheritance.[71] Once or twice descent, or pretended descent, from a slave was turned to positively good account: Tippu Tib, among the most celebrated of eastern Arab slavers and colleague of Stanley, was said to have been recognized king of Mbali, near Manyuema, early in his career, having claimed to be the grandson of the old king's sister, who had long before been sold into slavery.[72]

Race might be another dividing line amongst the women of the household, and in this case either the wives, or the

---

note 4, and Schultze, 1913/1968, 312; see p. 290 below.

[68] H. A. S. Johnston, *The Fulani Empire of Sokoto*, London 1967, 134-5.

[69] Slatin, 1896, 44-5. This concubine had been later promoted to the position of legal wife, before bearing Muhammad. Muhammad himself, as a child, had been placed in the care of the chief eunuch, Abu Shaikh Kurra.

[70] J. M. Gray, 'Mutesa of Buganda', and H. Mukasa, 'Some notes on the reign of Mutesa', both *Uganda Journal*, 1934, 23, 28, 128-9.

[71] Johnston, 1967, 152, 270.

[72] Ward, 1890, 183-4.

concubines, or both, might be split amongst themselves. As a general rule, lighter skin colours were preferred. Leo Africanus commented that, while all the maid-servants of the household of the king of Fez were black slaves, the king also had certain Christian captives, Portuguese and Spanish, 'most circumspectly kept by certaine Eunuchs, that are Negro-slaves'.[73] In nineteenth-century Katanga, the competing Portuguese and Arab parties each supplied the ruler, Msidi, with a wife at least partly white: one, Maria de Fonseca, was a Portuguese mulatto;[74] the other, Matayu, was brought from the east coast by the Arabs to offset Maria.[75] Maria complained that she had been sold as a chattel.[76] Matayu was ultimately strangled, for poisoning. Another variety much in demand, as well as the white woman, was the Ethiopian, prized for her beauty and amiability.[77]

This was the pattern also in Mecca. There, the white Circassian slaves, male and female, coming from Constantinople, were very expensive, and were never sold in the open market.[78] Black women were primarily house workers, and only secondarily concubines; Abyssinian women were regarded in the reverse order,[79] and may have excited more real enthusiasm than the Meccan women themselves.[80] In Brazil, several instances were reported in which the greater lightness in colour of a child or woman slave helped elicit more effective sympathy for emancipation.[81]

In Kuka in the mid-nineteenth century, the question of Circassian women having come up in conversation, the vizier al-Hajj Bashir told Barth with 'undisguised satisfaction, that he had a living specimen of that kind'.[82]

[73] Leo Africanus, A, II, 482; B, I, 238.
[74] Crawford, 1914, 183-5.
[75] ibid., 295-6.
[76] ibid., 191 n.
[77] A. E. Robinson, 'The Tekruri sheikhs of Gallabat', *Journal of the African Society*, 1926, 49; Harris, 1844/1968, I, 223-4, 233-5.
[78] Hurgronje, 1931, 10-11.
[79] ibid., 13-14.
[80] ibid., 107, 109.
[81] Verger, 1976, 454-6.
[82] Barth, 1965, II, 42. Doughty (1888/1923, I, 603), the English traveller in Arabia in the 1870s, was once taken, on account of his lighter skin, to his chagrin as the son of a Circassian bondwoman.

Nachtigal, though he was interested in skin colours, and in the colour scales worked out and applied by Africans within Africa—see the index entries for each of the four volumes of *Sahara and Sudan* —had very little to say about this with reference to wives and concubines. He did cite the Tunisian traveller Muhammad el-Tounsy, who said of the Qor'an people that they were so light-coloured that the Wadaians did not like Qor'an slave-girls.[83]

In one area, indeed, Nachtigal thought that a sense of racial purity discouraged concubinage. This was in provincial Darfur. Admitting that there were many concubines in Darfur, he urged a distinction between, on the one hand, the capital and the places where foreigners did their business, and on the other the provinces. 'In general the genuine Fur man does not like concubinage, for he is very proud of the purity of his race and seeks to preserve it.'[84]

In all this, we learn very little indeed of the way in which matters of race and colour were worked through within the household. There seem to be few visible signs of conflict: the home of Msidi, ruler of Katanga, may hardly have been a haven of peace, but neither was it Muslim.

Nevertheless, even when full allowance has been made for all these and many other possible problems, there is much evidence that slave and free could live in harmony together. At Hobbio, his point or re-entry into Borno territory in September 1872, after the horrific experiences of his Bagirmi expedition, Nachtigal and his companions were warmly welcomed. And,

> in addition, two neighbours, a slave woman of et-Titiwi [a Kuka notable], and a man who had been in Dr Vogel's service at the same time as Almas, strove most zealously to supply us with firewood, water and the like. We revelled again in Bornu's plenty, and rejoiced to the full in these proofs of the friendliness of an amiable people.[85]

The incorporation of concubines went forward at two other levels also. At an intermediate level, there were large collections

---

[83] II, 457 and notes.
[84] IV, 364.
[85] III, 448.

of concubines, each collection under a single master. There are the 14,000 slave-girls whom Mansa Musa in said to have taken on pilgrimage for his personal service (see above, p. 181), indubitably a mythical number. A little later in the fourteenth century, when Ibn Battuta was in Mali, he observed a prominent official in the capital city, the interpreter, attending the principal Muslim festivals with his four wives and about 100 slave girls, in beautiful robes, with gold and silver ornamented fillets on their heads, playing instruments and singing along with him.[86] Ibn Battuta also described the people of Takadda, vying with one another in the number of their slaves and serving-women, living in luxury and ease, just as the people of Mali and Walata did.[87].

In Timbuktu, just after the Moroccan conquest of Songhay at the end of the sixteenth century, a new official was appointed to replace one who had died in prison, and the new appointee appropriated a *harim* of 300 young girls.[88] Bawa, ruler of Gobir in the eighteenth century, received from the ruler of Nupe 500 female slaves, and 500 boys, each boy bearing 20,000 cowries. Bawa responded with a gift of 100 horses, and female slaves whose beauty out-shone the sun, 'beautiful, in form and character, and resplendent with ambergris and silk'.[89]

Such exchanges took place also between the Muslims and their non-Muslim allies, and amongst their opponents. When the Muslim ruler of Enarea, in Ethiopia, proposed an alliance to the Christian ruler of Gojam, the Christian replied: you are a Muslim and sell slaves, it cannot be; nevertheless he accepted 100 horns of civet and 50 female slaves, and sent in return 30 matchlocks, with men versed in the use of firearms.[90] The Pagan king of Segu, fighting Shehu Ahmadu, sought the help of a noted Bambara warrior, sending him, so the traditions tell, 6,000 horns of Arab powder, 15,000 of local powder, 6,000 slaves, 500 cattle, ten horses, two ostriches with feet encircled

[86] Ibn Battuta, 41; *Corpus*, 292-3.
[87] Ibn Battuta, 57; *Corpus*, 301-2.
[88] *Tedzkiret*, 278- 80.
[89] H. R. Palmer, 'Western Sudan history', *Journal of the African Society*, 1916, 269.
[90] Harris, 1844/1968, III, 53-5.

with gold, and a *vedette* whose gait was more supple than that of the female ostrich.[91] In this last case, though we may doubt round figures such as 6,000 slaves, the fact that the *coup de grâce* is given by a single woman of supple sex appeal is a reminder of the way in which attention may focus on an individual.

The emergence of a more militant puritan Islam, in the late eighteenth and nineteenth centuries, did not fundamentally alter the situation, though some of the leaders behaved with restraint. For Shehu Ahmadu, founder of the Masina theocracy, tradition apparently recalls only one concubine, a devout woman who could recite the Quran by heart and had studied the religious law.[92] Usuman dan Fodio was survived by wives and concubines, who lived on quietly together in Sokoto.[93]

We have already met (p. 196) al-Hajj Bashir, so proud of his Circassian concubine. Barth has a good deal to say about this man, whom he liked very much—'a most excellent, kind, liberal, and just man'.[94] Barth's description, from the outside of course, of the vizier's family circle, is very interesting, and most apt for our purposes here:

> He was certainly rather 'kamúma', that is to say, extremely fond of the fair sex, and had a harím of from three to four hundred female slaves.
>
> In assembling this immense number of female companions for the entertainment of his leisure hours, he adopted a scientific principle; in fact, a credulous person might suppose that he regarded his harím only a from a scientific point of view, as a sort of ethnological museum, doubtless of a peculiarly interesting kind, which he had brought together in order to impress upon his memory the distinguishing features of each tribe. I have often observed that, in speaking with him of the different tribes of Negroland, he was at times struck with the novelty of a name, lamenting that he had not yet had a specimen of that tribe in his harím, and giving orders at once to his servants to endeavor to procure a perfect sample of the missing kind. I remember, also, that on showing to him one day an

[91] Ba and Daget, 1962, I, 137-8.
[92] *ibid.*, I, 52.
[93] Clapperton, 1829, 207, 210.
[94] Barth, 1965, II, 43.

illustrated ethnological work in which he took a lively interest, and coming to a beautiful picture of a Circassian female, he told me, with an expression of undisguised satisfaction, that he had a living specimen of that kind; and when, forgetting the laws of Mohammedan etiquette, I was so indiscreet as to ask him whether she was as handsome as the picture, he answered only with a smile, at once punishing and pardoning my indiscreet question. I must also say that, notwithstanding the great number and variety of the women who shared his attention, he seemed to take a hearty interest in each of them; at least I remember that he grieved most sincerely for the loss of one who died in the winter of 1851. Poor Háj Beshír! He was put to death in the last month of 1853, leaving seventy-three sons alive, not counting the daughters, and the numbers of children which may be supposed to die in such an establishment without reaching maturity.[95]

The accumulation of slave girls in Bashir's *harim* is said on one occasion to have enabled Shaykh Umar of Borno, hard pressed by Sherif, the king of Wadai, to accept Sherif's offer to halt his threatened advance on Kuka if he were paid 1000 dollars. An Arab trader offered the Shaykh 600 dollars in exchange for young girls valued at 7 dollars per head, the current price in Borno being then 40 dollars, and on the Mediterranean coast 200. The Shaykh commandeered the most attractive members of Bashir's *harim*, and being able to make up the balance of 400 dollars by other means, could thus buy Sherif off.[96]

[95] Barth, 1965, II, 42. Barth accompanied an Awlad Sulayman slaving expedition undertaken on behalf of Bornu, on which the vizier was represented by an officer responsible for securing the vizier's share of the spoils. Alas, the most handsome—a Budduma—of these escaped during the night. Only her necklace, clothes, and the remains of her bones were found. It was supposed that her loss would affect the vizier greatly, he being rather fond of an ethnological variety of female beauty (*ibid.*, II, 280). See above, p. 166.

[96] A. Schultze, ed. and tr. P. A. Benton, *The sultanate of Bornu*, London 1913/1968, 266-7; for fuller details, see p. 290 below, note 220. According to the version of this story in *Documents scientifiques de la Mission Tilho*, 1911, II, 367, 'les bijoux de ses femmes' provided the other means which Shaykh Umar needed. Brenner (1973, 66 note) rejects the story of the payment to Sherif, for various reasons, including the fact that Barth does not mention it, nor is it a part of current tradition in modern times.

The third level at which the incorporation of concubines and slave-girls is significant is the national level. Here we need a wide screen, embracing thousands upon thousands of individual examples, plus many concubine concentrations particularly in the hands of the wealthy. Having sketched the original constituents of the Kanuri people, the main population group of Borno, Nachtigal goes on to argue that the young mixed people must have undergone changes, through climate and through living conditions,

> but also and in particular through the blood of the subjugated indigenous tribes. These delivered to the conquerors slave women, the mothers of their children, in numbers which with the successes in arms were ever increasing; moreover, while from generation to generation their own essence was losing something of its original nature, the foreign influence was constantly intensified.[97]

Nachtigal traces much the same pattern for the rise of the Bagirmi state and people. From the beginning, the young state faced great difficulties in holding out against neighbouring peoples, the Bulala and Kuka in the Fitri region, and the more powerful Borno and Wadai. Bagirmi turned to 'warlike enterprises against the disunited Pagan tribes around it and...the acquisition of slaves'. New elements of population were thus introduced every year, the assimilation was all the easier inasmuch as raider and raided were closely related tribally, while Islam had not yet raised the Bagirmi significantly above their oppressed Pagan neighbours.

> Later, when the country had become more densely populated, and all the inhabitants Muslim, so the contrast with their neighbours, Pagan albeit related, increased; these were no longer simply merged with the victors, but were rather sold and kept in slavery, although the mixture of blood went on continuously as a result of the large number of women and girls brought in every year from the south.[98]

Almost invariably, it has been the womenfolk of the conquered, the children and girls, the wives, concubines and mothers, who have had to face the challenge of assimilation,

[97] III, 164.
[98] III, 376.

whilst maintaining some of their own characteristics within the evolving society. Only once, I think, does Nachtigal mention slave-owners marrying their own daughters to their slaves: he alleges this of some Arab tribes in Wadai.[99] This is in the posthumously published final volume of *Sahara and Sudan*, and seems so surprising that one may wonder if an editorial error could have crept in.

A final note about slave-girls. In his discussion of the main Kuka market, Nachtigal refers to deaf-mute slave-girls, much in demand as servants for the wives of magnates of the more highly civilised countries of Islam, and commanding high prices.[100] I suggested to a colleague, far more knowledgeable than I about many such matters particularly in Hausaland, that such slaves might be especially valued as less likely to deal in scandal and gossip. He demurred: even the deaf and dumb would find ways to pass on information and rumour of this kind. Their real recommendation, he added, in some of the most hauntingly chilling words that I have encountered in so much reading and discussion about slavery: they could not even scream.

Cooks and cooking

'The same night a female slave of mine, named Awwa, refused to cook me my food, and gave as her excuse that she had no water. This made me a little angry.' (Hamman Yaji, p. 90, 4 March 1924; *cf.* p. 160 above)

Cooks did not dominate the domestic slavery scene in the same way that, as we have seen, concubines did. But, given that so much attention is paid to the pleasures of the bed, it would be surprising if those of the board did not figure also. Indeed, if we return to the eleventh-century source which commented in such vivid detail on the former, we find there commendation also of the latter:

> ...Sudan women, good cooks, one being sold for 100 mithqals or more. They excel at cooking delicious confections such as sugared nuts, honey doughnuts, various other kinds of sweetmeats, and other delicacies.[101]

[99] IV, 159.
[100] II, 218.
[101] *Corpus*, 68. See above, pp. 180-1.

In nineteenth-century Rio de Janeiro skilled cooks, black slaves, were in great request.[102] Even where such high standards were not maintained, female slaves might cook and even sell their creations on the market, as Clapperton noticed in Borgu and Sokoto—the food included fried fish, the fish having been caught by young slaves.[103]

Nachtigal's friend Lamino (see above pp. 34-5) was particularly proud to include among his several thousand slaves a group of skilled female cooks from all the countries between the Nile and the Niger.[104] Barth had travelled with a slave-raid against the Musgo, in 1851, on which this same Lamino was present, and had praised at that time the excellent cooking of one of Lamino's slave women who was accompanying her master.[105]

Lamino's interest in cooking—he seems to have done some himself, at least in the final stages of preparation—was unusual in a man, for cooking was widely regarded as very much women's work. In the later sixteenth century, Idris Alooma, the great warrior sultan of Borno, and his troops suffered from the lack of female kitchen staff on one of their many expeditions:

> We halted in the desert to feed the people and nosebags were tied on to the horses. But eating in this place was only possible with great difficulty, for cooking was always done by the women and girls [sic] slaves and could not be well done by men and men slaves. On this journey not one girl could come with us. For this reason cooked food was very difficult to obtain and very expensive.[106]

Both Barth's experience, when there was an excellent female slave cook in the travelling party, and that of Idris Alooma, who had no slave-girl at all on this particular expedition, point to the importance of slave women as mobile cooks. This is further confirmed by Hamman Yaji's diary entry, about 'the female slave I lent him [Sarkin Hausawa, a Madagali notable]

---

[102] J. Candler and W. Burgess, *Narrative of a recent visit to Brazil*, London 1853, 39.
[103] Clapperton, 1829, 94, 211.
[104] II, 137.
[105] Barth, 1965, II, 338-9.
[106] 'The Kanem wars. By Imam Ahmed ibn Fartua' in H. R. Palmer, *Sudanese memoirs*, 1928, reprinted by Frank Cass, London 1967, I, 41.

to prepare his food for him on a journey'. This third instance is additionally interesting for the light it throws on the manifold possibilities for dispute over slave ownership. Sarkin Hausawa said that the slave was now owned by him, 'because of the loan'. So Hamman Yaji sent him 'to the Kadi Amin, who said, "This slave belongs to a slave of the Sarkin Hausawa. Am I therefore to return her to him or not?" and God is knowing in this matter.'[107]

Nachtigal experienced similar difficulties on numerous occasions, despite having for a considerable time Moroccan servants, whose male aversion to cooking was much less than that among local people. Nachtigal's sojourn with the fugitive king of Bagirmi, Abu Sekkin, and his actively slave-raiding court-in-exile, illustrates this:

> Since in surroundings where slaves were so plentiful my people regarded it as beneath their dignity to prepare food themselves, or to perform the other usual domestic tasks, I asked the king to let me have two working slave women on loan. Their assistance was, however, not long available to us, for, although their feet were fastened together with short heavy chains, they soon, to my own sincere satisfaction, succeeded in running away.[108]

Later, during his second stay in Abeshr, capital of Wadai, Nachtigal found it very difficult to secure regular kitchen service, whether by hiring slave women belonging to his neighbours, or other women in his quarter. With the beginning of Ramadan, on 25 October 1874, 'no order of any kind could be maintained'. Finally Nachtigal's benevolent, resourceful and wealthy friend and travel companion, Hajj Ahmed Tangatanga, helped him out of this predicament, assigning him a slave woman to look after the household.[109]

Not that a slave woman necessarily solves the problem, as Hamman Yaji's diary makes clear.

> In the morning one of the women of my household refused

---

[107] p. 112; the reader's guess is as good as mine as to exactly what the judge meant. Maybe that is why Hamman Yaji falls back upon God's knowledge.
[108] III, 334-5.
[109] IV, 124-5.

to give me any food. —... I found that my slave girl in the absence of her fellow-slaves had said she would not prepare my food for me. Why she would not cook my food I do not know, but anyway the result was that I got no food from her and was obliged to buy it.[110]

This seems a remarkably mild response from a man perfectly content to kill in order to recruit such slaves in the first place. Lovejoy and Hogendorn, however, include the passage which heads this section amongst references to noisy complaints by his concubines against Hamman Yaji's harsh treatment,[111] and to concubines running away (see above, pp. 159-62); and, remembering extra-diary reports of the extreme cruelty practised by Hamman Yaji and his men (see above, p. 162 n. 98), we may well shudder when he himself admits to having been 'a little angry'.

But when the system worked well, it could work very well indeed. Nachtigal described a Jellabi *zariba* at Kobe, on the highroad between Wadai and Darfur, which was a positive hive of hospitality:

> The numerous women and slave girls [*Frauen und Sklavinnen*] of the house were busy the whole day in preparing food, for as soon as only two or perhaps more people had entered the courtyard where the reception was being held, a dish was at once set before them...[112]

Slaves, and cooks especially, facilitated hospitality.

I wonder whether Hamman Yaji's recalcitrant cooks, who downed tools so defiantly, were in a mild and muted manner expressing slave resistance? And I wonder whether, if a female slave could withhold her culinary favours in this way, she could ever do the same with her sexual favours (*cf.* pp. 76, 192 above)? The saga of Hamman Yaji's occasionally unreliable cooks ended happily, even on quite a touching note. He was deposed and arrested in August 1927, by the British authorities. After this, he at first refused to take any food at all. But when a female member of his household followed him, he agreed to eat the rice which she had faithfully cooked, and

---

[110] Hamman Yaji, 51 (20 September 1912), 52 (4 February 1913).
[111] Lovejoy and Hogendorn, 1993, 247.
[112] IV, 253. A detailed description follows.

the British officer in charge sent out for honey and milk at Hamman Yaji's particular request.[113] Hamman Yaji died two years later, in exile in Kaduna, on 8 May 1929.[114]

There are hints, even in Nachtigal's day, that external influences were beginning to open up career opportunities for male cooks. Almas, who had been taken as a child slave to Constantinople, returned to Borno as a young man, freed upon the death of his master—one of the few, in Nachtigal's opinion, 'who from a longish stay in Europe still benefit even after their return home'. A very practical man, much involved in high-level government activity—but also an excellent cook.[115] Almas was Nachtigal's principal escort on the visit to Abu Sekkin. Nachtigal describes, with evident relish, how he found Almas, at their first halt, busy with the preparation of a tasty meal of eggs, tomatoes, onions, and pepper, vividly reminding him of the *shuqshuqa* dish common in Tunis.[116]

At a very much lower level, but withal another pioneer in the field of male cookery in the heart of Muslim black Africa, there is Isiaku, one of Hamman Yaji's 'boys' (so he may not have been himself actually a slave). Following a visit by a British officer in December 1923, Hamman Yaji sent Isiaku to him, so that the officer might teach him how to cook Hamman Yaji's food.[117] Perhaps Hamman Yaji's late interest in European-style cookery had something to do with his long and troublesome dietary illness.[118] Isiaku, despite the somewhat enigmatic interest attached to him, is not indexed; there seems to be no indication of his return to Hamman Yaji. But just eleven months after the beginning of his cookery studies, the diary notes, 'Isiaku and others ran away.'[119]

That women, especially slave women, collected their own firewood is implied in the Darfur tale of a treacherous queen

---

[113] Hamman Yaji, 35; these details come from the editorial commentary added to the published diary; it seems to me very likely that the loyal woman was a slave, but this is not explicitly stated.
[114] *ibid.*, 41.
[115] III, 53-4.
[116] III, 218.
[117] Hamman Yaji, 86.
[118] *ibid.*, 19.
[119] *ibid.*, 103.

betraying the secret path to her consort's otherwise impregnable mountain stronghold, by the seemingly so innocent and natural gesture of sending many of her slave-women to collect firewood all along that path on a day agreed with the besiegers beforehand.[120]

---

[120] IV, 280-1.

CHAPTER VII

THE DOMESTIC SCENE, III: SLAVES AT WORK

Free and slave labour

'It was a fixture of anti-slavery doctrine that free labour would prove cheaper and more efficient than slave labour in the production of tropical staples.' (William A. Green, *Journal of African history*, 1974, 251)

It is generally accepted, and on the whole sound, doctrine in the western world that 'from the experience of all ages and nations...the work done by freemen comes cheaper in the end than that performed by slaves'.[1] There were, however, almost infinite variations of status and practice to be found in Africa, and slave-owners there, who had a scale of consumers' preferences quite different from anything that is now taken for granted in the west, were not easily persuaded by the generalizations, echoing Adam Smith, advanced by anti-slavery advocates—for example by Lugard, who quite reasonably maintained that 'from an economic point of view slave labour and forced labour are the least productive of results in proportion to capital expended'.[2] Clapperton shared this low regard for slave productivity, at least in Borgu, estimating that 'a smart English servant would accomplish their hardest day's work in one hour'; it was fair to recall, he continued, that, if the work was light, the food was light too.[3]

Nachtigal found that, especially in the larger centres of population, almost all the menial work was done by slaves, and

[1] Adam Smith, *Wealth of Nations*, book III, chapter 2.
[2] Lugard, 1933, 14.
[3] Clapperton, 1829, 94.

his firm adherence to the principle of employing only free wage-earners created great difficulties for him.

> The chief inconveniences for a traveller arise from his servants, especially if, in a country where all the work is customarily performed by slaves, he wishes to have free wage-earners around him. Even if in the north among the Arabs his servants have not felt ashamed of their subordinate serving status, it is only with reluctance that their self-esteem condescends to work under or with slaves. Their performance is much inferior to that of the slaves, and all the same they want to be better treated. During a quiet spell in a town, where the demands for their services were less, and opportunities for enjoying life were presenting themselves at every turn, their claims expanded considerably.[4]

Particularly intractable was the matter of female kitchen staff. Nachtigal believed that he should not buy a female slave to cook for him and his companions, so instead he hired a woman in Kuka. Quickly an intimate relationship developed between the cook and Ali from Mandara, a thoroughly unsatisfactory servant signed on in Tripoli, who had been released from Nachtigal's service long before as incorrigible,[5] but who continued a part of his household as a guarantee against falling again into slavery (see above, pp. 88-90).

> Soon the two of them were seen strutting around in new clothes, for whose splendour my generosity offered no explanation. My suspicions were aroused...kindly neighbours...gave me proof that, while my horses were getting thin, Ali was selling my grain in the market, and that the whole of the cook's family, her parents and brothers and sisters, were eating daily before my own people had their meals.[6]

Clearly Nachtigal's evidence of male disdain for female work, and the disinclination of the free to do the job of slaves, is persuasive; still, his problems were compounded by the natural, albeit disagreeable, tendency to 'rip off' gullible visitors. That such matters could be managed more effectively and more cheaply is demonstrated by Nachtigal's discovery,

[4] II, 165.
[5] II, 25.
[6] II, 166.

on his return from his journey back into the Sahara, that 30 dollars

> had sufficed to feed two servants and one horse for nearly a year, and also to pay a woman neighbour who had carried all the necessary water from the well, and cooked two meals each day,

demonstrating alike the cheapness of Borno life, and the thrift of Nachtigal's friend the Sherif el-Medeni, who had made all the arrangements.[7]

Nachtigal's own experience in respect of cooks and cooking on that excursion was less happy.[8] In Bagirmi he was in trouble again (see above, p. 204). The best solution seems to have been achieved only relatively late in his travels, in Wadai, where a friendly trader, Hajj Ahmed Tangatanga, assigned a female slave to care for his household again (p. 204).

In Kuka Nachtigal never succeeded in recruiting any satisfactory free local resident. He first employed men who had entered his service in Tripoli at the outset of his expedition, only one of whom had proved altogether, or almost so, satisfactory, Muhammad al-Qatruni. These initial employees were later gradually replaced in part by members of a troop of young Moroccan pilgrims, who were hoping to make their way to Mecca by putting on acrobatic displays in the towns through which they passed. By chance this troop joined the caravan with which Nachtigal travelled from Murzuq to Kuka. Some of them subsequently quarrelled with their leader, and eventually joined Nachtigal instead. The Moroccans were not ideal either. Nachtigal spoke of the unpleasantness of their 'stubborn disposition and brutal vehemence', whilst praising their love of 'energetic activity' and the fact that they were 'little troubled by the opinions of others'. One in particular, Hammu—'indolent,' Nachtigal called him, somewhat inconsistently, 'stubborn and stupid'—proved good-natured and loyal, and stayed with Nachtigal to the end.[9] A further step towards solving the servant problem was the device mentioned earlier (see above, pp. 67-8) of transferring to the traveller's service

[7] III, 45.
[8] II, 341.
[9] II, 165.

two of Shaykh Umar's slaves on the understanding that they would be freed after their arrival in Egypt.[10] The need for a slave-woman in Wadai shows that even Billama and Mohammedu were not a total solution.

A later observer noted deep-rooted convictions about the appropriate functions of free men and slaves producing some inconvenient short-run economic effects when in the twentieth century the French insisted that slaves in Niger should be freed. Men who had formerly been slaves did much less work than before; they decked themselves out as if they were great men, and, far from being grateful for their liberation, some even reproached the French for not permitting them to keep slaves of their own.[11]

Agricultural workers

'From inside the house, I heard drumming that sounded like his [my father's], but I was not allowed to leave the house except when I went to get water for the horses.' (Dorugu's narrative, Kirk-Greene and Newman, 38; see also p. 140 above)

Almost everywhere in Saharan and sub-Saharan Africa agriculture, including stock-keeping, was the foremost employment. And everywhere slaves participated in this. From the smallest to the largest establishment, slaves were incorporated into the domestic economy. We have already seen (p. 37 above) Nachtigal's report, that even less well-to-do households, even in small villages, could not well dispense with the help of a few slaves. Even at this very modest level, there are some signs of a specialised distribution of work: 'The domestic animals in particular are entrusted to the male slaves, who have to drive them to the pastures or cut fodder for them, while the female slaves help the mistress in all domestic duties.'[12] At the opposite end of the social scale, Nachtigal describes the assiduous care bestowed on horses in the homesteads of the great men of Borno. Instead of straw as in Europe, the horses stand on a thick layer of sand, which is freshly laid every day. 'It is regarded as indispensable for the animals' wellbeing, and

[10] III, 57-9 and notes.
[11] Marty, 1931, 214.
[12] III, 131-2.

is kept so clean that immediately after any pollution by a horse the affected part is at once removed by a slave and replaced by clean sand.' Nachtigal goes on to describe how the horses were fed, with dry grass, green fodder, and grain, and no doubt all this was done by slaves.[13]

The tending of livestock was a recurrent slave occupation: a visitor to Abeokuta, in southern Nigeria, in 1851 met a Fulani slave from Sokoto, apparently a Muslim, who had served his new masters for fifteen years, caring for their cattle.[14]

Judging by the heading to this section, the very first job to which Dorugu was assigned, perhaps only two or three days after his initial enslavement, was to help water the horses. Later, in the open space of the Bala district within Kano city, he saw camels, cattle and donkeys grazing, while slaves cut grass to take home.[15] It is ironical that slaves should so often have spent so much of their time tending horses—see also pp. 231-4 below—when it may well have been through horses that they were initially captured and enslaved.

The list of such varieties of slave agricultural work might easily be extended. Nachtigal several times noted the use of draw-wells in the Sahara: in Soqna, donkeys were used to work wells,[16] in Qatrun he saw only slaves employed,[17] while in Fezzan cattle, donkeys, and men served.

> Cattle are very scarce, and are therefore seldom used for this work. Donkeys and men are predominantly employed, the former of average quality, the latter of course slaves.[18]

That no more than an average quality of donkey might replace manpower rather suggests that these slaves were not emerging as irrigation specialists.

Among the Trarza Moors of the western Sahara, slaves were expert in the collection of gum arabic, principal export of the region. At harvest time, the Trarza went to the gum-bearing

[13] II, 152.

[14] Bowen, 1857/1968, 133. On one of the slave farms of a notable of Abeokuta Bowen met also a Hausa Muslim slave who, he was told, wished to escape from such servitude to a non-Muslim (137).

[15] Kirk-Greene and Newman, 76.

[16] I, 53. In Semnu, donkeys were 'essential for irrigation' (I, 63).

[17] I, 205.

[18] I, 86.

districts, and settled there. Daily the slaves were sent out to collect the gum. In the evenings fires were lit, to inspect what had been gathered. Should a slave have brought too little, his masters would reprove and perhaps beat him; but the slave himself would in any case be ashamed to see one of his colleagues surpass him in the work.[19]

We have already remarked the reluctance of the people of Tidjikdja to eliminate slaves lest there then be no one to care for the palm trees (see p. 93). On the east coast, tappers of coconut palm wine were among the most highly skilled and valuable slaves, comparable with traders, sailors and fishermen.[20] At Teyma oasis, in Arabia, where palm trees grew to a height of 15 fathoms, a few people only, and these all blacks, dared to climb them for the fruit.[21]

Perhaps the most important function of the slave as an agricultural specialist came in nomad economies. The traditional derivation of the name Timbuktu explains that it means 'the old woman', and refers to an old slave woman with whom the nomads left their goods when the place was just beginning to develop as an entrepôt.[22] This derivation is etymologically unlikely, but it does suggest the sort of settled role, within a primarily nomadic society, which slaves are believed to have fulfilled. Nachtigal, discussing reasons for the failure of suggestions that the nomad Awlad Sulayman might adopt a more settled life-style, thought that the relative scarcity of slaves in such poor regions might have encouraged the inhabitants in their devotion to the nomadic life: in effect, they were nomads at least partly because of the lack of slaves. But, he concluded, 'in the last resort everything foundered upon their nomad pride'.[23] Contrary to the view that slaves were in short supply,

[19] al-Shinqiti, 1911, 494; 1953, 116 (the French account is slightly abbreviated here).
[20] Beech, 1916, 148.
[21] Doughty, 1888/1923, I, 286.
[22] al-Sadi, 36.
[23] II, 379. Nachtigal refers to the generally good treatment of the Arabs in Wadai. Cattle-breeders for the most part, they can wander, 'and if they engage in agriculture, it is nearly always only with the assistance of slaves'. He continues; 'If their native wanderlust impels them to roam about even for years, the [Wadai] sultan allows them complete freedom. In Bornu the goods of such people would simply be confiscated, and a sojourn outside

it has also been suggested that nomads, for instance some of the Tuareg, feeling that the accumulation of slaves was inconsistent with the maintenance of their traditional way of life, kept the number of their slaves to a bare minimum, settling the surplus in villages where they had to pay tax.[24] It seems more likely, however, that the settled work of the slaves and the pastoralism of the nomads complemented one another in an essential fashion. The Tuareg, for example, cannot exist on pastoralism alone: good years are too few, and good times in each year too short—other food, from cultivation and the caravan trade, is necessary. Again, those in the Ahaggar mountains frequently have their camels grazing three hundred miles or more from their sheep and goats, and slaves were needed for these latter stock; indeed slave herdsmen, more knowledgeable perhaps than their Tuareg masters about certain varieties of livestock, might have considerable influence.[25]

Saharan nomads were not the only people to feel themselves above agriculture. Among the Vai, for example, trade was esteemed a more fitting occupation for freemen, while women and slaves farmed.[26]

Elsewhere, on the other hand, farming was sometimes combined with trading. At Iendwe, near Lake Tanganyika, in the later nineteenth century, both Arab and Wanyamwezi caravans, trading for slaves and ivory, used to halt and farm, slaves and wives doing the work, while subsidiary expeditions went in search of trade.[27] At nearly the same time Hausa traders in Adamawa sometimes stopped and farmed with their wives and slaves, thus feeding themselves and gaining some surplus for further trade with the local people.[28]

Thus far we have concentrated largely on slaves engaged in agricultural and stock-keeping activities, but within the

---

the country would, moreover, be regarded with suspicion.' (IV, 158-9).

[24] Deherme, 1908, 396-7.

[25] Nicolaisen, 1997, I, 160, 191; II, 604.

[26] S. W. Koelle, *Narrative of an expedition into the Vy country of West Africa...*, London 1849, 29.

[27] Thomson, 1881/1968, II, 16-18.

[28] H. Dominik, *Kamerun*, Berlin 1901, 76, ; *cit.* J. Lippert, 'Über die Bedeutung der Haussanation...', *Mitteilungen des Seminars für Orientalische Sprachen in Berlin*, 1907, *Afrikanische Studien* 208-9.

context of a household or even a family. With the oasis-minding slaves of nomadic peoples, the situation changes to one in which agricultural communities exist, more or less complete, more or less separate from their masters (apart from levies, taxes and the like, which could be very heavy), and more or less entirely slave. The diversity of conditions of life is, as so often throughout this entire discussion of slavery within black African Muslim society, immense. The slave tending horses in a great house of a capital city, and accompanying his master when he rode out to promenade, could hardly have been further removed from the desert slave, replacing an average-quality donkey as a drawer of water. Hamman Yaji, who so often opens a window on the actuality of things, mixed but so often bleak and bloody, provides a glimpse of the cruelty. Or rather, this is done in a British report of 1925:

> of how a gang of thirteen chained men had been found working on his private farms, eleven of whom had been sentenced to periods of imprisonment ranging from 25 to 45 days, all without trial.[29]

Hamman Yaji's own diary account makes up in discretion what it lacks in precise detail. On 3 September the Christian arrived, and various matters were discussed.

> He then ordered me to produce the people who were in chains and asked me about them. I told him about this matter, and he then went in person to Sarkin Shanu's house, but found no prisoners, as he had said.
> 4th September...The Christian went off to Duhu with the people who were in chains, and I followed along after him and stopped at Zu.
> 5th September...The Christian...ordered me to release the people in chains, if I wished, and I did so.[30]

It is not made clear whether the chained unfortunates were technically slave or free.

However, a great deal of agricultural slavery was organised much more on a plantation basis. For example, in the sixteenth century in Songhay it was normal practice for the *askiya* to appoint in each village a *fanfa*, presumably a slave, to dis-

---
[29] Hamman Yaji, 28 (editorial material). See also p. 171 above.
[30] *ibid.*, 116-7.

tribute the necessary seed to the slave farm workers whom he supervised, and in return a certain part of the harvest was delivered to the *askiya*.³¹ In the eighteenth century slave villages in Futa Jallon farmed the valleys, while their Fulani overlords lived above on hilltops or the edges of plateaux.³² In the Sokoto empire slave farming on the fiefs of great men reached massive proportions. In Adamawa province Barth contrasted the restricted position of the emir Lauwal, many of whose slaves were tied to farm villages, with the greater power of some marcher lords, receiving food supplies from tribute and hence having their slave hosts always available for other service.³³ One town near Sokoto, Magaria, with the villages around it, was inhabited mainly by slaves of the rich of Sokoto, raising grain and tending cattle. In one such village, visited by Clapperton in 1827, the slave-owner was the only free man in a population of 70.³⁴

Various systems were employed to regulate the pattern of such larger scale slave-farming. Clapperton described the general practice in the Sokoto empire in 1826. A male slave of 18 or 19 would be given a wife, and sent to a village or farm in the country. There he and his wife built a hut, and were fed until harvest by their owner. The owner explained his planting requirements; beyond these, the slave might enclose land for himself. He worked for his owner from daylight to midday, and thereafter used his time as he pleased. At harvest each slave received 'a bundle of different sorts of grain, about a bushel of our measure', plus his own produce. During off-seasons, he had to obey if his master called on him to travel or to go to war.³⁵ The organization of agricultural work among the Hausa Muslims in the latter years of the nineteenth century was still much the same:

> Each slave had his own farming land....In the early morning the slaves and their sons would go to their own farms. At

---

³¹ Kati, 179-80.
³² Trimingham, 1962, 170.
³³ Barth, 1965, II, 191; see below, p. 297.
³⁴ Clapperton, 1829, 192, 243.
³⁵ *ibid.*, 213-14; Reade, 1864, 582. Lovejoy and Hogendorn provide abundant detail on 20th-century Nigerian developments; see 'plantation' in their index.

this time of day (9.30 a.m.) they came back and went to the master's farm, the *gandu* fields until Azahar (2.30) when they returned. At noon food was taken out to them at the *gandu* farm. At Azahar they came in and rested, then in the afternoon the men went to their own farm-plots, and their wives and children went to their little plots too.[36]

In East Africa, slave cultivators worked under one of two arrangements. Some cultivated their master's land, paying him an *ijara*, that is a rent, each month, or perhaps annually; in this arrangement, the whole of the crop remained to the slaves, and the rent calculations took account of the abundance or paucity of the harvest. Under the other scheme, the master took the whole of the main harvest, sometimes even reaping it at his own expense; but he gave plots of land to his slaves, which they might cultivate for themselves on Thursdays and Fridays. Slaves under this arrangement paid no *ijara*.[37]

Somewhat similar schemes may survive the emancipation of the slaves. Among the southern Tuareg in the mid-twentieth century, many former slaves lived as independent farmers, or as nomads organized in clans rather like their former masters. Freed slave farmers cultivated land owned by the Tuareg, with half shares in the crops; the landowner must pay for the cultivator's food for six months, and must supply half the seed and other necessaries. Not many years before, the cultivator received only one-fifth of his harvest.[38]

The trans-Atlantic export trade and that from the interior of East Africa to the clove plantations of Zanzibar,[39] or the French island plantations of the Indian Ocean,[40] were also intended to supply mainly agricultural or plantation workers.

Occasionally the slave trade rendered valuable assistance in introducing new crops. Portuguese slavers brought the peanut from America to West Africa in the sixteenth century,[41]

---

[36] Mary Smith, 1954/1981, 41.
[37] Beech, 1916, 147-8; he adds that slave-owners on the second system appeared more prosperous than those relying on *ijara*.
[38] Nicolaisen, 1997, II, 264-8.
[39] J. Gray, in Oliver and Mathew, 1963, 216-17.
[40] Alison Smith, 'The southern section of the interior, 1840-84' in Oliver and Mathew, 1963, 268-9.
[41] M. A. Klein, 1968, 37.

and coffee is said to have been introduced first from Ethiopia into the Yemen—this was perhaps also a result of the slave trade, and Galla slaves might be found in the Arabian peninsula in the nineteenth century who told of the coffee trees at home.[42]

A final, rather miscellaneous, example of a slave task. A *sharif*, a descendant of the Prophet, and a member of Barth's household, died in Kastsina in 1853. The Emir being notified,

> he sent some of his slaves to dig a grave in our compound and they did so very nicely. They washed him, wrapped him in a new white cloth, and then laid him in a grave. After they had finished, they left us.[43]

Artisans

'Toiling slaves, who have put their garments aside and wear only a leather apron, are busy, under the direction of a master-builder in earth...or of an expert overseer, restoring the tumble-down walls of their master's dwelling.' (II, 158)

Of artisans, many of whom were apparently free men, Nachtigal gave no systematic account, though slaves are mentioned in a variety of occupations of which building was one of the most important. Judar Pasha, conqueror of Timbuktu for Morocco in 1592, used the services of slaves from various Timbuktu households to build a fortress in the city.[44] In Hausaland in 1826 Clapperton witnessed bands of men and women slaves, accompanied by drums and flutes and singing in chorus, passing to and from the river with water to mix clay for repairing the city walls; each great man had his part of the wall to build, as the Jews built the walls of Jerusalem each man opposite his own house.[45] In Timbuktu in 1828 Caillié saw slaves working as masons and bricklayers,[46] just as slaves in Mecca itself were often employed in building, and in other

---

[42] Doughty, 1888/1923, I, 247.

[43] Dorugu's narrative, Kirk-Greene and Newman, 55-6; see also 114 note 10.

[44] J. O. Hunwick, 'Ahmad Baba and the Moroccan invasion of the Sudan', *Journal of the Historical Society of Nigeria*, 1962, 319.

[45] Clapperton, 1829, 98; Nehemiah iii.28.

[46] Caillié, 1830/1965, II, 344.

heavier work such as quarrying. In Mecca, young slaves were sometimes put to such work in the hope that they would thus also acquire a more fluent command of the Arabic language.[47]

Dorugu, a young Hausa slave newly arrived in Kukawa, describes his initiation into building work:

> While I stayed in that household I didn't do anything, even though there was work waiting for me, since they wanted me to rest up from my journey from Zinder to Kukawa. When I had rested, they took me to where my master's slaves were house-building. They were building a new compound there. I carried earth along with those who were building the house. At certain times, we would go and look after the horses, but in the evenings I would always return to the house. Sometimes we would go into the city to get *tuwo* to eat. In Kanuri, they call this kind of *tuwo* with sauce *bargashi.* When we had finished, we would go back to carrying earth.[48]

Hardly a crushing load. A slightly blurred passage in Nachtigal's account of the history of Darfur suggests that there may perhaps have been a certain social symbolism, more sophisticated than simply dismissing it as slaves' labour, in building work. About the beginning of the nineteenth century, Abd el-Bari, the vizier, had been dismissed for treasonable speech, and was in danger of capital punishment. Prince Nuren, a son of the ruler, interceded for Abd el-Bari. Successfully. Abd el-Bari was entrusted to the Prince, in whose house he went to live. One day, the Prince had his own children help build his house, but scolded Abd el-Bari (who had continued to behave in a dissolute and arrogant manner) as an idle slave. This so upset Abd el-Bari that he committed suicide by poison. What was it that so upset Abd el-Bari? That he had been called a slave? Or, possibly that he had been excluded from the building programme, in which even the ruler's grandchildren were taking part, and that at a time when Abd el-Bari was living in the Prince's house, and was thus in some sense a member of the family? Or might both points have caused offence?[49]

---

[47] Hurgronje, 1931, 11.
[48] Kirk-Greene and Newman, 42-3.
[49] IV, 307. To my chagrin, I find a mistake here in our English *Sahara and Sudan.* It reads (wrongly) '...Prince Nuren had him help his own children in building his house and scolded him...', instead of (correctly)

One further slave building detail. When Nachtigal arrived in the war-camp of Abu Sekkin, he found no accommodation prepared for him. But a satisfactory dwelling was quickly provided.

> Exactly as my hut was brought complete from a hamlet in the immediate neighbourhood without consulting its owners, so had the whole village been set up within a few days. Immediately after the king has camped, everybody sends his slaves, if he has any, as quickly as possible into the neighbouring villages, or goes there himself, and poles, fences and roofs are immediately transferred to the camp site, set up there and arranged as a village. It goes without saying that the allies who are treated in this way, and who have in addition to take care of provisions for men and animals, do not view with exactly favourable eyes their friends and masters camping on their territory.[50]

The production of cloth and clothing was a second main theatre for slave artisans. Clapperton spoke of Nupe slaves in Sokoto in 1824, the men considered the most expert weavers in the Sudan, the women the best spinners.[51] Spinning was generally assigned to married women, or to some favourite old female slaves.[52] In Borgu also, where slaves were numerous, the men included weaving among their various tasks, while the women spun and prepared the yarn for the loom.[53] Female slaves were not always judged solely on their merits as concubines; south-east of Mandara the Musgo women were particularly disagreeable in appearance, but were very trustworthy and capable of great labour.[54]

Nachtigal observed how such work was often carried on within the family, in the capital of Borno, where, however, professionals in these handicrafts were gradually emerging, owing to the multifarious requirements of a large population, and to the demands for artistic workmanship.[55] Slaves coming

---

'...Prince Nuren had his own children help in building his house, but scolded him...'

[50] III, 315.
[51] Bovill, *Missions*, IV, 702.
[52] Clapperton, 1829, 221.
[53] *ibid.*, 94.
[54] Bovill, Missions, II, 250.
[55] II, 159. A roll of high quality cloth, collected by Nachtigal, still survives

from Massenya, capital of Bagirmi, were especially valued in Kuka as weavers.[56]

Nachtigal also visited Kinjalia, 'slave village', inhabited only at certain times of the year by slaves of the people of Ngigmi, the northernmost Borno town on the road from Murzuq to Kuka; the slaves were occupied with the production of salt from the ashes of *siwâk* wood.[57] Much higher quality salt came from the salt-mines of the Sahara; Ibn Battuta described the mining centre of Taghaza, in the fourteenth century, a very insalubrious location where only the slaves of the Massufa Berbers lived.[58] As late as the 1930s reports of peculiarly horrible conditions in the salt-mines of the western Jouf were still current.[59] Ibn Battuta observed slaves also mining and casting copper, in Takadda; both men and women took part.[60]

Among the Fulani, a people devoted to their cattle, the work of butchering was always left to slaves. This custom was used symbolically to stir up in revolt Ali, Sarkin Gobir, a Hausa chief who had collaborated with the Fulani after their *jihad*, and had received appointment by Bello, Fulani sultan of Sokoto. Hausa resisters sent Ali a set of butcher's knives, thus indicating that he was merely a slave of the Fulani. This device succeeded in persuading him to throw off his allegiance.[61]

Slaves took part in many other types of work also; Christian slaves sawed wood in Fez,[62] and there were slave drummers in

---

in the Museum für Völkerkunde in Berlin. Catalogue notes there state that material of such fineness, made in Borno by Hausa slaves, never came on to the market. See II, 181 n.1.

[56] III, 377.

[57] II, 103.

[58] Ibn Battuta, 23-4; *Corpus*, 282.

[59] W. Seabrook, *The white monk of Timbuctoo*, London 1934, 259; J. Wellard, *Lost worlds of Africa*, London 1967, 145-6.

[60] Ibn Battuta, 58; *Corpus*, 302.

[61] Johnston, 1967, 130 and n. In many parts of tropical Africa, where the need to guard against eating ritually unclean food is real, Muslims exercise a virtual monopoly of butchering. But in North Africa the trade is scorned: in Kabylia only the Akli, black or mulatto descendants of slaves, are butchers; and it is Homria, offspring of Mzabite men and black women, who form a separate caste at Ghardaia and act in Algiers as butchers or scavengers (X. de Planhol, *The world of Islam*, Ithaca, NY 1959, 66-7).

[62] Leo Africanus, A, II, 442; B, I, 203.

Sokoto.[63] Tremearne's Hausa stories include a passing reference to 'the market of the Filani Slaves who bring wood'.[64] Technically skilled people might, on being enslaved, pass at once into special service. In Tripoli, doctors went straight to the Dey, and were the best-treated slaves; one, a French naval surgeon, captured in 1668, has left an account of his experiences.[65]

Caravan workers

'I sent Burza and Ardhunga on a long journey with 1500 shillings to buy me rifles and cartridges. I gave them a slave so that they might sell him to buy themselves food.' (Hamman Yaji, p. 69, 17 May 1919)

The absence of adequate means of transport has often been adduced as one of the most important reasons for the persistence of slavery in Africa before the development of modern means of communication.[66] Leo Africanus twice mentioned slaves as essential for caravans in the Sudan: for caravans going in search of gold, over paths too rough for camels, slaves carried merchandise as well as food for their masters and guards (and presumably for themselves);[67] and large bodies of slaves helped to protect the merchants of Agades on the dangerous route between Kano and Borno, being speedily set to some useful business at each halting place to avoid idleness.[68] The most important function of the slaves owned by Mandingoes in the Boporo area in Liberia, where slaves in the 1860s were said to outnumber free men by three to one, was to serve as 'carriers for their masters in the trade of salt and country cloths'.[69]

[63] Clapperton, 1829, 254.
[64] Tremearne, 1913, 340. For non-Muslim examples, Newitt (1969, 76-7) mentions that slaves on the Portuguese *prazos*, or grants of crown land, on the Zambezi included among their jobs those of boatman, fisherman, trader, hunter, carpenter, basket-maker, goldsmith, musician, iron-worker, barber, cook, etc.
[65] De la Roncière, 1919, 73-4.
[66] A. McPhee, *The economic revolution in British West Africa*, London 1926, 126-7, 249-50.
[67] Leo Africanus, A, III, 832; B, II, 479.
[68] *ibid.*, A, III, 820; B, II, 473-4.
[69] Anderson, 1870/1971, 41.

In the employment of porters, as elsewhere, it was not always easy to draw a clear line between slave and free. Clapperton twice mentioned Hausa and Borno caravans whose carriers included both men and women slaves, as well as women working for hire.[70] European explorers might prefer hiring porters for wages, but many of those hired were in fact slaves.[71]

Some slaves possessed skills of advantage to an entire caravan. A German explorer, halted by a flooded river, 70 metres across, in Cameroon, watched a small Hausa caravan cross. All its goods were packed in small portions, and put one by one into a large gourd, which one slave, a powerful swimmer, ferried back and forth. Then the same slave helped over the men and women who could not themselves swim. All crossed safely, and the face of the slave, commented the explorer, Zintgraff, 'shone with proud satisfaction'.[72] A somewhat similar device, though not in slave hands, was described by Nachtigal in Logon.[73] Some slaves round Lake Tanganyika became seamen on Arab dhows,[74] and on the east coast dhow crewmen were one of the most highly valued categories of slave.[75] At Suez, too, slaves were employed on coastal sailing vessels.[76] Even on trans-Altantic slavers, sailing to Brazil, slaves purchased in Brazil were sometimes among the crews: nearly half the ships between 1799 and 1810 apparently carried some slave crewmen, averaging as many as 14 per vessel.[77] Some of the settlers in the colonies described above (see pp. 155-6 above), established in the nineteenth century, were runaway slave seamen. Not all slaves were gifted in this way; a young man whom Lander bought in Zaria was terrified at the prospect

---

[70] Clapperton, 1829, 68, 137.
[71] Thomson, 1881/1968, I, 67-8.
[72] E. Zintgraff, *Nord-Kamerun*, Berlin 1895, 308.
[73] III, 446.
[74] Speke, 1864, 230; Burton, 1860/1961, II, 96-7.
[75] Beech, 1916, 148.
[76] G. Baer, 'Slavery in nineteenth-century Egypt', *Journal of African History*, 1967, 421.
[77] H. S. Klein, 'The trade in African slaves to Rio de Janeiro, 1795-1811', *Journal of African History*, 1969, 541-3.

of crossing the Niger even in a boat. He was finally persuaded to do so, but fainted immediately on reaching the other side.[78]

The variety of languages which a miscellaneous group of slaves would speak might greatly help a caravan passing through several countries.[79] Slaves too might help to find the way for a caravan in areas which they knew well. Harris told how, on his way towards Ethiopia from Berbera, his caravan, travelling at night because of the extreme heat in the coastal plain, lost its way, until a female slave redirected it 'when all the lords of the creation were at fault'.[80] Slaves might also help market the goods of a caravan; Hausa caravans in Nupe sent slaves peddling small wares round markets and private houses.[81]

Such assistance was not confined to the secular: we have already mentioned (see pp. 92-3) the very real advantage accruing to a trans-Saharan caravan in this century from the fits of spirit possession of a freed slave women in the party. Nor was the assistance confined to the practical: Richardson recalled how, on a tedious journey in the central Sahara, a slave of the caravan 'amused us with playing his rude bagpipe through these weary wastes'.[82]

In addition to these and other services, sometimes indispensable, rendered by slaves as simply porters, they also sometimes played an important part in the organisation of caravans. Nachtigal mentioned two instances where a slave was assigned a position of responsibility. On the road from Murzuq to Kuka, his team of servants was supplemented by a Hausa slave of one of the leading men of Murzuq, who took the opportunity to send two camel loads of merchandise to Borno.[83] This slave, Barka by name, supported Nachtigal well, remaining by his side during a sandstorm in the desert,[84] and later formed part of his ceremonial escort on arrival in Borno.[85] Apparently—there is no specific reference to this—the man returned to his

[78] Lander, in Clapperton, 1829, 312-13.
[79] Thomson, 1881/1968, I, 29-30; Speke, 1863, xxvii.
[80] Harris 1844/1968, I, 214.
[81] Clapperton, 1829, 138.
[82] Richardson, 1848, I, 408.
[83] II, 26.
[84] II, 33.
[85] II, 115 and note.

master in Murzuq when he had disposed of the goods. Later, on the expedition to Bagirmi, the horse sent with Nachtigal by the Sherif el-Medeni to be sold to the king of Bagirmi was placed in the care of one of the Sherif's Hausa slaves.[86] When this man fell ill, Nachtigal was reluctantly compelled to let him ride, thus burdening the beautiful horse for which has was supposed to be caring, and which had been entrusted to Nachtigal.[87] The slave, his condition worsening despite riding, finally refused 'with the utmost resolution even to make the attempt to continue the journey'. Nachtigal, though hesitant to 'entrust him to people to whom in their poverty it must be very tempting to take possession of him', did in fact hand him over to a local village head, with one Maria Theresa dollar as an interim payment for board and lodging, and the promise of an additional payment on Nachtigal's return.[88] When Nachtigal did return, he learnt that the slave, called Afono—the Kanuri word, rather derogatory, for Hausa—had recovered within a month, and had returned northwards.[89] Dorugu, as a young Hausa slave in Kukawa in 1851, was asked by his Arab owner if he would take the Arab's horse to Kano, to sell it there. Dorugu refused: 'I'm a slave myself. If I should go to sell a horse, won't they sell me instead of the horse?' An interesting glimpse of slave life: how common was a slave's power to refuse? Afono had refused to travel further, and some women slaves could refuse to cook for their masters (see pp. 202, 204-5). The incident is also an indicator of Dorugu's unusual qualities: he was about 11 or 12 years old at the time.[90] Just a little before this incident, Richardson, in Ghadames in the 1840s, met a slave who was sent every year by his master to buy and sell, 'as if a regular free merchant'. The slave, a little apologetically, assured Richardson that he brought 'few slaves, and mostly goods'.[91] Nachtigal encountered another trading

[86] III, 216.
[87] III, 285.
[88] III, 288.
[89] III, 434. There is no further mention of him, so we do not know whether Nachtigal was able to confirm the host's report. See p. 125 above.
[90] Kirk-Greene and Newman, 44 and 4. The text continues with another Dorugu's refusal, equally firm, but this time entirely ineffectual.
[91] Richardson, 1848, I, 188; cf. 260.

slave, when his Awlad Sulayman nomadic Arab companions in the central Sahara plundered a passing caravan of peaceful merchants, including some even of their fellow-tribesmen, as well as a slave, Barqa Musgo, belonging to the Awlad Sulayman chief. Barqa Musgo, and one other member of the caravan, got their property back from the marauders, after negotiation.[92]

The attainment by slaves of command positions in caravans is particularly noted in the nineteenth-century East Africa trade. Cameron in 1874, west of Lake Tanganyika, met a caravan comprised of a few freedmen each with one or two slaves, two small traders with a dozen men each, and the main body of 250 porters divided between an Arab and the slave of an Arab.[93] Such situations were not rare.[94] A man might at the same time be the chief of a large village and the slave of an Arab.[95]

Caravan workers often combined private trade, and even private trade in slaves, with their group responsibilities. Nachtigal's supply difficulties on the road back to Kuka from Bagirmi were greatly increased by the investments in slaves made in Bagirmi by one of his servants and by the guide assigned to him by Shaykh Umar;[96] the story of the frequent and sometimes successful efforts of these slaves to escape is a constantly recurring theme in his account of this part of his travels (see above, pp. 123-30). Many early European travellers experienced similar difficulties. Burton told of porters investing their earnings, on reaching Lake Tanganyika, in slaves and ivory; those who bought slaves deserted as promptly as possible, in order to hurry home before the slaves escaped.[97] Speke, travelling with Burton, described how extra cloth had to be given to some of their caravan officials, who had bought slaves and had to make occasional presents to discourage escape.[98] Arnot in Katanga found his porters spending all

[92] II, 502-3.
[93] Cameron, 1885, 253; see also 230.
[94] *ibid.*, 58, 61, 218.
[95] *ibid.*, 49.
[96] III, 348, 361.
[97] Burton, 1860/1961, II, 74. See also pp. 165-6 above.
[98] Speke, 1864, 264.

their earnings on slaves, so that his camp became 'a regular slave-pen'.[99]

Royal or governmental slaves, though they have a separate section of their own (see below, pp. 256-80), deserve some mention also in the caravan context. Nachtigal first encountered such slaves on his journey to the Bagirmi court. Ten of the ruler's slaves,

> who had been in the north of the country on an errand for their master, had heard of my arrival in Logon and of my travel plans, and had waited for me in order, in return for small presents, to serve me as guides and escort, to reinforce our caravan, and themselves to travel in greater security. Their leader was a young man named Nyugo, that is, hyena, of the Sara tribe, whom in the course of the journey I learnt to value highly because of his good-natured kindness.[100]

Nachtigal goes on to elaborate in some considerable detail upon Nyugo's noteworthy, and meticulously tended, coiffure. His companions, still very young, came from a wide variety of Pagan tribes further to the south. Nachtigal was evidently favourably impressed with Nyugo, but the addition of this contingent was not an unmixed blessing to his caravan. 'The "Hyena" made a point in all the villages of practising the petty extortions customary there, in the name of his master but for the benefit of himself and of his companions.'[101] At the considerable village of Balenyere, less than a week after the newcomers had joined the caravan, Nachtigal could 'only with great difficulty...induce the king's slaves to move on in the afternoon, for they believed that they had a particular right to pillage this place, which is specially assigned to the queen mother'.[102] The very next day, more trouble, as the riverside locals declined to ferry the caravan across in dangerous proximity to their village: 'they feared the brutality and the demands of the king's slaves.'[103]

[99] Arnot, 1889/1969, 184-5.
[100] III, 273.
[101] III, 282.
[102] III, 284.
[103] III, 286. On the return journey, Nachtigal's 'Bagirmi guides' plundered a boatload of small Kanuri traders on their way to Abu Sekkin; the aggrieved traders followed Nachtigal to his next halting place, where, at the cost of a

A final specialized duty of caravan slaves was to be useful to their masters when they went on pilgrimage to Mecca. When Mansa Musa, emperor of Mali, went on pilgrimage in the fourteenth century, he was preceded by 500 slaves, each bearing a staff of gold.[104] In the nineteenth century, Momodu Lamine (see p. 188) had several slaves who carried before him the 300 Qurans which he had collected during his own long pilgrimage.[105] Other pilgrimage slaves might supply less spiritual paraphernalia: in 1876, in the pilgrimage caravan from Damascus, the Persian aga and his son were followed by a Galla slave, from East Africa, bearing fire in an iron sling, to kindle the nargilies, or hubble-bubble.[106] Slaves sometimes became a more permanent element in pilgrimage arrangements. At the end of the sixteenth century Idris Alooma, ruler of Borno, founded a pilgrim hostel in Arabia, with slaves as part of the endowment.[107] A freedman might achieve a post of real authority in pilgrimage organization: the *amir al-hajj*, conductor of the pilgrim convoy, which Doughty observed passing through Arabia from Persia in 1877, was a 'homeborn' Galla; his father had been a slave from Africa, but the son was born in the house of his master, Ibn Rashid.[108]

Some of these pilgrimage slaves might be used as a form of travellers' cheques, to help finance the trip.[109] It is possible that some of the slaves from distant lands, such as those from British India and from the Dutch East Indies who were observed in the slave market of Mecca in the 1880s,[110] may have served such a purpose. Colonial governments, even in the twentieth century, found the sale of slaves accompanying pilgrims,

---

small ransom, he got their property restored. It is not made clear whether these guides, well fortified with a royal letter and other instructions on Nachtigal's behalf, were slaves or not (III, 435 and 427).

[104] al-Sadi, 12-13.
[105] Fisher, 1970, 59.
[106] Doughty, 1923, I, 66.
[107] Ibn Fartua, 1926/1970, 11; 1987, 38.
[108] Doughty, 1923, II, 50; another son of the same slave father was a 'principal personage' in Hayil, where Ibn Rashid ruled (I, 603).
[109] Ibn Khaldun, II, 113; al-Umari, 90; Kati, 25-6; Harris, 1844/1968, I, 390; Trimingham, 1962, 32.
[110] Hurgronje, 1931, 13.

and disguised as servants or fellow pilgrims, particularly difficult to check. The Dutch attempted to deal with this, for pilgrims from Java, by a system of passports, coupled with a representative—Muslim of course—in Mecca. The British Indian government did the same.[111] In 1960 some Moor or Tuareg notables were reported to have covered part of their pilgrimage expenses by selling slaves in Arabia.[112]

On the other hand, the purchase of slaves sometimes involved the imprudent pilgrim in financial difficulties. Mansa Musa of Mali overspent on slaves and other commodities during his celebrated fourteenth-century pilgrimage (see pp. 181, 228) and had to borrow money in Egypt on his way home. A ruler, or *mai*, of Borno in the seventeenth or eighteenth century gave so largely in alms that he was unable to pay in full for certain slaves which were brought to him in the Hijaz, until the prayers of his accompanying clerics miraculously transmuted pebbles into gold: he then completed the purchase of the slaves, and resumed his almsgiving.[113] The pilgrimage caravan returning from Mecca to Damascus brought African slaves 'for all the north-west of the Mohammedan world'.[114]

Among these various pilgrimage slaves, some became pilgrims themselves, for the pilgrimage of a slave is valid if performed with the consent of his master (see above p. 67). An interesting tale is told of Askiya Daud, a sixteenth-century ruler of Songhay, who inadvertently kissed the hand of one of his own slaves among the returning pilgrims; on discovering his mistake, the *askiya* at first wished to have the hand cut off, but finally agreed not to punish its presumption for the sake

[111] Lugard, 1933, 13. He thought that investigation of the history of slaves liberated by Consular agents at Jidda and elsewhere might throw light on methods of enslavement, and he suggested that the permanent Slavery Bureau set up by the League of Nations in 1932 might undertake this work among other things (1933, 7).

[112] Froelich, 1962, 155; *cf.* A.H.M. Kirk-Greene, 'The major currencies in Nigerian history', *Journal of the Historical Society of Nigeria,* 1960, 141.

[113] el-Nager, 1969, 398-9.

[114] Doughty, 1888/1923, I, 209. But in 1877, he could not see five such slaves in the whole Damascus caravan. 'A stout negro lad' might be bought from the returning pilgrims for about 60 reals (then about £11), the price of two camels or a common riding camel (I, 553).

of the sacred rites it had performed in Mecca.[115] In the Hanafi school of law, which, however, is almost unknown in black Africa, a slave is allowed to perform the pilgrimage as deputy for someone else.[116]

The treatment of slaves who were serving as caravan workers sometimes partook of the cruelty accorded to slaves on the march as merchandise, and, of course, the slave as carrier, and the slave as commodity, were often one and the same. In the Congo area, for example, it was usual to kill slaves who fell ill while carrying ivory.[117] In 1827 Richard Lander, after death of Clapperton, travelled from Sokoto with a huge caravan of Fulani and Tuareg. The caravan included fifty slaves who had been sent as tribute to Bello, the sultan of Sokoto, from Bauchi, but were being returned to their original master since he had suffered heavy losses from attacks from Borno. These slaves were reported missing, and horsemen sent back in search of them found thirty-five dead on the road, unable while carrying their heavy burdens to keep up with the camels and horses. The other fifteen were presumed to have met the same fate.[118] German traders in Cameroon complained that their Hausa rivals loaded and overloaded slaves (and their own relatives) without government interference, despite a decree in 1908 regulating the maximum permitted loads.[119]

But there is evidence also to suggest that some degree of comradeship might be achieved amongst the working party on the road. Clapperton in the 1820s, watching a group of Gonja traders in a Hausa caravan passing through Bariba, observed how slave girls, though compelled to carry heavy loads on their heads, yet were 'as cheerful and good-natured as if they were at home grinding corn in their own native country'.[120] It was reported that in a caravan returning from the coast to Futa Jallon, 'even the slaves were relaxed into familiarity never permitted in the towns, while masters would

---

[115] Kati, 204-7; *cf.* p. 266 below.
[116] Umar al-Naqar, 1972, xviii, 80-1. See also p.67 above.
[117] Ruth Slade, *King Leopold's Congo*, London 1962, 87-8.
[118] Lander, in Clapperton, 1829, 282-4.
[119] Rudin, 1938, 334.
[120] Clapperton, 1829, 75-6.

sometimes be seen relieving the servants by bearing their burdens'.[121]

Luxury slaves

'I found this much feared but little respected man enjoying the cool of the evening in the courtyard of his house. He was reclining on carpets and cushions, his fat body covered with fine clothes, and surrounded by slave women, some of whom were massaging his unwieldy legs, while others kept him cool with fans, and all of them indulged his tastes with their lascivious chatter.' (II, 141; see also III, 42)

The wealthy might indulge in luxury slaves, whose work was often of a nature more frivolous than serious. Nachtigal had ample opportunity to observe this in the person and household of Ahmed Ben Brahim al-Wadawi (his father had come to Borno from Wadai), Nachtigal's landlord in Kuka and one of the top-ranking dignitaries in the country. It was Ahmed who sat amongst his slave women in the passage at the head of this section.[122] During Nachtigal's time in Kuka, a project was initiated for building a new royal residence some hour-and-a-half distant from Kuka, at a location more secure from the danger of flooding from Lake Chad.

Ahmed Ben-Brahim was responsible for this, and was accordingly in the habit of spending more time in Ba Dungu [the new site] than in Kuka. Several times a day a long row of his slave women moved out there with dishes on their heads to bring their master the means for good living to which he was accustomed.[123]

And it was Ahmed Ben Brahim, again, who needed six or seven slaves in attendance when he went out riding. One slave held the horse,

while on its right side, in order to provide a counterweight to his master as he mounted, another hung on to the saddle with the whole weight of his body, and four other slaves ex-

---

[121] Canot, 1928, 139.

[122] The passage continues; 'When I appeared the conversation became particularly piquant, for my single state gave the cheerful company much occasion for banter, and raised some questions which were difficult to answer.'

[123] IV, 17.

7. A slave in the block. J. Büttikofer, *Reisebilder aus Liberia*, Leiden 1890, II, 181.

erted themselves to lift him up. As soon as he was in the saddle, the animal slipped into the quick amble of a horse trained there, while his slaves trotted along on foot behind. The senior slave kept closest beside his master, keeping his right hand on the horse's back behind the saddle. A second carried his sword, a third his carbine, a fourth the usual riding whip of hippopotamus hide, and a fifth the halter; the two others jogged along behind without any visible purpose.[124]

Ahmed Ben Brahim was not exceptional in this display. Wealthy men, ostentatiously wearing, 'in glaring contradiction to the temperature that normally prevails', manifold and substantial luxurious garments,

> become colossal machines laboriously lifted on to their horses by their servants. With the corpulence which the climate and their mode of living seldom deny to them, they

[124] II, 124.

feel themselves to be wholly enviable personages as they hasten to the royal palace, followed by slaves trotting behind.[125]

Clapperton in Sokoto in 1824 had interceded on behalf of the slave of an official, whose job it was to run by the side of his master's horse carrying spears; for pretending lameness he had been heavily shackled, a severity however which Clapperton said was rare.[126]

Slaves on foot in attendance upon mounted riders are a recurrent feature. Entering Borno for the first time, in the early summer of 1870, Nachtigal observed the chief of the northernmost province of the kingdom, meeting the caravan and riding with it, while 'the two slaves who carried their master's sword and broadmuzzled carbine alongside their spears tried to keep up with us horsemen as in a long distance race'.[127] A tall, powerful slave, carrying the large yellow silk royal parasol, walked beside the horse of Shaykh Umar as he returned from the outdoor prayers of the *Id al-fitr*, the festival at the end of Ramadan, in Borno in 1870;[128] at the same festival, in Abesher, capital of Wadai, four years later, 'a gigantic umbrella, resplendent with all the colours, was held over the king's head by several slaves'.[129]

One of the grooms, young Dorugu, in Kuka, capital of Borno, speaks to us still, across 150 years:

> So I fell into the hands of a new master. His name was Bohal, I think, and he lived in the Arab quarter. Every day, he would go out for a ride and I would follow him, so that when he dismounted I could hold the horse for him. I liked this new master of mine because he was good-natured. He liked many people in Kukawa and many people knew and liked him.
>
> Sometimes when his horse was saddled, I would go with him to the house of the vizier, Haj Bashir, the Shehu's top

[125] II, 155-7; the influential slaves of distinguished households loved to follow the example of their masters, and to deck themselves out with similar extravagance.
[126] Bovill, *Missions*, IV, 692.
[127] II, 105.
[128] II, 281.
[129] IV, 128.

councillor. When we left there, he would go to the house of another friend of his named Alhaji, and then return home. Whenever he stopped, I would take care of the horse until he came out again, and so on until we finally returned home.[130]

Curiously, the first quotation refers to Dorugu as a slave, the second to Dorugu as a freedman. The job description does not seem to have changed at all. Clearly one slave only, following a rider, was not a luxury, but an essential attendant. Women did not usually ride, but in Wadai upper class women might wear hip shawls of such exaggerated length that they trailed for yards behind the wearer: such women were often seen followed by young slaves carrying the luxurious train.[131] To give an example of luxury slaves from the opposite end of Nachtigal's expedition, at the beginning, Nachtigal describes two such slaves attending the very much decayed Pasha or Governor of Fezzan. They were still boys,

> whom he had fitted up in scarlet cloth frock coats, and who in this remarkable costume seemed as if they were intended to simulate European footmen, though they did not know even how to serve coffee, [and they] presented the most grotesque appearance.[132]

Nachtigal himself had two very different close encounters with luxury slavery. He once enjoyed for a time the services of a luxury slave, Dunkas, originally from Bagirmi. Dunkas had worked as a boy with Eduard Vogel in 1854. After Vogel's death, Dunkas passed into Lamino's household. When Nachtigal arrived in Kuka, Dunkas introduced himself as 'slave of the Christians'. Nachtigal's first impression of him was fairly favourable: 'He talked indeed very big, but otherwise seemed to be a thoroughly good-natured young man.'[133] Later Nachtigal took Dunkas into his own service, 'out of politeness to Lamino'. Nachtigal was already modifying his first impression: 'I promised myself much profit from his local knowledge,

---

[130] Kirk-Greene and Newman, 48-50; Dorugu's employer was Adolph Overweg.
[131] IV, 196-7.
[132] I, 79.
[133] II, 113-4 and notes, 341.

LUXURY SLAVES 235

although in other respects his boastful character inspired no great confidence.'[134] This modification continued apace. Dunkas,

> who was to have been helpful to me because of his knowledge of the country,[135] soon proved to be completely useless. His services were in inverse proportion to the boastfulness of his nature. Under Lamino's generous protection and liberality, he had become completely unaccustomed to work, and had turned into a 'luxury servant', of which, in a country rich in slaves, as Bornu is, there is an endless number. I had wanted to attach him to my person; his own plan, however, was to spend the night in his house on the south side of the eastern town outside the walls, and he came to me in the mornings very late, or, if it was raining, not at all until the sky had cleared again. At last with naïve impudence he hired as a substitute for himself for a quarter of his wages a servant, by name Soliman, and himself lived like a lord.[136]

Dunkas, of course, 'proudly refused to make the slightest contribution to the preparation of meals';[137] and Nachtigal finally dispensed altogether with 'the useless Dunkas'.[138]

Nachtigal's other close encounter with luxury slaves was when he faced the prospect of becoming one himself. While effectively under tent arrest in Tibesti, a visitor from Borku thought it might be a good idea to purchase both him and his Piedmontese servant, who later turned Muslim and left Nachtigal's service. They would have some interest as curiosities, but as they would be worthless as working slaves, no more could be offered for them than one good strong camel. Nachtigal could not tell whether the rather unflattering

---

[134] II, 164-5.
[135] It was Dunkas who, when Nachtigal, in the main Kuka market, 'stared around in helpless curiosity, bewildered by the colourful picture, deafened by the muffled sounds of the crowd, overwhelmed by manifold impressions', could recognise at a glance the tribe to which any individual belonged (II, 221).
[136] II, 166; Soliman finally replaced Dunkas completely.
[137] II, 341.
[138] II, 320. Dunkas' exact status is not quite clear from Nachtigal, who only once (II, 341) calls him a slave, while describing Lamino as Dunkas' 'loyal guardian' (II, 114; see also p. 166).

offer made for him and Giuseppe by the Borku man indicated his contempt for them or rather the high value which he placed on his camel.[139] When the chips were down, far away from the effete opulence of city life, a luxury slave had no value compared with a worker. On the escape journey from Tibesti, at a particularly perilous moment, the anger of Muhammad al-Qatruni, Nachtigal's first and most effective assistant, burst out:

> 'Oh, these Christians, who, full of obstinacy, have much knowledge, but no understanding! By God, as you bear the chief responsibility for this, yours too is the greatest loss. You can choose now whether you will be killed'—and he made the ominous circular movement with his forefinger about his neck—'or will die of starvation. We others with our black skins at least get away with our lives, for at most we shall be made slaves. Only for you is there no escape.'[140]

Nachtigal's experience overall confirms the view that in many parts of Africa the possession of a large number of slaves had become a status symbol, a marker of conspicuous consumption. 'Slaves were valuable property, but they also had prestige value.'[141] Visitors to Bahia, in Brazil, early in the eighteenth century, were struck by the numbers of domestic slaves, and by the way in which slave-owners loved to make a parade of these to show off their wealth.[142] In a country such as Borno, rich in slaves, there was, as he observed, an endless number of luxury servants [143] who, serving only the changing whims of their masters, had lost almost completely any capacity they may have had for regular useful work. In Kano in 1851 Barth contrasted the host of idle, insolent slaves following a rich governor on horseback with the half-naked, half-starved slaves on sale, in rows like cattle, in a cattle shed.[144] The public deployment of luxury slaves is one of the more visible proofs of the principle enunciated by Adam Smith in his analysis of

[139] I, 308, and note.
[140] I, 325.
[141] F. Mahoney and H. C. Idowu, 'Peoples of the Senegambia', in Ajayi and Espie, 1965, 136.
[142] Verger, 1976, 50.
[143] II, 166.
[144] Barth, 1965, I, 497.

the economics of slavery, 'the pride of man makes him love to domineer'.[145]

Finally, though such a factor is scarcely susceptible of precise analysis, it is worth recalling the possible, or even probable, ill-effects on the masters, of having such slaves. Doughty in Arabia commented on a young prince: 'For his age he was corrupt of heart and covetous; but they are all brought up by slaves!'[146]

---

[145] *Wealth of nations*, book III, chapter 2.
[146] 1888/1923, I, 614.

CHAPTER VIII

THE DOMESTIC SCENE, IV: SLAVES AND THE STATE

Slaves, in addition to performing various duties such as those described in the previous chapter, on behalf of the ordinary slave-owning citizen, might also discharge important responsibilities on behalf of the state. This chapter discusses such state functions under four headings: as colonists, as soldiers, royal or government slaves, and the special category of eunuchs.

Colonists

'On his first pilgrimage he left in Masr (*i.e.*, Cairo) 300 slaves, and on his second a like number. When he was on his way to a third pilgrimage, and took ship, the people of Masr said to themselves "if this king returns from Mecca to his country, he will take from us our land and country without doubt." So they took counsel to destroy him. They opened a sea-cock in his ship, so that the sea drowned him by the command of God.' (concerning Sultan Dunama ibn Hume (mid-12th century), 'The Diwan of the Sultans of Bornu', Palmer, 1926/1970, 86)

Slaves have occasionally figured significantly in the African historical record as colonists. There are several famous, admittedly also rather obscurely documented, episodes in which slaves were sent out, chiefly from the Kanem/Borno area around Lake Chad, to settle in more or less distant locations. It has already been noted (p. 98) that merchants, maybe from as far away as Asia, were trading for slaves in Fezzan in the later ninth century. According to Borno records, at approximately the turn of the millennium, the ruler of Kanem, named Arki or Harki, established three slave[1] settlements in the same

---

[1] Perhaps not exclusively slaves: 'The Bornu people who were originally settled in Dirki, Gissebi and Bilma were for the most part slaves, but also to

central Saharan area, presumably also for trading purposes.² These colonies presumably strengthened southern influence upon Kawar and Fezzan, though whether they made an essential contribution is less clear. Nachtigal describes the easy interaction which existed:

> In Kawar...Bornu colonies, for the most part formed out of slave elements, have flourished for centuries, and have gradually mixed with the Teda. The ease with which the Kawar people can get to the Sudan from their oases situated on the great Bornu road, or can barter for slaves, both men and women, from caravans passing through, has particularly furthered this mixture of bloods.³

A later ruler, Dunama bin Hume, in the first half of the twelfth century, perhaps following his predecessor Arki's example, also adopted the policy of planting slave colonies to the north. A good deal further to the north, in Egypt in fact. With the result which is vividly described in the passage at the heading of this section. The episode is not as far-fetched as it might at first sight seem, for Egypt at this period was wracked by Fatimid decline and discord. A still later ruler again, Idris Alooma in the sixteenth century, established his slaves still further afield, in Medina (see above, p. 228).

The seventeenth- or eighteenth-century Borno *mai* mentioned above (p. 229), whose name is given, perhaps erroneously, as Ali bin Umar, he of the clerical alchemists, is remembered as having settled 5,000 slaves in Bagirmi, and 4,000 in each of two places in Wadai, leaving them there on his journey to Mecca and confirming them on his way home.⁴ What lay behind such settlements is not clearly known; perhaps the slaves were, through farming and other activities, to amass supplies for the use of the returning pilgrims.

After this sequence of regally planted slave colonies abroad, we may remember slave colonists throughout the desert, attending to oases and thus contributing to population mobility, in addition to supplying an essential economic counterpart to the

---

a less extent belonged to the Kanuri tribe of the Tura.' (II, 75).

² III, 137, 141-2; Palmer, 1926/1970, 67. See also I, 388, and II, 61.

³ I, 388.

⁴ el-Nager, 1969, 134-5, 395 ff., reproducing an unpublished manuscript.

nomadic activities of the original Saharans (see pp. 213-14). Without the oases the desert would have been a impenetrable barrier between the Mediterranean world and tropical Africa.[5] And without slaves many oases would have gone untended. Many, but not all, for, in Richardson's words, 'many a happy oasis is without a slave'.[6] He visited one, Sidi Mabed, near Ghadames. He had been told that the people of Sidi Mabed disapproved of slave-holding, and he went there in hopes of finding sympathizers with his own strenuous abhorrence of slavery and the slave trade; but the explanation of one of the villagers, was, alas, disappointing: 'If we had money we would have slaves; we have no slaves, because we have no money.'[7] In a geographical inversion, surrounded by water rather than husbanding it frugally, slaves were settled also as cultivators on the islands of Lake Chad.[8]

All the examples of slave colonies cited above are in the nature of outward-bound ventures, slaves for the most part being sent out of the host society, in order to establish useful footholds elsewhere. The colony pattern was also employed inside the host society, to marshall incoming human resources, or to strengthen the control of the central authorities over their territory, or to raise the level of crafts and culture at home. One aspect of the expansion of Kano in the fifteenth century was the establishment of imported prisoners in special towns: one official is said to have founded twenty-one such towns, of 1000 slaves, each, and from these settlements firstborn virgins later supplied the royal *harim*.[9] In the nineteenth century Adamawa was a country of slave colonies,[10] and slave agriculturalists helped more quickly to settle and absorb the territory surrounding towns newly conquered by the expanding

[5] N. Barbour, *A survey of northwest Africa*, London 1959, 2nd edn 1962, 342-3.

[6] Richardson, 1848, I, xxviii.

[7] *ibid.*, I, 285-6.

[8] III, 118.

[9] *Kano Chronicle*, 109-12; M. G. Smith, 'The beginnings of Hausa society', in J. Vansina and others, eds, *The historian in tropical Africa*, London 1964 (hereafter M. G. Smith, 1964 B), 351.

[10] Barth, 1965, II, 158, 195-6; not slave colonies only.

Fulani emirate there.[11] King Ali of Wadai's policy of settling the Bagirmians whom he had captured in 1872 with a view to accelerating the economic development of his country has already been mentioned (see pp. 54-7 above).

Although the re-location of conquered Bagirmi people to Wadai, after King Ali's victory over his western neighbour, has already been discussed in some detail (significantly, under the heading 'Slave and free status', for both slaves and free people were involved, in differing ways), it remains such an outstanding example of the mobilisation of demographic resources, and their assimilation into the host society, that is is well worthwhile reminding ourselves that this was deliberate, conscious policy.

> That King Ali of Wadai after the fortunate conclusion of his campaign carried away many thousand Bagirmi people to his county with the express intention of assisting his own subjects in agriculture, the aforementioned handicrafts, in the construction of earthen houses and the like, shows that in these respects they had a good reputation, and were superior to their eastern neighbours.[12]

There were also myriad minute examples of internal colony formation. The *Kano Chronicle* records this entry for the reign of Yakubu:

> In Yakubu's time the Fulani came to Hausaland from Melle [Mali], bringing with them books on Divinity and Etymology. Formerly our doctors had, in addition to the Koran, only the books of the Law and the Traditions. The Fulani passed by and went to Bornu leaving a few men in Hausaland, together with some slaves and people who were tired of journeying.[13]

The whole account of Yakubu's time is fascinating: several notables came, and were absorbed into high positions in the local hierarchy. Fulani from the west, as we have just seen, came. The Asbenawa came to Gobir, and salt became common in Hausaland.

---

[11] C. V. Boyle, 'Historical notes on the Yola Fulani', *Journal of the African Society*, 1910-1, 85.
[12] III, 377.
[13] *Kano Chronicle*, 111; see also above, pp. 5-6, 9-10.

Merchants from Gonja [the land of kola, though the chronicler doesn't mention this] began coming to Katsina. Beriberi came in large numbers. A colony of Arabs arrived, some settling in Kano, some in Katsina. Yakubu traded horses to Nupe, for eunuchs (see p. 112 above, p. 281 below).

One tiny sentence says it all:

There was no war in Hausaland in Yakubu's time.

Here and there in traditions about the origins of tribes, and the emergence of the founders of states, there are passing references to yet more internal slave colonies. The Kanembu Kajiti, for example, are not regarded as pure Kanembu, but rather as 'a mixture of these with the formerly numerous slaves, settled in Kanem, of the Magomi'.[14] There was an early relationship, more or less, between various autochthonous elements in the Bagirmi area, and the Fellata (or Fulani), 'as indeed with respect to Mabberate in particular it is said that it had been inhabited by former slaves of the Fellata, and had acquired a tincture of Islamic civilisation'.[15] Finally, and rather more clearly and explicitly, the immigrant founders of Bagirmi are said to have proceeded westwards through various places, in which they established colonies.

In the region of Hirla a slave was settled, whose name, Kherallah—which already allows the conjecture of Islamic influence, or of an origin in Muhammadan countries—was transferred to the village which emerged there (Hirla is nothing else but Kherallah).

Hence the saying, 'the people of Hirla are our slaves'.[16] Mbang Abdallah, ruler of Bagirmi in the late sixteenth century, a vigorous and constructive ruler, forbade marriage of Bagirmi with the inhabitants of Hirla, 'as being descended from slaves'.[17]

Soldiers

'Among the things which God (Most High), by his favour, beneficence, generosity and might, enabled him [Sultan Alooma of Borno] to have were

[14] III, 119.
[15] III, 398.
[16] III, 399-400.
[17] III, 403.

the Turkish musketeers present with him and the great number of his slaves of foreign origin who were trained and skilled in the use of muskets.' (Lange, 1987, 38; the chronicle refers to the period 1564-76)

Slave participation in Muslim military activities has had a long history in sub-Saharan Africa. For example, in the fourteenth century, when Yaji, the first Muslim ruler of Kano, failed to take an enemy town by means of the prayers of his newly arrived Muslim subjects, he then followed the advice of a shrewd slave and the expedition was crowned with success.[18] In the sixteenth century, Askiya Daud of Songhay reduced the whole army of the empire to slavery. Previously, the *askiya* had inherited only the horse, the shield and the javelins of each soldier; now he would inherit everything. As for the *askiyas'* continued habit of taking the daughters of their soldiers as concubines, the chroniclers resignedly commented, 'We are the Lord's and to Him we must return'.[19] The Funj, in the eastern Sudan, employed an extensive slave army. The growth of that empire led to the settlement of a standing army of slaves, mainly from the Nuba mountains of Kordofan, in villages around Sennar, where Bruce found them in 1772. These may have played some small part in spreading Islam among their own people, though Bruce thought that they were themselves hardly Muslim, and we do not know how many of them ever saw their homes again.[20]

In the nineteenth century the employment of slave troops continued, though some of the more thoroughgoing Islamic theocracies appear not to have relied on this device extensively. In East Africa, Arab and Swahili traders deployed slave soldiers. About 1840 a regular Arab colony was established in the Tabora area, in modern Tanzania, under Abdullah bin Salim, a recognized leader, with 200 armed slaves.[21] The armed slaves of the Arabs played a prominent part in the Muslim *coup d'état* which placed power in Buganda temporarily in Muslim hands in 1888.[22] Ngongo Lutete, a former slave

[18] *Kano Chronicle*, 105-6.
[19] Kati, 211; Rouch 1953, 206; Quran, Surah ii, 157.
[20] Stevenson, in Lewis, 1966, 210-11.
[21] Smith, in Oliver and Mathew, 1963, 270.
[22] Oliver, 1965, 106-7.

of Tippu Tib, became himself a powerful chief in the Congo. At first allied with the Arabs against the Congo Free State of King Leopold, he changed sides in 1892. He and his 1500 men, armed with guns were a help to the Belgians, despite the embarrassment caused by their rushing on to the field after each battle to eat their slain enemies.[23] Rabih, another noted slaver, may himself have once been a slave, but this is disputed.[24]

In the eastern Sudan, after the Egyptian conquest of the area by Muhammad Ali in 1821, Nubians were recruited into the administration's slave army, the *jihadiyya*, just as in Funj times; and this army was subsequently taken over by the Mahdists. Ex-soldiers, or runaways, returning home in this later period might thus have spent considerable time in a strongly Muslim environment.[25] Salih Shanqa, a Takruri notable at al-Qallabat, on the Sudan-Ethiopia border, had a personal retinue of 4,000 slaves, who carried firearms for him in war, and cultivated his villages in peace; with these, together with tribesmen and Egyptian government troops, he held the Mahdists at bay for some time.[26]

In Borno, in the central Sudan, there are repeated references to slave troops and officers. Al-Kanemi might be attended on his expeditions by about 100 chiefs and favourite slaves.[27] Not that such associates were a guarantee of success. Nachtigal included in his travel account a letter written by al-Kanemi on 9 September 1828, describing a defeat suffered by the Borno forces, under the personal command of al-Kanemi himself. Al-Kanemi was driven back to the Borno camp, but even there it proved impossible to make a stand.

> As we saw the camp stripped of its defenders and were convinced that a longer delay would be futile, we had the slave women and servants brought out and moved in front of us, while we remained behind them....Of the baggage of

[23] Slade, 1962, 108 ff.
[24] Trimingham, 1962, 218; Schultze, 1913/1968, 282, 300-1; Lippert, 1899, 243-4; MacLeod, 1912, 143-4.
[25] Stevenson, in Lewis, 1966, 211-12. See also p. 53 and note above.
[26] P. M. Holt, *The Mahdist state in the Sudan, 1881-1898*, 2nd edn, Oxford 1970, 167 ff.
[27] Bovill, *Missions*, III, 370.

my own tents was nothing saved, since not one of the slaves was to be seen. If only twenty mounted slaves had been available to me, nothing of my baggage would have been lost. But the slaves and Bornoese: women are better than they are!... of my thoroughbred horses none has been lost, but of the horses of the slaves and the councillors only a few were saved; not that they were taken by the enemy or lost their lives through weapons, rather they died as a result of excessive running. Praise be to God, whatever He may determine![28]

It is notable how slave-girls were a part of the expeditionary force, and also the care taken to prevent them from falling into enemy hands. Slaves had been among the losses which al-Kanemi suffered when his attack on the Fulani empire of Sokoto failed in 1827.[29]

The commander-in-chief of the Borno army about this time, Barca Gana, a devoted Muslim, had fallen to al-Kanemi as a slave when only nine years old.[30] Denham observed a crisis in the relationship between the general, and his master al-Kanemi, which admirably illustrates the uncertainty, but resilience too, inherent in slave status, even at the very highest levels. Barca Gana was al-Kanemi's favourite. He was governor of six large districts, owning more than fifty female slaves, and twice as many males, though a slave himself. Al-Kanemi by mistake gave Barca Gana a horse already promised to someone else, and accordingly asked to have it back. To this request Barca Gana took such great offence

[28] III, 455.
[29] Clapperton, 1829, 252. There is a remarkable poem by al-Kanemi, extolling, in term more reminiscent of the Song of Solomon than of the normal Muslim reticence concerning domestic and romantic details, the beauty of a young woman. The poem marks the return of al-Kanemi from a successful military expedition to Bagirmi: it is extremely tempting to suppose that the object of al-Kanemi's fervent desire was a concubine, who had accompanied her master to the field, and then been first lost in the fighting, and then safely recovered. But it is equally possible that she was a wife, not a concubine, and that her supposed loss may have been news from home of her death through sickness or some other cause, news later proved false. Since her relevance to our discussion of slavery remains thus unproven, I omit, regretfully, the rather vivid details of al-Kanemi's account. T. Hodgkin, *Nigerian perspectives*, London 1960, 208-9; or 1975, 275-6.
[30] Bovill, *Missions*, III, 321.

that he sent back all the horses which the sheikh [al-Kanemi] had previously given him, saying that he would in future walk or ride his own. On this the sheikh immediately sent for him, had him stripped in his presence, and the leather girdle (see p. 218 above) put round his loins; and, after reproaching him with his ingratitude, ordered that he should be forthwith sold to the Tibboo merchants, for he was still a slave. The favourite, thus humbled and disgraced, fell on his knees, and acknowledged the justness of his punishment. He begged for no forgiveness for himself, but entreated that his wives and children might be provided for, out of the riches of his master's bounty.

That the merchants to whom Barca Gana should be sold were specified as Tibboo, or Tubu, the people of Tibesti, presumably underlined the awfulness of the judgment (see above, p. 142). Next day, when the sentence was to take effect, all the courtiers and chiefs joined in interceding for the condemned man.

The culprit appearing at this moment to take leave, the sheikh threw himself back on his carpet, wept like a child, and suffered Barca Gana, who had crept close to him, to embrace his knees, and calling them all his sons, pardoned his repentant slave. No prince of the most civilised nation can be better loved by his subjects than this chief...[31]

General rejoicing: how would a free offender have fared?

Barth, approaching Borno from Hausaland to the west, through the Ghambaru district, potentially rich, but at that time reduced to ruins by the inroads of the Tuareg and Fulani, complained that

this condition of the finest part of the country is a disgrace to its present rulers, who have nothing to do but to transfer hither a few hundreds of their lazy slaves, and establish them in a fortified place, whereupon the natives would immediately gather round them and change this fine country...from an impenetrable jungle into rich fields, producing not only grain but also immense quantities of cotton and indigo.[32]

[31] Bovill, *Missions*, III, 178; quoted in Brenner, 1973, 46.
[32] Barth, 1965, I, 577. Slave soldiers could inflict devastation, as well as protecting against it : Barth in 1851 found Uba, the northernmost Fulani town in Adamawa, restricted in size after being plundered by Ramadan, a

Nachtigal, when he came to Borno some twenty years later, found much the same situation. There was, he reported, little effort to maintain a centralized armed force, and for his military expeditions the Shaykh for the most part depended on the contingents, mounted or on foot, which his leading dignitaries were prepared to equip. Nachtigal had the opportunity to observe such arrangements as these from his first arrival in Borno, when the caravan with which he was travelling was given a ceremonial military welcome.

> The main cavalry strength of the country is in these armoured horsemen, who carry as weapons a lance and usually a short, broad sword, and every dignitary seeks to equip as many as possible of his mounted slaves with this quilted armour....There were also slaves on foot, armed with spears and throwing-irons.[33]

Nachtigal laid it down a general rule that every courtier and official making any sort of claim to importance and prestige with the prince and the people, even when his position has no particularly military character,[34] would maintain armed men who were at the almost immediate disposal of the ruler. Even the chief *qadi*, for example, kept 100 cavalry.[35] But the list of semi-private military forces which Nachtigal gives does not quite justify this sweeping statement. Twenty-nine dignitaries are listed as maintaining some mounted soldiers, but of these seven were sons of Shaykh Umar, and another four were brothers, while three other brothers do not appear. And of fourteen representative courtiers listed earlier by Nachtigal, only six appear in the military list.[36]

Nachtigal includes this passage in describing his first visit to Lamino, foremost dignitary of Borno.

---

slave and officer of al-Kanemi (1965, II, 128).

[33] II, 119. This armour, padded or quilted, encased both man and beast. Nachtigal was told that, wherever possible, 'every man who is armed in this way must, when he goes into battle, have at his side a footsoldier, who, in case the horse falls or is killed, seeks to free him as speedily as possible from the constricting covering.'

[34] II, 263.

[35] II, 139-40 and note; II, 264.

[36] II, 263-4 and notes; II, 244.

Here in groups upon the ground sat Arab chiefs and the better dressed higher ranking slaves, who were described to me as the chief military men of the master of the house. Lamino maintained a regular mounted force of about 1,000 men, of whom at least 300 were armoured horsemen, and a bodyguard of forty to fifty mounted men.[37]

Nachtigal's arrival with Abu Sekkin, ruler in temporary exile of Bargirmi, provided a similar display, though on a much smaller scale, as greeted Nachtigal in Borno.

At the side of and behind Abu Sekkin were ranged his horsemen and footsoldiers, nearly all slaves, of the former about fifty, equipped with more or less complete quilted armour for themselves and their horses, and some hundreds of the latter, the lesser part armed with muskets, the greater with throwing-irons, lances and spears, and here and there with shields.

The chief military commander had some thirty horsemen and eighty footmen, other dignitaries with smaller contingents.[38]

Although it seems that none of these forces was made up exclusively of slaves, the military structure of Borno, Bagirmi and other states[39] did ensure a considerable permanent domestic demand for slaves, though it need not of course be assumed that all these men spent their working hours exclusively in martial manoeuvres.[40]

There are a few passing references to the garrison in Murzuq, in the Fezzan. In 1865, Rohlfs estimated this at about 500 infantry, mostly Fezzaners and some slaves pressed into service, and a few mounted men.[41] Nachtigal, a little later, mentions the garrison, nominally 500 Turks, actually 300 Fezzaners,

---

[37] II, 135; the 1,000 men were under fifteen captains (p. 263).

[38] III, 322. See picture on p. 51 above.

[39] Of Wadai, Nachtigal says, 'of soldiers in our sense of the word there are none', with the whole population aged from eighteen to sixty able to go to war. But at the same time he speaks of musketeers (including slaves), armoured cavalry, and so on, in very much the same terms as applied to other states (IV, 183-4).

[40] The guardian (not, however, described as a slave) of Shaykh Umar's rickety cannon could not live on his artillery commission, and combined with it a merchant's business (II, 283).

[41] Cited in I, 83 note; Rohlfs, 1874-5, I, 163-4.

but he does not mention slaves in this connection.[42] By 1896, the garrison was down to some 150 or 200 men, most of them, it was then reported, former slaves and very old, receiving no salary but a daily bread ration.[43]

Turning to the western Sudan, in Masina, which perhaps of all the theocracies kept closest to an orthodox model, Shehu Ahmadu, the head of state, kept few captives. Those that came to him, for instance as booty, he freed, often giving them posts which bound them to the community and made them sure auxiliaries. Captives who took part in the first battle, in 1818, which led ultimately to the establishment of the theocracy, were freed; Shehu Ahmadu bought and emancipated any whose masters would not release them in charity.[44] Celebrating the deeds of a slave warrior in the forces of Hadeija, a Fulani emirate in rebellion against Sokoto in the mid-nineteenth century, tradition states that the blood of his foes cemented his hand to his spear, so that after the battle it could only be freed with oil and hot water.[45] Some of the earliest followers of al-Hajj Umar, who launched a *jihad* against the Bambara in 1850, were slaves, whom he instructed in Islam and to whom he entrusted some of his most important military commands; it is likely that these men were freed.[46]

An example from the Sokoto empire indicates that not all the slaves engaged in military activities were men. Clapperton said of Bello's attack on the Gobir capital in 1826 (see p. 292), that the most useful person there, as well as being as brave as any, was an old female slave who had nursed five former governors of Zamfara, and who rode astride a scruffy horse giving water to the wounded and thirsty.[47] The sultan of Bagirmi possessed a large number of female slaves who accompanied him everywhere, even into battle, it being their duty there 'to taunt cowards to an assumption of courage'.[48]

[42] I, 166.
[43] Mohammed Ben Otsmane el-Hachaichi, *Voyage au pays des Senoussia*, 1903, 165; cit. II, 20.
[44] Ba and Daget, 1962, I, 40.
[45] East, 1934/1967, 79.
[46] H.M. Delafosse, *Haut-Sénégal-Niger*, Paris 1912/1972, II, 306.
[47] Clapperton, 1829, 188. See over, p. 250
[48] MacLeod, 1912, 169.

Special regulations sometimes applied to the weapons which slave soldiers might use. These regulations might be restrictive: among the Tuareg, the servile classes were not allowed to wear a sword, nor to carry an iron spear, these being distinctions of a free man;[49] but slaves did carry some sort of weapon, and in the old days, when cattle-raiding and warfare formed part of the Tuareg way of life, they often accompanied their masters on raids.[50] In other cases, however, slaves were encouraged in the exclusive use of certain weapons. We do not know if Alooma's Turks, mentioned at the head of this section were slaves, but clearly some, if not all, of the soldiers who carried the newly acquired firearms were. Clapperton, observing Sultan Bello's unsuccessful attack on the Hausa capital of Gobir in 1826, noticed that all the forty-one muskets were handled by slaves, not one by a Fulani.[51] Such arrangements may reflect the desire of the ruler to keep these weapons strictly under his own control; the king of Ethiopia did not like to let the guns of his matchlockmen out of his sight.[52] Perhaps also the old aristocracy found the new weapons undignified and unworthy. A parallel instance, though not involving firearms, appears among a branch of the Danakil, in the area of modern French Somaliland. They deemed unlawful in their own persons the use of the bow, and maintained some 100 Somali archers; these were originally prisoners of war, who, though naturalized among their captors, retained their own language and never intermarried with the Danakil.[53] Slaves themselves were not always exempt from a similar conservatism, as the inability of the Egyptian Mamluk dynasty to adjust to firearms, in attempting to resist the rise of the Ottomans, indicates.[54] Distinct foreign groups serving special-

---

[49] Barth, 1965, I, 204.

[50] Nicolaisen, 1997, II, 603.

[51] Clapperton, 1829, 186. See just above, p. 249.

[52] Harris, 1844/1968, I, 382-3; II, 58, describes the general of the gunmen, riding a gaily caparisoned mule, richly attired, followed by fifty attendants —'but he too is a slave, as was his father before him and as his son will be after him'.

[53] *ibid.*, I, 231.

[54] D. Ayalon, *Gunpowder and firearms in the Mamluk kingdom*, London 1956/1978, 47.

ized military functions and sometimes carrying particular weapons, were of course not necessarily slaves. In Ashanti, for example, a royal bodyguard of Hausa, hired by the king, used the Snider rifles in the royal armoury.[55]

One common specialised use of slave soldiers was as raiders for slaves. Nachtigal's 'slave raids' chapter included at the end of this volume begins with 'the Bagirmi people and their slaves' setting out on the hunt.[56] Such employment was of considerable antiquity in the area; Alooma used slaves in slave-raiding, and sometimes to massacre prisoners, in the late sixteenth century.[57] In East Africa slaves, or ex-slaves, were often their masters' most effective agents in slaving.[58] The few cases of deliberate cruelty to slaves which Cameron observed were perpetrated not by Arabs but by owners who were themselves slaves or had recently been freed.[59] On the other hand, there are occasional instances of ex-slaves being used in anti-slavery operations. In 1832 the Liberian authorities in Monrovia mounted a column against a Muslim potentate, called the Sultan of Brumley, on the St Paul's river. He had started raiding when the Monrovians refused to send back some of his slaves who had escaped to Monrovia (see also p. 317 below). The Liberian force was accompanied by 120 freed slaves, serving as scouts.[60]

The prospect of acquiring slaves was also sometimes a sort of pay supplement scheme for soldiers on active service, an African army equivalent to the prize money of western navies. Al-Kanemi rewarded his followers with the slave produce of

[55] A. B. Ellis, *The land of fetish*, London 1883, 188-91, 215; also 202.
[56] III, 341. *Slavery* 1970, 135, citing this reference and also pp..344-5, claims that on these raids slaves, with no less zest than their masters, helped to tear to pieces the bodies of the victims. In fact, except for the general reference to 'the Bagirmi and their slaves' just above, slave actors (apart from one slave carrying an emblem to inspire the troops) are not mentioned in these passages, where the most savage brutalities are attributed not to the Bagirmi, but to 'their heathen allies', who were probably not slaves at all. See also below, pp. 353-4.
[57] Ibn Fartua, 1928/1967, 22-3, 28; 1987, 54, 63.
[58] Speke, 1864, 210-12.
[59] Cameron, 1885, 256.
[60] Johnston, 1906, I, 151-2.

Borno's wars.[61] The Arabs fighting Mirambo, in East Africa, gave a slave and a concubine to anyone bringing in the trophy of a fallen foe.[62]

Such largesse, and this was indeed true of all booty, required some regulation. Such regulation touched upon slaves in three major respects. First, who might properly be enslaved as part of the booty, and who, despite having been defeated and captured, should still be protected by his or her Muslim faith against enslavement; this is a major issue, discussed extensively in the Introduction to this volume, and we shall not spend more time on it here. Second, how should booty in slaves be divided? And third, should such division be adjusted according to whether the captor was slave or free?

Such matters were discussed by Muslim scholars in sub-Saharan Africa. Usuman dan Fodio spells out some of the detail in a fascinatingly complex chapter, 'Oh how the booty should be divided'. Usuman's son, Bello, sultan of Sokoto, once attempted to apply the proper legal division of booty, but after three expeditions his troops went on strike, refusing to fight for another man's booty and Bello reverted to the old practice whereby each man took what he could lay his hands on. Even at the height of his reforms, Bello had not gone so far as actually to stockpile women and children captured by individual soldiers for later redistribution, but merely included them in his calculations of the total value of the booty.[63] As a contrary example, a poem of Futa Jallon describing a raid by the *almami* about 1863, in conjunction with the clerics of Touba, one of the main Islamic religious centres of that area, mentions 12,000 captives who were assembled and then distributed, each participant in the campaign receiving his share.[64]

Often there were local rules, bearing little or no relationship to recognised Muslim models; it may even be that there were different rules for different groups of subordinate raiders within a given state, e.g. the Shuwa Arabs in Borno:

[61] Bovill, *Missions*, II, xxx.
[62] Cameron, 1885, 111-12.
[63] Haj Said, *Histoire du Sokoto*, attached to *Tedzkiret en-Nisian*, 306-7.
[64] Alfâ Ibrâhîm Sow, *La femme, la foi. Écrivains et poètes du Foûta-Djalon*, Paris 1966, 231-3.

For military enterprises, all Shuwa tribes have to render military service, and each man is entitled to half his booty if it consists of slaves, horses or cattle, and to the whole if it is a question of inanimate objects (clothing, ornaments, etc.); only the captured weapons fall exclusively to the government.[65]

Amongst the Bagirmi and their allied raiders, at the battle of Koli, each attacker 'sought to seize, on his own account, people or domestic animals, half the former and all the latter belonging to the man who made the capture'.[66]

Nachtigal did not explain how this 50% rule was interpreted when, as presumably often happened, a warrior captured an odd number of the enemy, three, or perhaps only one. Among the Hausa, whose raid into Gwari country initiated the adventurous story of the hero of Sir Abubakar Tafawa Balewa's novel, *Shaihu Umar*, the rule was that 'if a man were to capture three slaves, the Chief would take two of them, and he would be allowed to keep one'.[67] A sad decline from the days of Usuman's ideal theorising, and Bello's ill-fated attempts at practical reform.

The third instance of intersection between booty and slavery—that is, should the division of the spoils distinguish between slave and free recipients—is discussed in Shehu Usuman's chapter 'On how the booty should be divided':

As for the unbeliever....if he fights, there are three different opinions; [one allows it, another denies it and] the third draws a distinction between whether the Muslims were in need of his help or not; if they were, he is to be given a share, if they were not, then he is not to be given anything. The slave is to be treated like an unbeliever.[68]

The passage is interesting, reminding us of the flexibility inherent in the choice amongst divergent legal opinions, even within the context of utmost obedience to the letter of the law. And unsatisfactory, inasmuch as it makes no reference to the rights of the slave-owner: the slave was not a free agent.

[65] III, 178.
[66] III, 355.
[67] *Shaihu Umar*, 22; see also p. 366 below.
[68] Usuman dan Fodio, 1978, 108, editor's brackets.

The principal practical instance of controversy over slave and free shares occurred in the *jihad* of al-Hajj Umar. In the 1860s his men had marched to the attack, confident of either conquering slave-women here (men prisoners were regularly killed), or winning the large-eyed girls of paradise,[69] a comforting no-lose prospect. But in al-Hajj Umar's army itself there was discontent with the rules for booty distribution: free Muslim soldiers were required to surrender the canonical one-fifth of their captured slaves and goods; slave warriors, or *sofa*'s, had to give up one half; while the *tuburu*, those who had been forced to convert and follow al-Hajj Umar, received nothing by right, but only by somewhat arbitrary grant.[70]

Slave soldiers also formed a special category in foreign trade, with black soldiers—or untrained slaves specifically intended to become soldiers—being exported from sub-Saharan Africa, and with European and Asian slave soldiers being brought in. Al-Umari, in first half of the fourteenth century, mentions black slave soldiers in North Africa,[71] and such troops were significant in Egypt. Slaves from East Africa were important in India, especially as soldiers, in the fourteenth or fifteenth centuries.[72] Ahmad Graan, Muslim scourge of Ethiopia in the sixteenth century, sent Ethiopian slaves to the Turks in Arabia and received a large body of Janissaries in return.[73]

Idris Alooma of Borno, in the same century, also had Turkish help, as recorded in the chronicle at the beginning of this section. That translation is the most recent, published in 1987, by Lange. A much earlier rendering, by Palmer, in 1926, is quoted in *Slavery* 1970, p. 130. Palmer attributes the acquisition of the Turkish musketeers to Alooma himself, while Lange (38, note 40) argues that it is more likely Alooma inherited the Turks from one of his predecessors. I imagine that there must have been new recruits and replacements from time to time, to keep numbers up. The other musketeers,

[69] Mohammadou Aliou Tyam, *La vie d'El Hadj Omar*, tr. H. Gaden, Paris 1935, 95-6, 132-3.
[70] Willis, 1970, 152-4; 1989, 130.
[71] Ibn Fadl Allah al-Omari, *Masalik el Absar*, I: *L'Afrique, moins l'Égypte*, Paris 1927, 114-15, 131, 147.
[72] Mathew, in Oliver and Mathew, 1963, 121 and note.
[73] Harris, 1844/1968, II, 236.

explicitly slaves, whom Lange describes as 'of foreign origin', Palmer calls 'domestic'. The Arabic (p. 6 of Lange's Arabic text) is *muwalladun*. It is difficult to see see exactly what 'of foreign origin' might mean, applied to slaves within black Africa, but not to the Turks who are clearly a separate category. It may be a technical term, brought into black Africa by the local chronicler, but having no precise applicability there. Palmer's 'domestic' (p. 11) may be closer to the truth.

In the seventeenth century the pasha of Tripoli sent fifty young Europeans to Borno in an exchange which included, among other things, 200 horses and some muskets from Tripoli, and 100 young men and 100 girls from Borno. The succeeding *mai* of Borno, in view of the satisfactory performance of these Europeans, sent to ask for some more, accompanying his request with 200 young slaves and several eunuchs. He received the solicited Christians, and fifty horses too.[74]

Several features of the preceding discussion carried over into the period of European colonialism. Abd er-Rahman, king of Darfur at that time, thought it prudent to send Napoleon Bonaparte a congratulatory address after his invasion of Egypt. In June 1799 Napoleon acknowledged this address, and asked Abd er-Rahman to send with the next caravan 2,000 black slaves, over sixteen years old, strong and vigorous. 'I shall buy them all,' he assured the Darfurian ruler, 'on my own account.' Another letter, twelve days later, repeated the request. Heavy casualties in the Syrian campaign explain Napoleon's anxiety.[75]

Again, the native battalions of the Italians in Eritrea contained many Galla, mostly freed slaves. Freed Galla slaves fought too in the Italian forces in Libya against the Arabo-Turks.[76] And, in muted form, the same tradition crossed the Atlantic; in Brazil in the 1860s, for example, some citizens, confronted with the possibility of being drafted for military service, the country then being at war with its southern neighbours, sent instead slaves who had been specially liberated for this purpose.[77]

[74] De la Roncière, 1919, 79, 83-4.
[75] IV, 296, note 2, citing J. Christopher Herold, *Bonaparte in Egypt*, London 1963, 212.
[76] Cerulli, 1922, 14.
[77] Verger, 1976, 456.

Finally, even in the sphere of booty it is sometimes a delicate task now to distinguish between local practice and that followed by some European colonialists. For example, after a battle in 1887 in which the French defeated the army of Momodu Lamine, the Soninke leader on the upper Senegal, seventeen women of Momodu Lamine fell into French hands. The French commander, Galliéni, asked them, through his interpreter, if they would like to marry instead some of his African *tirailleurs*. Their answer is not recorded. Galliéni, assuming that they would not mind—*que leur importait de changer d'esclavage?*—distributed them to the seventeen men who had most distinguished themselves in the battle just finished, giving each his choice in descending order of valour.[78]

Royal and other government slaves

'My slave asked me for the donkey road, for which he gave me a striped upper garment, a gown, a donkey and 37s[hillings]. The agreement was that the people of Madagali should take their donkeys at an appointed place and pay to him only.' (Hamman Yaji, 119, 17 November 1925)

At least in the larger political units visited by Nachtigal—Borno, Logon, Bagirmi, Wadai and Darfur—the heads of state deployed huge slave establishments, both household and military. No clear distinction was made between slaves who were the ruler's personal property and 'slaves of the state'. We have seen some figures, not precisely verifiable but assuredly indicative, of large slave followings in the chapter on the size of the slave population. In 1866, shortly before Nachtigal's visit, Rohlfs, visiting Borno himself, estimated the number of the ruler's personal slaves at around 4,000.[79]

The vast majority of these royal, and other government, slaves performed routine, often menial tasks, just as did the slaves of lesser owners, though royalty may have done things on a grander scale. Here is Nachtigal's description of the stables of Loël, an eighteenth-century king of Bagirmi,

---

[78] Lieut.-Col. Galliéni, *Deux campagnes au Soudan français, 1886-1888*, Paris 1891, 120-2. M. A. Klein, 1968, 167, mentions another case, which became notorious when one soldier so rewarded later offered his bride for sale.

[79] 1874-5, II, 3, cited in II, 248, note 1.

passionately devoted to good horses, for one of which he would, it is said, pay up to 1,000 cattle.

In the interior of the extensive royal dwelling, he is said to have made room for five hundred horses, each of which had, in addition to its rider, three slaves to wait upon it (that is, for feeding, for watering and for cleaning), and on the royal square (*fâsher*) he installed a bodyguard of a thousand slaves. These round numbers are, of course, not to be taken literally; in those countries they have become general terms for a large number, but they have all the same some relative significance.[80]

At the other end of the size spectrum, but still within the royal sphere, are a variety of minor tasks, requiring only a handful of slaves. Shaykh Umar of Borno needed slaves, for example, to look after the collection of wild animals kept in some huts near the west gate of his palace.[81] And there are many references, scattered throughout *Sahara and Sudan*, to slaves and free courtiers lounging about at court, or, particularly the slaves, busy fanning the king their master with giraffe tails, or performing other luxury-style duties.[82] Such ostentatious display through slaves, and the hidden agenda symbolised by such performance, can be discerned as early as the middle of the fourteenth century, when Ibn Battuta was in Mali. The king's wife had fallen into disfavour for her excessive pretensions; one sign of her ostentation was to ride each day with male and female slaves, with dust on their heads, in attendance. Finally one of her female slaves informed against her, and the unruly queen sought sanctuary in the house of the *khatib* or preacher.[83] The ubiquity of such slaves at the heart of government led Nachtigal into a case of mistaken identity. On arrival at the court of Abu Sekkin, fugitive king of Bagirmi, he was sent to lodge with the Fastsha Alifa, the highest dignitary of the king. Finding

> that no preparation of any kind had been made for my accommodation, I complained loudly, and demanded of a

[80] III, 408.
[81] II, 172.
[82] For example, III, 253, 316-17 and note 1; IV, 46, 262, 265, 317.
[83] *Corpus*, 294-5; Ibn Battuta, 44-5.

man whom I took to be a slave, who was resting comfortably on the dry straw under the roofed shelter of the *fatsha's* horses, that he summon the master of the house. He listened to my expressions of displeasure very tranquilly without changing his position, and then introduced himself as Fatsha Alifa.[84]

The widespread use of royal umbrellas, with their slave bearers, has already been mentioned under the heading of luxury slaves (see above, p. 233). Perhaps that is too dismissive, for the umbrellas may better be regarded as a symbol or signal of centralised political power. Another example of such ritual demonstration, observed by Nachtigal, was at a military parade, attended by Abu Sekkin, king of Bagirmi, mounted, with on either side a slave carrying, with difficulty, on a long pole an immense scarlet silk sunshade fringed with green silk.[85] The symbolism of the umbrella was exploited in a practical way during civil strife in Wadai, when the ruler Abd el-Aziz, in battle against rebels,

> made use of the stratagem of having umbrellas, one red and the other blue, carried by his slaves without himself making any use of them. When the insurgents supposed him to be under the blue umbrella, they directed all their efforts towards this point, and thus diminished their strength elsewhere.[86]

Slaves also had an important part to play in the distribution of royal gifts. Nachtigal, who often received these himself, particularly in Borno, had considerable personal experience of the varying facets of the system. Even before actually entering Kuka, the capital of Borno, on his first arrival there, when the caravan with which he was travelling paused outside the city the day before, he first encountered slave gift-bearers.

> In the evening a long train of slaves appeared from the Shaykh's household bearing the customary meal, some 50 or 60 dishes, of which ten were set down before my tent, while Bu Aïsha [the caravan leader] distributed the remainder....Like hungry beasts of prey, the bearers awaited

---

[84] III, 314. Unusually, Alifa was a free man; see p. 275 below.
[85] III, 321.
[86] IV, 218; I do not know whether the colours also made some significant symbolic statement.

the moment when our hunger would be appeased—and we could not polish off the third part of the sumptuous meal—in order to throw themselves upon what was left over; for, in accordance with custom, this, instead of the otherwise customary gratuity, is their right when their master's first guest meal is delivered.[87]

After entry, royal food was supplied for several days. On the first evening, three slaves (two of them eunuchs) presented Nachtigal with a supper of ten dishes, with rice, wheat and *dukhn* grain by the hundredweight, containers of butter and honey, and finally 'two uncommonly fine fat rams'.

> The enjoyment of the Shaykh's liberality was, to be sure, burdened with considerable expense, for Bornu is the promised land of speculators in gratuities. This practice, or malpractice, has become so obligatory that the head eunuchs and other slaves have regular schedules, which it is impossible to avoid, for foreigners and for natives. In this connection I could rely completely on the experience and expertise of the old Qatruner [Nachtigal's foremost servant and companion], but despite his parsimoniousness I had to give to the first eunuch four Maria Theresa dollars, to the second three, and to the third slave two.

These tips were for the supervisors only; the actual carriers were much more easily satisfied with hand-mirrors, the cheapest cloth, and 'the incredibly cheap Steiermark razors with which the Sudan countries are inundated'. The gratuities rate tapered off. On the second day, a eunuch bringing Nachtigal two garments received only two dollars. Payment for the third day's services

> could, in accordance with custom, be still further abated, except those for the horse [delivered after midnight, to avoid the evil eye], which amounted to twelve Maria Theresa dollars for one of the highest ranking eunuchs, Abd el-Kerim, the treasurer, *mâla* [see below, pp. 288-91], who appeared in person, and two for the groom who had conducted the animal.[88]

That so great a man as the *mala* appeared on such an occasion

[87] II, 114.
[88] II, 142-4.

is a measure of its importance, and that not only for the *mala*'s own purse.

Nachtigal's experience in Wadai differed from that in Borno in two respects. First, while the royal hospitality, though less than that of Shaykh Umar, was quite adequate for Nachtigal, comprising foodstuffs, sheep, the local cloth currency,[89] yet there was never a prepared meal for the German visitor, despite the fact that it was part of Sultan Ali's daily routine to decide in the late afternoon to which guests or magnates meals should be sent, even fixing the number of dishes, not infrequently one or even two thousand, all delivered by slaves.[90] The second difference concerned tipping.

> In this connection I could again observe the stringent control which the king exercised over his subjects. The eunuch who brought his hospitable gifts steadfastly refused to accept the gratuities offered to him, not because he thought them inadequate, but because his master had forbidden it. The king could not endure that his generosity to foreigners should be made a source of profit for his servants. What a difference between King Ali's officials and those of Shaykh Umar and of the king of Darfur, who could discuss for hours whether the gratuities offered to them corresponded to their dignity and to the value of the presents conveyed by them![91]

During Ramadan in Borno, the pattern of royal hospitality changed somewhat, placing an even greater strain upon the resources of the ruler,

> for not only does he supply his guests before the fast begins with stocks of wheat, rice, butter, honey and cattle, but in accordance with an old custom, he sends daily an evening meal to every foreigner in the town who has paid his respects to him or has been introduced at court. A list is drawn up beforehand of all who are entitled to this, and every evening an official rides through the streets of the town on horseback, at the head of more than 100 slaves

---

[89] IV, 55.

[90] IV, 176. How profound is the symbolism of the meal unshared. Just what message, however, the king, otherwise so amiable and supportive to Nachtigal, was sending by this exclusion, I do not know.

[91] IV, 55.

carrying the dishes on their heads for distribution according to the rank and social importance of the foreigners and the degree of favour which they enjoy with the Shaykh.[92]

In the capital of Mali, in the mid-fourteenth century, a somewhat more balanced arrangement was in place. The custom was for the commanders to break their fast each day in the sultan's house, each having his food brought in by twenty or more of his own slave-girls. Only on the most sacred night of the 27th did Ibn Battuta, visiting Mali at that time, see about 100 slave-girls, plus two of the king's daughters, carrying food out of the palace. Ibn Battuta, however, makes no comment on this export/import balance: he was utterly scandalised by the fact that all these womenfolk, even the two princesses, went stark naked.[93]

The slave as the bearer of royal gifts is very well documented in *Sahara and Sudan*, because Nachtigal was so often and so directly personally involved. However, the slave as royal messenger had a wider role: the Sokoto ruler sent orders to fief-holders by eunuchs or throne slaves.[94] One of Sultan Bello's messengers was an old female slave, herself owning nearly forty men and women slaves; she was, Clapperton observed, 'a shrewd old woman, of strong natural sense'.[95]

The clearest single instance, in Nachtigal's account, of the royal slave messenger is provided by the *tuweïrat*, literally 'birds', royal pages at the court of Wadai. Nachtigal does not explicitly say that all the *tuweïrat* were slaves, but that is certainly his implication. He calls them 'the king's personal servants', and refers to the *tuweïrat* 'and other slaves'.[96] They had their own overseer, the *aqid gerri*, a very senior figure amongst the sultan's domestic household officials. Nachtigal attended the truly sumptuous wedding of the *aqid gerri* to a daughter of the king.[97]

[92] II, 279; this was 1870; IV, 11 gives a very similar description for 1872.

[93] Ibn Battuta, 48. The usually impeccable *Corpus* (296-7), like Homer, nods, giving the 25th, and about 200 slave-girls (unless the Arabic text of Defremery and Sanguinetti, IV, 424, is itself mistaken).

[94] M. G. Smith, 1964 A, 177.

[95] Clapperton, 1829, 249.

[96] IV, 46.

[97] IV, 85.

He has the king's books and documents in his care, and is his chief messenger, but, as overseer of the *tuweïrat*, he usually makes use of them, and this is probably the origin of their name, Birds. The *ayâl el-qedâba*, i.e. those used for important messages, form one section out of about 500 'Birds'. They are slaves, boys from twelve to sixteen, about twenty in number; from them the *aqîds* and other high officials are frequently appointed, and they are used especially by the sultan on important commissions. Anyone who is summoned directly to the sultan by one of the *ayâl el-qedâba* recognises immediately the significance of the order from the demeanour of the messenger. If the messenger crouches submissively at a distance with a friendly greeting, a favour may be expected, but if the boy approaches him aggressively, and in summoning him to the royal citadel, actually touches him, the man has every reason to be concerned for his head.[98]

The *aqid gerri* also led the *tuweïrat* in war.[99] Nachtigal was summoned for his first audience with King Ali by one of these pages, 'who, kneeling down and gently clapping his hands, addressed to me the words, "The king, our master, calls for you".'[100] Abeshr, capital of Wadai, was a rough town, not at all a place in which the visitor might choose to wander alone. However, even the smallest of the king's *tuweïrat*

> was as effective as the most numerous armed company in assuring complete safety for foreigners, and the vigorous prince had succeeded in the heart of the country in creating among the raw inhabitants at least so much fear that any one who was accompanied by one of the *tuweïrât* would have been able to travel throughout the region with tolerable safety.[101]

The slave as messenger is an interesting social concept. He is in a sense an extension of the king's presence, the long arm of the ruler, whether benign, coming at midnight, to present the drowsy and bemused recipient with a fine horse, or at midday, a page seizing one's arm as prelude to some ghastly

---

[98] IV, 177-8. The Arabic phrase, *ayal el-qedaba*, means literally, and appropriately, 'the family of striking' (see p. 404).

[99] IV, 184.

[100] IV, 47; but see also p. 45.

[101] IV, 50.

ROYAL AND OTHER GOVERNMENT SLAVES   263

royal punishment. But at the same time the slave messenger acts as a kind of *cordon sanitaire*, interposed between the ruler and the recipients of his messages.

Individual slaves might also rise to some of the very highest positions in national government. The earliest instance of this which Nachtigal mentions concerns Ahmed Bokkor (or Bukr), king of Darfur probably early in the eighteenth century, who was the first in Darfur to bestow the title of vizier upon a slave.[102] One of the last slave viziers in Africa was also in Darfur, the foremost official in the kingdom under Sultan Ali Dinar— he had begun his career long before as Ali Dinar's slave boy, and he fell in 1916, in the final battle in which independent Darfur was overwhelmed.[103] In Nachtigal's Borno, most court officials were slaves.[104] Some court offices, however, were always held by free men, and why different offices were treated in different ways Nachtigal does not explain.[105] At least some slave officials owned their own slaves.

> We find, accordingly, the most important court offices in Bornu in the hands of slaves, while posts which are remote from the seat of government are in the hands of the princes, and indeed overwhelmingly in the hands of the sons of princesses...who could scarcely ever become dangerous.[106]

Similar arguments applied elsewhere.

> The slave element, of course, played the same important role in Darfur as in the other Sudan countries. A ruler there will usually be careful not unnecessarily to make an enemy of a distinguished free man, but as a rule his real confidants are slaves, whose prosperity depends on his, and who on his death can be thrown into the insignificance of ordinary slave life.[107]

Most important, in Nachtigal's opinion, for the ruler of

---

[102] IV, 330; for the date, see also O'Fahey and Spaulding, 126 and 206 note 4.

[103] Theobald, 1965, 212.

[104] II, 247. But most non-military members of the *nokena*, or State Council, were free (II, 117).

[105] II, 248-56.

[106] II, 248.

[107] IV, 333.

Borno, than most of the (mostly slave) court officials, and most of the (mostly free) Councillors, or *kokenawa*, were the military chiefs, *kashellawa*. These men, nearly all slaves of the head of state, commanded forces always prepared, the nearest thing to a standing army which Borno knew.[108] Nachtigal listed the names of 30 *kashellawa*.[109] Though called slaves, at least two were described as chiefs of Kanuri tribes,[110] two others had succeeded to their fathers' positions, and they were allowed a great deal of latitude in determining the size of the military contingents which they would recruit. Nachtigal believed that on the whole the strength of the forces under their control had diminished; by 1870 the detachments commanded by one or two had fallen to an almost derisory figure, and the total number of soldiers under the *kashellawa* was less than the total maintained by non-military dignitaries (see p. 247). The military commanders in Logon similarly had been originally slaves.[111] Historically the highest military commander of Borno, the *kaigamma*, was always of slave origin.[112] By Nachtigal's time this title was slipping out of use, though some old-fashioned people still applied it to Kashella Bilal. Nachtigal described Bilal as the most outstanding among the *kashellawa*,

> an old man stricken in years who had the reputation of being the most energetic and courageous warrior in the country, and for half a century had enjoyed the highest esteem. He was the chief of the Kanembu tribe of the Sugurti, and ruler of a large part of southeastern Bornu.... Nearly as important as Bilal was Kashella Abdullahi Marghimi, chief of the Kanembu Kuburi, who from Gujeba guarded the frontier in the southwest of country. To a certain extent he shared the power of the former *kaigamma* with Bilal, to whom, however, the title of that office had passed. Both of them had a seat in the *nôkena*, and accompanied the royal processions, one on the sovereign's right hand, and the other on his left.[113]

[108] II, 117, 247-8, 259-63.
[109] II, 262-3.
[110] II, 259.
[111] III, 265.
[112] II, 249; III, 483.
[113] II, 259.

It is a little difficult to reconcile these men with any standard picture of slaves, still less of slaves who were on the one hand contributing to the ruler's despotic power, while on the other they lived under the daily threat of the ruler's disfavour. That they were slaves is I believe Nachtigal's clear implication, and Barth explicitly includes Bilal (and an Abullahi) in a list of royal slaves.[114]

Of course, the fortunes of an individual slave might rise or fall. Nachtigal's account of the origins of the Dalatoa tribe in western Kanem illustrates the possible preference for slave officers. After the seat of government moved from Kanem to Borno, about 1400, the Tunjur Arabs were made guardians of Borno's eastern flank. Later, when they adopted 'a disagreeably independent attitude',

> the Bornu government became suspicious, and confided the post to...Dala, a Hausa slave who had achieved honour and dignity, and who was invested with power sufficient to inspire the Tunjer with respect. The Kanem government has ever since remained in the hands of the descendants of this governor,

from whom the Dalatoa take their name.[115] The Dalatoa, although thus actually of ignoble descent, were in Nachtigal's time well regarded nonetheless.[116]

For a decline, a Fulani slave, Ibrahim, with the title *digma*, provides an interesting example.

> In the old days the *digma*...had been far from enjoying the fullness of power with which...Ibrahim was invested at the time of the German travellers, Barth and Rohlfs [shortly before Nachtigal]. I in turn saw this same *digma* completely stripped of his authority, in the midst of slaves who used in front of his to throw the dust of the streets upon their heads, sitting outside by the door of the great reception chamber within which he had in earlier times had one of the first places. He was still always called *digma*, he still retained some functions originally characteristic of that office, nonetheless his authority was gone. That he owed the outstanding importance, with which Gerhard Rohlfs formerly saw

[114] 1965, II, 638.
[115] III, 9 and note 1.
[116] III, 73.

him invested and which Rohlfs attributed to his office, only to his personal qualities, is evident from the fact that his successor, Hajj Bezzem, though very well regarded by the Shaykh, had attained to nothing like the same powerful position.[117]

The key words appear to be 'personal qualities': for some, at least, being a slave was a career open to talents.

Bezzem, or Bazam, though he may not have matched Ibrahim in the latter's heyday, did have an extraordinarily interesting relationship with his master. He had been, during Shaykh Umar's early years, his closest companion among the royal slaves who had been captured on a Borno expedition on the western frontier. He is said to have deputised for Umar on pilgrimage to Mecca. After the ceremonies there, Bezzem reportedly wrapped up his right hand, unwrapping it again only to greet Umar and thus to convey to him directly the blessings of his contact with the holy places.[118] After his return, Hajj Bezzem was freed, and continued to serve his master as personal chamberlain.[119]

Slaves might care even for dead kings. In Darfur, in Nachtigal's time, almost all the Muslim kings were buried at Torra, where more than a hundred slaves lived, guarding the tombs. Each year, before the annual great drum festival, a specified number of cattle were taken to Torra, for sacrifice as *sadaqah*.

> The slaves of the dead kings had to slaughter an appointed number of cattle for each of them, to eat as much as possible of the flesh in honour of and as a memorial to their masters, and to distribute the rest among those who lived around, while the Quran was read several times by *faqihs* so that the dead might rest in peace.[120]

Slaves seem often to have been associated in one way or another with death. At the drum festival just mentioned, the princes and princesses of Darfur sat down together to a particularly revolting meal.

---

[117] II, 247; Rohlfs, 1874-5, II, 3. Had Nachtigal known earlier of Ibrahim's fall, he would have been less eager to look him up (II, 132-3).
[118] al-Naqar, 1972, 80-1; *cf.* pp. 229-30 above.
[119] Brenner, 1973, 76.
[120] IV, 338.

Armed slaves stood behind them so that no one could withdraw from the duty of eating it. Woe to him who, overcome by nausea, or irritated by the pepper, made any movement that suggested vomiting, or gave way to a fit of coughing; the slaves who were on guard had the duty of killing him, since his behaviour was considered a sign that he did not wish well to the king and his government.

At the time of Nachtigal's visit, this death penalty was apparently no longer so strictly imposed.[121] In Nachtigal's discussion of the (sometimes rather horrible) judicial penalties in Wadai, slaves are mentioned several times amongst the various categories of executioners.[122] Dorugu, the slave boy in the mid-nineteenth century, describes how slaves buried a dead *sharif* (see above, p. 218).[123]

Slave soldiers were often an important element lending strength to the state, and reliance on such soldiers, and on slave officials of all kinds, was a recurrent feature of African governments aiming at centralization and, often, at despotism. An early example is perhaps ancient Mali, where slaves may have played an important part.[124] For Hausaland from about 1350 onwards, M.G. Smith has argued persuasively the importance of the inter-relationship of many factors—among them Islam, slave raiding, slave tribute, slave export, slave settlements, slave officials, eunuchs and concubines—in the development of centralized and sometimes dictatorial governments.[125] The sultan of Kano, about 1500, was threatened by a revolt by one of his chief officials, the *dagachi*; the sultan survived this and subsequently dismissed the *dagachi* and replaced him with a slave.[126]

This general line of argument, linking slavery with centralised government, is clearly strong, but at the same time certain qualifications need to be kept in mind. Let us look at three of

[121] IV, 340-1.
[122] IV, 182-3.
[123] Kirk-Greene and Newman, 56.
[124] C. Monteil, *Les empires du Mali*, Paris 1930, 141; N. Levtzion, 'The thirteenth- and fourteenth-century kings of Mali', *Journal of African History*, 1963, 351; Mauny, 1961, 341, 374.
[125] M. G. Smith, 1964 A, 164-94; 1964 B, 346-52.
[126] *Kano Chronicle*, 112.

these: first, the widely differing characteristics of states incorporating extensive slave infrastructures; second, some of the shortcomings of slaves as a means to effective government; and third, the extent to which slave and free strands can become so intertwined within the state hierarchy that unpicking them is sometimes difficult.

Borno and Wadai were, in the third quarter of the nineteenth century, both powerful, effective states, in which slaves made divers and major contributions. Both were states which Nachtigal had enviable opportunities to observe. And they were very different states, in nature and character. Wadai had many features tending towards despotism and dictatorship (though not random, neither in many cases unjust), such as might be associated with a major slave-owning society. Borno, despite its intimate and far-reaching involvement with slavery, was a much more ramshackle, even bumbling affair. Nachtigal attributed the treading softly approach of the Borno government to that fact that comparatively recently centuries-old dynasty, which free men might still cherish and respect, had been displaced by the family of al-Kanemi, an outsider, though friendly, called in to rescue a weak and despairing monarch from Fulani attack, early in the century.

> The new rulers had obviously taken it to heart that, for the old order of things which recalled overmuch the former dynasty that had ruled Bornu for more than half a millennium, a new order should be substituted, but also, since the old institutions were too firmly rooted to be suddenly overturned, that this should be done gradually; most of the court and government offices therefore survived, though their order of precedence and importance had undergone changes which were often substantial.[127]

Even if Nachtigal's analysis is correct, it shows that slave states, in this case Borno and Wadai, could adopt very different policies. It could be argued, however, that, precisely because a new regime was taking over from a predecessor, a really firm hand was needed, something more on the Wadaian model of King Ali. Indeed, in 1835, a combination of foreign interference against Borno, in collusion with the former,

[127] II, 247.

legitimate (as many citizens might have regarded it) dynasty, did force Shaykh Umar momentarily into a resolute policy of suppression.[128] But Umar quickly reverted to his habitual mildness. Nachtigal respected King Ali of Wadai; I think he loved Shaykh Umar of Borno.[129] Differing individual styles of government, between one leader and another, differing historical heritages, political needs, economic desiderata, anthropological contexts, and many other such variables intervene to modify overarching generalisations about slave states.

The second qualification to the efficacy of the slave state concerns the unreliability of the slaves themselves. As a weapon of strong government, slaves were a delicate instrument. There are many episodes in which the excesses of slaves provoked a popular, or even a divine, reaction. The iniquity of slaves, arousing divine vengeance, was one of the causes assigned for the defeat of Songhay by the Moroccans in 1591, but we are not told exactly in what this iniquity consisted.[130] In Kayor, now part of modern Senegal, the exactions of the *tyeddo*, or royal slave soldiery, finally drove the Muslims of Kayor to revolt, instigated by their *qadi*, at the end of the seventeenth century. On this occasion the rising was successful, and the prince who had converted to Islam took the throne.[131] The Kayor Muslims again revolted a century later; this time the *damel*, or ruler, put them down, and sold them into slavery.[132]

In the mid-eighteenth century the ruler of Darfur was said to have completely alienated free men by the preference which he showed for slaves, showering upon them riches and positions of honour. He was eventually defeated in an expedition against Wadai, when his free subjects, already exasperated by the burdens imposed upon them to facilitate his military preparations, and also resentful of the slight inflicted on them

[128] III, 151-4.
[129] 'Shaykh Umar received me as always with such moving, truly fatherly kindness that I was guilty of no exaggeration when I assured him that I felt as I would if in my home country I had returned to close relations, and he overwhelmed me with evidences of his friendly feelings.' September 1872, returning from Bagirmi to Kuka (III, 451).
[130] Kati, 272.
[131] Cheikh Tidiane Sy, *La confrérie sénégalaise des Mourides*, Paris 1969, 39.
[132] V. Monteil, 'Lat Dyor...et l'Islamisation des Wolofs du Sénégal' in Lewis, 1966, 343.

when slaves were placed in the front line of the battle, free men being relegated to the second place, refused to rally to his support when his slave guards began to waver in the final decisive conflict.[133] In 1760 the Funj dynasty in the eastern Sudan lost the last remnants of its power, having during its decline relied more and more on a slave army.[134]

With a mass of rather intractable detail, Nachtigal traces the story of two early nineteenth-century rulers of Wadai, who met violent death as a result of the real or alleged overdependence of the Wadaian throne upon its slaves.[135]

Nachtigal adds further examples, drawn from his own experience, of the resentment aroused by overbearing royal slaves. We have already mentioned the fraught relations between royal Bargirmian slaves, accompanying Nachtigal, and local villages which the slaves visited—or wished to visit: sometimes the local people were able to fend off the would-be intruders (see above, p. 227). In Borno, anti-Wadai rumours circulated:

> In Wadai itself, the principles of administration followed by the young king [Ali], his preferential treatment of foreigners and slaves, his violation of old custom and his cruel harshness were said to have made him more feared than loved by the Maba tribes.[136]

After Nachtigal's own Wadai visit, summing up his experience there, Nachtigal was very positive; he admitted some popular resentment, directed, however, against foreigners, while slave appointments he saw as much as an attempt to choose the best man for the job, as to engross more power to the ruler.

> With the usual arrogance of their nation, the people of Wadai indeed reproached him [Ali] for showing too much favour to foreigners, and for violating the ancient customs

---

[133] IV, 285-6; A. J. Arkell, *A history of the Sudan from the earliest times to 1821*, London 1961, 221.

[134] Trimingham, 1968, 25.

[135] IV, 216-17; or possibly even three cases—see also IV, 212-13. Another source, Fresnel, attributes one of these deaths to poisoning by a favourite concubine, in a garden (IV, 216 note—see also pages 196 and 219 above in the present volume).

[136] III, 51.

of the country. King Ali in fact often chose his officials contrary to the old practice, not from this or that tribe, or this or that family, but gave an office, which perhaps only a freeborn Maba had previously held, to a slave, if he thought that he would be more competent. This wise prince, however, by the firmness of his government and the justice of his principles of conduct, established such a reputation and a position of such power that any thought of violent discontent was ruled out.[137]

Nevertheless there was clearly abuse of power further down the hierarchical ladder. Poor people in southern Wadai, for example, were frightened of going to the capital, fearing 'above all the extortions of all kinds practised before ever they could get to Abeshr, by men in authority, the slaves of the sultan and other officials'.[138] Later, early in 1874, travelling on from Darfur to Egypt, Nachtigal heard Arabs comparing the treatment of their people in Darfur and Wadai. In the former, they were treated just like other inhabitants, while in Wadai they suffered oppression. A young Mahamid shaykh, himself a refugee from Wadai,

> recalled the numerous encroachments of King Ali's slaves and officials, while at the same time acknowledging King Ali's own integrity; the thing that was finally decisive for him was the abduction one day of his wife, the mother of his children.[139]

In 1873, while Nachtigal was still in Wadai, the king of Darfur, Muhammad el-Hasin, (more correctly al-Husayn) died. He had designated as his successor the youngest of his three sons, Ibrahim. Early reports to coming to Wadai spoke of popular resentment against the dead king, who had 'placed the whole administration in the hands of slaves', and of support for one of his brothers, Hasib Allah, as his successor. 'It was therefore very probable that there would be a conflict between the slaves and soldiers under Ibrahim, the claimant to the throne, and the free Fur under Hasib Allah.'[140]

However, when Nachtigal himself arrived in Darfur, the

[137] IV, 226.
[138] IV, 111.
[139] IV, 248.
[140] IV, 70-1, 74.

chief complaint against the late king seemed to be that he had been too much a trader himself, more mercantile than regal and warlike.[141] A pious Muslim, but an ineffectual ruler. Royal slaves had taken advantage of this, often to the detriment of the king's own commercial concerns. Nachtigal found many of the houses in Kobe, the traders' town, empty and ruined, as many trading families had emigrated eastwards, or had simply been ruined and died out. A small section had moved to the capital, 'where under the eyes of the king they found themselves less exposed to the extortions of his slaves'.[142] But it was as much members of the royal family and other title-holders who usurped power for themselves, particularly the king's sister Zamzam; she virtually ruled the country after her brother became blind towards the end of his life.[143] Another example of the difficulty of disentangling slave activity from free.

Between 1870 and 1880 the Fulani rulers of Zaria, within the Sokoto empire, appointed slave generals to command their standing armies, as much in this instance through fear of internal revolt as a means of defence against invaders.[144] In Katsina city, also within the Sokoto empire, towards the end of the nineteenth century royal slaves 'so troubled the market that its members rebelled and thrice drove back the royal slave cavalry'.[145] In a situation not exactly parallel, since the slaves were not his own, Kalema, the late nineteenth-century Muslim *kabaka* of Buganda, losing popular support, relied increasingly on the Arabs and their bands of armed slaves.[146] The first emir of Adamawa appointed by the British, though he was the correct legal successor, was unpopular because he preferred court favourites and slaves to the old Fulani aristocracy, and he was deported in 1901.[147] In some cases, however, where the

[141] IV, 308, 320; O'Fahey and Spaulding confirm the increasingly close links between traders and the court (p.161).
[142] IV, 255-6.
[143] IV, 315-16 and 365; O'Fahey and Spaulding, 150, 175.
[144] M. G. Smith, 1959, 242.
[145] M. G. Smith, 1964 A, 178.
[146] J. M. Gray, 'The year of the three kings of Buganda', *Uganda Journal*, 1950, 37-8.
[147] Boyle, 1910-11, 88-9.

Fulani leaders clung closer to the nomadic tradition, and preferred to tend their farms and cattle rather than to dance attendance at court, the advancement of slaves to high political office was not so much resented; Sambo, founder of the Fulani emirate of Hadeija, obtained from his colleagues express consent for such aggrandisement.[148]

Where it was a Muslim government that evoked such resentment, we may guess that the cause of the faith sometimes suffered. But in other cases, when it was the hand of non-Muslim, slave-supported, rule that lay heavy upon the people, popular resistance sometimes found succour in Islam: this was true in the Woloff states of West Africa, where tension between royal slaves on the one hand, peasantry and marabout leadership on the other helped speed up Islamization of the peasants.[149] There was, moreover, also a danger that the royal slaves might come themselves to dominate, or to undermine, their master. At the end of the thirteenth century the imperial throne of Mali was seized by a freed slave, Sakura.[150] An exiled royal slave played some part in encouraging, presumably for revenge, the Moroccan conquest of Songhay.[151]

One of Muhammad Bello's sons apparently died of disgruntlement after quarrelling with the slaves whom his father had settled on him.[152] While several subordinate rulers in the Sokoto empire of the nineteenth century tried to govern their respective emirates independently of the Fulani aristocracy, relying largely on eunuchs and slaves, the abler despots, in order to encourage rivalries, frequently redistributed offices among their slaves, gave critical functions to freemen or kin when advisable, and sometimes summarily executed senior royal slaves. Nevertheless, as a member of the dispossessed Haùsa dynasty of Katsina observed of the throne slaves: 'These were the rulers, the Fulani had power in name only. The king

[148] J. M. Fremantle, 'A history of the region comprising the Katagum division of Kano province', *Journal of the African Society*, 1911, 314.
[149] Klein, 1968, 19 note.
[150] Levtzion, 1963, 345 and note; *Corpus*, 323, 334—the Arabic is *mawla*, translated once as 'freed slave', once 'client'.
[151] H. de Castries, 'La conquête du Soudan par el Mansour', *Hespéris*, 1923, 445-6, 452; al-Sadi, 215-16.
[152] C. E. Whitting (tr.), *History of Sokoto*, Kano [1948?], 25; Said, 341.

was in the hands of his slaves.'[153] In the later nineteenth century, there was a revolt of the palace slaves of Kano, which was however quelled.[154] The potential unreliability of slave support is further illustrated in the case of Tukur, who succeeded his father as chief of Tibati, one of the major principalities within the Adamawa emirate. Tukur drove out his rival brother, Ardo Hammadu. But Hammadu later sent secret messages to the chief slaves in Tibati; some deserted to him, while others, remaining at their posts, became his clandestine supporters. Finally Hammadu attacked Tibati, and Tukur, abandoned by his slaves, was defeated and killed.[155] And to turn again to Kayor, which we have already cited for other slave difficulties, in the later nineteenth century the royal slaves wished to depose the *damel*, Lat Dyor. Lat Dyor frustrated this conspiracy, and dismissed the chief of the slaves; but this man did in the end contribute to Lat Dyor's overthrow.[156]

And finally, slaves might present a threat at any time of a change of government. Referring to the accession of Muhammed el-Hasin, the king of Darfur whose death in 1873 has been mentioned above (p. 271), Nachtigal remarked,

> when there is a change of government the princes of the royal family must always have the greatest anxiety about their own lives, and on this occasion Abu Bekr [eldest son of king who had died] and his brothers [el-Hasin among them] were also afraid of the treachery of the dead king's domestic slaves.[157]

In fact it was the leading slave official, Adam Tarbush (see below, p. 321), who successfully manipulated the succession in favour of el-Hasin.

A third qualification to slave state generalisations arises from the sometimes exceedingly intricate interaction between slave and free in the structure of the state. In Borno, the State Council, or *nokena*, consisted

---

[153] M. G. Smith, 1964 A, 179.
[154] *Kano Chronicle*, 131.
[155] East, 1934/1967, 47-9.
[156] V. Monteil, in Lewis, 1966, 345.
[157] IV, 305-6.

of members of the royal family, that is the sons and brothers of the Shaykh, and of the State Councillors (*kokena*, plural *kokenawa*), some of whom were freeborn representatives of the various sections of the population, while others were military commanders (*kashella*, plural *kashellawa*) of slave origin.[158]

The free kokenawa are, of course, sensible of their free origin in contrast to the Shaykh's slaves, but the Shaykh took no account of noble birth, and the free man bowed before the slave if the latter stood higher in the sovereign's favour.[159]

While there are clearly many instances in which the distinction and difference between free persons and slaves were deeply felt, this is hardly surprising. What may be less expected is the extent to which the slave and the free were apparently equally eligible for certain posts, or, if not quite equally, slaves might be preferred as a general rule. In Bagirmi, for instance,

the highest dignities and the most important offices, that is those of the *mbarma, fatsha, alîfa Moito* and *krêma*, are usually entrusted to slaves, though examples are not lacking of the appointment of freeborn men, such as for instance my host, the Fatsha Alifa, who was of free descent.[160]

In Darfur, any official, whether slave or free, could be appointed to the office of *maqdum*, commissioners sent out into the provinces from time to time by the king. The appointment was usually for two or three years, though it became permanent in the northern province. After completing their mission, these special appointees returned to their former positions. Their function as *maqdum* was quite exalted: they were to obviate any kind of encroachment upon the royal authority, and, in some measure representing the king in person, they took charge of the supervision of affairs, in the area to which they were sent.[161]

[158] II, 240.
[159] II, 245.
[160] III, 330.
[161] IV, 326. One *maqdum*, defeated in a raid against the Rezeqat Arabs, was captured and subsequently killed by slaves of the Rezeqat, perhaps a glimpse of slave soldiers being deployed against the central government (IV, 310). For another senior Darfur official who may be either free or slave, see IV, 335.

THE DOMESTIC SCENE, IV: SLAVES AND THE STATE

In Wadai, too, there were very senior positions which could be filled by free men or slaves. The royal stables were supervised by four masters of the horse, who were at the same time important administrative officials.

> The *jerma toluk* is the senior master of the horse; he may be either a free man or a slave, and the west of the country, i.e. Kanem, etc., is assigned to him. The *jerma luluk*, who is next to him in rank, is always a freeborn man.[162]

Nachtigal calls the *aqids*, that is, the military leaders, the most important officials in Wadai adding that they 'may be free men, slaves or even eunuchs'. However, he goes on to say that an *aqid* and a *jerma* have approximately the same rank, that they perform the same functions, and enjoy the same income. Beneath both these groups come the *teraqina* (singular *turqenak*) of whom there are sixteen, 'invariably freeborn men'.[163]

Another slave/free balance in the Wadai royal domestic household concerns the two principal officials, the two *umena* (singular *amin*), one of whom is free, the other slave.

> The first *amin* has part of the royal treasure in his custody, actually in his own house, and is also director of the merchants, the Jellaba. The second *amin* has the greater part of the treasure in the palace itself under his care. He is the Sultan's special groom of the chamber, and serves his food.[164]

Much further down in the Wadaian hierarchy of officialdom, at village, level, a similar counterpoint occurs. There is

---

[162] IV, 178. Nachtigal refers several times to Jerma Abu Jebrin, calling him (on p. 180) 'the most powerful man in the country' when Nachtigal was there. Abu Jebrin was brother of the Queen Mother (pp. 51, 54, 75), and thus clearly not a slave. Only once does Nachtigal specify that Abu Jebrin was *luluk*, (p. 180), and thus technically the lesser of the two foremost masters of the horse; such deviations from strict hierarchical models are frequent, reminding us of the scope which existed for the display, and recognition, of individual talents.

[163] IV, 180. It is interesting that in both the Wadai examples, the second in rank, the *jerma luluk* and the *teraqina*, must be free, while those above them may be free or slave.

[164] IV, 177; see also p. 175.

a village headman, the *manjak*, a free man, who shares his office with a slave official; both these are appointed by higher officials, perhaps both by the same man, perhaps by two different men. The principal task of the free headman and his slave colleague is the distribution of cultivable land, 'a matter in connection with which intrigues and attempts at bribery are of course not absent'. It is not in any way regarded as an honour to be appointed *manjak*, headman, waxing fat at the expense of other people.

> His colleague, the slave, who quite naturally is in government service, is more highly respected than the *manjak*, the free citizen who who stoops to receive a salary.

In the absence of the higher appointing officials, the *manjak* (but not, at least by implication, his slave colleague)

> may judge minor offences, and impose fines, but he has so little authority that accused persons are seldom content to accept his verdict, and usually appeal to a higher court.[165]

Patrick Manning, in his useful book *Slavery and African life: occidental, oriental and African slave trades*, acknowledges, very briefly, the importance of slave soldiery and slave officials. Somewhat grudgingly, too:

> The meaning of this upward mobility and of the power of individual slaves should not be distorted. In one sense, it did represent a finite chance that certain slaves might rise above their menial position to one of power and influence. More important, however, was the obverse side of this message: these slaves could be allowed to rise only because many more were held in utter subjection. They could be trusted because they were absolutely dependent on their patrons, and they could be sent back to the fields, the mines, or to the executioner for any reason whatever or no reason at all.[166]

I hesitate over this. Fundamentally it suggests too sharp a distinction between slave and free. In the preceding discussion, there are too many instances of offices being available indifferently to free men and slaves. Slaves were indeed

---

[165] IV, 187.

[166] Cambridge University Press, first published 1990, 3rd reprinting 1995, 116.

vulnerable to the wrath of the ruler, but so too were free men. Indeed, in some situations and for certain groups, the slave's lot might be preferable to that of a free royal. In both Bagirmi and Wadai, for example, it was the practice for a newly-installed king to have his brothers blinded.[167] Some slaves were trustworthy, but others could be unruly, even treacherous—or, simply by abusing the authority entrusted to them, they could so stir up resentment as quite to undermine the position of their masters. It is difficult to see precisely what, in practice, is meant by slaves being 'allowed' to rise, and still more difficult to understand how this is possible *only* 'because many more were held in utter subjection'. How would these considerations apply, say, to a bright twelve-year-old lad being recruited into the ranks of King Ali's *tuweïrât* in Wadai?

It is not only the too sharp demarcation in Manning's summary above, but also the absence of any reference to the scope for individual initiative, over which I stumble. My father and I struggled with these points in our annotation of *Sahara and Sudan*, where we suggested

> that there was a good deal more flexibility in the structure of *de facto* administration than would commend itself to a modern 'expert' with his natural prejudice in favour of clearly defined chains of authority and responsibility. And this would be most easily understood in the case of the slaves of the royal household, who were at least in theory entirely dependent upon their royal master, and whose effective influence must have depended even more than is normally inevitable upon their personal qualities.[168]

We can conclude with one further example from Nachtigal, quoted at length both because there is a certain piquancy to the word-picture he sketches, and because it inverts some

---

[167] In Bagirmi, this dated from the later eighteenth century (III, 411-12); there, only one eye was blinded (p. 327). In Wadai, Nachtigal says that the custom dated only from the beginning of the nineteenth century (IV, 174-5); King Ali, on his accession in 1858, is said, perhaps contradictorily, to have been following 'an old Wadai custom' in blinding potential rivals (p. 52—he spared some brothers, relying on their better nature, but blinded some other close relatives as well as ambitious brothers). A hot iron or boiling butter was the usual instrument.

[168] II, 248, note 3; we were referring to Borno, but the observation could equally well be applied more widely.

stereotypes, as the king intervened to appoint a free man rather than a slave, while the appointee's prospective subjects protested against the elevation of one of their own number, rather than a customary slave. The passage also illustrates the importance of how relationships between individuals worked. The top administration of Nimro, the traders' town in Wadai,

> is in the hands of the *kursî*, an office formerly always held by a slave of the king, and with an *amîn* serving under him. My host, however, the present *kursî*, came from a good Jellabi [trader] family, and when he was twenty-six had inherited from his father a property which in the circumstances of that place was quite substantial. As he himself told me, he offered his inheritance to the king in return for the office of *kursî* of the Jellaba. The king, who knew the young man and appreciated him because of his energetic character, granted his wish despite the lively opposition of the Jellaba. It was years before the young *kursî* succeeded in establishing his position, but his strong, tenacious nature enabled him to overcome all difficulties. The office of *kursî* is indeed very lucrative, for he receives taxes from the Jellaba, who are almost continuously on the road, two *maqta tromba* for every laden camel on their return from Darfur, and one *turkedi* on their arrival from the west. The *kursî* also has jurisdiction over robberies, adultery, police offences and bloody brawls, and the penalties nearly always take the form of fines which accrue to him. In criminal cases of importance, half the fine goes to the king. It was characteristic of my host's strong constitution that he could endure the life which he led; when one looked at him, one could not avoid the conclusion that *merrîsa*, the beer of that country, has a much less devastating effect than our alcoholic drinks, for he drank it from daybreak until the time of the evening meal, *ashâ*, about 8 p.m., eating almost no farinacious food, but only some roasted meat. He practised this vice, moreover, not secretly, but in the yard, surrounded by his friends and subordinates, while he attended to the details of administration, settled disputes and judged offences.[169]

There is also in this episode more than a hint of the power

---

[169] IV, 62; the *maqta tromba* and *turkedi* are both pieces of cloth often used as currency (see, for example, IV, 55).

of something akin to bribery; this, being reminiscent of the quotation which opens this section, neatly rounds off this discussion.

Eunuchs

'I have hung one man in Obeid for mutilating a boy, and hope to hang five more in a couple of days.' (Charles G. Gordon, Khartoum, 19 August 1878, in R.W. Beachey, *A Collection of documents on the slave trade*, London 1976, 71)

Though the making of eunuchs is said to have been strictly forbidden to his followers by the Prophet Muhammad, African rulers, in their search for reliable civil servants, sometimes found eunuchs attractive, in the lower ranks for looking after the *harim*,[170] but in higher political offices also, since there could be no temptation to found a rival dynasty. Around 1800, for example, the prince of Muscat, fearing lest his African dependency of Zanzibar become too independent, appointed eunuchs as his representatives there, dividing civil and military power between them.[171] And this steady, extensive market within Africa has been complemented by an even longer-standing export demand from the Muslim heartlands.

The best-known early source of eunuchs in Africa was in Ethiopia. Here, despite the efforts of the king of Amhara to forbid the practice, castration continued to be performed in the fourteenth century in the town of Washlu, the care of the survivors being the speciality of the Muslim principality of Hadya.[172] Ethiopian eunuchs were already well-known in

[170] The status of harem keeper was sometimes a degraded one, and might be alleged in insult: Amda Seyon, conquering ruler of Ethiopia in the fourteenth century, had been incensed by his lowland Danakil enemies taunting him as a eunuch, fit only to care for women (Harris, 1844/1968, II, 232).

[171] Freeman-Grenville, 1962/1976, 198.

[172] In *Slavery* 1970, on p. 143, we suggested that the Ethiopian slaves whom Mansa Musa and his suite bought in Cairo were presumably eunuchs. The more recent and more accurate *Corpus* text (p. 351) reads: 'The members of his entourage proceeded to buy Turkish and Ethiopian slave girls.' (See also p. 181 above.) The early fourteenth century, in fact, seems too soon for a lively interest in Muslim western Africa in eunuchs: Ibn Battuta, perfectly cognizant of eunuchs from his other travels, and who spent a considerable time in the empire of Mali at mid-century, does not mention eunuchs there.

Arabia, for the servitors and doorkeepers of the mosque in Medina, all eunuchs, included Ethiopians. The head of these, not himself an Ethiopian, in Ibn Battuta's time, confronted with the temptations of Joseph in Potiphar's house, had followed the example of Origen.[173] An Ethiopian eunuch was in charge of the Zanzibar customs at the beginning of the nineteenth century, and later became *hakim* or magistrate as well.[174] In Ethiopia itself, the market was dependent on domestic demand as well as on exports. Harris, visiting in the nineteenth century, found many eunuchs among the king's servants.[175] Many supervised women slaves, but one commanded a garrison town during the king's absence, and the whole court went into deep mourning for the chief eunuch's death.

Another important early source was Nupe. The exchange of ten horses for twelve eunuchs between the rulers of Nupe and of Kano in the mid-fifteenth century has been mentioned above (see above, pp. 112, 242). Queen Amina of Zaria, variously dated as early fifteenth or mid-sixteenth century, also received eunuchs from Nupe.[176] The institutions of mass-slavery and of eunuchs both flourished in Kano. The first to appoint eunuchs as important state officials there was Muhammad Rimfa, in the later fifteenth century.[177] In the time of Abubakr Kado, who in the later sixteenth century concentrated exclusively on religious duties, both eunuchs and clerics became very numerous in Kano.[178] Early in the seventeenth century, Wombai Giwa, presumably a eunuch, became so powerful and likely to revolt that he had to be dismissed from his office.[179] Kutumbi, ruler of Kano in the second quarter of the seventeenth century, was always attended by 100 eunuchs handsomely dressed and with gold and silver ornaments.[180]

[173] Ibn Battuta, Gibb and Beckingham, I, 175; Defrémery and Sanguinetti, I, 279-80.
[174] J. Gray, in Oliver and Mathew, 1963, 212 n.
[175] Harris, 1844/1968, II, 27, 57-8, 76, 167, 168, 376; III, 306.
[176] Alhaji Hassan and Shuaibu Na'ibi, *A chronicle of Abuja*, Lagos, 1962, 3; *Kano Chronicle*, 109.
[177] *Kano Chronicle*, 111-12.
[178] *ibid.*, 114.
[179] *ibid.*, 117.
[180] *ibid.*, 119.

In Songhay, too, eunuchs had an important place in the civil service. Leo Africanus spoke of a private palace of the *askiya*, containing a great number of concubines and slaves, kept by eunuchs.[181] He also said that Askiya Muhammad I attacked and killed the Hausa king of Gobir, and made eunuchs of his grandsons.[182] A eunuch was in charge of the *askiya*'s extensive wardrobe.[183] The chief of the palace eunuchs, Ali Folon, played almost the part of regent towards the end of Askiya Muhammad I's reign.[184] Askiya Ishaq II, defeated by the Moroccans, attempted to slip away with gold and silver, royal emblems, thirty of the best horses in the royal stables, and forty eunuchs.[185] A little ironically, some of the early leaders of the Moroccan expeditionary and occupation forces were themselves Andalusian eunuchs.

Nachtigal, who gives a great deal of information about eunuchs in the central Sudan countries, is imprecise about the earliest origins of the institution there. Introducing his extensive discussion of eunuchs in Bagirmi, Nachtigal refers in passing to earlier production in Borno.

> The Bagirmi kings, who seem all along to have bestowed special attention upon their harems, had to be sure always employed eunuchs to manage them, but these were bought in Borno, and because of their high price could be kept only in very small numbers.[186]

More than this, about Borno as pioneer eunuch producer and exporter, Nachtigal does not say.[187]

The transition in Bagirmi from importer to producer and exporter, Nachtigal dated as during the reign of the *mbang*, or king, Muhammad el-Amin, also called Haji, 1751-85.

---

[181] Leo Africanus, A, III, 827; B, II, 471.

[182] *ibid.*, A, III, 828; B, II, 473; Rouch, 1953, 204.

[183] Kati, 260-1.

[184] Rouch, 1953, 192 & n; al-Sadi mentions Ali Folon several times, but not as a eunuch.

[185] Kati, 273.

[186] III, 411.

[187] Ibn Battuta refers once to *fityan*, and beautiful slave-girls, coming from Borno. Hamdun and King translate *fityan* as eunuchs (p. 58), the *Corpus* as young men slaves (p. 302). Neither volume gives a fully adequate index reference. See also p. 98 above.

On one occasion when Mbang Haji had acquired several of them [eunuchs] at fifty slaves apiece, Araueli [the *fatsha* or chief minister] complained about this extravagance, and proposed to proceed with production himself. He installed a hundred boys at Kolle on the Ba Laïri [river], and carried out the cruel operation on them with his barber—*wanzam* in Kanuri and Bagrimma. Thirty of them came through alive,[188] and could be presented to the king as his own manufacture. Delighted, he went to work, now supplied on his part the Sudan markets with this prized article which brought to his coffers a considerable income, and also repeatedly sent eunuchs to Mecca, where they were gladly accepted as presents, although Islam in fact strongly condemns the operation.[189]

A later account, published in 1907, also gave King Haji the credit for inaugurating the making of eunuchs in Bagirmi; this account, though recognizably based upon the same popular traditions as those upon which Nachtigal had drawn, differed in some of its details from his story. Haji, it was said, learnt the value of eunuchs either while he was in Mecca or from some of the potentates whose courts he visited while on pilgrimage. Returning from Mecca, he purchased a eunuch in exchange for fifty slaves from the sultan of Mandara, and then when it was pointed out to him that this was a rather expensive procedure, he took instruction in the techniques of castration, and subsequently made his own eunuchs.[190]

Exactly what happened to the domestic production of eunuchs during the nineteenth century in Borno is not clear. Gaden says that it was rare, no eunuchs being made there during the first forty years (though Muhammad el-Kanemi's campaigns brought in a considerable number from Bagirmi),

[188] Other estimates have put the mortality rate at 80% (Deherme, 1908, 373).

[189] III, 411.

[190] H. Gaden, 'Etats musulmans de l'Afrique centrale et leurs rapports avec la Mecque et Constantinople', *Questions diplomatiques et coloniales*, XXIV, 1907, 441. Commandant Gaden had lived in Bagirmi, and was resident at Zinder from June 1901 to December 1902. He wrote after Bagirmi had come under French control, his information being derived from conversations with Bagirmians, and with political refugees who had come from the neighbouring countries into Bagirmi during the troubled years at the beginning of the twentieth century (436).

Shaykh Umar himself indulging in the practice only once, with a score of captives taken on a raid against the southern Pagans, and none of his successors making any eunuchs at all.[191] Nachtigal's information suggests that Gaden was concentrating too much on rulers. At the same time as emphasising, as we shall see, the more or less monopolistic control over the making and ownership of eunuchs exercised by local rulers, Nachtigal attributes a surprisingly free hand to Lamino, admittedly a very powerful figure in the Borno hierarchy.

> Lamino...appears to have been sufficiently devoid of conscience to collect from time to time hundreds of boys, and subject them to castration, condemned though this is by Islam. Under the pretext of wanting to circumcise the boys, the barbers who perform the operation are accustomed with a quick grip to grasp the whole of their external genitals in the left hand, and with the right to amputate them with a sharp knife. Boiling butter is kept in readiness and poured on the fresh wound to staunch the bleeding of the unfortunate boys. Very many of them, of course, succumb to the horrible operation.

Nachtigal, indeed, in this same passage goes further, extending the same license to an indefinite number of notables:

> many a mighty man of Bornu...has not been ashamed to increase their [the eunuchs'] number, either with a view to immediate profit, or in order to keep them in readiness as a costly present for the Shaykh.[192]

It is difficult to combine this do-it-yourself approach, at least among the great men, with a royal monopoly. It may perhaps be that such activity, of its nature a discreet and delicate matter, remained somewhat in the shadows, allowing exaggerated rumours to circulate about it.

In Wadai, castration was sometimes inflicted as a judicial punishment on local wrongdoers, and the royal corps of eunuchs was also reinforced by young Tubu and Bideyat captured by Mahamid Arab raiders from Wadai.[193] Castration was occasionally self-inflicted, as in the case of Muhammad

---

[191] Gaden, 1907, 437-8.
[192] II, 217.
[193] Gaden, 1907, 438-40.

Kurra, who eventually became for a time *de facto* ruler of Darfur.[194]

Turning from the making of eunuchs to their use, eunuchs were prominent in all the states of the central Sudan which Nachtigal visited. Bagirmi, the production and export centre, was pre-eminent, at least in the number of eunuch dignitaries in proportion to the size of this relatively small state. Mbang Burkomanda, who died not long before mid-century, is said, with rather implausible (and Mozartian) precision to have had 1,003 of them, while never allowing any of his subjects to maintain any.[195] The chief eunuch, the *ngarmane*, was in close attendance when Abu Sekkin, the ruler, first received Nachtigal.[196] The *ngarmane* commanded nearly as many troops as did the chief military commander.[197] The next eunuch in rank was the *katurli* or *katurluli*, having the oversight of many Pagan districts and tribes, his familiarity with these regions and their political conditions making him a successful expedition leader and tax-gatherer there.[198] Nachtigal remarks that only the *ngarmane* and the *katurluli*, among the eunuchs, had 'achieved a certain importance'; but he says also that eunuchs were 'especially numerous at the court of Bagirmi', and he lists thirteen titles (among others) held by eunuchs, for the most part administering Pagan districts.

> It is surprising to find in Bagirmi and in Wadai likewise that it is precisely military posts that are held by eunuchs, of whom one is inclined to suppose that, after the loss of their virility, they would gradually assume an effeminate character not only externally, but inwardly.[199]

Some fifty eunuchs still survived in the early twentieth century, relics of the days of Bagirmi's independence, but by that time no further additions were being made to their number.[200]

Only in Logon, despite its proximity to Bagirmi, did Nach-

---

[194] IV, 294.
[195] Gaden, 1907, 441.
[196] III, 317.
[197] III, 322.
[198] III, 330.
[199] III, 330-1.
[200] Gaden, 1907, 442.

tigal, to his surprise, find apparently no eunuch officials at court.[201] This may have been a mis-observation on his part, or a temporary glitch in the local court arrangements, for Barth, not long before, did report court eunuchs at the time of his visit in 1852.[202] In Darfur, eunuchs were important and numerous in government circles: the keepers of the royal stores, for example, were all eunuchs,[203] and eunuchs were of course deeply involved on the women's side of the royal household.[204] Nachtigal's analysis of the eunuchs of Darfur, however, is rather overshadowed by the dramatic career of Muhammad Kurra, *abu shaykh* or *abu shaykh dali* of Darfur. Kurra had entered government service as a youth, perhaps as a slave, more likely as a free, royal, spear-bearing page. He became a favourite of the king, whereas a rival colleague told the king that Kurra was spending too much time with one of the royal concubines. To avert the anger of the jealous ruler, Kurra castrated himself. An eventful, roller-coaster career followed, culminating in Kurra's appointment as *abu shaykh*, the highest administrative title in the realm. When the king under whom he had risen to power died, Kurra became regent, and ruled with an iron hand. Finally he was killed in a fracas with supporters of the young king, engineered by some of the eunuch's many enemies.[205]

The Wadaian eunuch establishment is presented in a more balanced way in Nachtigal's pages, and less as a one-man show.

> Closely associated with the harem are, of course, the eunuchs (called Masters, *Shuyukh* [or Shaykhs], of whom there are about forty to fifty, mostly imported from Bagirmi; some, however, are from Wadai itself, though these have been made eunuchs only as a punishment. Some are confined

[201] III, 265.
[202] 1965, II, 445.
[203] IV, 338.
[204] IV, 337.
[205] The details, some of which come not from Nachtigal but from the Arab traveller, el-Tounsy, who visited Darfur seventy years before Nachtigal and stayed there about eight years, are given in IV, 294-301. Slatin (1896, 44-5) adds that Kurra had been tutor to the new king, Muhammad al-Fadl, before his accession to the throne. For more on Kurra, see R. S. O'Fahey and J. L. Spaulding, *Kingdoms of the Sudan*. London 1974, 137-40, 171-2 (the above story), 178.

strictly to the service or supervision of the women. Others, however, are high officials or military leaders, and frequently have distinguished themselves by their warlike spirit. The Aqid of the Salamat, for example, who has one of the major and militarily most important appointments, is always a eunuch, just as in Bornu, too, eunuchs occupy some high posts which have nothing at all to do with their original vocation. The senior eunuch at the court of Wadai is the Aqid Duggu Debanga, who administers the supplies of the inner palace, and arranges the sultan's relations with the apartments of his wives; in addition he has the Arab tribes and villages under his control, which makes him a very influential and wealthy man. Next to him comes the *millek artan*, '*ornang shuyukh*', i.e. the overseer of the eunuchs, whose most important function is to carry out the sultan's commissions concerning his wives. To these are added five or six others with less important duties.[206]

The house of the chief eunuch, one of a select group of individuals sharing the highest rank in Wadai, that of a *kamkolak*, stands in front of the 'women's way' entrance to the royal residence. Every visitor who has not been directly summoned by the king must notify the chief eunuch before entering the palace; otherwise entry will be denied by the guard at the gate.[207] The holder of this office in Nachtigal's time, Kamkolak Fotr, died of a lance-thrust sustained in a drunken brawl between himself and another senior eunuch, and their respective partisans.[208]

It was, however, in Borno that the most elaborate and effective eunuch hierarchy existed, and it was also here that Nachtigal had his best opportunities for close observation of the system. Interestingly, while Nachtigal won the respect and affection of a wide range of people on his travels, from rulers to (eventually) his own slave boys, and particularly of several notables and officials of importance, he does not seem to have been similarly close to any of the eunuchs, despite knowing a good many. More important, and of greater prestige, than

---

[206] IV, 176-7. Nachtigal does not give any fatality rate for those punished by castration, compared with figures up to 80 per cent among young boys.
[207] IV, 46.
[208] IV, 121, 126.

most of the other government officers whom Nachtigal mentioned

> were and are the officials of the innermost household of the sovereign, the eunuchs. The highest in rank among these is the *yurôma*, who within the residence is not concerned with the women, female slaves and children, but is in change of the women taken along on any military expeditions or journeys of the ruler [—a further reminder of the great importance of the mobility of women slaves: see for example pp. 183, 203, 245]. In former times the *yurôma* collected one tenth of the grain in the west of the kingdom; he still has general supervision over the region of the *ghaladîma* and of the ruler of Mashena or Matyena, and was often sent abroad on confidential missions as being so to speak his master's representative.
>
> The second in rank, but in ordinary times the most important eunuch, is the *mistrêma*, the real commander of the women's section and governor of all the non-adult princes and princesses.
>
> The third eunuch, scarcely less important, is the *mâla*, who is the custodian of the royal palace itself, and of all the goods and chattels in it. He shuts the palace every evening, and opens it at the crack of dawn. He is keeper of the royal privy purse, and from this on instructions from his master he gives the appointed gifts to foreign guests (see above, 259).[209]

Eunuchs also played a part in provincial administration. Ngornu, the second largest town in Borno, was under a governor with the title *fugoma*, who was, 'as is customary', a eunuch. 'He was a tall, powerful man, of lively temperament and pleasant manners', and received Nachtigal hospitably as the traveller set out on his visit to Abu Sekkin, king of Bagirmi.[210] The *fugoma* was away when Nachtigal and his party next called at Ngornu, returning from Abu Sekkin, but they were nonetheless excellently catered for in the *fugoma*'s own dwelling.[211]

With some at least apparent inconsistency, Nachtigal does

---

[209] II, 256-7. Rohlfs (1874-5, II, 3) uses the term similarly, though saying only that the office was important, not specifying its rank.

[210] III, 217-18.

[211] III, 451.

not include the *fugoma* amongst the eunuch officials of the government. He is listed among the other officials, where nothing is said of him or any of his predecessors being eunuchs, though they were 'formerly' slaves. Earlier the *fugoma* had been 'governor of the capital, remaining there when the king was absent, and administering justice then with power over life and death', but his standing and office at the time of Nachtigal's visit had been 'not immaterially changed', and only Ngornu was under his sway.[212]

Another office, this time one of Nachtigal's explicitly eunuch appointments, but which it seems no longer existed, was that of the *udima*,

> who was responsible for the administration of the most northerly villages in the country on the Chad from Ngigmi to Barua. He received caravans and messages coming from the north, and despatched those going in the opposite direction.

Udi or Wudi was a village south of Ngigmi, where once the earlier Borno kings had temporarily resided.[213]

Nachtigal sums up his discussion of eunuch officialdom in Borno with considerable confidence:

> Of all the court officials the eunuchs have maintained most completely the lustre of their position in earlier centuries.... [While only some other officials] still occupy the offices of their predecessors more or less in their earlier form, the position of the eunuchs has remained exactly as it was in former times, and their incomes have been the least curtailed.[214]

With too much confidence, maybe, since on the basis of his own evidence the office of the *fugoma* had been substantially cut back, and that of the *udima* closed down altogether.

One royal eunuch, the *mala*, Abd el-Karim in Nachtigal's time and for years later, deserves special mention. Nachtigal encountered Abd el-Karim chiefly as purveyor of gifts from Shaykh Umar, and as chief recipient of the substantial gratuities which those receiving such largesse were supposed to give to

---
[212] II, 253.
[213] II, 257 and note 3.
[214] III, 257-8.

its bearers.[215] That Abd el-Karim had weightier importance is indicated by his commanding 150 light cavalry and 40 heavy, more than any other non-military dignitary except Lamino and some members of the royal family.[216] Abd el-Karim's star seems to have continued more and more in the ascendant after Nachtigal's final departure in 1873. P.-L. Monteil, who visited Kuka in 1892, described Abd el-Karim as a man of great intellectual and moral strength to whom Shaykh Umar had given all his confidence during his last years. After the Shaykh's death in 1881, four years before Nachtigal's, Abd el-Karim took the initiative in ensuring the succession for Aba Bu Bekr.[217] It is noteworthy that both Abd el-Karim, and Muhammad Kurra, both very senior eunuchs in their respective countries, Borno and Darfur, became centrally involved in royal successions: perhaps a eunuch, with no direct lineage associations of his own to forward, was well suited to the king-making role. Monteil called Abd el-Karim the Shaykh's 'first eunuch', giving him the title of *settima*.[218] A more recent African scholar, C.C. Ifemesia, presumably influenced by Monteil if not fully dependent upon him, calls Abd el-Karim, the *shetima*, 'the real ruler of Bornu', '*de facto* master of Bornu for nearly half a century'.[219] It is presumably the same man who appears as Malla Karim in Schultze's account, as the chief eunuch and the commander of the Borno troops against Rabih. The Bornoese were defeated, and by Rabih's orders Abd el-Karim was 'sewn up in a freshly-flayed bullock hide, and so found a horrible death exposed to the rays of the African sun' in 1893.[220]

[215] II, 127, 143 and note 3; III, 42, 45.
[216] II, 264, 257 and note 4.
[217] P.-L. Monteil, *De St Louis à Tripoli par le lac Tchad*, Paris 1894, 342.
[218] Nachtigal (II, 257) mentions *shitima* as another eunuch title, but very much inferior in rank to the more superior offices, including that of the *mala*.
[219] 'Bornu under the Shehus', in Ajayi and Espie, eds, 1965, 291. Ifemesia classifies all Borno *kashellawa* (see above, p. 264), overexuberantly, as 'eunuchs of servile origin'.
[220] A. Schultze, *The sultanate of Bornu*, ed. and tr. P. A. Benton, London 1913, reprinted 1968, p. 30; the original German was published in 1910, Schultze having worked in the area on boundary demarcation in 1903-4, only a decade after Rabih's devastating incursion.

Just to illustrate how tenacious some of the old ways and titles might be, after Rabih had overrun and desolated the empire, and then the European powers, British, French and German, had divided it up, the *mala* was still listed in German Borno as first among the sultan's eunuchs, with part of the sultan's mounted bodyguard under his control, and with the duty of supervising the dwelling places of the king's women and looking after his wardrobe.[221]

Eunuchs also, to a limited extent, penetrated into social levels a little below royalty. When Nachtigal made his first visit to Lamino, foremost dignitary of Borno at that time, he was 'announced and introduced by Mesa'ud, Lamino's head eunuch—the powerful man allowed himself eunuchs, an uncommon luxury among the subjects of Bornu'.[222] Shaykh Umar is said to have given several eunuchs to Lamino, and one to Hajj Beshir, vizier of Borno, who met a violent death during civil unrest in the country in 1853.[223]

This attention to the detail of very small numbers of eunuchs must raise again doubts concerning the independent production of eunuchs by 'many a mighty man' of Borno, mass production indeed in the case of Lamino (see above, p. 284).

Trade in eunuchs is similarly a rather elusive subject. Nachtigal includes boy eunuchs in his price list for the Kuka market, 50 to 80 dollars, higher than the price of any other slave (even deaf and dumb girls) except a *surriya* or concubine, for whom there was a wide quality, or consumer preference, differential, from 40 to 100 dollars.[224] This price information suggests at least some dealing on the open market, though Nachtigal also says that this was very rare:

> Eunuchs, *adim*, have an exceptional value, but they scarcely ever come on to the open market. The demand for them on the part of foreign merchants who seek them for the great men of the Mohammedan world of Europe, Asia and

[221] Adolf von Duisburg, *Im Lande des Cheghu von Bornu*, Berlin 1942, 61.
[222] II, 135; see note 2 here for another reference to a senior Borno official including a eunuch amongst his slaves.
[223] Gaden, 1907, 438, cited in II, 217, note 2. Two lines in this note are wrongly placed: in the full paragraph on p. 218, lines 16 and 17 should be moved up to follow line 2.
[224] II, 226; the deaf-mutes are on p. 218, and see also above, pp. 36, 202.

Africa is so great, while indeed the supply of them can only be limited, that they are very quickly sold privately.[225]

The international trade in eunuchs is also difficult to trace in precise detail, partly because many circulated more as special gifts, or tribute, than as trade commodities. Bagirmi, as the main source of supply, is the starting point for the trade. Nachtigal, as we have already noted (see above, p. 283), thought that the export of eunuchs provided the Bagirmi ruler with a considerable income;[226] and most of the eunuchs who came up for sale in Borno were from Bagirmi.[227] But at the same time Bagirmi repeatedly sent eunuchs to Mecca, where they were gladly accepted as presents (again see above, p. 283), and it is said that Shaykh Umar preferred to get eunuchs from Bagirmi, whose sultans sent them to him on demand.[228] Hajj Bashir took several eunuchs with him, as presents, on his pilgrimage; and Hajj Bezzem, another Borno notable, sent several to Mecca. Presents which included eunuchs were sent from time to time from Borno to Constantinople and Mecca, in Shaykh Umar's time; those gifts ceased after his death, although Sultan Abd el-Hamid is said to have asked more than once for a revival of the practice.[229] The ruler of Wadai also sometimes sent a number of eunuchs to Constantinople, 'as a kind of homage'.[230]

The eunuch tradition flourished in many other areas of Muslim black Africa. Denham witnessed the sultan of Mandara accompanied by thirty of his sons and six favourite eunuchs.[231] Sultan Bello's house in Sokoto in 1826 had two entrances, one, presumably because his *harim* was there, guarded only by eunuchs, of whom he had a great number.[232] Eunuchs attended Bello's army in the attack on Gobir in that year (see

[225] II, 217.
[226] III, 411.
[227] II, 217.
[228] Gaden, 1907, 438, cited on II, 218 note.
[229] *ibid.*, 442-3.
[230] IV, 175; *Slavery* 1970, p. 148, speaks of the Wadaian ruler having given eunuchs to several of his dignitaries; the source, not given there, is Gaden, 1907, 436, 440.
[231] Bovill, *Missions*, III, 342; see also pp. 335, 336-7.
[232] Clapperton, 1829, 208.

above pp. 249-50).[233] Atiqu, Bello's successor, sent a eunuch to enlist al-Hajj Umar's prayers on behalf of a besieged Fulani town.[234] The chief eunuch of the sultan of Agades called on Barth when he arrived in town.[235] Eunuch officials in Borno were mentioned by Barth.[236] In 1910 a eunuch was monitor at the French government-controlled *madrasa* in Timbuktu.[237]

Eunuchs were not peculiar to Muslim societies in black Africa; in Yoruba traditional government, for example, they also played an important part.[238]

In summary, the production of eunuchs contributed significantly to the fatality statistics (even though these can never be established precisely) of slaving operations overall: although relatively few slaves, of the huge total numbers captured, were castrated, it was a high-risk procedure, with heavy losses. The production, ownership and distribution of eunuchs was on the whole a jealously guarded royal monopoly, though occasionally, through gifts from the crown, or, more rarely, through non-royal making of eunuchs, possession of these highly prized individuals did penetrate also into the uppermost ranks of officials and nobility. They were a luxury item, very costly, seldom sold on the open market, and frequently circulating as tribute or gifts, rather than trade goods. They were much in demand in the heartlands of Islam. There, their work seems to have been partly in the service and supervision of women in the palaces and great houses, and partly in the care of shrines and holy places. Nearer home, in black Africa, the domestic role obtained, but was supplemented by a wide range of official, even military appointments, sometimes at the highest levels. Specifically religious roles for eunuchs are hardly mentioned in black Africa, though, according to Gaden,

[233] Clapperton, 1829, 185.
[234] Said, 328-9.
[235] Barth, 1965, I, 318; he summoned Barth to the sultan.
[236] *ibid.*, II, 40, 592.
[237] Seabrook, 1934, 190.
[238] R. Smith, 'The Alafin in exile', *Journal of African History*, 1965, 69; S. Johnson, *The history of the Yorubas*, Lagos, 1921, reprinted 1956, 59-60; P. Morton-Williams, 'An outline of the geneaology and cult organization of the Oyo Yoruba', *Africa*, 1964, 253-8; Clapperton, 1829, 38; Lovejoy, 1983, 119.

eunuchs in Bagirmi, Bornu and Wadai were feared and respected by everyone, as having a kind of sacred character. Instead of cherishing a futile rancour against their masters, they served them, he said, with a fidelity which the sultans were glad to recognise. Their fidelity was, moreover, further stimulated by the substantial rewards which they received, and the prospect of attaining high office.[239]

---

[239] Gaden, 1907, 437, cited on II, 217 note. Eunuchs seem today a somewhat sensitive issue for academic discussion. They are not indexed at all in Lovejoy and Hogendorn, and Manning has only a single mention—'the medieval Oriental demand for slaves...included demand for soldiers, laborers, and eunuchs' (p. 36).

CHAPTER IX

THE DOMESTIC SCENE, V: SLAVES AS A MEANS OF EXCHANGE

With so many different uses for slaves, it is not surprising that they circulated sometimes as a means of exchange, even almost as a form of currency. In any predominantly barter economy it is often difficult to differentiate clearly between transfers of goods in discharge of legal obligations to pay tribute or taxes, conventional or courtesy presents, and exchanges of goods which are definitely barter. Slaves have been widely used for all these purposes, and provided it is remembered that in practice one category shades almost imperceptibly into another, it will be helpful to comment on this use under various heads separately.

Tribute

'When the tribute to King Ali [of Wadai] was due, Abu Sekkin [of Bagirmi] sent, as if in mockery, the oldest, ugliest and most useless slaves that he could muster.' (III, 422)

From the earliest period of the history of Islam in Africa, slaves were frequently mentioned as tribute or taxes paid to political superiors. Uqbah bin Nafi, who conquered several places in North Africa and Fezzan in the 660s, imposed on various rulers an annual tribute of 360 slaves, cutting off an ear or a finger of some of the rulers as a lifelong reminder of their obligations.[1] Even earlier, the Muslim conquerors of Egypt had begun levying slave tribute from Christian Nubia. This continued, with some interruptions, into the fourteenth

[1] al-Bakri, 33-5.

century, and was discontinued only when a Muslim became king of Nubia. In this case, as in some others, the payment of tribute was not easily distinguishable from exchange, for Nubia at the same time received annually from Egypt grain, cloth and horses.[2]

Here are some later examples. About 1400 Kanajeji, a son of the first ruler of Kano to adopt Islam, received slave tribute from the Kwararafa in exchange for horses; he oppressed some of his enemies to the extent of obliging them to surrender many of their own children as slave tribute.[3] From about 1450 each ruler of Katsina on his accession sent 100 slaves as tribute to Bornu, though his sovereign rights do not seem otherwise to have been affected.[4] Leo Africanus described the presentation around 1500 to the king of Fez by a neighbouring prince of 100 black slaves, men and women in equal numbers, ten eunuchs, twelve camels, a giraffe, ten ostriches, sixteen civet cats, a pound of civet, a pound of ambergris, and almost 600 oryx skins.[5] Ngolo, the powerful eighteenth-century king of Segu–Segu and its rulers, however, were but slightly tinged with Islam–began his career when his village used him to pay the government in lieu of tax.[6] On the east coast, the sultan of Pate used to receive from each of the heads of some subordinate tribes tribute of one slave and 20 dollars.[7]

In the nineteenth century, slave tribute was very common. A Bornoan, kidnapped and sold into slavery at the opening of the century, said that his country had received an annual tribute of 1000 slaves from the Kwararafa kingdom to the south-west.[8] The Kwararafa in turn may have received some slaves in the tribute which their own vassals paid to them.[9] The newcome ruler of Dar Fertit, a vassal state neighbouring Darfur, kept in his overlord's good graces by an annual gift of

[2] Arkell, 1961, 186-9, 199-200; Y.F. Hasan, *The Arabs and the Sudan*, Edinburgh 1967, 21-8, 91, 107-10.
[3] *Kano Chronicle*, 107.
[4] Barth, 1965, I, 476; M.G. Smith, 1964 B, 348 ; Palmer, 1928, III, 83.
[5] Leo Africanus, A, II, 308-9; B, I, 139. See below, p. 326.
[6] C. Monteil, 1924, 44-6.
[7] Freeman-Grenville, 1962 /1975, 248.
[8] Koelle, *Polyglotta Africana*, 1854/1963, 21, 10.
[9] Ruxton, 1908, 380.

200 slaves, together with a little myrrh and ivory.[10] Much of our information for this period concerns the Fulani empire of Sokoto. From eight of the ten Fulani emirates listed by Clapperton as paying tribute to Sokoto in 1826, the offerings included slaves.[11] A visitor to Ilorin in 1855 reported the presence there of a messenger from Sokoto, with a demand for 200 slaves.[12] Such emirates themselves received slave tribute; at least one freed slave in Sierra Leone had been paid to Bauchi in this way.[13] Pagan enclaves or neighbours acknowledged the paramountcy of the Fulani by paying a capitation tax, supplying armed levies, or giving slaves.[14]

In 1851 Barth was told that the emir of Adamawa, the main slave centre for the Fulani, received in annual tribute about 5,000 slaves as well as horses and cattle, a figure which Barth thought rather high.[15] From this tribute, and the produce of its own raids, Adamawa passed a part to Sokoto. As many as 2,000 slaves might be sent from Adamawa, perhaps half of them reaching Sokoto.[16] Zubayr, emir of Adamawa 1890-1901, having received permission from Sokoto to war against Hayatu, a dissident member of the Sokoto ruling family, set out in company with a Sokoto agent, and on the way stopped to capture some slaves, sixty of whom were handed over to the agent for the sultan of Sokoto.[17]

Earlier, when Adama, first Fulani emir of Adamawa, died, one of his chiefs, in semi-rebellion, refused to come to the capital to acknowledge Lauwal, Adama's successor. Lauwal sent a messenger to summon the recalcitrant chief, Buba Njidda. After a somewhat unsatisfactory parley, Buba Njidda's

[10] G. Douin, *Histoire du regne du Khédive Ismail*, Cairo 1936, vol. III, part 1, 451; the newcomer was Muhammad al-Hilali, who had set out from Morocco intending pilgrimage, but was distracted by the needs and opportunities in Dar Fertit, and settled there. Rabih killed him in 1872.

[11] Clapperton, 1829, 215-16.

[12] C.S. Groves, *The planting of Christianity in Africa*, London 1954, reprinted 1964, II, 62.

[13] Hair, 1965, 197.

[14] M.G. Smith, 1964A, 185; Lacroix, 1952, 29; Hogben and Kirk-Greene, 1966, 450.

[15] Barth, 1965, II, 191; Lacroix, 1952, 34.

[16] Boyle, 1910-11, 82, 86-7; Zintgraff, 1895, 291; East, 1934/1967, 21.

[17] East, 1934/1967, 113-15.

head slave offered the messenger 500 slaves as something with which to buy kola nuts, an offer which the messenger treated with scorn.[18] Again, when Buba Njidda retook possession of a certain territory he gave 1,000 slaves to Sokoto, 1,000 to Yola, the capital of Adamawa, and 100 to a one-man boundary commission.[19] Examples outside the Sokoto sphere include a present of 500 slaves to the pasha of Tripoli in 1822 from an Arab who hoped thus to persuade the pasha to remove the sultan of Fezzan,[20] and tribute in slaves and ivory paid to Darfur by the Bahr al-Ghazal tribes.[21] In this last instance, and probably in many others, a delinquent tributary could be raided, with equally gratifying results, if tribute were not forthcoming.

Nachtigal offers a considerable amount of evidence concerning slaves as tribute. This material is distributed widely throughout *Sahara and Sudan*, often interwoven with wider discussions of relations between states, or peoples, or regions. Tribute was an important element in the history, and the current politics, of Fezzan, Nachtigal's first major port of call. The ruler of Fezzan, Nachtigal said, had been compelled during the seventeenth century to accept an obligation to pay an annual tribute to Tripoli 'of 4,000 *mithqals* of gold, payable half in gold dust and half in slaves'. An attempt later in the century to refuse tribute led to Tripolitanian intervention, which 'collected a rich booty, 15 camel loads of gold and a countless number of slaves'.[22] Since it is highly unlikely that all these captives had been slaves before the northern invasion, it seems that the whole exercise must have involved the extensive, and illegal, enslavement of free Muslims. According to Hornemann, at the very end of the eighteenth century, the tribute due from Fezzan to Tripoli, which had once been set at 6,000 dollars, had since been reduced to 4,000. An official of the Tripolitanian pasha, the *bey el-nobe*, travelled annually to Fezzan to collect this tribute, whether in

[18] East, 1934/1967, 35-7.
[19] Lacroix, 1952, 34.
[20] Bovill, *Missions*, II, 147.
[21] Slatin, 1896, 47.
[22] I, 154-5; see also 164.

gold, senna or slaves. Hornemann himself travelled to Murzuq from Tripoli, at the very end of 1799, with this official.[23]

An early sub-Saharan illustration of tribute, this time as a highly significant marker in the game of power relations between states, occurred in the interaction of two of the most remote kingdoms in the central Sudan, Wadai and Darfur. In the first half of the seventeenth century, a new dynasty seized power in Wadai, displacing the former Tunjur rulers. The usurping king, Abd el-Kerim, throughout his reign,

> paid tribute to Darfur as the Tunjur had done before, mainly in the form of a princess despatched every three years, and to Bornu, whose intervention in favour of the Tunjur he thereby averted.[24]

Around 1700,[25] the king of Wadai was Ya'qub Arus. The following passage in Nachtigal's account illustrates very well just how deeply the symbolic impact of even a slight tribute payment might cut.

> When Ahmed Bokkor, the sultan of Darfur, had payment of the customary tribute demanded from Wadai, and a princess had been chosen for this purpose, a poor ragged man named Kirdi came forward, obstructed her departure, and described this tribute as a disgrace for the land of Wadai. Arus, delighted that there were still real men in his country, ordered the princess to remain, and sent instead of her two men with a message to the sultan of Darfur that, if he wanted to have his tribute, he could collect it for himself. The messengers carried out their dangerous commission, but Ahmed Bokkor did not allow anyone to lay hands on them, sending them home without any answer.[26]

Emboldened by this mild response from Darfur, Arus invaded, establishing a camp within Darfur and raiding in all directions.

[23] Bovill, *Missions*, I, 100, 109n.; also cited in Nachtigal, I, 158 n.
[24] IV, 207-8. This is the Wadai account; Nachtigal does not specify what the tribute to Bornu was. In the Darfur account (p. 281), the princess was an annual obligation.
[25] *Slavery* 1970 (152) wrongly locates these events in the late eighteenth century.
[26] IV, 209. Kirdi is a generic term, referring to southern Pagans.

On learning of these attacks, the long-suffering sultan of Darfur sent a messenger to Arus to ask him what he wanted in his country; to this the insolent man replied that he was on a pilgrimage to Mecca. Bokkor then sent him one of his daughters as wife 'for the long road to the holy land', asking him to set forth on his journey. Arus, however, remained where he was and on her arrival the unfortunate princess was treated with contempt.[27]

A neat inversion of the customary tributary relationship, leaving Darfur in undisputed control of the moral high ground. Or so at least it seems to us today, though this is the story as told to Nachtigal in Wadai, the Darfur version omitting this particular detail of the exchange between invader and invaded.[28] When Ahmed Bokkor's grandson, Omar Lele, who ruled in the 1730s, demanded the tribute from Wadai, he too received the answer that he could come and get it himself. A warlike man—'a great scourge of the country on account of his brutality and wild, warlike temperament', according to Nachtigal[29]—Omar Lele accepted the challenge and invaded Wadai, only to be defeated and captured, eventually dying still in captivity.[30]

These princesses were obviously free women, girls of royal blood intended for the *harim* of the King of Darfur.[31] This was not slave tribute, and could quite well be regarded as a recurrent matrimonial alliance between the two royal houses.[32] The princesses, however, arriving annually or even triennially, would have become too numerous all to be wives of the Darfur ruler. Yet, neither could they, as free women, become his concubines. If they were in fact treated as concubines, that would, strictly speaking, be tantamount to enslavement—illegal, of course, since a free Muslim cannot be enslaved. How far such

[27] IV, 209.
[28] The Wadai and Darfur statements of these events are respectively IV, 208-10 and 281.
[29] IV, 283.
[30] IV, 210, 283-5.
[31] IV, 281.
[32] Abd el-Kerim, as part of the build-up of his power before seizing the Wadai throne from the Tunjur, ensured for himself a substantial following among the Arab population by marrying the daughters of his family to various Arab chiefs; IV, 207.

scruples were present in participants' minds at the time difficult now to judge. Slaves were unambiguously involved when newly enthroned Wadai kings sometimes, 'as a kind of homage', sent a number of eunuchs to Constantinople, and pious gifts of money to the holy cities of Mecca and Medina.[33]

In 1874, when Nachtigal was himself in Darfur, and had just come from Wadai, the relationship between the two states was no longer expressed in tribute, but rather in the exchange of gifts. Even in such gift exchange, however, coded messages could be sent. The two states had recently been close allies, both threatened by external forces from the northeast. Now, with the accession of a new king of Darfur, Brahim, the previous good relations appeared, so Nachtigal observed,

> no longer to be maintained with the same warmth. First Shems ed-Din, the messenger of the new king of Darfur, had brought as a present to the neighbouring sovereign only one horse and one slave girl; the king of Wadai had responded, indeed, to this modest gift with several hundred camels, four horses, and several female slaves, etc., but on the other hand he had spoken only in general, though friendly terms, and had decisively declined any formal renewal of the earlier alliance. He had also presented to the envoy Shems ed-Din only one horse and one slave girl.

So dissatisfied was King Brahim at the outcome of the embassy, that the hapless Shems ed-Din got no presents for himself at all on his return.[34]

The dividing line between taxes levied on subject groups, and tribute levied on neighbouring groups, is often hazy. Revenue was certainly flowing into the hands of the governments of both Darfur and Wadai. The *diwan*, levied in Darfur every four years, varied according to the occupation of the tribes and the yield of the region in question. It might be paid in horses, camels, wheat, cloth, tobacco, honey, salt, butter. And several tribes, the Sula, Bego, Daju, Gulla and others, paid in slaves.[35]

The Salamat Arabs, living in and to the south of Wadai,

[33] IV, 175; curiously, slaves are not mentioned among the 'usual presents' given by Borno and Darfur to the new ruler of Wadai.
[34] IV, 372.
[35] IV, 359.

made frequent raids further south to get slaves, of whom they had to deliver a considerable number, never fewer than 100 a year, to the ruler of Wadai, in addition to cattle, cloth, honey, ivory, rhinoceros horns, crocodile skins, and the like.[36] Every year, the *aqid* of the Salamat, the tribe's representative in Abeshr, the capital of Wadai, travelled south

> to supervise his extensive district, to keep up the warlike spirit of the people of Wadai by raids to the south, southwest and southeast, and to supply the sultan's requirements of slaves and ivory.[37]

Later, summarizing the Darfur sultan's revenues, Nachtigal speaks of some 4,000 slaves, apparently from the Salamat and from another Arab tribe, the Rashid, together, payable every third year. Nachtigal says one-half of the slaves go to the sultan; where the other half go he does not make clear. The sultan receives in addition the produce from his officials' raids.[38]

According to a report, not from Nachtigal himself but cited in a footnote, says that, just before the middle of the nineteenth century, the districts of Fongaro and Goula, the former belonging to Darfur, were paying an annual tribute of 1,000 slaves each to Wadai, in order to escape being raided for slaves themselves.[39]

Bagirmi was the principal tributary of Wadai, an obligation dating from 1806, when King Sabun of Wadai sacked Massenya, capital of Bagirmi. Nachtigal reports Bagirmi's tribute as 500 slaves, thirty young slave girls, 30 horses and 1,000 tobes, payable every third year.[40] Barth gave the triennial tribute as 100 ordinary male slaves, thirty handsome female slaves, 100 horses, and 1,000 garments, besides an additional payment, for the official responsible for this province, of ten female slaves, four horses and 40 garments.[41] According to el-Tounsy, the traveller closest to the event, whose father had accompanied Sabun's expedition, the original tribute, annual,

[36] IV, 98.
[37] IV, 141.
[38] IV, 181-2.
[39] Fresnel, 'Mémoire', 19, cited in IV, 357 n. See also IV, 50.
[40] IV, 214 n. 3 (Nachtigal's own note).
[41] 1965, II, 552, 657.

was 1,000 slaves, 1,000 horses, 1,000 camels and 1,000 garments, a heavy load, which Sabun later reduced by half on the appeal of the Bagirmi ruler.[42]

Not surprisingly there was sometimes trouble over the quality of the slaves offered as tribute; the custom of the king of Bagirmi of sending his oldest, ugliest and most useless slaves to Wadai was one of the various provocations which moved the king of Wadai to attack him in 1870.[43]

Bagirmi was not only a tribute-payer, but a receiver of tribute, and a very successful one in Nachtigal's opinion, for he identifies the tributary Pagan tribes as the main sources of the development of Bagirmi power, 'great in proportion to the limited extent of the country'.[44] Birni Besse, the first Bagirmi king, in the sixteenth century, imposed tribute of cattle and horses on some conquered groups, but Maje, a small domain, paid in slaves: Birni Besse had married the daughter of the ruler of Maje, and had then killed him.[45] By Nachtigal's time, a wide variety obligations had been imposed. The northern Sokoro domains delivered more or less precisely defined annual taxes in horses, cotton strips, and garments. This tribe does not possess many slaves, nor do they enslave their own people. Busso and Sarua also appear to pay regular tribute, in slaves and cotton strips. Miltu and others were subject to tribute of 100 slaves each, but paid only when an armed force arrived to collect it; smaller numbers might be similarly demanded from yet other groups. Somraï, when reminded of its tributary duty, by military intervention, is said customarily to yield one of its own villages for plundering.

> More productive for the Bagirmi kings than these larger Pagan districts with more or less fixed taxes are the tribes dispersed in individual local communities, whose disunity makes impossible either resistance in common, or tribute in common. A single conquered village of the Sara, Gaberi, Kuang or Musgo often yields more slaves than the whole tribute amounts to of one of the larger little countries

---

[42] Muhammad el-Tounsy, *Voyage au Ouaday*, Paris 1851, 171, 182.
[43] III, 422. See the opening quote on p. 295 above.
[44] III, 388.
[45] III, 400-1.

mentioned, and often involves less trouble since, in order to ward off disaster from themselves, neighbouring fellowtribesmen not infrequently lend a helping hand against their own brothers.[46]

Borno patriots, apparently, liked to regard Bagirmi as tributary to their own country. Nachtigal denied that any such dependent relationship existed, adding however that Bagirmi did make an annual gift of slaves to the ruler of Borno, which courtesy was 'suitably requited' by him.[47]

Nevertheless, Borno was surely a major consumer of tribute, even if not, strictly speaking, from Bagirmi. The slaves in the Bornu markets came from raids, trade, and through 'tribute from vassal princes on the periphery of the country, who likewise carry on continuous warfare for this purpose against their Pagan neighbours.'[48] The little country of Logon, which Nachtigal visited twice, lying between Borno and Bagirmi, illustrates very well the circumstances of a tributary state, and the possible advantages of such a position.

> From the beginning of its existence as a state Logon has probably been subject to the overlordship of Bornu, and perhaps even first took shape under the aegis of this powerful neighbour. It could be nothing but welcome to the kings of Bornu that on the southern borders of their domain there should be formed a Muhammadan state, paying tribute regularly, which would spare them the trouble of penetrating all too frequently the swampy Musgo country to capture slaves. But this tributary relationship appears always to have weighed less heavily upon the country than [did] the vexations to which it was exposed on the side of Bagirmi....The tribute which is paid to the king of Bornu seems now to consist of only a hundred slaves and a hundred tobes; and in addition to this there are at most demands for provisions for the Bornu troops when these undertake occasional raids into the Musgo countries.[49]

Tribute might also be imposed on a one-off basis, as a form of punishment for national misdemeanour. An example

[46] III, 388.
[47] III, 214.
[48] II, 233.
[49] III, 264.

concerns Tanemon, ruler of Zinder, an independent and turbulent state between Borno and Hausaland further to the west. Tanemon had killed one of the most loyal vassals of Shaykh Umar of Borno, behaving in general with obstreperous insolence. The Borno war machine was gradually set in motion, to prepare for punitive action. But there was no spirit for a fight on the Borno side, and when Tanemon sent an apologetic envoy, inviting Shaykh Umar to impose any punishment whatever, the Shaykh, 'breathing a sigh of relief', fined Tanemon 1,500 slaves, 1,000 for Umar himself, 300 for the principal councillors of the state, and 200 for the messenger whom he would send to collect this corrective tribute. 'Lord Tanemon has easy and reliable access to slaves, for he sells his own natives and makes them slaves.'[50]

Selling one's own people, or surrendering them, into slavery is clearly a bad thing. Nachtigal, recalling the days before the penetration of Islam into Darfur, that is, before the Tunjur immigration, says that there is no doubt that the Daju formed then the most powerful section of the population. Now, however, '...they are regarded as being very nearly Pagans, so that during the last century part of their tribute still had to be paid in the shape of their own subjects', despite their glory days in the distant past.[51] There is however a grey area, in which handing over some of one's people to the government might be acceptable, provided that those so handed over be treated with appropriate respect. The Birgid people in Darfur provide an illustration, in Nachtigal's pages. The Birgid were evidently rather a stiff-necked people: the king of Darfur, Suleman Solon, conquered them in the seventeenth century;[52] in the early eighteenth century, King Omar Lele defeated rebels in Dar-Birgid, the region of the Birgid;[53] Nachtigal defines the Birgid as 'a tribe which consists of slaves of the sultan, and has not mixed with other people', 'sultan's slaves'.[54] In the reign of Muhammad Tirab, in the later eighteenth century,

[50] II, 284 and n. Richardson (1853, II, 204-5) also reported this disagreeable practice of the Zinder government, selling its own subjects into slavery.
[51] IV, 347.
[52] IV, 279.
[53] IV, 284.
[54] IV, 152, 165.

there was a revolt of the Birgid, who charged the king with selling to the Jellaba as slaves their daughters, of whom they had to deliver each year a number of concubines for the king, wives for his dignitaries, or servants for the royal household in the residence.[55]

It was not the payment of fellow tribesman in tribute which caused the trouble, but rather that some of these were then sold abroad, rather than being incorporated into the royal residence. Tirab finally firmly incorporated the Birgid into Darfur: the goat's hair brush which decorated spears carried before king of Darfur is said to derive from the beard cut from the face of the defeated Birgid ruler.[56]

One final sub-heading, already indicated here and there in the preceding discussion: something very much akin to tribute, but operating within the national framework. On the appointment of a new *bash-shaykh*, or Arab tribal chief, in Borno, the ruler claims from the tribal section concerned a certain number of horses; of these, the head dignitary, presumably the representative of the tribe at the capital, receives his share, usually claiming also a slave-girl into the bargain.[57] The payment on the accession of a new chief might be replicated when a chief dies. When two Pagan village heads died on the same day, within Hamman Yaji's jurisdiction, he ordered one village to pay three calves and thirty goats, and the other two slave-girls.[58]

And again, though here the border situation seems ill-defined, the district where Nachtigal gave up his abortive attempt to visit Runga, south of Wadai, during the rainy season in 1873, the district of the Jeggel people, paid taxes to its representative in Abeshr, of 150 jars of honey, 300 cotton strips, and ten slaves.[59]

Nachtigal's comments throw no light on reasons for using slaves for these purposes in some cases but not in others, apart from the obvious consideration that slaves might sometimes

[55] IV, 287-8.
[56] IV, 288.
[57] III, 178; the text might also be read as identifying the head dignitary, *Chef-Würdenträger*, with the newly appointed *bash-shaykh*.
[58] Hamman Yaji, 54, 12 August 1913.
[59] IV, 110.

be the most easily accessible means of payment. In any case, slave tribute was not exacted merely, or even in most cases mainly, because the slaves might later be advantageously exported to Tripoli, Cairo or Constantinople. It was also believed that the recipients of such tribute would find the slaves really useful at home. Slave tribute was an unusually predictable, and controllable—though far indeed from being perfectly so—procedure within the broader policy of population mobility, the marshalling of demographic resources.

Alms and presents

'My son Hasan [got married] to the daughter of Bulama Abba. I gave as her marriage present a cow, a female slave and 11 woollen mats. The cow, though, I borrowed from Hassan.' (Hamman Yaji, p. 131, 29 August 1926)

The general acceptability of slaves under this heading was another element which helped keep up demands for them. We have seen in the preceding section how alike, in some instances, the payment of tribute, and the exchange of gifts, might seem. The difficulty of defining the exact difference between one transaction and another (see above, p. 295) arises with gifts, just as at other points in this chapter. Tributary obligations for which there was no ready means of enforcement tended to become a little hazy, and it might be difficult to determine whether there was any element of tribute in the transmission of such things as the eunuchs sometimes sent by the kings of Wadai to Constantinople as a mark of respect (see p. 292). Similarly, the slaves presented to the official in charge of the Darfur frontier post by the caravan with which Nachtigal travelled from Wadai to Darfur in 1874 might be variously classified as a gift or a transit-toll.[60]

Gifts including slaves certainly played an important part in many political transactions. In 1584, for example, the ruler of Songhay, receiving an embassy bearing gifts from Morocco, responded with still more costly gifts, chiefly slaves and eunuchs.[61]

All kinds of political business might be facilitated by supererogatory gifts of slaves. Slaves were among the gifts with which King Ali of Wadai tried, unavailingly, to seduce the

[60] IV, 247.
[61] al-Sadi, 193; he specifies 80 eunuchs.

volatile Awlad Sulayman from their somewhat uneasy allegiance to Bornu.[62] In the time of Zubayr, emir of Adamawa 1890-1901, the chief of Gabow died and left four sons, who, seeking the succession, repaired to the emir. One, Atiku, had nothing to offer; but he promised the *wazir* fifty slaves, and thus gained admission to the emir; he promised the emir 300 slaves, and gained the inheritance. Then, to meet his commitments, he enslaved some even of his fellow Fulani, even clerics. Zubayr, angry, summoned his chiefs, Atiku among them. No chief came with a gift of more than thirty slaves, except Atiku who brought 100, in fine gowns, trousers and fezes, each on a horse. Zubayr was thus mollified, and Atiku lived out his days in peace.[63] Hamman Yaji acted on the same principle, though with little confidence:

> Bula gave me a slave girl as the price of his getting the pagans of Dubulum. I do not think that they will be in his control for 12 months, for he is a mischief-maker in the land.[64]

Letters found in Sokoto after the 1902 British occupation often mention presents which originally accompanied the correspondence, mostly written to chiefs, including the Sokoto caliph (all the requests for blessing or prayer are to him, except one to the *waziri*). Letter 38 refers to five slaves and ten rolls of cloth, sent 'for your blessing'; letter 41, ten slaves, 'to seek your blessing'; while letter 15, from Bauchi, mentions the 'usual annual present of seventy slaves and ten bags of cloth', evidently more tribute than gift.[65]

[62] II, 336.
[63] East, 1934/1967, 107 ff.
[64] Hamman Yaji, p. 63, 7 November 1917. See also p. 76, 24 April 1921.
[65] Backwell, 1927/1969. Just for interest, the most common gift, appearing in nearly half the cases in which gifts are mentioned, is cloth or clothing; horses come next, including one 'as requested', and one case of someone asking *for* a horse, rather than giving one; cowries, kola and slaves all figure several times; once each are scent, paper, prayer-beads, silver coins, cows, and a coat of mail. Often a special request is attached to the gifts, usually religious: 'to ask your blessing' (as also in two of the cases quoted in the main text), 'to seek for your blessing', 'for the benefit of your prayers', 'I desire your prayers which are always favourably heard by Allah'. In one case, the offering 'is my acknowledgment to you as chief'—in another, 'that you may buy wood'.

Often presents were built into fixed political rituals: for instance the high Darfur official who places the turban on the head of the new king at his investiture received for this a horse with harness, a robe of honour, and a concubine.[66]

The religious dimension mentioned just above, gifts for prayers, echoes our earlier discussion of slaves as presents to clerics, and to teachers and students of religion (see above pp. 59-63). Similar generosity might be exercised on behalf of lay as well as religious recipients, whether prompted by religious or other motives. Of the sultan of Kilwa, who was surnamed Abu'l-Mawahib, the giver of gifts, Ibn Battuta reported in 1331 that he once gave away his own clothes to a beggar, perhaps a religious mendicant; the sultan's son took back his father's clothes, and gave the beggar instead ten slaves, and the sultan was so impressed by the popular acclaim evoked by this generosity that he himself added ten more slaves and two loads of ivory.[67] Leo Africanus, then aged sixteen, once deputized for his uncle, visiting a prince in North Africa, and reciting poems, some by his uncle and some by himself, in honour of the prince. Leo received 100 ducats and two slaves for his uncle, 50 ducats and a good horse for himself, and 10 ducats for each of his two servants.[68] Later, at the court of Gaoga in the central Sudan, Leo saw a merchant of Damietta give the king a gallant horse, a Turkish sword, a royal robe and several other articles, receiving in return five slaves, five camels, 500 ducats and nearly 100 ivory tusks.[69] Usuman dan Fodio too, founder of the Sokoto empire in the nineteenth century, was renowned for his generosity in slaves, camels and provisions, especially to *sharifs*, descendants of the Prophet.[70] A *sharif* named al-Habib once came to Ali, a later sultan of Sokoto, and explained that he would not pretend to have come on pilgrimage to the tomb of Usuman or for any other pious purpose, but honestly admitted that he had come for money. Commending his frankness, Ali gave him drafts for five horses on Zaria, and for 200 slaves on Adamawa; honouring

[66] IV, 330.
[67] Ibn Battuta, 20-1; Freeman-Grenville, 1962, 108.
[68] Leo Africanus, A, II, 305-7; B, I, 136-8.
[69] *ibid.*, A, III, 835; B, II, 483.
[70] Clapperton, 1829, 205.

the draft, the emir of Adamawa added fifty slaves as a personal token.[71] When Canot, the nineteenth-century slave-trader, left Futa Jallon after his visit there, he was given various presents by the ruling family, including five slaves. The son of the *almami* of Futa Jallon, 'like a gentleman of taste, despatched for my consolation the two prettiest handmaidens he could buy or steal in Timbo', capital of the state.[72]

Slave-girls were, of course, a particularly piquant gift, or means of settling accounts, or acknowledgment of one's superiors, or whatever. Hamman Yaji's diary gives examples, numerous enough indeed to suggest quite a hive of activity in this rather localised sub-heading of population mobility. In September 1912, some Pagans of the Matakam tribe from Buba Magawa's village brought Hamman Yaji a female slave.[73] Such arrangements might be fitted into dealings with the European administration (though Hamman Yaji does not record anything comparable to Canot's experience in Timbo):

> I sent two messengers...to Ngaundere with two horses for the White Man; one was a present for him and the other was for sale. There was also a female slave for the interpreter.[74]

This was in December 1912. A double entry in the same month, three days later, suggests that peaceful exchange might sometimes work better than violence:

> the pagans called Shikawa brought me 10 slave girls. I also sent soldiers to Kamale, but they did not reach the Arnado's compound and only got a female slave whose hand had been cut off and who was as stupid as a goat. This made me very angry with them.[75]

Hamman Yaji seems not to have noticed the contrast between the two policies; or, if he did, he certainly did not act on it. And in any case, receipt of slaves peacefully, as gifts or tribute, merely moves the violence one step further down the line: how did the pagans called Shikawa get their slaves whom

[71] Said, 351-3.
[72] Canot, 1928, 173.
[73] Hamman Yaji, 51; this is the very first diary entry.
[74] *ibid.*, 52.
[75] *ibid.*, 52. The *arnado* is the village chief.

they were so courteously to pass on? The typed English translation of the diary omits pages of the original Arabic (now lost), as of lesser interest. Between 10 February and 17 March 1913, for instance, a manuscript page of Hamman Yaji's activities is excised with this summary: 'concerned mainly with entries regarding trading expeditions, gifts to him of slaves, and his own visits to his "country houses".'[76] Rather frustrating for us. In August 1917, the Madagali raiders seem to have run amok (see above, p. 180), killing women and children. Nonetheless eighty slaves were captured, of whom Hamman Yaji gave away forty.[77] The whole incident is mysterious.

In August 1918:

> Bajam and Maliki returned from their journey to Marua and said they had fought the case against Bakari Duhu and had defeated him and had got back for me the pagan girl. So I gave them a slave girl.[78]

This seems to have been a case of disputed ownership, of 'the pagan girl'. We may hope that Bajam and Maliki did not themselves fall out over the single slave-girl given to them as a reward. In October 1918:

> Bakr Guldum brought me the stocks (?) of two rifles and I gave him ten shillings. I decided I would give him a slave girl.[79]

In July 1919:

> I caused the name of my land to be changed and gave away two slave girls on the occasion of changing the name, and I fixed a fine of 5s. for anyone who made a mistake in this name.[80]

In December of the same year Hamman Yaji gave the Emir of Rei a horse, two six-year-old cows and a female slave;[81] the

---

[76] Hamman Yaji, 52. See pp. 44-5 for the history of the text. On p. 75, 'gifts of slaves to his sons' are among the items dropped.
[77] ibid., 63.
[78] ibid., 66.
[79] ibid., 67.
[80] ibid., 70.
[81] ibid., 71.

Sarkin Arewa was given a slave-girl two years later.[82] A final gift example, on 1 April 1924:

> I gave my son Abd al Rahman a small slave and I said to him: 'Listen, I am not going to clothe you any more.'[83]

Not only Muslims gave slaves as alms or gifts. King Jesus I of Ethiopia, 1680-1704, sent back a few slaves and a young elephant with emissaries who had visited him from France, though by various misadventures all the gifts were lost.[84] Amai, Christian ruler of Nubia, who visited Cairo early in the fourteenth century, included slaves among the gifts which he took with him on that occasion.[85]

Over a wide area, and a long span of time, slave-girls were regarded as an entirely appropriate component within a bride's dowry. Leo Africanus reported that in Fez 'the meaner sort' usually gave for a daughter's dowry 30 ducats and a black female slave worth 15 ducats.[86] That added touch of feminity might occasionally go too far. In Sokoto in 1826 the dowry given by a family of good condition consisted of young female

---

[82] *Hamman Yaji*, 78.

[83] *ibid.*, 92. My first thought here was, was this Abd al Rahman's first slave? and, if so, did possessing a slave of one's own mark the achievement of a certain maturity and independence? However, the small slave seems unlikely to have been such a novelty for Abd al Rahman, as he had received from his father the chieftainship of Kova two years before (p. 78). Events in Kova later got out of hand, requiring the direct intervention first of Hamman Yaji (p. 87) and then of a British official, W.O.P. Rosedale (p. 88). Immediately after this, Rosedale ordered Hamman Yaji to send Abd al Rahman to him, and Abd al Rahman was despatched forthwith to Yola (p. 88). After the small slave incident, which followed the Kova troubles, Abd al Rahman is mentioned only once, sent on a minor errand by his father (95). Maybe the small slave was in fact a symbolic reproach to a son not fulfilling his father's expectations. Abd al Rahman had been sent 'to the school of the Christians at Garua' at the very end of 1916 (61). On Abd al Rahman's return (presumably not for the first time) 'from the school of the French Christians', four years later, Hamman Yaji noted, 'I told him: "There are three things for you to look after—the mosque, your dress and your food."' (74) Another reproach? for it is a very modest agenda. Hamman Yaji almost never quotes his own spoken words in his journal, but he did this twice in the case of Abd al Rahman.

[84] Arkell, 1961, 217-20.

[85] *ibid.*, 197-8.

[86] Leo Africanus, A, II, 448; B, I, 209.

slaves, and many household and personal goods which were carried in procession on the heads of the wife's female slaves when she first went to her husband's house. If the husband slept with one of his wife's dowry slaves, he had next day to supply a new virgin slave of equal value; this, it was said, never occasioned any dispute.[87]

Nachtigal noted two instances where slaves figured as part of a marriage dowry, though he does not specify that these should be female slaves. It was, he said, standard practice among the well-to-do of Borno for the bride's father to include a slave among the presents given to a prospective son-in-law, who however will already have given his father-in-law to be the bride-price, which 'depends entirely on the wealth of the two men, and consists of money, slaves, horses and the like'.[88] In Wadai, on the wedding day the groom presents the bride with a gift, 'the right of the bride's bed', 'in the shape of slaves, horses, cows, according to his wealth, but he has the right to take this back if the bride does not come up to expectations.'[89]

Nachtigal also himself witnessed a double wedding, in Abeshr in August 1873, just before setting out on his abortive attempt to visit Runga. Two daughters of the king of Wadai were marrying important notables, and the royal dowry provisions were lavish in the extreme. Nachtigal admired the arriving camels,

> laden with clothing, ornaments, and especially with all the property in the shape of gold, silver and cloth, with which their royal father had endowed the brides....Slave girls, who followed the young mistress out of her father's house, were enthroned on the loads. Those camels which carried the most valuable loads of this kind were decorated with ostrich feathers on their heads, and with silver foot-rings.

The sister and envoy of the *momo*, or Queen Mother,

> led a singular procession which carried the *momo's* presents for her granddaughter....A slave led the horse on which she was sitting, while at her side two others made a dreadful din with a gourd full of stones....Thirty slave girls brought up

[87] Clapperton, 1829, 213.
[88] II, 275-6.
[89] IV, 192.

the end of the procession, who were not only neatly but richly dressed and ornamented, all carrying on their heads large baskets with covers, the contents of which were of course not visible to the spectators. The baskets themselves were decorated with cowrie shells or beads in the most varied and tasteful patterns, and the whole scene gave an impression which was as varied as it was charming and interesting.[90]

Hamman Yaji's gift of a female slave, even as late as 1926, to his prospective daughter-in-law is quoted at the head of this section. On 2 July 1921 he had sent a daughter to wed the Emir of Adamawa, and with her 'large quantities of goods and horses, so that they could not be counted for their large numbers.'[91] No mention of slaves: yet it is hard to imagine that none were included. The explanation for this reticence, if reticence it be, may lie in the visit of a British official to Hamman Yaji in the latter part of December 1920, just over six months earlier.[92] The editors, Vaughan and Kirk-Greene, suggest that it was on this visit that the British ordered Hamman Yaji to cease raiding for slaves.[93] So soon after this, he may have deemed it prudent not to record the presence of slaves is so public a context as a huge wedding party sent to the ruler of Adamawa.[94]

Two final examples, to illustrate again the time and geography span of the dowry slave. In the seventeenth century, it was reported that, among the coastal Vai people of west Africa, the bride was purchased with presents and slaves, and the

[90] IV, 85-6.
[91] Hamman Yaji, 76.
[92] *ibid.*, 75.
[93] *ibid.*, 15.
[94] The argument here is speculative on two counts. First, Hamman Yaji does not relate exactly what the Britisher said: 'he told me what he had to say.' The editors claim that this wording 'is unlike any other description of interaction in the diary, and in this oblique fashion he calls attention to the importance of the transaction'. In fact, very much the same phrasing is used of two other encounters with the British, on 27 March 1924 (p. 91), and again on 25 July 1924 (p. 97). And second, it would seem surprising for Hamman Yaji consciously to censor his own account of the wedding preparations, when at exactly the same time he records gifts of slaves to his sons, flogging female slaves, receiving slaves as a present, and retrieving a woman runaway slave (pp. 75-6). See also pp. 342-3 below.

dowry included a slave.[95] And, at least until the mid-twentieth century, among the Saharan Tuareg, it was customary for the bride-price to include a slave girl.[96]

Nachtigal himself had to fend off repeated efforts by Abu Sekkin, the Bagirmi ruler in temporary exile, to bestow gifts of slaves upon him (see below, p. 378). A somewhat similar, and rather melancholy, incident occurred in Wadai. There, a slave who had not long before come to Wadai from the Pagan regions to the south, and suffering from leprous ulcers affecting the joints of his fingers, attached himself very closely to Nachtigal and his party. Nachtigal treated him, indeed amputating one finger completely. King Ali of Wadai, seeing the patient's attachment,

> wanted to make a present of the poor man to me, but I had to refuse him, in spite of the fact that I was sorry to see him left behind in the royal palace in the utmost despair, for with my departure close at hand I should not have known in the least what I should do with him.[97]

Finally, the eunuchs despatched to Mecca and Medina for the service of the holy places there consitute a rather special category of gifts or alms. As marks of respect comparable with the eunuchs sent to Constantinople, Nachtigal mentioned only pious gifts of money as being despatched to Mecca and Medina.[98] Eunuchs were, however, also sent there, as they were to Constantinople, only rarely from Borno, but more frequently, though irregularly, from Bagirmi and Wadai. In 1852 Barth met an envoy from Medina in Massenya, who had come to ask for eunuchs to guard the Prophet's tomb.[99] The last such despatch was about 1895. The satisfaction which the eunuchs who went to Mecca at that time found in their work there seems still to have been as sincere as ever. Another old Bagirmian eunuch, freed after many years of service in charge, he said, of the Zam-Zam well, returned from Mecca in the later

---

[95] Ogilby, 1670, 392-3. When Sau, the father of Doalu Bukara who in the nineteenth century invented the Vai script, died, Sau's son-in-law received among other presents a slave (Koelle, 1849, appendix, 5).
[96] Nicolaisen, 1997, II, 600.
[97] IV, 78-9.
[98] IV, 175.
[99] Barth, 1965, II, 505.

years of the nineteenth century to end his days peacefully in Abeshr.[100]

Slaves as currency

'I heard that I was to be given away because of a debt.' (Dorugu, in Kirk-Greene and Newman, 43).

This is the most difficult section in the whole book to separate out from the others. Slaves as cooks, for example, are distinct; slaves as curency are not. The entire 'Slaves as tribute' discussion could be included here. 'The contribution of slaves to religious activity' includes many payments of slaves to members of the religious establishment. And so on. In several respects slaves were an unsatisfactory currency: they were high value, and could not be cut up as Nachtigal saw done to the Maria Theresa dollar; they were perishable, or elusive; and they varied enormously in quality. Nevertheless, it seems worthwhile to try to focus, however unsteadily, on the currency dimension.

The leader of a trading caravan from Futa Jallon to the West African coast in the nineteenth century, too sensible to fall captive under the romantic spell of the mere name of Timbuktu, did nevertheless prefer the market of that city.

'Ah!' said the astute trafficker, 'no market is a good one for the African, in which he cannot openly exchange his slaves for whatever the original owner or importer can sell without fear! Slaves . . . are our money.'[101]

Nachtigal also noted how slaves came to be regarded as one of the more useful substitutes for money. They became, in effect, a store of value, albeit one which medical hazards made extremely risky.[102] Nachtigal's friend, the Sherif al-Medeni, had for several years been trying, in vain, to return to North

[100] Gaden, 1907, 439-40, 442-3, 445.
[101] Canot, 1928, 135-6.
[102] *cf.* J.F. Ade Ajayi, 'West African states at the beginning of the nineteenth century', in Ajayi and Espie, 1965, 254: 'Slaves were used in large transactions as a form of currency.' Also, *Report on Lagos for 1891*, 58, *cit.* McPhee, 1926, 234: 'The slave has become the cheque book of the country, and has been necessary for all large payments. Unfortunately, he has a trick of dying, while passing from hand to hand, and it is possible that the less perishable currency [silver coin] will oust him from the commercial field.'

Africa, or to his home in Arabia. Several times he collected sufficient in slaves, ostrich feathers, and ivory, to enable him to depart. But always something interfered. Among such stumbling-blocks were the epidemics which thinned the ranks of his slaves.[103] Human as well as medical factors might complicate the utility of slaves as a form of money. In the mid-nineteenth century, in Sama, an increasingly Muslim centre in Liberia, one man lent another a slave to take on a journey in the direction of Monrovia. Near Monrovia, once within which slaves were by law free (see above, p. 251), this slave ran away, and the lender had later to bring an action in Sama against the borrower, trying to recover the lost value.[104]

The discharge of debts is one of the clearest 'currency' uses of slaves. Payment in slaves was in itself quite a respectable financial operation, sometimes used by Lamino who enjoyed a high reputation as an honest and trustworthy debtor.[105] The possession of a good supply of slaves not only strengthened the social standing of men of rank, but also made them better credit risks. By great good fortune, we have the account of someone—Dorugu, in Kukawa in the mid-nineteenth century—who was himself used to pay a debt.

> I heard that I was to be given away because of a debt. I was told this by a boy who spoke Kanuri.[106] I said all right. One day when an Arab came, the boy said to me, 'Do you see that white man? That's who you are going to be given to.' I said to myself, 'What can I do? I don't know what to do.'

[103] II, 176-7.
[104] Bowen, 1857/1968, 81-2.
[105] II, 139.
[106] Dorugu was Hausa, and, having just arrived in Borno, spoke no Kanuri, the principal language there: 'It was just as if I were deaf', the same sensation he had later in his life on arriving in Marseilles (Kirk-Greene and Newman, 40, 88): the other boy was presumably Hausa too, since he could communicate with Dorugu, but had lived long enough in Borno to learn Kanuri. The language problems, sometimes amounting to to total linguistic isolation, confronting slaves deserve more attention; the remark that a variety of languages amongst slaves might help a caravan on the march is correct (see above, p. 224), but does not by any means take the measure of the difficulty. Slave-owners might also be constrained by language barriers. Dorugu, who became a linguist himself, working with Africanists in Britain particularly on Hausa, was perhaps unusually sensitive to language circumstances. See also Pipes, 1981, 80.

The boy said to me, 'When you see that white man coming, go into the bush and hide and don't come out until evening.'

But I didn't pay close attention to what he was saying. Some time later, the man came when my master was also there. All of us slaves assembled and then they called me. The Arab examined my eyes, my tongue, my hands, and even my feet. When he had finished looking, they began to talk, although I didn't know what they were saying. The Arab mounted his horse. Then they said to me, 'Go with him.' 'Why?' I asked. They said to me in Hausa, 'Go and fetch some wood from his house.' I told them, 'You're lying. I know that you've sold me.'[107]

The Arab who accepted Dorugu was clearly getting good value, better than he could ever have realised, and he took care to check Dorugu carefully beforehand. Other creditors, particularly among the foreign merchants, might not be so lucky. A favoured device of the defaulting debtor was to sacrifice, even before a judge, 'an old, almost unsalable and overpriced slave'.[108] Such transactions as these, and that involving Dorugu, were taking place in Kuka, a major trading city, where a more or less satisfactory currency system existed, based on the Maria Theresa dollar and the cowrie.

Even when there is no dispute about quality, slaves may be unacceptable as a non-convertible, or otherwise unsatisfactory, currency. Nachtigal himself confronted this problem. Three hundred dollars were due to him, from Belaid, a merchant in Kukawa,

> a thoroughly honest man whom I had known for a long time, [who] was so short of cash of any kind that, with the best will in the world, he had only slaves to offer me, which I could not convert into money again.[109]

Nachtigal was under far greater pressure still to accept slaves, offered to him by the king, Abu Sekkin, when visiting the Bagirmi court in exile. In succession, Nachtigal fended off

---

[107] Kirk-Greene and Newman, 43.

[108] II, 236; or the debtor might, before the creditor's very eyes, 'give the order to sell at any price this slave woman and that horse', but nothing would be done.

[109] IV, 7; on p. 19 Nachtigal declines camels also, as well as slaves.

ten elderly men and women, ten *sedasi* slaves, a comparatively richly dressed royal concubine surprised in an indiscretion (Nachtigal calls her a wife of Abu Sekkin, but this seems almost certainly wrong), and finally a sixteen-year-old Pagan maiden (whom the king eventually gave to Almas, Nachtigal's guide— whether the girl was one of the party who finally returned to Kukawa, or whether she died, or ran away, is not made clear: see above, p. 127).[110]

Even before getting to Abu Sekkin at all, Nachtigal had had the prospect of some dozens of slaves held out to him by a chief along the way, who, impressed with the weaponry and gunpowder of Nachtigal's party, thought that the visitors might be lured into slave-raiding against neighbouring enemies.[111]

At the other end of the slaves-as-currency spectrum is the situation in which the seller insists upon slaves. In Kobe, the second city of Darfur, in 1874, 'horses were dear and mostly had to be purchased with slaves'.[112]

There are several instances in which a *sedasi* slave is mentioned, though not altogether unambiguously, more as a unit of account, then as a medium of exchange: the value of a woman's long necklace in Wadai (IV, 197), in the purchase of cotton clothing (IV, 373), the price of a camel in Kawar (I, 418).

> In the use of slaves as currency, or in any other commercial transaction in which they served a role somewhat akin to currency, it is difficult, just as it is at many points in this survey, to distinguish how much arises from the original Islamic heritage, and how much from the local African custom. The legal texts repeatedly make special mention of commercial regulations applying to slaves. The law of

---

[110] III, 364-5; see below, p. 378. *Slavery* 1970 (p. 157) says that the proprieties were eventually observed by a gift of ivory; more careful study of the text indicates that, while Nachtigal did have some ivory, which he sold for 130 dollars after getting back to Kuka (IV, 19), this was part payment for Nachtigal's own horse, sold to Abu Sekkin; the further ivory, promised in place of the rejected slaves, never materialised.
[111] III, 309-10.
[112] IV, 254.

sale includes frequent references to slaves;[113] purchase *en bloc* is forbidden for slaves, clothing, or anything else that can be counted easily;[114] a guarantee for a slave is valid, if explicitly stipulated or part of local procedure, for three days at the total responsibility of the seller—such a guarantee, extended to a year, insures only against madness, elephantiasis and leprosy;[115] anything may be made the object of a loan, save slave girls and silver dust,[116] if a female slave is given as security, a child born to her after the contract is agreed becomes part of the security, but her goods do not unless special provision is made for this.[117]

In these and other like provisions, it is clear that the religious law provides considerable precedent for regarding slaves in an economic, almost a fiscal way. Yet at the same time there are similar precedents to be found in parts of Africa where there has been little Muslim influence. For example, an American traveller near Badagry, in Yorubaland, in 1850 saw the corpse of a slave bound in mats and suspended, several feet above the ground, between two stakes. This, he was told, was the customary mode of burial for a slave who died while in pawn for debt, so that his original owner, the debtor, on returning from the interior, should know that the creditor had not sold him.[118] In Katanga and the surrounding area, a system called *nkole* was in force, whereby the aggrieved party might seize someone, someone perhaps only very remotely connected with the offender, in any dispute. If the offender still declined to offer adequate compensation, the innocent third person who had been seized might be enslaved, and thus himself provide the compensation.[119] An introductory survey—which does not, however, mention Islam—has been made of

---

[113] Ibn Abi Zayd, 200 ff.
[114] *ibid.*, 212.
[115] *ibid.*, 210.
[116] *ibid.*, 206.
[117] *ibid.*, 236.
[118] Bowen, 1857/1968, 101.
[119] Crawford, 1914, 9 ff. He tells of a family of four taken as *nkole*; the father was killed, and the two daughters made concubines of the aggrieved chief. Just after, the chief died, and one of the girls was buried alive with him. Crawford (195-6) also mentioned two boys bartered for one man.

sometimes called it debt slavery, or even domestic slavery; the pawn owner in many instances acquired hereditary rights, and the status of pawn was itself heritable. Pawns, in this area, seem to have been more important as compensation for an injury, leading to a strengthening of the pawn owner's lineage, than in any narrower economic sense. A somewhat parallel system, called panyarring, obtained in West Africa, where it was apparently much abused in order to provide recruits for the Atlantic trade.

A slave who might be used as a medium of exchange, in any of the forms just described, was peculiarly liable to that insecurity which has been noted earlier as inherent in slave status (see pp. 147-9). One of the favourite slaves of King Muhammad al-Fadl of Darfur, Adam, who attained a position of great importance shortly before Nachtigal's visit to that country, acquired the nickname of Tarbush from an episode which vividly illustrated this hazard. Having been presented with a tarbush by a passing merchant, the king gave instructions to express his thanks by the counter-present of a slave. An official, who had a grudge against Adam, handed him over to the merchant, and it was with some difficulty that he was retrieved to resume his career in the king's service.[121]

---

[120] Mary Douglas, 'Matriliny and pawnship in Central Africa', *Africa*, 1964, 301-13.

[121] IV, 307-8. On p. 333, Adam, and Abd al-Bari his predecessor as vizier of Darfur, are classed as half-slaves.

CHAPTER X

THE SLAVE MARKET IN KUKA

'It was at Keffi [in 1901] that I first saw slaves for sale in a market—men, women, and children too—all seated with their legs stretched out. The trading for slaves was just the same as today's bargaining for buying a horse or a cow or a donkey.' (Maimaina, in Kirk-Greene and Newman, 1971, 142)

The slave section, an important part of the great market held every Monday in Kuka, was supplied from three main sources. Some were captured in government raids in the surrounding Pagan territories south, west and south-west of Borno; others came from tribute paid by vassal princes, who carried on continuous warfare against their Pagan neighbours to discharge this obligation; and some came through trade with nearby Hausa countries, Adamawa, and especially Bagirmi.[1] These channels of demographic replenishment depended in considerable measure on high-level organisation, governmental, military and economic. But they could not have functioned as effectively as they did, had they not been able to draw upon grassroots support among ordinary people. Nachtigal's experience in Borno, as he prepared for his remarkable expedition to the court of Abu Sekkin, ruler of Bagirmi, illustrates the extent of popular interest in at least the trading alternative.

As soon as the news had spread abroad in Kuka that I should probably, with the Shaykh's assistance, succeed in getting by the land route to King Abu Sekkin, the spirit of enterprise of many Bornu people, who had a saleable horse or a few dollars to spare, was aroused. It was known that the fugitive king was intent above all on increasing his military

---

[1] II, 233.

potential, so that he might to able to resume the war against Wadai, that his followers needed supplies of clothing, and that, with his superabundance of slaves, he himself was in a position to pay the highest prices. I fended off a numerous company as much as I could, for I did not wish to make my caravan too unwieldy; for if, on the one hand, a reinforcement of men who could bear arms must have suited me well, yet I had, on the other, more confidence in the swiftness and secrecy of my journey than in force of arms. Fortunately only a few of those who wished to join the expedition were able to complete their preparations speedily enough.[2]

Nachtigal made a point, early in his time in Kuka, of visiting the great Monday market, 'one of the most magnificent spectacles that this Negro capital has to offer', as often as possible.[3] He scrutinised every aspect of the market. Our concern is with the slaves.

> In the eastern section of the south side of the market slave dealers have set up large stalls where, protected from the sun and rain, their wares, with or without chains, are displayed in long rows. There await their fate slaves of both sexes—*kinji* means slave without regard to sex, *kalia* means male slave, *kir* female slave—of every age and price from the most diverse Pagan countries to the south of the states of the Sudan. Old men, tired of life, sit alongside small children snatched away from the tender care of a loving mother before they could retain any picture of her in their memories. Among repulsive-looking women, whose faded skin hangs loosely on their fleshless bones, and who have

---

[2] III, 219; see also p. 225. A private and personal zeal for trade in slaves might operate also at the very highest levels. Nachtigal's later departure from Abeshr, capital of Wadai, on his way eastwards to Darfur, was held up, owing to the roads being closed. One rumoured explanation was that the king's favourite wife was to have two sons circumcised in a few days, on which occasion presents would come in from all directions. 'She intended, at the conclusion of the festivities, to exchange these and other goods which she had previously accumulated, for slaves, and to send them with our caravan to Darfur, and she did not wish to have the market there spoiled.'. In fact, the rumour was false: the road was closed because the king of Darfur had died: but no one seems to have found the story of the commercially astute queen implausible. (IV, 70.)

[3] II, 204.

become apathetic through toil and misery, there are bright young girls, their full well-rounded figures in the first bloom of youth, with coquettish head-dress, washed clean and glistening with butter, who look hopefully into the future.[4]

Dorugu, visiting Timbuktu in 1853, briefly described the markets there, contrasting them with Borno in size:

I saw the Timbuktu market where they sell different kinds of meat, firewood, bread, and many other things as well. There were also various slave markets. I went to see the slaves there—boys and men, women and their children—but not very many, as one sees in Bornu; there you will see hundreds in one place.[5]

Slatin provides a comparable picture of the slave market in Omdurman during the Mahdiya.[6] Hurgronje described the slave market in Mecca in most amiable terms.[7] Comparing Mecca and Cairo, in the 1880s, he said:

No unbeliever comes to Mekka, while the Azhar Mosque [in Cairo] has been defiled by the feet of English men and women. In Mekka there is a slave market. In Egypt slaves can only be bought in secret, as if it were a sin.[8]

An African Muslim cleric, visiting Freetown in 1792, told the Governor that Freetown 'ranks next in holiness to Mecca and Medina, for no slave lives or is sold here'.[9] The visitor, it seems likely, had studied a little what it might please the Governor to hear.

The price structure in the Kuka market clearly indicated the general supply and demand situation. It seems probable, though Nachtigal did not specifically say so, that most slaves were females. Long ago, in September 1353, Ibn Battuta left western Africa on his way home northwards across the Sahara, joining a caravan of some 600 women slaves.[10] In more recent

[4] II, 215-16.
[5] Kirk-Greene and Newman, 66.
[6] Slatin, 1896, 557-8.
[7] Hurgronje, 1931, 14-15.
[8] *ibid.*, 185.
[9] Diary entry of 3 November 1792 of Lt. J. Clarkson, in *Sierra Leone Studies*, March 1927, 95-6.
[10] Ibn Battuta, 60; *Corpus*, 303.

times, of those who eventually got through to the caravans for the Mediterranean, it has been estimated that some 60 per cent were young women, and 10 per cent of the rest children under the age of ten.[11] In one caravan of 400-500 which passed

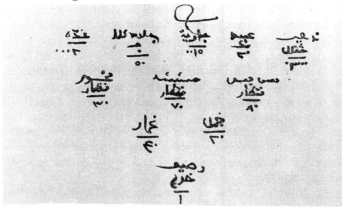

A Ghadames bill of sale, including gold, slaves, slave-girls, hides, pillows (or pillow-cases?), ivory, herbs (senna?), perfume, camels, sacks (or perhaps sheaths, scabbards), and household slaves (perhaps eunuchs). Richardson, 1848, I, 114.

through Qatrun from Bornu to the coast when Eduard Vogel was there towards the end of 1853, most of the slaves were girls or children under 12. Vogel saw at most fifteen men, and was told that they would not be relieved of their chains until they reached Murzuq.[12] As men were more likely than women to be killed during a slave-raid, women and children would usually be in a majority when the booty was rounded up at the end of the day. Even at the end of the day, there are a good many references to the slaughter of grown male prisoners (see above, pp. 179-80, and index, slaves: execution of).

At the same time the demand for women, both as concubines and for domestic service, was much livelier than the demand for men, so much so that at all ages, despite the disparity in supply, the price of women was usually higher than that for men. In East Africa, too, Burton in 1860 reported the

[11] Boahen, 1964, 128.
[12] 'Eduard Vogel's Reise nach Central-Afrika', *Petermanns Mitteilungen* 1855, 251; a rare mention (see pp. 101-2 above) of head-loads, up to 25 German pounds.

price of females as everywhere about one-third higher than that of males.[13] This was in contrast with the conditions in the United States, where female slaves usually brought about three-quarters of price of male slaves of similar age.[14] On the West African coast, where the pattern of American demand had some effect, Canot reported that women slaves who were aged over twenty-five were subject to a 20 per cent. price reduction, though if such 'were staunchly-built, and gave promising tokens for the future', their price was the same as that of able-bodied men. Children, he added, were rarely purchased at the coastal factories, but might be traded advantageously in the local towns.[15] Somewhat surprisingly, Leo Africanus, costing presents given to the ruler of Fez in the early sixteenth century, valued men above women: good men slaves he put at 20 ducats, women slaves at 15, eunuchs at 40, and civet cats at 200.[16]

Much of the demand for women depended a good deal on the individual tastes of the buyer; in the Kuka market young women commanded prices ranging from 40 to 100 Maria Theresa dollars. Consumers' freedom of choice in this connection might lead to unexpected consequences; in accordance with the principle that only the testimony of people of the highest moral probity was admissible in a court of law, an otherwise respectable citizen of Cordova was once rejected as a witness on the ground that on one occasion he had been so smitten with desire for a slave girl as to pay for her a sum far in excess of her real value.[17]

The *sedasi*, the boy who measured six spans from the ankle to the tip of the ears—the word comes from the Arabic *sudasi*, applied also to a six-letter word, a hexagon, and so forth—aged usually from 12 to 15, was a more standardized item of commerce in Borno, and movements in his cost indicated the general situation in slave prices. A foreign merchant, enquiring about the state of the market, would ask, How much are

[13] Burton, 1860/1961, II, 376.
[14] *Encyclopedia of the Social Sciences*, New York 1934, vol. 14, 86.
[15] Canot, 1928, 90 n.
[16] Leo Africanus, A, II, 308-9; B, I, 139. See above, p. 296.
[17] N.J. Coulson, 'Doctrine and practice in Islamic law', *Bulletin of the School of Oriental and African Studies*, 1956, 220, 213-14.

sedasi? *Sedasi* figure in the popular songs and poetry of the central Sudan: a Shuwa Arabic poem, recounting the deeds of the folk hero Abu Zayd, tells how he offered, for a splendid white mare which he eventually acquired by the cheaper method of murdering its owner, ninety-nine old women, ninety-nine slaves of five spans, and ninety-nine *sedasi*.[18] A praise singer at the court of Borno claimed that the *galadima* had rewarded his poetry with a present of twelve slave girls and twelve *sedasi*.[19]

There was, in addition, a brisk demand in Borno for both boys and girls in the five-span group; from ten to thirteen, the girls again generally more expensive than the boys; seven-span boys, fifteen to twenty, brought good prices, though they were more difficult to train, and more likely to run away. Older men suffered even more from these defects, and were not much in demand.[20] They were, moreover, likely to keep up a spirit of discontent among their womenfolk, and one case was actually recorded in Bagirmi where, partly for exactly these reasons, some captured men were resettled, with an appropriate number of women, on the site of their own devastated village (see below, p. 375).[21] For older women who could be used in household work somewhat higher prices were paid than for men of the same age.

Eunuchs, mainly from Bagirmi, seldom came into the open market, as they were usually sold privately to dealers who were confident that they could dispose of them among the

[18] J.R. Patterson, *Stories of Abu Zeid the Hilali in Shuwa Arabic*, London 1930, 24 and 3.

[19] J.R. Patterson, *Kanuri songs*, Lagos 1926, 22.

[20] Daniel Pipes argues that a master seeking prospective military slaves, in the Muslim heartlands, will accept boys as old as seventeen, but prefers them about twelve, corresponding very closely to the preferences which Nachtigal observed in sub-Saharan Africa. 'In contrast, a master seeks ordinary slaves among young adults, when they are at the peak of their economic activity.' (*Slave soldiers and Islam: the genesis of a military system*, New Haven and London: Yale University Press, 1981, 8) But the preference in favour of the very young applies in western Africa across the board, no distinction being made between male slaves intended to become soldiers, and those who would do other work. Indeed, it would be interesting to know what evidence there is of slaves being bought there specifically for military training; Nachtigal does not mention this at all.

[21] III, 362.

magnates of the Muslim world in Europe, Asia and Africa.[22] Nachtigal also saw offered for sale in the Kuka market, for export to the north, deaf and dumb slave girls, much sought after as servants for the wives of these magnates, and dwarfs, a favourite play-thing for Muslim princes, particularly if trained as court jesters. Deaf-mute girls fetch good prices, though not so high as for eunuchs; Nachtigal tells us nothing about the prices of dwarfs. The Dinka deaf-mute, male, whom al-Hajj Ahmed Tangatanga, Nachtigal's patron on the road from Wadai to Darfur, purchased from a young Arab in 1874 has already been mentioned (see above p. 36). Borno dwarfs evidently enjoyed widespread popularity. In 1653 the *mai* of Borno sent some 125 slaves to the pasha of Tripoli, including twenty eunuchs and five dwarfs.[23] Clapperton's party found a Borno dwarf near Badagry in 1825, and tried to buy him his freedom; but the slave did not wish to be sold, and his master therefore refused to part with him.[24]

Nachtigal's price list for slaves in the Kuka market in 1870[25] follows. The Maria Theresa dollar, in which all prices were quoted, was at that time worth about 4 marks.[26]

An old man	4 to 5 M.T. dollars
An old woman	6 to 10
A robust man	12 to 14
A middle-aged woman	10 to 15
A young bearded man	15 to 18
A 7-span youth, aged 15 to 20	16 to 22
A 6-span boy, 12 to 15, or a 5-span girl, 10 to 13	20 to 25
A 5-span boy, 10 to 13	16 to 20
A *surrya* or concubine	40 to 100
A boy eunuch	50 to 80

[22] According to Gaden (1907, 436), the sultans never sold eunuchs, but sometimes presented them to other sultans or sent them to Mecca and Medina for the service of the holy places. Ivory and ostrich feathers also did not usually come to the open market (II, 234).

[23] De la Roncière, 1919, 82-3
[24] Clapperton, 1829, 16.
[25] II, 225-6; see also p. 216.
[26] II, 234.

It is interesting, for purposes of comparison, to note that at the same time the price of a fine riding horse, bred by the Shuwa or Tubu, was 20 to 40 dollars, and of a good strong riding-horse of the usual local breed, 15 to 25 dollars. A northern camel which had come through the desert sold for up to 15 dollars, a camel from the Tuareg, or from Kanem or Wadai, for 15 to 40 dollars.[27] There is thus an approximate equivalence in price, between a *sedasi*, the standard slave unit, and a good horse or camel, though the range of prices for the animals, which are not much sub-divided into categories, is considerably greater than the range for each category of person. Elsewhere in his account, Nachtigal observes that a good camel could be exchanged for a *sedasi* at any time in Kawar.[28] The highest prices for horses are higher than the cost of a good *sedasi*, and there seems to be a tendency for this gap to widen, as horse prices creep upwards. In Darfur in Nachtigal's time a *sedasi* cost about 30 dollars; a goodish horse which the king gave for his departure Nachtigal reckoned was worth about 50 dollars, apparently including handsome harness; the price of a horse there might rise to 150 dollars.[29] This figure is confirmed in Kobe, the second city of Darfur, where horses had to be purchased with slaves, up to the value of 150 dollars for a good beast.[30] This is a very high price indeed, about five slaves for a single horse. In July 1918, Hamman Yaji fixed the price of Yerima Baba's horse at three slave girls.[31]

One other comparative price: in 1871 Nachtigal paid 30 dollars for the maintenance for more than nine months of two servants and horse left behind by him in Kuka while on his expedition to the Awlad Sulayman; this included paying a woman to carry water and cook two meals daily for his men.[32]

Clapperton quoted prices in cowries in Sokoto which showed

---

[27] II, 226.

[28] I, 418; there is a mistake in the published English translation here: in line 9, read 'at any time', not 'at that time'.

[29] IV, 373-4.

[30] IV, 254.

[31] Hamman Yaji, 65. Other slave prices he received were 50 shillings and two gowns for a slave girl (p. 61), or 260 shillings for an unspecified, and thus possibly male, slave (p. 68).

[32] III, 45.

very much the same ratio between men and women as in Nachtigal's Kuka; a youth aged thirteen to twenty cost from 10,000 to 20,000 cowries; a virgin girl of fourteen or fifteen commonly cost about 30,000; an exceptionally handsome woman might fetch 40,000 or 50,000.[33] At the Yoruba capital in the same year, he found horses selling for from 80,000 to 100,000 cowries, while prime slaves were 40,000 to 60,000.[34] By 1852, prices in the Sokoto market had apparently risen: a lad 'of very indifferent appearance' was sold for 33,000 shells, while a pony fetched 30,000.[35]

Somewhat more elaborate comparisons of relative slave prices are available for the Cairo market in the nineteenth century. The price of black girls was usually, though not always, a little higher than that of boys. The price of black adults was higher than that of boys by 50 to 100 per cent.,[36] and eunuchs fetched double or three times the price of black male adults. Abyssinian boys were a little more expensive than blacks, the difference rising to 100 per cent in the higher age brackets. Abyssinian girls cost from 25 to 600 per cent more than black girls, and white Circassian girls were sometimes ten times as expensive as Abyssinian girls.[37]

Oversupply cut prices. In the glutted market of Bagirmi in 1872, old men could be purchased for the equivalent of two or three dollars, while older women, better adapted for work and always more docile than men, might fetch 5 dollars. Young girls cost at the outside twice as much, but only because

[33] Clapperton, 1829, 222, 232.
[34] *ibid.*, 59.
[35] Barth, 1965, III, 132.
[36] Following on from p. 327, n. 20 above, the higher price of adults than children here may reflect that black slaves in Egypt were too far away from home ever to flee, and too much acclimatised to slavery ever to resist; thus their greater immediate economic potential was reflected directly in their price.
[37] Baer, 1967, 427. Al-Maqrizi, an Arab historian who died in 1442, said of Mansa Musa and his entourage, on pilgrimage from Mali in 1324, that, among many other things, they purchased 'Turkish and Ethiopian slave girls' (*Corpus*, 351). The *Corpus* editors hesitate: 'Did the people of Mali really buy Ethiopian girls? Or is the reference to Turkish and Ethiopian slaves merely conventional?' (p. 428). The evidence of prices, and the frequency of references to Ethiopian and non-African slave-girls as up-market goods, suggest to me that al-Maqrizi's report may well be correct.

the king and his dignitaries still had the means to pay so much. The price of children from six to eight years old never exceeded than of an ordinary shirt, costing in Kuka about three-quarters of a dollar. Smaller children one might obtain almost as a gift (see below, pp. 375-6).[38]

A comparable glut was recorded after a successful campaign by Samori's troopers in the west, at about the same time: six chickens were sold for one slave, a sheep for three slaves, a cow for ten[39]—but these prices may have been the consequence also of a shortage of food on that occasion.[40] In Katanga in 1887 Arnot saw Arab slavers buy a man for 10 yards of calico; he was told that women and young lads would fetch 12 to 16 yards.[41] Children too small to walk were usually thrown away; Arnot soon acquired a small family of them.[42]

Dorugu, on his first march after enslavement, went on, crying. 'I saw a pair of twins lying on the road. They were crying but they were too young to talk. And then we arrived in Zinder.' An editorial footnote comments:

> The Hausa, unlike many tribes in southern Nigeria, consider twins to be good luck. Special pairs of names, such as Hassan and Husseini, are used for twins.[43]

---

[38] III, 363. For horse prices here, up to 12 slaves each, see p. 379 below.
[39] Kouroubari, 1959, 563.
[40] V. Monteil, *L'Islam noir*, Paris 1964, 101; 2nd ed., 1980, 130.
[41] Arnot, 1889/1969, 205.
[42] *ibid.*, 183-4, 213-15, 243.
[43] Kirk-Greene and Newman, 38, and n. 21 on p. 104.

CHAPTER XI

CONCLUSION: ANTI-SLAVERY MEASURES

'I welcomed the Judge Mai Madubi. He spent the night and then on Monday I met him and *he told me what he had to say*....On [the following] Monday...I left the Judge Mai Madubi in view of his evil words and conversation....' (Hamman Yaji, p. 75, 19 and 27 December 1920)

In countries actually or nominally under the control of the Sultan of Turkey, more or less vigorous efforts were being made at the time of Nachtigal's travels to enforce anti-slavetrade edicts. It was, however, nowhere easy to ensure the effective administration of these, partly because many people benefited materially from the trade, which to them appeared perfectly legitimate and natural. Early in 1826 the British Consul in Tripoli estimated that the Pasha there had lost about £10,000 during the lull in the slave trade resulting from nothing more serious than the presence of British missions in the interior.[1] For governors and other officials in distant provinces, both the temptations to evasion and the difficulties of supervision were increased. Some provincial officials, very poorly paid, indifferent to the broader political considerations which weighed with their distant masters in Cairo or Constantinople, and perhaps with a direct monetary concern in the trade, accordingly made only perfunctory efforts to enforce the law.

Richardson's experience in Ghadames, in the 1840s, although no anti-slave-trade laws applied there at the time, shows the financial importance of the trade. The market in

[1] F.O. 76/20, Warrington to Hay, 29 January, 1826, Public Record Office, London.

Tunis had already been shut, and slave-dealers were seeking outlets in Algeria.[2] The governor of Ghadames levied a duty of 10 dollars per head on slaves; this was a very heavy tax, apparently 25 per cent or even more of the sale value of the slaves.[3] At one time, the governor had to borrow money from Richardson, and was able to repay it only when a caravan of forty slaves arrived and the tax on them had been paid.[4]

The tolls levied in Murzuq upon the slave trade varied. In the last years of the eighteenth century, the tax payable on slaves coming in for sale from Borno and the Sudan was two *mithqal*'s per head, about a quarter of an ounce of gold.[5] According to Eduard Vogel, the rate in the latter part of 1853 was three *mahabub* per head, a *mahabub* being worth, in Nachtigal's time, a little less than a Maria Theresa dollar. Just as Vogel was leaving Murzuq, the Pasha added another *mahabub* to the toll. Vogel estimated that the three *mahabub* toll was equivalent to an *ad valorem* tax of about 5 per cent. The general transit toll levied on other goods on their way to the Mediterranean coast was 12 per cent, except on ivory, on which 3 per cent was paid.[6]

In 1865, just over a decade later, Rohlfs reported that for each slave the Governor got two *mahabub*, just half the final rate when Vogel had been in Murzuq.[7] In addition, for each outgoing slave the Governor's son-in-law, described as the police minister, received an additional 2½ groschen—the implication being that the Governor got his payment on all incoming slaves, whether in transit northwards, or intended for permanent employment within Fezzan.

The garrison physician at that time engineered a private

[2] Richardson, 1848, I, 269, 355.
[3] *Ibid.*, I, 253-4, 355. The price of slaves in Ghadames which Richardson mentioned ranged from twenty to fifty dollars (I, 253-4, 258-9, 263, 293).
[4] *ibid.*, I, 269, 293.
[5] Bovill, *Missions*, I, 102, from F. Hornemann's Journal.
[6] *Petermanns Mitteilungen*, 1855, 251-3; see also II, 16 note 2.
[7] In Vogel's time, Borno was racked by internal discord. Abd al-Rahman, a brother of the ruler Shaykh Umar, had briefly seized power for himself, and had executed Hajj Beshir, the foremost dignitary under Shaykh Umar (III, 154-5). It may be that the increased rates of duty in Murzuq were somehow related to supply difficulties in Borno.

CONCLUSION: ANTI-SLAVERY MEASURES

meeting with Rohlfs in the hope of inducing him to report to the consuls in Tripoli, who might be expected to complain to Constantinople, the inefficiency with which anti-slave-trade ordinances were being administered in Murzuq. He was not, indeed, at all objecting to the slave trade as such, but merely to the failure of the Governor to share his gains from the tolls with any of his official subordinates. The commandant of the garrison, he said, had told him that during the twelve months that he had been with the garrison 4,048 slaves had been brought into Murzuq. He knew the exact number because slave caravans entered Murzuq only at night, and the corporal of the watch who opened the town gate to let them in had to report to the commandant each morning how many had entered during the night. As many slaves [again] were believed to enter Fezzan at other points, and everywhere the *qaimaqam* collected the same tax, making in all, it was thought, a total of 20,000 *mahabub* a year, from which neither the commandant, the *katib el-mal* [or treasurer]... nor the garrison physician received anything. The Governor, Halim Bey, it was said, was careful to send good presents to the *mushir* in Tripoli, and had just recently presented twelve slave girls to him.

According to the local gossip, the Maina Adam [a Kawar notable] had once in one year paid 10,000 Maria Theresa dollars to the *qaimaqam* on account of slaves which he had purchased.[8]

When Nachtigal arrived in 1869, the charge—'according to the old regulations'—was still two *mahabub*, which earlier could easily have produced an annual income of about 40,000 marks (implying an annual intake of rather more than five and a half thousand slaves), in which the official administering the control in the most southerly oases of Fezzan received his modest share. The Governor's income from this one tax exceeded his regular income.[9]

Officials were obviously reluctant to abandon such a lucrative source of revenue, particularly if there were no realisable alternative at hand. 'While I was in Murzuq,' Nachtigal observed drily,

[8] I, 121 note, citing Rohlfs, 1874-5, I, 169-70 and 184, also *Petermanns Mitteilungen*, Ergänzungsheft 25, 1868, 6.
[9] I, 121; II, 233.

the ordinances against the slave trade were, as used to happen from time to time, renewed and made more stringent. Inasmuch, however, as a caravan from Bornu was expected at the same time, the ordinance was held up until the caravan had arrived and the slave tax [been] paid. Only then was it made public, gradually to be allowed again to fall into oblivion.[10]

Nachtigal gives another *vignette* of a slave caravan arriving in Murzuq (or possibly both descriptions relate to the same caravan—the first description is undated, the other comes fairly late in Nachtigal's protracted Murzuq period).

> Towards the middle of December...there arrived a company of Mejabra from Bornu, whose human merchandise was, in view of the intensified prohibition of the slave trade, at first brought into the town secretly by night, after Hamed Bey to be sure had not neglected to collect the usual sum of two *mahabub* per head, *râs*,—it was even said that, in view of the difficult conditions, he had demanded, and received, double this amount.[11]

Early in 1869, approaching Fezzan from the north, Nachtigal's party met small caravans almost daily.[12] While slaves by their hundreds could no longer be brought into town markets openly, prohibition measures could still be evaded by minor merchants concealing small groups of slaves in the suburban gardens of Murzuq and Tripoli, or in nearby villages, where they could be safely disposed of clandestinely.[13]

There was still in 1874, near the end of Nachtigal's journey, considerable uncertainty about the rigour with which the ban upon the slave trade would be applied in practice in the outlying provinces of Egypt under the regime of Khedive Ismail. As Nachtigal was now travelling with the export tide, not against it, he had much better opportunity of observing the difficulties, devices and deviousness involved. The large caravan which set out from el-Fasher, the capital of Darfur, on 6 July, included an 'immense number of slaves whom we brought with us, either as servants or with the intention of

[10] I, 121.
[11] II, 16.
[12] I, 58; see also above, pp. 84, 104 and note.
[13] I, 120.

selling them'.[14] Eight days on from el-Fasher, on the road towards el-Obeid in Kordofan, disquieting reports gave the travellers pause.

> News about the monopolisation of the ivory and ostrich feather trade by the Viceroy of Egypt and the complete impossibility of selling slaves there greatly depressed my travelling companions. ...They debated for days what should be done with their slaves, until to the majority it seemed best first to get more accurate information in the great merchant entrepôt at Omm Meshana, and in the most unfavourable case to sell as much as they could of their human wares there, or else to send the slaves back home. Some of the Jellaba, who came from Dongola, but had been waiting a long time with the Kababish Arabs in order to get the most recent and certain information, arrived the day after us. All they knew was that exports of slaves had become impossible; of any monopolisation of trade in the other two items they knew nothing.[15]

On arrival at Omm Meshana, detailed and authentic news about trade conditions in Egypt

> filled the members of our caravan with great concern. The prohibition of the slave-trade appeared actually to have been intensified to the extent that in el-Obeid, the capital of Kordofan, the *mudir* had confiscated all the slaves in the town, both those which had recently been purchased and those which had been bought a long time before...the latter were, however, subsequently returned.

The situation with regard to feathers and ivory, on the other hand, was not as serious as had at first been feared. But worry about slaves had kept many merchants back in Omm Meshana, among whom Nachtigal found some whom he had met a considerable time before in Wadai. Other merchants had left, but remained in uncertainty and fear at the frontier.[16]

The following days at Omm Meshana

---

[14] IV, 376-7. Nachtigal does not mention here 'hot' and 'cold' slaves, a distinction which earlier aroused anxiety (see above, p. 56). That had been a question of rightful and wrongful enslavement within a Muslim slave-owning world: the traders now confronted a world without slaves.

[15] IV, 381.

[16] IV, 382-3.

were completely taken up with discussions about what ought to be done in relation to our journey to Egypt, and on this opinions in our camp were very contradictory. Some wanted to abandon the journey altogether, others to wait for further news, while others again, who were carrying goods that had been entrusted to them, wanted first to send back to Kobe and el-Fasher [both towns in Darfur] to ask those who had commissioned them for instructions. Finally the eloquence and prestige of Hajj Ahmed [Tangatanga] were successful in establishing general agreement that the members of our caravan should either sell their slaves in Omm Meshana or send them back to Kobe, that is Darfur, but that they should continue their journey unperturbed by the ostrich feather tax or the import duty on ivory.[17]

Hajj Ahmed was truly, in Nachtigal's words, 'a prudent and resolute man'. In addition to his crucial standing in the general deliberations of the merchants amongst themselves, he was eager to dispose of his own slaves, and it was only in Omm Meshana that he could not only sell his slaves, but also turn the proceeds from their sale into ostrich feathers.[18] He was also engaged in negotiation with the Darfurian border authorities under their *khalifa* or chief, in transmitting orders from the ruler of Darfur, and in marshalling military resources for the defence of Darfur, already within the shadow of the jaws of external enemies who would, before the year was out overrun the country, kill the king, and capture the capital city. Hajj Ahmed used the opportunity of his enforced halt in Omm Meshana

> to increase his prestige, respresenting himself as a confidant of the king, but he also knew immediately how to combine what was useful with what was pleasant. While he promised to mediate with the [local] Hamr Arabs, he sold to the *khalifa* at a high price the robes of honour which he had received from the king as well as a slave girl.[19]

Some of the caravan's slaves, intended for sale, still remained, and a Nile merchant who had come out to meet the caravan took possession of them all, confident that his knowledge

[17] IV, 387.
[18] IV, 384, 388.
[19] IV, 384, slightly amended.

of the road, and his skill in concealing slaves unnoticed in the villages of his district, combined with the venality of Egyptian officials, would make it easy to hold the slaves until the government once more relaxed the strict application of the latest edict prohibiting their import.[20] Entering Kordofan, on the way to el-Obeid, some of Nachtigal's companions left the caravan, in order to get to the capital by an indirect route, avoiding villages, as village officials might confiscate their slaves.[21] Nachtigal's final halt before el-Obeid, where his independent travels effectively ended, was at a country house of Muhammad en-Nur, his guide since Omm Meshana. 'We had an excellent reception, the more so as they [Muhammad en-Nur's family] enjoyed tolerable prosperity and possessed about 100 slaves.'[22]

Similar smuggling was described on the road from Gondar to the Egyptian Sudan in 1855. Doka, a Sudanese village, had formerly been an important slave-trade centre between Ethiopia and Sennar. By 1855, the trade was illegal. (It was also illegal in Ethiopia under Theodore, but smuggling went on there too.[23]) In Doka there were no European consuls to receive information and make the necessary representations to the authorities. The Coptic civil servant and the Muslim *kashif* or judge were not so remorseless. The Muslims of Gondar were said to keep their slaves concealed in cellars under their houses. (Slave pits were not uncommon, witness the caves under Cape Coast Castle on the coast of modern Ghana, and the remains in Darfur.[24]) The slaves were moved only at night, and then with their mouths stuffed with rags lest they should cry out.[25] Cameron, west of Lake Tanganyika in 1874, observed the use of a wooden snaffle to gag slaves, in an area where there was considerable local kidnapping and slaves might be offered for sale to a passing caravan when still quite close to their own homes.[26]

[20] IV, 389.
[21] IV, 391; see also 392.
[22] IV, 393.
[23] Krapf, 1860, 466-7.
[24] Arkell, 1961, 213-4.
[25] Krapf, 1860, 470.
[26] Cameron, 1885, 256.

CONCLUSION: ANTI-SLAVERY MEASURES 339

It is clear from Nachtigal's experience that there were serious problems in implementing anti-slavery policies in both the Sahara and the eastern Sudan. Financial incentives to circumvent such policies were as strong as the power of central governmental authorities to impose them was weak. Even among the high authorities responsible for issuing edicts against the slave trade, there was in Nachtigal's time a certain ambivalence of attitude. The institution of slavery had been abolished in Tunis in 1846,[27] but there was clearly a continuing and lively interest.

> The slave trade has ceased so completely in Tunis that in my farewell audience on my departure from there the Bey and his then Prime Minister jokingly asked me to bring along with me as many little *usfan* (plural of *usif*, Negro) as I could. When the great men of Tunis wish to expand their households by the addition of black servants, eunuchs or domestic slave-girls, they send to Tripoli and have them purchased there at high prices.[28]

At the beginning of 1870, as Nachtigal was waiting—in fact, more than six months elapsed between his return to Murzuq from Tibesti, and his departure from Murzuq towards Borno—in Murzuq for some southbound caravan to which he might attach himself, word came that the Governor of Tripoli intended to send an envoy to Borno. The envoy would carry gifts to Shaykh Umar and through the Shaykh's good offices collect lions, tigers and similar animals, to be sent from Tripoli to the Ottoman Emperor. Such little courtesies were very necessary for any provincial governor, to bring himself from time to time to the friendly remembrance of His Majesty. In addition, Nachtigal continued, and this despite the fact that the black slave trade had been formally abolished throughout the Ottoman domains, except the Hijaz, in 1857,[29]

> some eunuchs could be brought along, for whom there was a considerable demand in the palaces of the great men of Constantinople, and which form the most acceptable present to the powerful men responsible for the dealings of dignitaries

[27] Boahen, 1964, 140.
[28] I, 16.
[29] Boahen, 1964, 155-6.

who live far from the capital with the Commander of the Faithful.[30]

In Kuka, Bu Aïsha strove tirelessly to turn his visit there, and the goodwill of the generous ruler, to material profit. Gradually he collected slaves, as well for himself as for the Governor of Tripoli, Ali Riza Pasha; he also exchanged many presents of slaves for ivory and ostrich feathers.[31] He also gathered in many other items, and when, two years after leaving Tripoli, he set out on his homeward journey, he took with him considerable wealth, including ordinary slaves, eunuchs, deaf-mutes and dwarfs.[32] On the other hand, despite the openness of these transactions, there was also perhaps a desire to avoid awkward publicity: Nachtigal thought, for example, that the initial reluctance to allow him to join Bu Aïsha's caravan might have been based on a wish to restrict his opportunities of seeing how even the highest authorities still connived at the trade in eunuchs and other slaves.[33]

In the slave markets in the Sudan countries themselves, there was no objection in principle to the slave trade, nor any effort, however half-hearted, to abolish it. The difficult adjustments created in these countries by an enforced steadily diminishing export demand for slaves have already been noted (see above pp. 107-8), and Nachtigal drew attention to this as an important contributory cause of the decline of Murzuq. In earlier years no Murzuq merchant could engage in trade with the Sudan without buying and selling slaves, so that, as part of their business contracted, the incentive to maintain their trading connections correspondingly weakened.[34]

Underpinning all these considerations—the profitablility, to distant provincial officials, of the slave trade as a source of

[30] II, 17.
[31] II, 306.
[32] IV, 4. The caravan was attacked in the desert by Arab raiders, who despoiled it utterly, leaving only the gifts from Shaykh Umar direct to the Tripoli Governor. The Shaykh and his courtiers rejoiced heartily at this news, for Bu Aïsha, after leaving Kuka, had written most discourteously to his former hosts. (IV, 13-4).
[33] II, 18.
[34] I, 23-4, 119-20.

tax revenue; the extreme difficulty which central authorities had in controlling such officials; the lack of total commitment even amongst the central authorities themselves; the dependence of Sudanese and Saharan states upon slaves as the central sector in their export trade—underpinning all these was religion. Even if the central governments, reflected Nachtigal,

> not indeed impelled by conviction, but moved by political considerations, also actually have the will to impose control, the provincial officials, lacking the higher political interests of their prince, still follow their religious convictions and their own interests. Every Muslim is bound to regard slavery, and therefore also the slave trade, as lawful. Gritting his teeth, he endures the yoke of European demands, but in his heart there is a profound regret that he can no longer deal with Christians in the way which they wish to prevent him from applying to Pagans. If he can do it without being punished, a provincial governor will therefore turn a blind eye to, and even favour, a contravention of the law, when his own advantage requires it, and the merchants take care that this will be the case. The governments, with their finances in disorder, pay their officials poorly or not at all; does it not seem natural that they should seek a profit in a trade which according to their religious convictions appears to them quite legitimate?[35]

However much officials might drag their feet in carrying out the perhaps reluctant instructions of their masters, and whatever other obstacles stood in the way of anti-slavery reforms, the trade was none the less clearly on the way out. The number of slaves which earlier had passed annually through Fezzan Nachtigal believed to have been between 5,000 and 8,000. By 1869 this had been reduced by at least two-thirds.[36] A caravan which went north with two of Nachtigal's servants after his first arrival in Kuka carried with it 1,400 slaves, but by that time such caravans were rare.[37] Slave parties were encountered much later, but they were very small. In 1906, a little south of Qatrun, a British traveller met a trader from Tibesti who had with him

---

[35] I, 120, See also II, 233.
[36] I, 121-2.
[37] II, 233 and note. The next caravan north from Kuka left eighteen to twenty-four months later; see above, p. 105.

half a dozen slave children whom he had brought from Wadai in the hope of selling them in North Africa.[38] In 1913 a Tubu raid carried off some Arab women and children, who were then sold as slaves and for the most part sent away to the Sanusiya in Cyrenaica; it is not clear from the reference whether the Sanusiya were themselves buying the slaves, or simply receiving them.[39] Numerous sales of slaves in Murzuq and Zella were reported during the First World War after the Italians had withdrawn to the Mediterranean coast.[40] The last known consignment of slaves is said to have arrived in Murzuq in 1929 before the Italian reoccupation.[41]

The trans-Saharan slave trade is now virtually a matter of ancient history. The subsequent course of domestic slavery in the Sudan countries, as they collapsed under the pressure of superior European power, is another story. Many of Nachtigal's African friends were more or less aware that among the numerous unaccountable eccentricities which they attributed to Europeans an antipathy to slavery was often to be found; nevertheless, just as the ancient Greeks had done, and whatever their social status, they 'always took slavery for granted as one of the facts of human existence', and none of them a century ago was able 'to imagine that there could be a civilized society without slaves'.[42]

The quotation from the diary of Hamman Yaji, at the heading of this section, needs elucidation. Judge Mai Madubi is a nickname for a European wearing glasses, clearly a colonial officer. The editors of Hamman Yaji's diary argue that the phrase, he told me what he had to say (the italics are mine on p. 332 above), 'is unlike any other description of interaction in the diary', and that in this oblique fashion Hamman Yaji 'calls attention to the importance of the transaction'.[43] We are

---

[38] Vischer, 1910, 195.

[39] Jean Tilho, 'The exploration of Tibesti, Erdi, Borkou and Ennedi in 1912-17', *Geographical journal*, Aug./Oct. 1920, 183; see also I, 364n.

[40] Enrico Petragnani, *Il Sahara Tripolitano*, 1928, 161 and 220.

[41] James Wellard, *The Great Sahara*, 1964, 117.

[42] M.I. Finley, 1960, [53], [61].

[43] Hamman Yaji, 15; there is in fact a similar turn of words, also relating to Europeans, 'they told me that which God ordered that they should say' (97), and an identical one, European again, 'he said what he had to say'

never told just what it was that Judge Mai Madubi said, but it was clearly something which seriously upset Hamman Yaji; there was also simultaneously a dispute between the two men about boundaries, but the editors' suggestion that the two strands can be distinguished seems persuasive. And there is no further reference, in all the remaining years of the diary, to any more slave-raiding by Hamman Yaji. Hardly a change of heart: Hamman Yaji seems to have been one of the gritters of teeth: but the interruption of slave-raiding seems to have been effective.

Nachtigal's first grave, in Liberia. Büttikofer, 1890, I, 440.

---

(91), but the editors' argument overall is not thereby undermined. See also above, p. 314, for this passage in a marriage context.

APPENDIX A

OUTLINE CHRONOLOGY OF NACHTIGAL'S TRAVELS

1834	
23 February	Gustav Nachtigal born in Eichstadt, a village north of Stendal, west of Berlin (III, xvii)
1862	Went to North Africa, seeking relief from tuberculosis (III, xviii)
1868	On the eve of returning home to Europe, his health restored, Nachtigal agreed to carry presents from the King of Prussia to the Shaykh of Borno (III, xviii)
1869	
18 February	Departure from *Tripoli*, for *Murzuq*, capital of Fezzan (I, 38)
27 March	First arrival in *Murzuq*, from *Tripoli* (I, 72)
6 June	First departure from *Murzuq*, travelling east into *Tibesti* (I, 195)
8 August	Arrival at Bardai, in *Tibesti* (I, 286)
3/4 September	Flight from Bardai (I, 318)
8 October	Return to *Murzuq*, following *Tibesti* expedition (II, 3)
1870	
18 April	Second departure from *Murzuq*, this time southwards towards *Borno* (II, 27)
26 May	Arrival in *Kawar* (II, 52)

CHRONOLOGY OF NACHTIGAL'S TRAVELS

10 June	Departure from *Kawar*, on the way to *Borno* (II, 78)
28 June	Arrival at Ngigmi, northernmost village of *Borno*, on the shore of Lake Chad (II, 99)
6 July	First arrival at *Kuka*, capital of Borno (II, 115)

1871

6 January	First news reports reach Kuka of Wadaian military preparations (II, 295)
4 February	Death of Lamino, foremost Borno notable and a friend of Nachtigal, in Kuka (II, 300)
20 March	First departure from *Kuka*, capital of Borno, travelling to *Kanem*, north-east of Lake Chad (II, 319)
24 April	Departure from *Kanem*, travelling north-east back into the Sahara, to *Borku* (II, 343)
23 September	Beginning of the return journey from *Borku* to *Kuka* (II, 481)
29 November	Beginning of a detour into south-east *Kanem*, lasting until 9 December (III, 3)

1872

9 January	Second arrival in *Kuka*, capital of Borno, returning from *Kanem* and *Borku* (III, 40)
28 February	Second departure from *Kuka*, travelling south-east into the *Bagirmi* region (III, 214)
11 March	Arrival in *Logon*, en route from Kuka to Bagirmi (III, 240)
4 April	Arrival at the war-camp of Abu Sekkin, temporarily displaced ruler of *Bagirmi* (III, 310)
14 April/13 May	Slave raiding with the Bagirmi (III, 340-59)
30 July	Departure from Abu Sekkin, on the way back to *Kuka* (III, 427)
6 September	Third arrival in *Kuka*, capital of Borno, returning from Abu Sekkin (III, 451)

1873

1 March	Third and final departure from *Kuka*, going east towards *Wadai* and *Darfur* (IV, 23)
7 April	First arrival in *Abeshr*, capital of Wadai (IV, 45)

APPENDIX A

17 August	First departure from *Abeshr*, going south towards *Runga* (IV, 89)
12 September	Attempt to reach *Runga* abandoned (IV, 112)
1 October	Return to *Abeshr* (IV, 119)
1874	
11 January	Second and final departure from *Abeshr*, going east towards *Darfur* (IV, 229)
7 March	Arrival at *El-Fasher*, capital of *Darfur* (IV, 257)
6 July	Departure from *El-Fasher*, for *Cairo* (IV, 376)
22 November	Nachtigal's odyssey ends in *Cairo*, after five and a half years and approximately 10,000 kilometres (III, xviii)
1879	Vol. I of *Sahara und Sudan* published in Berlin
1881	Vol. II published in Berlin
1885	
20 April	Gustav Nachtigal dies at sea, off the coast of West Africa
1889	Vol. III published in Leipzig

APPENDIX B

BOOK 5, CHAPTER 6, OF *SAHARA AND SUDAN*
(vol. 2, pp. 626-58 of the original German;
vol. 3, pp. 338-66 of the English)

The main text of the chapter is as published in the English *Sahara and Sudan*; the footnotes have been adjusted where necessary to the present volume. Mbang Mohammedu, or Abu Sekkin, the Bagirmi ruler, has temporarily been displaced by a usurper, Abd er-Rahman, supported by Wadai.

SLAVE RAIDS [1]
April to July 30, 1872

[626] Mbang Mohammedu's continued sojourn in Broto did not bring him any appreciable benefit. No noteworthy success attended his military enterprises, and political negotiations were constantly frustrated by the local people's justified mistrust. Even in the immediate neighbourhood of Broto, the inhabitants of Kimre, also Gaberi by tribe, had [627] withdrawn to the secure heights of their cotton-trees,[2] and paid no

[1] This chapter, in many respects the most dramatic, and moving, in the whole of *Sahara and Sudan*, is the only portion of the book which was translated at once into English. 'Slave-hunts in central Africa' appeared in April 1874 in *Harper's new monthly magazine*, vol. 48, no. 287, pp. 710-17. The English is based on Nachtigal's letters, and a German version, 'Sklavenjagden in Centralafrika', appeared in the *Kölnische Zeitung*, 20 and 28 July, 1873. Gourdault, *Tour*, 391-408, gives a French account. It would be interesting to prepare a text collating all the divergent details (of which there are many) of these several accounts, as a case-study of the reliability, in details, of even eye-witness accounts. That was my hope, for 'the near future' when Volume 3 of the English translation appeared in 1987; it is, alas, still no more than a hope now. Only a few examples are cited in the following pages.

[2] For cotton-trees, see III, 299. Trees were similarly used for defence purposes in Kanem (III, 15).

347

attention to either the fine words or the threats of the Bagirmi. From experience Abu Sekkin knew that he was practically powerless against these aerial fortresses; in a nocturnal interview shortly after my arrival he had sought advice and assistance from me, who could not at first understand this difficulty of dealing with enemies who had simply fled into the trees. On April 14, however, when a new attempt was made to bring these people into subjection by force, I had the chance to see for myself, as an eye-witness, the inadequacy of my associates' means of attack.

An hour after midnight there sounded one of the long trumpets, several of which are also among the insignia of the *fatsha*. All who were eager for plunder assembled in front of the camp, though not exactly with military precision, and about an hour later we were able to set off. Our march took us in a southeasterly, and later a southerly direction, as far as could be judged in the darkness, first through the cultivated fields of Broto, then across a treeless plain where even the growth of grass seemed rather sparse, further through bush, and finally through the grain fields of Kimre. By sunrise we had before us the wood, the natural fortress of those whom we were pursuing. The neighbourhood was distinguished by a black clayey soil, rich in humus, dotted with pools of water, and crossed by elephant tracks. With the scanty rainfall of this time of year, the young seedlings were sprouting in the grain fields. Clouds of smoke rose here and there from the wood, as warning signals to those who lived further away, and as evidence that our approach had not remained secret.

Before we entered the wood, the *fatsha* mustered his warriors, who gradually came together there. Of the Bagirmi people and their slaves, we numbered perhaps 60 mounted men, many of whom were equipped with quilted armour, and about 400 footsoldiers, whose armament comprised lances and hand-irons, sometimes shields as well. Approximately the same number of Pagans—Sara, Bua, Ndamm, Tummok—but without any cavalry, accompanied us. The *fatsha* called a halt, seized a staff, his marshal's baton as it were, perhaps 30 centimeters long and covered with dark cloth, and took from the hand of a slave a fan-like [628] emblem preserved likewise in a cloth container. After the *fatsha* had unfolded this emblem, he waved it enthusiastically, leaping up and down in front of the crowd. After this ceremony, the origin of which neither the *fatsha* nor anyone else could, or would, explain, and which took the place of any rousing oration, and after the emblems, once more in their containers, had been given over to a slave for safe keeping, our forces were set in motion,[3] and we entered the wood.

There were still cultivated fields in the clearings, and the deserted dwellings of the people lay scattered about attractively over a wide area beneath the shade of the magnificent trees. Where the houses had not already suffered destruction—the inhabitants had already taken to their lofty war dwellings some weeks before—the most delightful landscape scenes unfolded, in the simple grace of the straw and mud structures, the fresh grass in their immediate surroundings, the vigour and luxuriance of the forest trees, and the cosy intimacy of the spots, upon which here and there the rays of the rising morning sun were stealing.

Soon we came in sight of those whom we were pursuing, and who were watching, apparently with great composure, from a safe height the approach of their cruel hereditary enemies. Above all the trees towered the *Eriodendron*, which seems to be chosen there as an abode only in times of danger. Its height, its dead straight hardwood trunk, the whorl-shaped arrangement of its branches, stretching out nearly horizontally at successive levels, make this tree appear especially suitable for this purpose. The lowest tier is, for the most part, left unused, as being much too accessible to attackers. At the level immediately above this, however, adjoining branches, as near as possible horizontal, were joined by poles laid across them to form a platform, to which some solid thick straw matting was made fast, and on this the household was set up. It consists usually of one small hut, which also contains stores of grain, water-pitchers and household utensils, such as wooden mortars for preparing flour; even domestic animals, goats, dogs and fowls, were taken up there with them.[4] Above this division

---

[3] *Harper's*, 711, says that, after the ceremony, '... all order, all common action of the wild horde, was over. Riders and foot-soldiers crossed the plain at a gallop, and especially the Baghirmi and their slaves, eager for prey, ran a race together toward the forest.'

[4] *Harper's*, 711, adds that horses are sent 'to distant villages until quieter times return'.

Tree-dwellings under siege in Kimre. III, 342.

of branches, a basket, like a crow's nest, made of stout wickerwork of boughs and straw, is frequently attached to the trunk itself; it can hold one or two persons, and the greater [629] part of the store of weapons of the people situated in the tree is kept there. The chief warrior, or warriors, of the tree are in this receptacle, the sides of which are about a meter high; from there they hurl the innocuous reed projectiles already mentioned,[5] keeping their hand-irons and lances ready in case the attackers should succeed in climbing up to the lowest storey. One or several families live in a tree, according to its girth and height. During the night, when no attack is to be feared, the inhabitants climb down as necessary to replenish their supplies of water and of grain, which is kept hidden in concealed pits. For climbing up and down primitive ladders are used, made of thin tree trunks, creepers and cords of plant fibre.

There was no question of any systematic attack or combined operations on our side. As soon as we confronted the inhabited trees, most of our men were content to brandish their spears and lances threateningly, and to protect themselves carefully with their shields, or, in default of shields, with pieces of straw matting taken from the half-destroyed huts, or with stronger mats. Others scattered into the wood in the hope of finding a forgotten goat, a dog or a couple of hens, or stumbling on a grain pit, or even discovering some poor human soul who, having come down from his tree and been surprised by the sudden attack, had perhaps been unable to regain his place of refuge. Both the Bagirmi and their Pagan allies were at a loss to know what to do in the face of such a situation. Hundreds of armed men were standing around the separate refuges, with threatening words and gestures, but without the courage to risk an attack, since those who were the first to climb a tree would have to be considered lost, as long as its armed defenders were at hand. There were no tools

[5] 'The Gaberi, especially those sections of them who in times of war are in the habit of shifting their dwellings to the high trees in their woods, carried with them in baskets of woven bark some peculiar, very primitive and ineffective throwing weapons. I took these at first for arrows, but failed to see the appropriate bow, and on closer investigation found them to be hand-missiles, about half a meter long, made from stout reeds cut sharp and pointed in the manner of a quill at one end, and weighted near the other with a spindle-shaped lump of clay encircling the reed.' (III, 324)

for felling the trees, and the besieged were too high to be reached by ordinary weapons. The king and the *fatsha* had, to be sure, a number of slaves armed with flintlocks, but of these not one was competent to handle a musket, to aim and to hit the mark. Holding the deadly weapon as far as possible from their bodies the moment they contemplated firing, the only lives they were likely to endanger, if any, were those of their own [630] comrades. The easiest way in which the besiegers could succeed seemed to be to destroy the straw constructions of the fugitives by fire, thereby driving the defenders higher in the trees and thus gradually overcoming them; where adequate cover made it possible to climb without much danger into the lowest branches of an inhabited tree, an attempt was also made to set the huts and 'crow's nest' on fire with lighted bundles of straw fastened to long poles. The attempt, however, was seldom successful; when the straw and wood did actually ignite, the besieged with their supplies of water extinguished it without difficulty.

I was just beginning to feel reassured about the fate of our poor adversaries when to my distress it appeared that the tables might be turned upon them by my own men. Almas and Hammu joined in the fight, which to be sure for them was only a hunting diversion, neither bringing with it the dangers or the exertions of other hunts, nor, in view of the immobility of their targets, requiring any great skill. My indignation at this dastardly inhumanity made no impression whatever upon the two fanatics; my authority found here its limits, since for them it was a matter of religious justification, about which the Christian was not competent to judge. Neither did they feel the slightest regret about killing like guinea fowl these 'accursed heathen': after all, they had refused submission to a Muhammadan king and to the laws of Islam! If Almas had fortunately not been only a mediocre, and Hammu a very incompetent, shot, and if both had not used up their ammunition very early on, many of the hapless Kimre people would have paid that day with their lives for their inflated confidence in the cotton-trees.

I was an eye-witness of the first victim of the day. From the height of his crow's nest, the tall young champion of one tree inhabited by several families was hurling his harmless reed-darts, protecting himself as far as he could with a shield, or with the breastwork of the basket. He occasionally raised himself to his full height, clenched his fist angrily at his persecutors, and assailed them with expressions of derision and contempt, accompanied by encouraging cries from the women in the immediate [631] vicinity. At one such moment, he collapsed without a sound, hit by a bullet from Almas. Soon after a second defender of the tree, who was on a side-branch further up, was also mortally wounded. For a few seconds he clung in desperation to the limb, and then, a lifeless weight, plunged from the height. An atrocious scene ensued. Our men fell on the corpse, and in a trice it was slashed and torn to pieces with their hand-irons. And the most savage in this connection were not the Bagirmi, but their heathen allies, who were in a way fellow-tribesmen of the victim, and some other time were bound to confront the same fate themselves. A third, the last grown man in the tree, was wounded by a shot; with the final exertion of his strength, he climbed with his family to the top of the tree, and clung there in silence, while his blood trickled down in a long trail on the gray bark of the tree trunk. Then the cowardly attackers dared at last to scale the tree. Soon the goats, dogs and fowls were passed or thrown down. The dead man and the wounded man were flung below and given over to the comrades standing beneath to be torn bestially to pieces. The women and children, with one old man, were pulled down one by one. No cry, no complaint passed the lips of the survivors. With despairing resignation they allowed themselves to be bound together with cords, in order to take the road into slavery, in anguish over the death of their families and the loss of their home.

One single tree was climbed gradually without the assistance of firearms, and thus, as it were, conquered. There was only one active fighter there, and he surely was disheartened when he saw in the neighbouring tree the catastrophe just described. After his hut had been set on fire, he withdrew to a greater height; some attacked him there with lances, while others seized the women and children hidden here and there in the branches. As soon as the man had been thrown down wounded, and had breathed his last whether as the result of his plunge from the height, or beneath the hand-irons of our men, two 14 or 15 year old boys fled to the extreme top and branches of the tree, and when their pursuers had nearly caught up with them, threw themselves into the depth with desperate [632] heroism. Scarcely had I for a moment involuntarily closed my eyes to the terrible spectacle, which wrung my heart, when, on looking up again, I saw already instead of human corpses only shapeless lumps. In a few minutes the barbarians had removed the heads of their victims, torn out their entrails, dismembered them and hacked them to pieces.

Finally the tree which served as a place of refuge for the chief of Kimre was discovered. Small livestock, crowded closely together on a lower level, looked down over the edge of the platform with innocent curiosity. From his basket the principal defender warded off the fire-brands of his enemies with great skill, and with remarkable wariness prevented those who, encouraged by the unusual successes of the day, had climbed up to the lowest storey, from penetrating further. The chief himself, with two women and four children, was sitting at the intersection of three vast branches, and from there he hurled his inadequate darts. The limited supplies of the Bagirmi in powder and shot were exhausted against this tree, and fortunately without substantial success, though the chief and his people had little cover. After they had succeeded in wounding the younger warrior and compelling him to retreat to the regions above, the Bagirmi too tried to climb higher; the chief, however, did not for a moment lose his coolheadedness, but strove to maintain his position, desperate as it must have appeared to him. Exposed to gunfire without any protection, the women and children were taken to a still higher position, not easy in view of the tender years of the children, each of whom had to be carried separately by its mother, while the brave man grasped his lances and throwing-irons and kept his pursuers in check. If the ammunition of our people had lasted longer, the fate of the chief and his family could scarcely in the long run have been in doubt. But, though the tree was defended by only one man, its conquest by handweapons alone would have demanded from the foremost attackers a willingness to sacrifice themselves which could not be generated by the prospect of a modest booty of a goat, a dog or a small child. Thus to my great satisfaction, the chief and his family were saved.

[633] Since the Bagirmi were very satisfied with their successes which, in comparison with earlier efforts of the same kind, were considerable, the hunt was called off towards midday. Most of the tree-fortresses were left unassailed, and we turned back towards Broto, which we reached towards evening. I had not exactly captivated the Bagirmi by my behaviour; quite the contrary, I had bitterly disappointed the hopes which they based upon my assistance. I had refused either myself to fire the breech-loading carbine on my back, or to allow others to fire it; nor in my deep depression did I seek to conceal my disgust at the cowardly cruelty of my companions, using language which was, in view of my own defenceless position, dangerously imprudent. Unfortunately I had later to hear that my peaceable character had not found due recognition among those who were attacked. They had, on the contrary, been inclined to regard the harmless telescope which I had directed towards their tree-dwellings as a not inconsiderable aid to their enemies, though they were unable to perceive any material effects from the instrument.— For the rest, the day's success comprised only some fifty slaves, but not the submission of the people of Kimre, who abandoned their beautiful wood, and withdrew towards the southeast to a neighbouring village, named Kariatu, which was protected by an earthen wall.[6]

When similar expeditions in the neighbourhood, from which I succeeded in holding my own men back, produced no more noteworthy results, the Bagirmi no longer spared even those of our nearest neighbours who had submitted to the King. Thus one day they decided to attack the village of Be-Delüm, some three hours roughly southeast from our

[6] *Harper's*, 713: 'The total result of the expedition consisted in perhaps forty slaves and seven or eight dead, which almost all fell victims to Almas's rifle. I was surprised on our way back at the resignation of the captured women and young men, who did not show the least signs of pain or affliction, some of them walking along even with cheerful countenances. Half of them belong to the sultan, the other half remain the property of their captors, while the yield in cattle and other objects belongs entirely to those who seize them. Sometimes the sultan claims all the slaves captured in an expedition, but more frequently the members and leaders of the latter find means of delivering up to the sultan less than half.' See also p. 366 and n. below.

camp, and since Almas and Hammu had promised me not to participate in the fighting, I attached myself to the expedition. Since those who were threatened by the raid could easily have been forewarned of our purpose, and were almost completely without the comparatively safe places of refuge of the cotton-trees, the raid had to be carried out with the utmost possible speed. After trotting or galloping for some two hours over difficult terrain, full of holes and furrows, and covered with scrub, we reached our objective, and with a loose rein rushed upon the village, [634] which, however, to my satisfaction, we found already deserted. Since the inhabitants had apparently fled only at the last moment—of the domestic animals they had been able to save only the horses—there now began on the part of our mounted men a horrifying round-up in the adjacent woods, while those on foot made it their business to plunder the village. Soon numerous smaller children were picked up here and there, women and older children who had not been able to run away fast enough were seized and bound together, and men who had allowed themselves to be delayed by the attempt to save their families were killed in the thicket, often only after a desperate resistance. Although the booty amounted after all to at least 100 women and older children—smaller children are less welcome, since without maternal care it is easy for them to perish or to create transport difficulties—many of our people were left empty-handed, and it was accordingly decided to attack on the way home a Gaberi village lying somewhat more to the west. Fortunately the inhabitants had already fled in good time, but they had left exposed considerable supplies of grain, so that we reached our camp laden with *durra*.

In the meantime the king's slaves who had stayed behind in Broto, annoyed that they had to remain that day without any spoils, had sought to compensate themselves by a shameful act of treachery against the Gaberi of Mode. Indignant at this perfidy, I sought first to remonstrate with the *fatsha*, and then, since the only answer I had from him was the counter-question, 'Is *amân* then, *i.e.* good faith, necessary in dealing with the heathen?', I betook myself to the king, from whom I obtained at least the return of those persons of the people of Mode who had been abducted. Unfortunately his undisciplined slaves again thwarted my success the same evening by seeking another quarrel with their Mode neighbours, and thoroughly pillaging their village. The burning huts and the resounding war-cries caused great uneasiness in our camp. Sometimes the rumour spread abroad that the people of Be-Delüm were in the neighbourhood with the intention of attacking us, sometimes people said that the combined Gaberi of Mode and Broto were approaching, thirsting for revenge.

The Bagirmi would scarcely have allowed themselves to behave with such treachery [635] against their nearest neighbours if the rapid diminution of the grain supplies, and the impending impassability of the region which was a consequence of the increasing rainfall, as well as the failure to register any material or political successes had not in any event made our transfer to some other district desirable. Our position in the place where we were was no longer tenable. The more the immediate surroundings were plundered, and the hatred which our neighbours felt for us intensified, the further afield the foraging expeditions had to be extended, the more meagre was their yield, and the more they acquired the character of military operations. When in the morning before daybreak those who were in need of food were called together, it was already proving difficult to induce them to come along. Since it ended every time in bloody murder, each individual was therefore willing to join up only if everybody else participated; but if everybody went, the camp was left exposed defenceless against the enemy. Tightening our belts more and more we waited longingly for the return of our men, which was often delayed until evening, and seldom were their exertions and our hopes rewarded with grain. Today there was a little bag of beans, tomorrow a little basket of groundnuts or a small quantity of sesame, and we often had to go to bed hungry.

Earlier the people from the neighbourhood had held a market in our camp for firewood, fowls, sesame, etc., now there was nothing. I sadly missed especially the fowls and a root tuber, probably yams *(Dioscorea)*, in shape and taste much more like our domestic potato than is either the sweet potato *(Batatas edulis)*, or the tuber, probably a wild potato, which in Kanuri is called *bürma*. When at last one of my two draught oxen fell ill, and had to be slaughtered, I began in the midst of our other difficulties to contemplate the future with some concern, since no substantial service, either as riding or as baggage animals, was to be expected from the horses, which were growing thin on an exclusive diet of the fresh grass which the increasingly frequent summer rains caused to spring up everywhere. And as our privations increased, so too did my household, for apart from the two slave girls whom I had borrowed from the king, and who, as I have said, had soon found an opportunity to run away, [636] Almas had sold his Bornu horse for four slaves and a pagan horse, all having been delivered immediately.

No less did the advancing season threaten to make our situation disagreeable. After we had had the first rainfall in Somraï, rain continued throughout April to be fairly infrequent, but during May it became quite abundant. The clay soil of Somraï must soon become impassable, and if there were still almost two months to go to the height of the rainy season in Bornu, it was to be feared that before long the road thither would confront us with great difficulties. An immediate departure, however, seemed inadvisable, for disquieting rumours to the effect that Abd er-Rahman's forces had appeared north of us on the Ba IIi, and that a small Bagirmi caravan, thirty strong, had been massacred in Somraï, testified to the insecurity of the road and the unreliability of the Somraï.[7] Besides, Abu Sekkin had right at the beginning taken possession of all the horses which our caravan had for sale, but he had not yet paid anything for them.

My objective, moreover, was still far from being attained. Already at the outset Abu Sekkin had promised me that he would soon shift his camp to the sandy region near the Shari, and would then send me to the Bua of Korbol, to the Nyillem and the Sara of Dai. When after several weeks we were still in Broto, I earnestly enquired about my journey to Dai; and, as a deaf ear was turned to this request, I sought at least to obtain permission to visit Lai, which was only a few days' journey away

---

[7] Gourdault, *Tour*, 395, says that the caravan, of ordinary travellers, were killed to the last man by 'our people', in order to procure provisions. This seems likely to be another instance of faulty translation into French.

on the western Shari (Ba Bai or Ba Logon).[8] Trustworthiness was not, however, exactly one of my royal friend's virtues; evasions and excuses to explain why this and that could still not be carried out were easily found, especially for a Bagirmi king for whom custom made any intercourse with the outside world very difficult, and whom one could not assail day after day with reproaches and entreaties.

Thus my mood gradually became bitter and gloomy, and my talks with Abu Sekkin, when once I had succeeded in getting to him—usually our business was transacted through intermediaries—were not always very friendly. After the treacherous treatment described above, [637] which on May 13[9] and the following days his own people had inflicted upon our very nearest neighbours, had turned them into our open enemies and had seriously changed our position for the worse, he asked me one day my views on the best way of getting out of these difficulties. Without sparing him I said in reply that Almighty God did not bless princes or people who were without *amân*, and that we Christians involved ourselves only in matters that were honourable. He would have to see for himself how to get things right; as for me, God would at the right time rescue me from such a perfidious society. Observations of this kind, which must, to be sure, have sounded very unusual to him, he took by the way in no bad part, but no more did they make any serious impression upon him.

The inhabitants of the villages of Mode and Broto had withdrawn with those of Be-Delüm to the neighbouring village of Tshire, which was surrounded by a protecting wall, and from there they harried the country round our camp. An attempt to surprise them there did not seem to have been seriously intended by us. I took part in this expedition in order to satisfy myself of the existence in Tshire of the date-palms which had been reported to me from all sides. Scarcely, however, had a march of about three hours roughly south-westwards brought us to the neighbourhood of the village,

---

[8] Lai is today the centre of the prefecture of Tandjile which was established in 1962; P. Fuchs, *Tschad*, 1966, 40.

[9] This was about a week before the birthday of the Prophet; it is perhaps indicative of conditions in the Bagirmi camp that Nachtigal makes no reference to this important Islamic festival. See also II, 80 and note.

and five women, surprised while gathering herbs, had been taken prisoner, when at the sight of 50 to 80 Pagan horsemen we hastily beat a retreat. All the more frequently did we have unpleasant visits from that quarter. About us hostile horsemen prowled continually on their swift little steeds, stole every head of cattle that was not pasturing actually before our eyes, and killed the slaves who had wandered too far from the camp, and did not belong directly to their tribe. Even in the immediate neighbourhood of the camp, it became day by day more dangerous for women and girls to collect the herbs and leaves, a decoction of which had to make our miserable porridge of groundnuts or bean flour in some measure tasty; many of them never returned, and were found killed days afterwards.

When at last even the haughty Abu Ṣekkin had become convinced of the untenability of our position, it was decided to withdraw to the east. Shortly before, we had the pleasure [638] of seeing a caravan of petty Bornu traders arrive. Among them there were to my great surprise a *mejebri* (inhabitant of the Jalo oasis south of Benghazi) and a Murabid from Qatrun, who had been brought into this dangerous region by the love of adventure and the lure of profit. To receive them was to me like greeting fellow-countrymen, and the news which they brought from Kuka, Fezzan and Kanem moved me as if it had been news from home. And as a joyful or a sorrowful event seldom comes alone, so the day before our departure, a deserter from Abd er-Rahman's camp also appeared with the news that, with the advancing rainy season, both Abd er-Rahman and Knetishe, the *aqîd el-bahar*, the leader of the auxiliary troops from Wadai, were about to withdraw to the north into the region of Lake Fitri. Knetishe, whose sympathies for Abu Sekkin were known, had, moreover, quarrelled with his protégé, and realising his complete inadequacy, had seriously threatened to break with him altogether, since he had neither following in the country, warlike spirit, nor political understanding. Everybody prepared with fresh courage for shifting our camp to the east.

When, long before daybreak on May 29, the great drum gave the signal to break camp, we in my household had already been busy for a long time in making the most essential preparations. This foresight was quite in order, in the first instance because, apart from the king and the very highest dignitaries, I still had the largest quantity of baggage; then, in place of my slaughtered ox, I had obtained from Abu Sekkin a pagan horse, for which quite a different method of packing was required; and finally it seemed important that we should not be among the last to leave the place. Dense hordes of armed Pagans were in fact assembling in menacing proximity, and surely not merely as innocent spectators of our departure. Any hut on the periphery which had been abandoned by its inhabitants they were able to set on fire, and at the very moment when with my people I was able to leave our huts, the Pagans were pressing forward with loud war-cries into the *fatsha's* enclosure. Fortunately, in order to cover the withdrawal, the king and his captains, with their contingents were holding themselves in the *fâsher* ready for battle. Otherwise, although there was no [639] wind, the whole place would have been ablaze even before we could leave it, and I should probably have fared badly myself, for the load of the ox had to be repacked scarcely fifty paces from my dwelling. In the fantastic illumination of the burning huts, we saw, not without a feeling of uneasiness, how the black forms, brandishing their weapons with cries of rage, were darting hither and thither, and giving expression to their justified hate by the destruction of the huts and of the most trifling objects that we had left behind. Their wild cries rang in my ears for a long time.

By sunrise the camping place lay behind us, and after marching eastwards for about an hour, we reached the rendezvous, still in the territory of Mode. As soon as the king arrived with his escort, we continued in the same direction, at first through grain-fields, and then over pasture land with low bushes, and after a few hours entered the woods and arable land of Murki, the inhabitants of which are still Gaberi. But these, after Abu Sekkin with his usual perfidy had laid waste this place also a few months before, had still not returned again to their domestic hearths. Towards midday we camped on the former campsite of the Bagirmi, where separate huts still gave the favoured ones among us protection against two violent thunder-storms which broke over us in the afternoon and evening.

On the following day, May 30, we marched along the edge

of a thick wood; to the right of our path lay some low-lying pasture land, dotted with pools of water, which I was told belonged to the Ba Ili system. To my astonishment we camped after only a few hours, ostensibly because water was close at hand, but mainly, as became evident during the course of the day, to avoid getting too close to the village, Koli, which belongs to the Tummok section of the Palem, since it was intended to surprise these people early the following morning.[10] Just as earlier the inhabitants had repeatedly successfully resisted the king and his father, Abd el-Qadir, so now too they sent no token of submission. While during the afternoon we marched in a generally southeastern direction through a somewhat sparser [640] wood, we were surprised by a frightful thunder-storm which made our situation very disagreeable, and compelled us to camp. Only with difficulty did we succeed in kindling here and there a small fire for a makeshift drying of our clothes, and, cold and wet, in continuous fear of renewed rain, for the sky remained heavily overcast, we spent an extremely uncomfortable, sleepless night.

Long before daybreak we set off again, and at sunrise entered an open wood; among the leafy trees, with tall trunks, there was however no *Eriodendron*. The dwellings of the natives lay scattered about in the shade of the trees, the cultivated fields here and there in the clearings. The houses for the most part had either been recently destroyed by fire or were still burning. Of the inhabitants there was at first nothing to be seen. At the sight of the dwelling places our people scattered to look for any domestic animals or other property which might have been left behind, while I myself rode on with gloomy reflections about this scene of destruction which sharply contrasted with the luxuriant beauty of nature and the magnificence of the sun rising in the clear sky. I longed for peace and homely conditions, equally nauseated by my companions who believed that they could derive from their religion the justification for robbery and murder, and by their victims who, instead of uniting against their hereditary enemy, were ready to destroy each other. Suddenly I was roused from

[10] *Harper's*, 713: Nachtigal thought Abu Sekkin might have been encouraged in this attack 'by the firearms of my companions, which had already been of great service to him on several emergencies'.

my gloomy thoughts by some of the reed missiles, one of which tore my clothing. I looked around and saw in front of me a broad clearing on the edge of which Abu Sekkin and the *fatsha*, surrounded by our mounted men, had halted, and in the middle of which were the people of Koli who were threatened by us.

To the side huts were going up in flames here and there, or clouds of smoke were rising from their burnt-out ruins. In front of me I saw a wide clay wall, only 1 to $1^{1/2}$ meters high, which at the point nearest to me formed a right angle. On the other side of the wall lay a few more huts, and the middle of the field of vision was occupied by a dense wood. Except for the burning huts and those few isolated darts, everything made an impression of the most profound peace. Many of the natives were sitting on the wall, throwing-iron carelessly on the shoulder, and [641] now and then exchanged greetings with people in our company with whom they might share a common origin. Some small piebald horses were grazing in the interior of the enclosure, men lay chatting on the grass, while others wandered up and down with their weapons in their hands, apparently in the greatest peace of mind. Only for women and children did the eye seek in vain. That this calm was an indication not of peace and friendship, but of resolute preparedness for war, the subsequent course of events during the day was to show.

Soon the picture changed. Tribally related messengers went from the side of Abu Sekkin to the leading men of Koli to demand submission, but met with the most determined refusal. The men climbed down from the wall, assembled with their comrades inside the enclosure to take counsel; all provided themselves with an abundance of throwing-irons and javelins, many with shields. The horses had disappeared into the background; small groups of defenders formed along the wall; all were ready for the fight. A shallow trench ran along the low wall, which formed a broad, almost square rectangle, with an opening on each of the sides visible to us. The thicket in the middle, I was told, had been made as impenetrable as possible by planting brambles on its periphery; in its interior, it sheltered the village of refuge.

The openings in the wall were carefully barricaded with tree

Battle for Koli. III, 353.

trunks and our assault parties were for the most part posted near them. The harmless darts of the besieged could not seriously disturb us, and their spears and throwing-irons, indispensable for the later fighting, could not be thrown out over the fortress wall, for they would then have been lost. Only once, apparently as a result of my strange appearance, did a Koli warrior allow himself to be induced to make use of a throwing-iron. Standing right on the wall, and mockingly and threateningly brandishing his weapons at us, he took aim at me, and hurled his iron as I was riding quietly from one of our parties to another. I saw it coming, and would have avoided it easily, if my horse had not been somewhat hard-mouthed and I myself had had spurs; as it was, I succeeded only in moving sideways, and the iron hit the stirrup, though not without at the same time injuring my horse.

[642] In the meantime those of our people who had gone off without any noteworthy success to plunder the outlying village turned up again, and the assault began. The capture of the outer works presented no difficulty. With the help of their firearms and the protection of their shields, the more daring of our footsoldiers soon succeeded in scaling the wall at various points and capturing the barricade at the northern entrance. After this had been destroyed and cleared away and even our armoured horsemen could break through, the enemy without delay abandoned the defense of these fortifications, ran nimbly away, and disappeared into the central thicket. This too was surrounded by a shallow trench, the earth from which had been piled up to form a low wall, and it proved in fact to be almost inaccessible. Here began the crisis of the day. From early morning until afternoon, the defenders of their domestic hearth maintained here an unequal struggle, at once glorious and doomed to fail.

While the defenders were fighting for their most precious possessions, life, family and freedom, the Bagirmi had no more lofty motive than greed for booty, or at most a crude delight in fighting. Their objective was not the ultimate victory, but only personal gain; from this arose the lack of any united action, a fact which was of substantial advantage to the besieged. As soon as the hatchets at hand had cut entrances into the edge, artificially reinforced, of the protecting grove—

inside this was less dense and intersected by regular paths—
and the besieged were concentrating their attention exclusively
upon these points of assault, there began on all sides the
private enterprises of the attackers. Each sought to seize, on
his own account, people or domestic animals, half the former
and all the latter belonging to the man who made the capture;[11] on all sides greedy men were seen disappearing as they
crawled under the thick bushes, or returning by the same path
with a child or a goat. In such confusion, and since in any case
the armoured horsemen who were generally very much feared
by the Pagans were unusable against the thicket, Koli would
not have been defeated that day if an all too great superiority,
and the firearms, had not been on our side.

[643] The *fatsha* with his people took up his place on the
east side of the thicket; the *ngârmâne* operated on the north,
the *mbarma* on the west, and the Sara, Ndamm, Bua, Nyillem
and Tummok bands who were with us surrounded the wood
without any order on the look-out for booty. I remained in the
entourage[12] of the *fatsha*, for here the decisive conflict was to
be expected. After an entrance had been made which permitted several warriors to get through at the same time, our
men gradually forced their way into the interior of the grove
under the protection of the musketeers,[13] who found cover
behind the thick trees. The wood was becoming more open,
and a broad path which was being defended by the besieged
led to the war village. When some of the foremost men had
been shot by Almas, the troop fell back; the women and girls

[11] Nachtigal did not explain how this rule for the distribution of booty
was interpreted when a warrior captured an odd number of the enemy,
three, or perhaps only one. According to an incident in Sir Abubakar
Tafawa Balewa's novel, *Shaihu Umar*, the rule among the Hausa was that 'if
a man were to capture three slaves, the Chief would take two of them, and
he would be allowed to keep one' (Hiskett's translation, p. 22). See also III,
346, note 1, and p. 253 above.

[12] The German is *Umgebung*, and might here equally well mean 'vicinity'.
This is a recurrent problem: for example, on III, 71, we have 'Daza
environment', which could as well be 'Daza companions'. See also III, 43
note.

[13] *Harper's*, 714, adds that the two Arabs who had arrived shortly before
(p. 360 above) played, together with Almas and Hammu, a leading part in
the attack on Koli, because of their firearms.

nevertheless came out of the village, refreshed their warriors with *merissa* and fresh water, and with fiery speeches spurred them on to renewed endeavour. The men too took heart, and drove their pursuers out to the thicket, only to be driven back again themselves immediately afterwards. Thus there ensued an almost regular surge of battle back and forth, in which, to be sure, the poor Pagans gradually lost ground. For each enemy whom they killed or wounded, many of their own men fell, and their losses bore all the more heavily upon them because of their inferiority to the attackers in numbers of warriors.

The day was very hot, and since we had not been so fortunate as to find a well in the vicinity, we suffered severely from thirst. Hammu, who had succeeded in creeping through the bush from the side as far as the village, brought me thence a vessel with some water, and told me of the large supplies of grain and fruits of the earth[14] stored in the village. Since I cherished a wish to see the places of refuge before they must be destroyed, I too entered the wood, and, along a bypath, from which I could see our warriors at some distance, I reached the outermost huts of the village. In the huts there were only small children, for the women were just carrying fresh drinks to their warriors. As I was then withdrawing again with the utmost despatch, I took to the main path, and exactly at a moment when the people of Koli took heart for a furious attack. The Bagirmi [644] were compelled to resort to wild flight, in which of course I too was caught up; they very soon overtook me, for in running I lost the only pair of shoes that I still called my own, and the tender skin of my bare feet was as ill-suited to the roots and branches on the ground as my wide Bornu garment was to rapid locomotion. My imposing blue spectacles, the last unbroken ones which I possessed, fell to the ground, and my tarbush, with its waving tassle, was left hanging in the branches of a tree. Anxiously looking back, I saw my black pursuers storming ahead, brandishing their weapons, and clad in leather aprons with the tails attached to

[14] In his wording here, *an Getreide und Bodenfrüchten*, Nachtigal seems to distinguish between two categories of crop; but on III, 69 he apparently includes *Getreide* among the *Bodenfrüchte*. *Bodenfrüchte* is now obsolete in German, and has a rather Biblical flavour.

them. I heard their war-cries, already at close quarters, saw their spears and throwing-irons flying past me, and an early termination of my career as a traveller seemed to me certain, when suddenly the ground disappeared under my feet, and I rolled into the shallow trench in front of our horses' feet. Humiliated I crept away to my horse, barefoot, bareheaded, and bleeding from a superficial cut on the right foot, tied a piece of cotton cloth on my head as a protection against the sun, and cursed my ill-timed curiosity.[15]

The catastrophe was hastened by success in setting fire to one of the huts, closely packed together, of the village of refuge. Although it was a windless day, the efforts of the besieged to put a stop to the fire were nevertheless in vain; the village with its abundant stores of grain was reduced to ashes. The confusion and despondency of the inhabitants increased, and the efforts of our people to get possession of the enemy's women and children became ever more frequent and more audacious. The number of Pagan warriors was visibly shrinking, and the strength of the survivors diminished; their dwellings, reduced to ashes, could no longer be held. By midday the village was deserted, and all had withdrawn into the thickest part of the wood, not far from the point occupied by the *mbarma*. The struggle was now concentrated there, a struggle of despair, the frightful scenes of which have remained among my most painful memories.

Caught between two fires—for our men were pushing forward from the burning village—the desperate little band repeatedly sought to break through on the side of the *mbarma*, and to seek safety in the certainly admirable speed [645] of their legs. But when the foremost had paid for this intrepid effort with their lives the others crawled back again disheartened to the temporary shelter of the thicket. I saw one tall man, covered with blood, who succeeded in breaking through the ranks of the Bagirmi and fled in colossal leaps across the plain. His strength, however, gave out as the blood streamed from him. Hunted half to death, he breathed his last under the blows of the Pagans—his fellow-tribesmen!—who were with us. The badly wounded were dragged out from the

[15] According to Gourdault, *Tour*, 398, Nachtigal's fortunate escape was attributed to his occult knowledge, and to his magic.

bushes and killed. Women and girls were pulled half-fainting from their hiding places, and not infrequently a bloody struggle developed to get possession of them. Despite their black skins, the pallor of fear and of terror could be clearly seen on the young girls and small boys. Tender children—useless as plunder—were torn without pity from the arms of their mothers, and if there was any dispute about their distribution, their limbs were tugged hither and thither so brutally that one was compelled to fear that they would be literally torn to pieces. A foal, still very young, died at the hands of those who were greedily competing for it even before it had found a master; its skin was at once stripped off, and the Pagans, to whom custom permits the consumption of horseflesh, roasted it over the fire and ate it.

At last about 2 p.m. the survivors were reported to be willing to surrender and to appear before the *fatsha*, if he could bind himself to restrain the furious Bagirmi and their Pagan allies. With the best will in the world the *fatsha* was in no position to do this. He had lost control of the mob, which had divested itself of all human feeling. His people managed, indeed, to bring before him two of the unfortunate enemy, who had bound their unsheathed daggers to their necks as a sign of submission: a young man wearing a tobe, and an old man with a gunshot wound on the upper thigh. There was no success, however, in mollifying the rage of the mob sufficiently so that the others too could have come out without endangering their lives. The two emissaries returned to their people, and the forlorn little band seemed willing to die fighting. Once more there followed the affecting [646] scenes of frantic efforts to break through the compact ranks of the enemy, the short final act of the tragedy. But now that it was possible without danger to search the thicket through for women and children who might still be hidden, general interest was diverted from the last of the fighting men; and while quarrels, more loathsome even than the crude horror of the actual fighting, were breaking out on all sides about the possession of the unfortunates who had lost parents, home, freedom and hope, twenty or more men, the last defenders of Koli, could come forward and surrender unconditionally without being exactly manhandled. The king of Bagirmi was in possession of a few hundred more slaves, but a happy and prosperous village had vanished from the face of the earth.

I rode sadly through the grove past the bodies of the fallen, among whom I also recognised several of the people who had come with us from Bornu,[16] and across the site of the burnt village, where the signs of a superhuman heroism, such as only the deepest despair could have evoked among the women of Koli, wrung the heart of the onlooker. Twenty-seven half-burnt bodies of infants I counted there, whom their own mothers had given over to a violent death to save them from the almost certain slow extinction which was to be expected for them in the war-camp of their enemies, or from prolonged slavery.[17]

After some hours we left this scene of bestial destruction. My two boys, Mohammedu and Billama, were nearby with the baggage animals and the baggage, and soon there also appeared most of our travelling companions from Bornu, who almost without exception had secured a share of the human booty. Through a sparse wood, where the deleb palms predominated, we marched eastwards beyond a Palem village, in which the houses lay scattered over a wide area, and which we reached after sunset. Although Abu Sekkin's *amân* had been assured to them, the inhabitants had either moved their families to safety up in the few cotton-trees in the neighbourhood, or had shut them up behind the makeshift barricades of their farmsteads. In nervous defiance the men stood well armed in front of their [647] barricaded doors, guarding their people whom from the height of my horse I could sometimes see crouching in anxious suspense together in the courtyards.

[16] See III, 219.

[17] Manning, 1995, 89, 112, 114, mentions Nachtigal three times, all in connection with the Koli battle. He attributes bows and arrows to the defenders, says that children were left behind, and adds that, while men were killed or captured, and women captured, 'the remaining casualties were among the Baghirmi raiders themselves as they struggled for control of the captives'. Footnote references are deficient, inasmuch as Manning (first published in 1990) was still awaiting Volume III (1987) of Nachtigal. This almost total neglect of Nachtigal, together with the trifling errors which have crept into even that snippet of Nachtigal material which is used, show how far Africanist scholarship still is from taking adequate account of so major a source as is *Sahara and Sudan*.

From a distance were heard from time to time the anguished cries of women and children, as unscrupulous marauders forced an entry to their hiding places and were plundering them or taking them prisoner.

In outward appearance the Palem are not very different from the Somraï and Gaberi; they are robust, often tall, and symmetrically built, their skin colour is more or less black, usually without any shades tending towards reddish or yellowish, and for the most part they too appear to understand the Bagirmi language.

The sky was thickly overcast with clouds, with thunder rolling on every side, as we pitched our camp for the night at the foot of some deleb palms without other sheltering trees. I spent half the night in surgical treatment of the wounded. I stitched flesh wounds together with horse-hair, and bandaged the more seriously injured as well as I possibly could. Many, however, had deep breast or stomach wounds, or open shoulder- or hip-joints, and some gave up the ghost even that night.

Next morning, June 1, we set off an hour before sunrise, and crossed, still in a generally easterly direction, a depression with a rich growth of grass, which was pointed out to me as *komodugu*;[18] at it lowest points it exhibited marshy ground with small scattered pools of water, and, according to what people said, it was supposed to extend to the north towards Mul and to the northwest to the Ba Ili. Towards evening on the day before we had crossed a similar grassy treeless valley, where in summer there was abundant water, and which appeared to stretch from southeast to northwest. Both these valleys, as well as the valley-like depression near Murki and another lying southsouthwest of Gundi, which we caught sight of later, appear to be parts of the network of marshes from which eventually the Ba Ili emerges. One hour after sunrise we turned to the south, passed numerous scattered barricaded farmsteads, which already belonged to Gundi, marched beyond the centre of this principal village of the tribe of the Tummok, and camped about 8 a.m. Everybody immediately went off into the [648] surroundings to look for roofs and wall-coverings for huts, for stakes and fencing, wooden mortars

[18] Valley with pools of standing water, as *hénderi* (Nachtigal's *enneri*), or more commonly river (Barth, *Vocabularies*, II, 162-5; I, 435, and III, 481).

and other household gear, in short for all the requisites necessary for a dwelling. The insolent slaves of the king and of his highest dignitaries duly came back richly laden, but the booty of my people was only one piece of straw fencing, sufficient at most for the walls of one hut, and we had to content ourselves for the time being with a lodging of leafy branches. With a light southeast wind the forenoon was overcast, but about midday the sky cleared, so that I indulged the hope of a rainless night. But at this season downfalls of rain had become so frequent, and I could so little afford any damage to my scanty belongings that, after neither Almas nor Hammu had succeeded in the afternoon in getting hold of a roof for a hut in the neighbourhood, it was not without anxiety that I lay down to sleep.

A bad night followed, of which the beginning especially has remained a disagreeable memory for me. Without suspecting it, we had erected my stopgap hut on a termite nest, which was however no higher than the level of the surroundings, and during the night the detestable little creatures paid me a most unwelcome visit. Scarcely had I passed half an hour in uneasy sleep—ever since Somraï I had suffered from severe rheumatic pains—on my bed, set up as always flat on the ground, than I awoke with a peculiar feeling on the skin all over my body. At first I tried to ignore it, and to go to sleep again, but then I decided, since my pain promised me no rest anyway, to get up and strike a light. This last was by no means an easy undertaking, for while, with the help of a little scrap of *khâm* rolled up to form a wick, I had made a lamp out of a small dish containing butter, our cooking fire had gone out, and I had to kindle dry rags in the touch-pan powder of one of our flintlock muskets. At last, however, I got a light, and then by the dim gleam of my primitive lamp saw my bed submerged by thousands upon thousands of white ants, many of which I had already crushed. My shirt and the surface of my bedcover were covered with insects which had been squashed to a pulp, and fresh swarms were continually [649] creeping out of the ground. All the cloth within their reach had already been riddled with holes, and a square piece of *khâm* which I used as a pocket handkerchief had disappeared into insignificant fragments. I started up overwhelmed with disgust, woke Hammu from his sleep, and with his help established myself inside the piece of hut walling acquired that morning, and over which I threw a mat and lion skin. Scarcely had I recovered from my alarm when a heavy gale arose from the eastsoutheast, with masses of cloud which threatened disaster. The wind then moderated, and with rolling thunder and flashing lightning torrential rain burst over us, reducing me to a lamentable condition, and giving my baggage a severe battering.

Only after a few days did I succeed, with the help of king, in getting possession of an excellent hut which gave me security against the inclemency of the weather. Not only did it let no drop through, of even the heaviest rain, yet it was constructed with rare art. The peak of the roof consisted of a large, slightly arched rosette, which was made up of roundish straw wreaths, closely plaited and tightly bound one with another, and fastened to the body of the roof proper with strips of leather. The roof inside appeared smooth; while the free ends of the straw used in the plaits projected densely outside, here they were carefully cut away to form a uniform surface. This acquisition was important, for humidity and rainfall were continually increasing. Rain fell during more than half the days of the following months, June and July. Covers and clothing were always damp, all leather grew mouldy, all iron rusted, and even instruments which were used regularly could only with difficulty be kept free from rust. The atmosphere of the hut was as damp as that of a cellar, and the essential fuel was lacking to keep up a fire which would keep things dry, as the natives are accustomed to do at this time of year, since dry wood was scarce, and a search for it at any distance entailed, with the hostility of the inhabitants, putting one's life in jeopardy.

Tummok had been represented to me as the Promised Land. *Durra, dukhn,* maize, sesame and groundnuts were said to be there in profusion, and goats and hens to be indescribably cheap. [650] The sandy soil, mixed with humus, which at once absorbed rain after it had fallen, suited us, to be sure, in view of the time of year, better than the previous clay soil, and seemed to hold out to us the prospect of conditions for our return northwards more favourable than Somraï's muddy tracks. Of the superfluity of foodstuffs, however, there was at first no sign. Already on the second day after our arrival an expedition for grain brought in only a meagre quantity of groundnuts, and the natives had received our people with weapons in their hands. The villages of the Tummok recognised without reservation the supremacy of Bagirmi, and paid their taxes, but they relied in return on the agreement which promised security for their lives and property, and were not at all willing silently to let themselves be plundered. Every foraging expedition thus became a ghazzia, in which some people on both sides lost their lives. And these raids had to be pushed out to such great distances that, with the uncertainty of success, it was difficult to get people to participate in them.

It was a difficult time, which made an early return to more favourable conditions seem more than desirable to me. I had now about twenty persons to feed, for my people had gradually come into possession of slaves whom I had all the more to leave to my people, so little was I in a position to offer them any compensation for the slaves. After some time, indeed, grain came into the market, but it was difficult to get the number of throwing-irons needed to purchase it, and the Tummok definitely refused to accept payment in any other form. For my household I needed grain daily to the value of two throwing-irons, equivalent to half a Bornu tobe, and I could calculate with some certainty the day when my property would be reduced to nothing. I had already renounced altogether the consumption of poultry, eating only soups made from the flour of cereals or of groundnuts. We were really starving.

During the month of June I did not completely abandon hope of making shorter expeditions from our camp, especially since Abu Sekkin was still always representing them to be an assured prospect. Now, when we were scarcely two days' march from Sara Kumra, the chief there could not, so Abu Sekkin asserted, delay longer [651] in paying his respects, and this chief should then also guide me to the Sara of Dai who live south of Kumra. Abu Sekkin refused, however, to let me go without the chief, just as he was also unwilling to permit a visit to the Nyillem and Bua without their commanders as escort, for I was a pledge entrusted to him by Shaykh Umar, for whose life and security he was responsible. Nor, as I could easily see, was there now any longer any question of a journey to the southwest through the region of the Gaberi. When the whole of June passed without the prospects for my journeys becoming any more assured, I abandoned my hopes, but all the more eagerly gave consideration to my return to Bornu.

Gundi was the principal village of the Tummok and the residence of the chief, Bai; there was nothing in the construction of its houses to distinguish it from the villages which we had earlier passed through of other tribes. The chief Bai had purchased the devastated Koli for 100 slaves, and to repopulate the village he got back the men who had survived, together with a corresponding number of women. This restitution was no exceptional act of generosity, since apart from the fact that it was surely in the interests of the Bagirmi king himself to bring about the repopulation of the district, men are nowhere much in demand as slaves. They are no longer educable, make endless efforts to escape, and keep up among the women and the younger people too the spirit of resistance and the hope of returning home. As a result of the purchase of Koli, the levy which Bai owed to Abu Sekkin had, however, together with his own tribute, risen to 200 'heads', and it is not easy for a minor chief to collect such a number of slaves. Absolute ruler as he is in most things, he naturally has great misgivings about handing over into slavery people of his own tribe, and to abduct 200 people from neighbouring districts demanded in this case a force sufficient to insure him, after the Bagirmi had withdrawn, against reprisals from those whom he had injured.

As the Bagirmi king also cherished the wish soon to transfer his residence to the north, the usurper having left the south, so the tribes which were living close by were being energetically [652] pressed to discharge their tributary obligations. With the instalments which were gradually coming in, and the yields from the smaller expeditions which went on without interruption, some led by the *fatsha*, others by the *ngârmâne*, but especially by the *katurluli*, our camp was seriously overcrowded with slaves, and with their number and the difficulty of maintaining them, their value naturally fell. Older men could be bought at price which in the market of Kuka would have corresponded to two or three Maria Theresa dollars. Older women, who are better adapted for work and always more docile than the men, reached a value of five Maria Theresa dollars, while young girls cost at the utmost twice as much, since the king and his dignitaries were still in a position to pay such a price. Small children who probably had little capacity for the march one might obtain, in view of the scarcity of means of transport, almost as a gift. The price of those from six to eight years never exceeded that of an ordinary Bagirmi or Bornu shirt, which in Kuka cost about three-quarters of a Maria Theresa dollar.

The crowding together of a large number of people, the inadequate and bad food, the inclemency of the weather—only a few could get shelter against the sun's rays and the almost daily rain—grief about lost happiness and fear for the future, soon produced among the slaves a debility and despondency which undermined all powers of resistance to the diseases which were sure to come. It is well known throughout the Sudan that the slaves from the far south, especially the young individuals, are often attacked by intestinal diseases which easily take on an epidemic character. In the miserable conditions which prevailed in our camp, such a state of affairs was unavoidable, and a diarrhoea was soon raging which swept away many victims. Since the wretched sick could not, because of their weakness, leave the camp circuit, or were prevented by their masters from doing so, so that they should make no attempt at escape, new sources of infection were always being accumulated in their excrement. They scraped out superficial hollows for themselves near the huts of their masters, and dragged themselves there and back as long as their strength lasted. At the same time they remained fastened together with their companions—the shortage of iron chains [653] being made good by broad strips of raw hide twisted axially, which formed neck-rings at regular intervals—so that whenever any individual wanted to relieve himself, the whole row had to accompany him. If the strength of a sick person was so far exhausted that an attempt at escape became inconceivable, so he was released from his bonds, and usually did not move again from the edge of his hollow until his miserable life was at an end. The unhappy victim of man's bestiality was then dragged to the outskirts of the camp, and the body left to the effects of the atmosphere and to the vultures and hyenas. The poisoned atmosphere can be imagined which gradually developed in our camp, partly as a result of the excrement, lying almost uncovered, of the sick, and partly of the corpses continually decaying in the damp air.

On July 1 I was myself stricken by this intestinal disorder, from which I recovered only on the journey back to the north. The condition of my digestive organs, weakened by a prolonged unattractive diet, made me susceptible to the illness, and the aftereffects of the malaria which had not spared me since the beginning of the rainy season, had left me with only diminished powers of resistance. The farinaceous interior of the fruit of the *Parkia biglobosa* seemed for a time to produce favourable results, but because of the scarcity of this tree in our neighbourhood this remedy was not always to be had; and indeed, because of its harmful effects on the stomach, it ought to be used only occasionally.[19] My strength faded away with alarming rapidity, and I had now only the one wish, the one hope, to be able to depart as soon as possible. Sometimes I had myself lifted on to my horse, and rode to the dwelling of the king nearby, in order to excite his sympathy by my wretched appearance and to induce him to send us back. But I found that I had nothing to oppose to his simple Muhammadan logic, when to my complaint that I was near to death, and did not wish to die among the heathen, far from my friends in Bornu, he replied, 'If God has decreed death for you, o Christian, it seems to me a matter of complete indifference whether you die here or in Bornu or along the road. But if the Almighty has granted you life, [654] you will again recover your health. God is great, and the fate of all rests in His hands!'

Among Abu Sekkin's reasons for continually postponing my departure was the fact that he had not yet paid in full for the horses which he had purchased from our caravan; he desired, moreover, when opportunity offered, to obtain some unusually intelligent counsel or other from my presumed supernatural knowledge of all things; but he was also influenced

---

[19] A tree with dainty feathery leaves and velvety dark blood-red blossoms on long hanging stalks, and seeds of which form the ingredients of the 'dadawa' cakes, said to be relished all over the Sudan; 'they have a nauseous smell, however, and are only digestible by a negro's stomach' (Schultze, 1913/1968, p. 102; see III, 300).

by a more worthy motive. I had brought him valuable presents, and he had been unable either to entertain me in a suitable manner or to satisfy my desire to travel. His sense of royal dignity and the wellknown generosity of his disposition made the thought of dismissing me without a guest-gift intolerable to him, and yet for the time being he possessed nothing but slaves. Repeatedly he sought to persuade me to accept some slaves, for, despite all my insistence, he could not bring himself to believe that anybody would not aspire to property, or would be genuinely scandalised by human merchandise. Thus he sent to me one day ten elderly slaves, men and women, who became a source of infinite vexation for me. The eunuch who brought them refused to take them back, for he much less still could understand the reason for a return which would be so mortifying to his master. But the *fatsha*, whom I then asked to take the people back again to the king with my thanks, wanted to bestow them upon my servants, from whom he had received a promise of some material demonstration of their gratitude. My servants, finally, whose good will was of the greatest importance to me in these difficult conditions, accused me of wanting to deprive them of that which the favour of fate and the liberality of the king were offering to them. The rejection of ten *sedâsîya* (that is, six-span high slaves) created no less complication for me; these were sent as a substitute for those which I had refused, for Abu Sekkin could not resist the conviction that I had declined to accept the earlier ones because of their poor quality. Only after even one of his wives, who, surprised in an indiscretion, was to have been consigned to the Christian by her brutal husband as a sort of punishment, had, despite her handsome appearance, despite her comparatively rich clothing, and despite the good will towards me which the gift of [655] her person was said to demonstrate, been rejected, did Abu Sekkin seem to be convinced of the firmness of my principles in this matter. Even then he sought once more to entice me with the beauty of a recently captured Pagan maiden of about 16. However he took her back without difficulty, especially as the poor girl nearly died of fright on seeing me, and he then let Almas have her.[20]

[20] Rohlfs was confronted with a similar embarassing situation in 1866 as he was leaving Doloo, the capital of Mandara; the sultan of that country

In the meantime my companions from Bornu were gradually being paid for their horses. As I have said, the prices had been settled by the king himself, and indeed to the great satisfaction of the sellers. The best animals fetched eight to twelve slaves, those of medium quality five to eight, the less good three to five. The animal which the Sherif el-Medeni had entrusted to me had unfortunately arrived in Broto in very poor shape, since it had been unable to get used to the *durra* diet, and was afflicted besides by a long-festering ulcer. Its master had counted on getting at least eight slaves in exchange for it, but Almas who was looking after this business in the place of Afono who had been left behind,[21] had to be content with getting only half as many. Of course, it fell to me to feed these slaves too. I had responded all the more gladly to Abu Sekkin's desire to purchase my horse also, as I was unable to feed it. As purchase price I received two centners of ivory and a pagan horse for the return journey. Instead of the slaves which I had persistently declined, the king now intended to give me as a guest-gift [*Gastgeschenk*—token of hospitality?] some more beautiful elephant tusks, which he was expecting from the chief of the Sara Kumra. The latter, however, was in no hurry to make his visit of homage, since he was not in a position to pay the tribute, which pressed heavily upon him, of 100 slaves. He had repeatedly requested that Bagirmi troops might be sent to him so that with their help he might meet his obligations. Abu Sekkin, however, could not make up his mind to go to Kumra in person, since his ancestors had never gone south beyond the territory of Tummok, and his people did not wish to hear anything of further expeditions and would scarcely have followed the *fatsha*.

---

sent him a 20-year-old male slave, whose value in the Kuka market was estimated at 25 dollars, and a pitch black 12-13-year-old girl from the sultan's *harim*, perhaps worth twice as much. (Almas was given a 25-dollar woman, and Dunkas, maybe already inclined to uselessness (see p. 235 above), a 10-dollar young girl.) The official who brought these slaves to Rohlfs said that to return them would be regarded by the sultan as an insult; Rohlfs therefore took them with him to Kuka, where, instead of selling the girl, as his friends advised, he presented her to Shaykh Umar (*Pet. Mitt.*, Ergänzungsheft No. 34, 1872, 20 and 26). See also p. 127 above.

[21] III, 288. See also pp. 125 and 225 above.

July dragged slowly on in hunger and misery. Privation and disease increased. On one foraging expedition twenty of our people were killed in one day, including [656] seven women whom hunger had driven to take part. With the increasing rainfall, there were again added to my intestinal disorders daily attacks of fever against which I could not fight with a single dose of quinine. For my bed I had built up in my hut a fairly high bench of sand, the disintegration of which I tried to prevent as effectively as possible by side-supports; over the sand branches were laid, and on top of these were spread out my mats and coverlets. However, wood and mats rotted away, coverlets and cloths were constantly covered as if with dew, and the more violent downpours not infrequently washed my sand bench away. When rain set in during the night, the possession of my bed also became a subject of dispute for me. My greyhound, who of course suffered from shortage no less than the humans, had had puppies, and had prepared a hole for them in the soft sand within my hut. The less capable of feeding her young the poor creature was, reduced to a skeleton and able to offer them only a few drops of milk, the greater was the affection with which she looked after them. It was heartrending to observe the old dog when the little ones sought again and again, in vain, to be fed, and our efforts to keep them alive with gruel could not, of course, succeed. As soon as fairly heavy rain set in at night, and the hole began to fill with water, the anxious mother lifted the pups as quickly as possible on to my bed, and in spite of her normally mild disposition, resisted with resolute hostility any opposition from me.

During this time our position improved in some measure, because the grain in the fields was now far enough advanced in ripening to be used as food. These resources were, however, of little use to me personally, since the young roasted grains seemed only to make my condition worse. And for the same reason I could profit as little from the favourable circumstance that the few Arabs who were following Abu Sekkin actually had some milk cows. An unexpected and interesting visit from the district of the Bua Korbol supplied with butter those who possessed small children for purchasing it.[22] The visitors were Fellata (Fulbe), who in their [657] noteworthy urge as cattle breeders to pass through north equatorial Africa from west to east, and to establish colonies far from their home country, had been driven as far as the Bua. They felt themselves so much strangers in that region, and were so convinced that their ancestors had come from the Mediterranean coast countries, that immediately after their arrival they came to greet me as a cousin—*uled ammi* [literally, child of my uncle] in Arabic. All spoke broken Arabic, and had the characteristics of their race; that is, their skin-colour was a dirty yellow, they had well-formed noses, straight or curved, and their hair was longer and less matted than that of the Negroes. According to their account, their colony in Korbol consisted of perhaps 200 men; some Arabs also were living alongside them there, and both nations were said to have settlements among the other Bua sections and among the Sokoro.

After all that I had seen of the Bua, and now heard about them from the Fellata, I should have been glad to go to Korbol, and it was indeed very probable that Mbang Mohammedu would be going there himself in person. It was, however, likely still to be a long time before he could enforce his claims on the chiefs of the Tummok and the Sara Kumra, and after that collect the tribute due from Ndamm and Miltu. Nor did he at all want to arrive before the end of September in the northern part of Bagirmi, where he intended again to hold his court in the security of Bugoman, for one could not count on the grain harvest there earlier than that, and it was all too certain that there were no grain stocks in existence. For the rest Abu Sekkin would probably have been able without overmuch anxiety to return also to other parts of his country, for Abd er-Rahman's retreat into the district between Chad and Fitri and his quarrel with the Wadai army leader were now established facts. The difficulty lay to be sure not with the usurper, but with the King of Wadai, whose inflexible spirit was known

---

[22] An out-of-the-ordinary reference to a specific demand for small children, who were usually regarded as expendable. Nachtigal's phrasing is so matter-of-fact here that, in *Slavery* 1970, we entirely failed to notice that this is in fact another example, admittedly of an unusual kind, of trading in slaves.

far and wide. I strongly advised Abu Sekkin to throw himself into the arms of Shaykh Umar of Bornu, to ask him to intercede with the king of Wadai, and through his mediation to have rich gifts of reconciliation transmitted to the king. It was in fact not improbable that King Ali, who [658] must for a long time have been well aware of the inadequacy of the ruler whom he had set up, would have gladly made use of intercession from Shaykh Umar, with whom he had just established new relationships of friendship, in order to extricate himself from the difficult situation in Bagirmi, and not completely to undermine the productive capacity of the country which owed him tribute. Mbang Mohammedu, however, was much too arrogant to accept my advice. After the fall of Massenya Shaykh Umar had forbidden him entry into the territory of Bornu, and for that he could never forgive him.

The discussion of these matters formed the last conversation which I had with Abu Sekkin. Since there was no prospect whatever of any early expedition by him from Gundi; besides, I lacked strength and opportunity for other journeys; and all my Bornu companions had been paid—I was willing to try to depart even without the king's permission. Instead of the ivory for which he had waited in vain, and which I had repeatedly told him that I neither wanted nor could even transport, I succeeded in getting as a present a transport ox, and I was now determined that only force would prevent me from setting out. After my attempts on several days in succession had failed, as the king each time had my baggage removed from the laden animals, he at last allowed me to depart on July 30, not without assurances at the last moment that the ivory which he had intended for me would be sent after me.

STUDENTS' BIBLIOGRAPHY

An all-inclusive bibliography, often many pages long, bears witness to the painstaking industry of the author of a book, and allows fellow-specialists to see quickly which sources have been used or, rarely, omitted. Such a bibliography may also be more overpowering than user-friendly. Ordinary readers, and in particular students embarking on a new field of study, need more focussed help. A 'bibliography for students' should in one way be much more selective and compact, concentrating on the most relevant and important complementary sources, and in another more expansive, commenting on the items which are included. This is what is attempted below. At the same time, every source cited in the book is traceable through the index: every author is indexed, every reference to every author is listed, and italic figures in the index indicate where in the present volume the full publication details are to be found. The only exception is Nachtigal's *Sahara and Sudan*, cited too often for each reference to be indexed.

Baba of Karo, Mary Smith, ed., Faber & Faber, London 1954, 2nd edn. 1981. A delightful Africanist classic, the autobiographical narrative of which everyone interested in Africa should read; the supporting anthropological critical apparatus is more demanding. Slavery is not a major theme, but there are many passing, or more than passing, references throughout. Baba's memories stretched back to pre-colonial days.

Backwell, H.F., ed., *The occupation of Hausaland 1900-1904: being a translation of Arabic letters found in the house of the Wazir of Sokoto, Bohari, in 1903*, Government Printer, Lagos, 1927, reprinted by Frank Cass, London, 1969. A handy short collection of documents concerned chiefly with administrative affairs within the Sokoto caliphate just before the British conquest. Explanatory commentary has been added, but some of the material remains difficult to understand in detail. Slavery is one theme among many; it is fascinating to see, through the eyes of administrators and rulers, something of how the institution functioned within a major Muslim black African state.

Balewa, Alhaji Sir Abubakar Tafawa: see *Shaihu Umar*.

Bovill, E.W., ed., *Missions to the Niger*, 4 vols, published by the Hakluyt Society and Cambridge University Press, 1965-6. The last three volumes are used extensively in this book. They reproduce, together with much other material, the *Narrative of Travels and Discoveries in Northern and Central Africa in the Years 1822, 1823, and 1824*, by Denham, Clapperton, and Oudney, first published in 1826, by John Murray in London. The account is very readable, but it is not so substantial and scholarly as *Sahara and Sudan*.

Corpus: see Levtzion and Hopkins.

Dorugu: see Kirk-Greene and Newman.

Fisher, A.G.B. and H.J.: see *Slavery* 1970.

Fisher, H.J., 'A Muslim William Wilberforce? the Sokoto jihad as anti-slavery crusade: an enquiry into historical causes' in S. Daget, ed., *De la traite à l'esclavage. Actes du Colloque International sur la traite des noirs: Nantes 1985*, Paris 1988, vol. 2, pp. 537-55. My hypothesis here is that one important contributory cause of the Sokoto, or Fulani, *jihad*, which broke out in northern Nigeria in 1804, was the increasing (and in Muslim eyes illegal) enslavement of free Muslims. Evidence is gleaned from a variety of sources, ranging as far afield as Ashanti and Brazil. The article is mentioned in the present volume (see p. 30 above), but the material is not discussed here.

Fisher, H.J., 'Population mobility, especially in Islamic black Africa' in P.E.H. Hair, ed., *Black Africa in time perspective*, Liverpool University Press, 1990, pp. 38-56. A somewhat fuller elaboration of the 'population mobility' thesis summarised in the opening pages of the 'Introduction' above.

Gourdault, J., 'Voyage du Bornou au Baguirmi, par M. le docteur Gustave Nachtigal', *Tour du monde* (Paris), 1880, vol. XL, pp. 337-416 (identified in the notes to this volume as Gourdault, *Tour*). This is a translation of a *résumé* manuscript kindly supplied in advance by Nachtigal (see pp. 337 note, and 416). For my as yet still unfulfilled intention to prepare in parallel texts the five published versions of the Bagirmi slave-raiding chapter (two German, two French, and one English), see above, p. 347. Gourdault is neither as complete, nor as reliable, as the English *Sahara and Sudan* which is now readily available.

Hamman Yaji, *The diary of Hamman Yaji: chronicle of a West African Muslim ruler*, James H. Vaughan and Anthony H.M. Kirk-Greene, eds, Indiana University Press, Bloomington and Indianapolis, 1955. A unique, and uniquely interesting, account by another crucial eye-witness, and a source used extensively in the present volume. The diary runs from 16 September 1912 to 25 August 1927, direct, brief and unadorned entries on a daily basis (though missing many days, and in addition some sections, apparently less interesting, of the original diary were omitted when the translation was first made). Slaves and slaving comprise the most important single theme in the diary, although just over halfway through, at the very end of 1920, slave raiding seems to have ceased, apparently as a result of British intervention.

Hanson, John H., *Migration,* jihad, *and Muslim authority in West Africa: the Futanke colonies in Karta,* Indiana University Press, 1996, 159 pages of main text. A study of Muslim, mainly militant, migration from the Senegal valley into Karta, and the subsequent refusal of most immigrants to go further, even when strongly encouraged by their leaders to do so, during the second half of the 19th century. Very detailed, sometimes densely so, but well arranged and clearly argued. Slavery is a minor theme, but the book is a major contribution to the study of population mobility, which I argue is the overarching context within which slavery inside black Africa may best be studied.

Ibn Battuta. *Ibn Battuta in black Africa,* Said Hamdun and Noel Q. King, eds, first published in London in 1975 by Rex Collings; there is a more recent printing by Markus Wiener in America. This excellent little book, of under 100 pages, should be in the library of every Africanist student. Ibn Battuta was a 14th-century world traveller. His full account runs to several volumes, not quite as long as Nachtigal, but still very substantial, very interesting and very valuable. Hamdun and King have extracted the complete account of Ibn Battuta's travels in black Africa, east and west. The west African material is also available in the *Corpus,* and in almost all cases both books have been cited for any reference in the present volume; only on p. 281 has it been necessary to cite the two complete translations, by Defrémery and Sanguinetti into French, and by Gibb and Beckingham into English. Ibn Battuta had no specific interest in slavery *per se,* but he has a good deal to say about it, insamuch as it was a prominent component in the African societies which he visited, and also a significant element in his own life-style.

Johnson, Walter, *Soul by soul: life inside the antebellum slave market*, Harvard University Press, 1999. This book appeared too late for account to be taken of it in the main text here. Two major points in the argument of *Soul by soul* are echoed in the present study: the immense importance of the mobilisation of demographic resources internally, in the American case after the banning of further importation from Africa, in the African case when trans-Saharan exports, probably never as important as internal demand, were shrinking still further; and secondly, the pivotal role of slave markets. An early review (in London's *Financial times*, 8/9 Jan. 2000) complains that the market was 'not the real face of slavery', which is to be found in the overseer's lash, the runaway in the swamp, the sundered family. All these, and worse, are to be found in the internal slavery of Muslim black Africa — but in combination with an extraordinary diversity of slave experience. The internal American market was part of the real face of slavery, just as was Thomas Jefferson's fruitful liaison with Sally Hemmings. The 'fancy' in America, the concubine in Africa, provide another point of comparison, as does the conspicuous consumption illustrated by luxury slaves — and the actual danger of wrongful enslavement or re-enslavement.

Kirk-Greene, A.H.M., and P. Newman, *West African travels and adventures: two autobiographical narratives from Northern Nigeria*, Yale University Press, New Haven and London, 1971. The major narrative is that of Dorugu, which tells the story of his childhood, his enslavement, his work and social experiences as a slave, his manumission by European travellers and his transfer to their service, and his eventual visit to England where he helped early linguists in their study of the Hausa language. A remarkable instance of the voice of a highly intelligent slave, speaking vividly and at length.

Levtzion, N., and J.F.P. Hopkins, eds, *Corpus of early Arabic sources for West African history*, Cambridge University Press, 1981. An extremely valuable source book, including, in annotated translation, practically every external Arabic reference, up to about 1500, concerning western Africa. Slavery is one theme among many, and may be traced through the elaborate indices.

Lovejoy, Paul E., *Transformations in slavery: a history of slavery in Africa*, Cambridge University Press, 1983. An impressive and wide-ranging historical attempt, by a prolific and much respected scholar. The Islamic factor is carefully studied, but is necessarily a minor component of the whole picture. As often happens in broad studies, theoretical generalisations may sometimes obscure the relative chaos of eye-witness reality. Lovejoy suggests, for example, that eunuchs 'were especially dependent, without even the chance of establishing interests that were independent of their master' (p. 17). But some eunuchs, such as Muhammad Kurra in Darfur (pp. 284-6 above), or Abd el-Kerim in Borno (pp. 288-91), seem to have pursued their own personal agendas quite vigorously - and who was the eunuch's master, when the king died?

Nachtigal, Gustav: for bibliographical details, see p. xix above.

Savage, Elizabeth, ed., *The human commodity: perspectives on the trans-Saharan slave trade*, Frank Cass, London, 1992. A collection of interesting and useful essays, by no means confined to the trans-Saharan dimension. Joseph C. Miller has contributed 'Muslim slavery and slaving: a bibliography', 23 pages.

Shaihu Umar, a tiny novel written in Hausa by Alhaji Sir Abubakar Tafawa Balewa, first Federal Prime Minister of Nigeria, killed in 1966 during a military coup; *Shaihu Umar* was translated into English by M. Hiskett, and published by Longmans, London, 1967. A very short and easy read, some 60 pages. Set in the late nineteenth century, before European colonialism, and filled with intriguing slavery details. A second edition published by Wiener, 1997, with the subtitle 'Slavery in Africa', and with a new introduction by Beverly Mack (a contributor to the Elizabeth Savage volume).

Slavery 1970. A.G.B. and H.J. Fisher, *Slavery and Muslim society in Africa: the institution in Saharan and Sudanic Africa and the trans-Saharan trade*, London, C. Hurst & Co., 1970. Now superseded by the present volume, which includes everything of substance from *Slavery* 1970, much of it rewritten and with a great deal of new material, resulting in a new book more than twice as long. Nachtigal is much more fully represented in the new volume, and the emphasis on direct evidence, from participants and eye-witnesses, is a distinctive feature.

Usuman dan Fodio (Hausa form), Uthman bin Fudi (Arabic), *Bayan wujub al-hijra ala'l-ibad* [Concerning the obligation of *hijra* upon worshippers], F.H. El Masri, tr. and ed., Khartoum and Oxford 1978, ISBN: 0 19 822703 5. A fascinating volume, with full critical apparatus: a substantial introduction and bibliography, the Arabic text, a complete English translation (120 pp.), and an English index. Oddly, slaves are not indexed, although a good many references are scattered throughout the book. Two chapters cite slaves in their titles: 'On the law concerning giving freedom to the slaves of unbelievers dwelling in the Abode of War if they flee to us, and the permissibility of taking as concubines the women who have been captured from them, after waiting for the passing of one menstruation; even if they have husbands in non-Muslim territory', and, 'On the law concerning one who has been found as a slave in the hands of the unbelievers and claims to be a free-born Muslim or one who has been captured in a *jihad* and claims to be a free-born Muslim [but] has not emigrated; or one who has been brought from a land where the selling of free men is commonplace and claims to be a free-born Muslim'.

Verger, Pierre, *Trade relations between the Bight of Benin and Bahia from the 17th to 19th century*, Ibadan University Press, 1976, originally published in French in 1968, translated Evelyn Crawford. A huge book, full of detailed information. Chapter IX, 'Slave revolts and uprisings in Bahia, 1807-1835', is of special interest for students of Islam.

Willis, J.R., ed., *Slaves and slavery in Muslim Africa*, 2 vols, Frank Cass, London, 1985, being papers presented in 1977 to a conference, 'Islamic Africa: slavery and related institutions', at Princeton University. Contributions cover a wide range of topics, and are in some cases of variable quality. Anyone who has responded positively to one of the main aims of the present volume, that of allowing as far as possible active participants, and eye-witness observers, to speak for themselves, will find the paper by Mervyn Hiskett, 'The image of slaves in Hausa literature', including material translated from both Arabic and Hausa, in the first volume particularly rewarding.

INDEX

In all entries, all page numbers giving full bibliographical details of any source cited in the book are printed in italic type (e.g. see under Ajayi).

Aaisha, Lamino's cook, 152, 203
Abdallah, 16th-century Bagirmi ruler, 242
Abdallah, Y.B. (1919), *109*
Abdallah Ben Salim, Awlad Sulayman slave owner, 168-70
Abdullahi dan Fodio, 18, 23
Abd el-Ati, cleric, friend of Nachtigal, 184
Abd el-Aziz, Wadai ruler, 258
Abd el-Bari, 19th-century Darfur vizier, 219, 321
Abd al-Hamid, Ottoman sultan, 292
Abd el-Jlil, Awlad Sulayman chief, 50
Abd el-Karim, treasurer, *mala*, 35, 259-60, 288-90
Abd el-Kerim, usurped royal power in Wadai from Tunjur, 299-300
Abdul Karim, Barth's Arabic name, 94
Abdulkarim, Shaihu Umar's master, 190-1
Abd al-Malik bin Marwan, 180
Abd Masuma, slave poet, 69
Abd er-Rahman, usurping Bagirmi ruler, 347, 358, 360, 381-2
Abd al-Rahman, usurping Borno ruler, brother to Shaykh Umar, 333
Abd al-Rahman, returner from Brazil, 91
Abd er-Rahman, king of Darfur, 255
Abd al-Rahman, Sokoto caliph, 171
Abd al-Salam, rebel against Sokoto, 20-1
Abdullah bin Salim, Arab leader in Tabora, 243
Abdullahi Marghimi, senior military Borno slave, 264-5
Abeokuta, Nigeria, 91-2, 212
Abeshr, Wadai capital, 36, 55-6, 137, 148, 188, 193, 204, 233, 262, 271, 302, 306, 313, 316, 323, 345-6
abolition of slavery, anti-slavery: 19, 39, 52-4, 63-4, 83-4, 100-1, 105, 175-6, 182, 208, 251, 332-43; *firman*, 100-1; Quranic prohibition of slavery, 47; *see also* British: anti-slavery, emancipation
Abubakr Kado, pious Kano ruler, 281
Abu'l-Mawahib, generous Kilwa sultan, 309
Abu Muhammad, 12th-century trans-Saharan trader, 137
Abu Sekkin, literally Father of the Knife (*see* III, 421), Mbang Mohammedu, ruler of Bagirmi: 51-2, 54, 95, 105-6, 113, 122-4, 126-7, 133-4, 163, 165, 204, 206, 220, 227, 248, 257-8, 288, 295, 315, 318-9, 322, 347-82; his father Abd el-Qadir, 362
Abushiri, Muslim opponent of Germans in East Africa, 188
Abu Yazid, leader of 928-9 slave revolt, 194
Abyssinia, *see* Ethiopia
acrobats, Moroccan, 210; *see also* Hammu
Adamawa: 25, 54, 65-6, 71, 73, 102, 104, 132, 161, 169, 214, 240, 246, 272, 274, 297-8, 309-10, 314, 322; Adama, emir, 71, 187-8, 297; Gabow, 308; Lawal, emir, 104, 216, 297; Yola, capital, 71, 241, 298; Zubayr, emir, 25, 308
Adeleye, R.A., 1971, *12*
adultery, 19, 115-17, 121, 148, 162, 186, 279; *see also* sexual relations, wives
Afade, near Kuka, 125, 127
afia, 135; *see also* Lafia
Afigbo, A. E. (1965), *120*
Afonja, Yoruba Muslim revolutionary, 157

Index

Afono, 125, 225, 379
Agades, 222, 293
agriculture: *see* farming
Ahaggar, 38, 214
Ahmad Baba, Timbuktu scholar, 26-8, 218
Ahmadu, Shehu, ruler of Masina, 63, 198-9, 249
Ahmed Ben Brahim al-Wadawi, Nachtigal's Kuka landlord, 231-2
Ahmed Bokkor (or Bukr), Darfur king, 263, 299-300
Ahmed el-Medeni, Sherif, 106, 113, 124-5, 127, 210, 225, 316-17, 379
Air, place name, 100
Ajayi, J.F. Ade: (1965), *316*; and I. Espie, eds (1965), *120*, 236, 290, 316
Ajia, Hamman Yaji's head slave, 160, 177
alcohol: 19, 146, 279, 287; coconut palm wine, 213; *merissa*, 279, 367
Alexander, B., 1908, *108*
Algiers, Algeria, 221, 333
Ali Dinar, last sultan of Darfur, 13, 26, 263
Ali, the Fezzaner, Nachtigal's servant, 182-3
Ali Folon, Songhay eunuch, 282
Ali, Nachtigal's servant, *see* Mandara
Ali Riza Pasha, governor of Tripoli, 340
Ali Sarkin Gobir, 221
Ali of Shiraz, 194
Ali, sultan of Sokoto, 309
Ali bin Umar, alchemical Borno *mai*, 239
Ali, King of Wadai, 19, 20-1, 32, 35, 54-7, 69, 100, 136, 148, 193, 241, 260, 262, 268-71, 278, 295, 307-8, 315, 381-2
alifa ba, 166; *alifa Moito*, 275
Aliyu Babba, son of Sultan Bello of Sokoto, 195
Alldridge (1901), *52*, 116
Allen, J.W.T. (1960), *188*
Almas, Nachtigal's guide to Abu Sekkin, 74, 95-6, 123-8, 164, 197, 206, 319, 352-3, 355-6, 358, 366, 372, 378-9
alms, *see* presents, sacrifice
Alooma, Idris, 16th-century Borno ruler, 19-21, 49, 203, 228, 239, 242, 250-1, 254-5
aman, good faith, promise of security, 356, 359, 370, 374
ambassadors, messengers, 96, 159, 261-3, 288-9, 297-301, 310, 312
America, U.S.A., 7, 30, 49, 149-50, 176, 217, 320, 326

amin, pl. *umena*, two senior Wadai royal household officials, one free, one slave, 276; see also 279 Amin, Madagali scribe, 61-2
amulets, talismans, 56, 61-2, 157; *see also* supernatural powers
ancestry, *see* genealogy
Anderson, B.: (1912), *149*; (1870/1971), *157*, 222
animals, domestic: 1, 14, 15, 37, 58, 59, 211-2, 214, 253, 354, 356, 362, 366; baggage, 126, 357-8, 361, 370, 382; *see also* camels, chickens, cows, dogs, donkeys, goats, horses, sheep
animals, wild: 339; crocodile, 302; giraffe, 257, 296; guinea-fowl, 352; hippopotamus, 123, 152, 232; hyena, 127, 227, 376; lion, 192, 373; rhinoceros, 192, 302; tiger, 339; vultures, 376
Anti-Slavery Society, 19; *see also* abolition of slavery
apostasy, 'kaffering', 29; see also Pagans
aqid, 193-4, 261-2, 276, 287, 302, 360
Arabia, Arabian peninsula: 17, 43, 64-5, 74, 101, 145-6, 196, 213, 218, 228-9, 237, 254, 281, 304, 317; Hijaz, 101, 229, 332; Jidda, 229; Ta'if, 174
Arabic, language: xvii, xviii, 30, 34, 65, 69, 90, 137, 145, 157, 182, 219, 255, 261, 262, 273, 311, 326-7, 381; *Arabian nights*, 36, 67; literacy, 30; records, 19, 22, 30, 57, 103; *see also* chronicles, Quran
Arabs: xviii, 6, 17, 20, 22, 25, 32, 34, 38, 53, 71-2, 85, 88, 134, 139, 145, 151, 153-4, 182, 190, 192, 194, 200, 202, 209, 213-4, 225, 233, 242, 248, 271, 286, 287, 298, 300, 306, 317-8, 328, 331, 340, 342, 366, 380; eastern, 22, 53, 107, 116, 138, 153, 156, 195, 196, 223, 226, 243-4, 251, 272, 296; gunpowder, 198; Hamr 337; Kababish, 26, 336; Khozzam, 194; Mahamid, 77, 271, 284; Mgharba, 79; Rashid, 302; Rezeqat, 275; Salamat, 287, 301-2; *see also* Awlad Sulayman, Shuwa, Tunjur
Arami, Nachtigal's Tubu guardian, 143
archaeology, 43, 338
Ardo Hammadu, of Tibati, 274
Arkell (1961), *270*, 296, 312, 338
Arki (or Harki), early Kanem ruler, 238-9

Index

arnado, village chief, 179, 80, 189, 310; *see also* chiefs
Arnold, T.W. (1913/1961), *54*
Arnot, F.S. (1889/1969), *109*, 169, 226-7, 331
Arus, Ya'qub, king of Wadai, 299-300
Asad, Muhammad, Quran exegete, 47
Asbenawa, 6, 241
Ashanti, 251
Asia, Asians, 98, 254, 291, 328
askiya, ruler of Songhay: 215-16; Daud, 60-1, 229-30, 243; Ishaq II, 282; Muhammad I, 19, 21, 23, 29, 60, 112, 282
'ataqa: *see* emancipation
Atiku, chief of Gabow, 308
Atiqu, Sultan Muhammad Bello's successor, 293
Atlantic slave trade, xx, 29-30, 45, 49, 65, 91, 99-100, 107, 108, 113, 119-120, 134, 180, 182, 217, 223, 255, 316, 321, 326
Awdaghast, 34, 180-1
Awjila, Saharan oasis, 100
Awlad Sulayman, 20-1, 41, 50, 77-9, 88, 139, 150, 166, 168, 184, 200, 213, 226, 307-8, 329
Awwa, Hamman Yaji's recalcitrant cook, 202; ?see also his fugitive concubine Awu, 160
Ayalon, D. (1956), *250*

Ba, A. H. and J. Daget (1962), *63*, 71, 199, 249
Baba of Karo: *see* Mary Smith, 1954
Backwell, H.F. (1927/1969), *xvii*, 58, 80, 82, 163, 171-2, 308, *383*
Badagry, 92, 320, 328
Baer (1967), *223*, 330
Bagdad, 36, 86
Bagirmi, xix, 12, 19, 36, 41-3, 52-6, 70, 74, 87-8, 92, 95, 99, 103, 107, 121, 123, 125, 132, 137, 163, 166, 170, 174, 197, 201, 204, 210, 221, 225, 226-7, 234, 239, 241, 242, 245, 248, 249, 251, 253, 256-8, 269, 270, 275, 278, 282-3, 285-6, 288, 292, 294, 302-4, 315, 322-3, 327, 330-1, 345, 347-82
Bahr al-Ghazal, eastern Sudan, 195, 298
Bai, Tummok chief, purchased devastated Koli, 375
Ba Ili, river, 358, 371
al-Bakkai, Shaykh Ahmed, Timbuktu scholar, 57
al-Bakri, 98, 115, *180*, 295

Baldé, M. S. (1975), *184*
Balenyere, Bagirmi village assigned to Queen Mother, 227
Balewa, Alhaji Sir Abubakar Tafawa, *xvii*; *see also Shaihu Umar*
Bambara, 52, 70, 93, 145, 198, 249
Barade, 62; Barade Umaru, 160
Baraghwata, sect, 77
barber, *wanzam*: 283-4 (for castration); slaves, 222
Barbour, N. (1959/1962), *240*
Bardai, in Tibesti, 144, 344
Barde (a name to Hamman Yaji, but in *Shaihu Umar* (24) 'a mounted attendant of the chief'), 33, 179
Barka, Hausa slave, with Nachtigal, 224-5
Barka Gana, Borno commander-in-chief, a slave, 245-6; Dorugu's Kanuri name, 191
Barka-ngolo, Borno cut-throat, 151-2
Barqa Musgo, trader, slave of the Awlad Sulayman, 226
Barth, Heinrich: 7, 85, 87, 90, 94 (Abdul Karim), 134, 140-1, 218; (1965), *19*, 25, *33*, 38, 41, 93, 99, 103-4, 106, 112, 131-2, 136, 150, 151-2, 166, 180, 183, 186, 196, 199-200, 203, 216, 236, 240, 246-7, 250, 265, 286, 293, 296-7, 302, 315, 330; Vocabularies, 371
Bashir, al-Hajj, *wazir* of Borno, 131, 166, 196, 199-200, 233, 291-2, 333
Basra, 86, 98, 152-3
Bauchi, 16, 25, 89, 230, 297, 308
Beachey, R.W.: (1967), *109*; (1976), *280*
Be-Delŭm, tribe, 355, 357, 359
Beech, M.W.H. (1916), *73*, 77, 84, 213, 217, 223
Beeljie, enslaved Fulani princess, 118
Begu people, Darfur, 195
Bello, Muhammad, Sultan of Sokoto: 11, 20, 22, 27, 72, 195, 221, 230, 249-50, 252-3, 261, 273, 292-3; 'Tanbih al-raqid', 72
Benghazi, 100, 131, 360
Benton, P.A.: (1911), *194;* (1917), *17; see also* Schultze (1913/1968)
Benue river, 102, 107
Berbers: 26, 43, 112, 145; Massufa, 183, 221
Beriberi (Hausa name for Borno immigrants), 6, 242
Berlioux, E.F., 1872, *155*
bey el-nobe, tribute collector, 298-9
Bideyat, people of Ennedi, 79, 168, 284

Index

Billama, Nachtigal's slave servant, 67-8, 83, 211, 287, 370
Bilma, 132, 238; Dirki, Gissebi, 238
Binger, L.G. (1891), *54*
Birgid people, Darfur 305-6
Bir Meshru, 130-2; *see also* wells
Birni Besse, first Bagirmi king, 303
Bivar, A.D.H.: (1961), *29*; and M. Hiskett (1962), *19*, 27
blindness, 16, 272; illness, 124, 133; punishment, 278
Blyden, E. W.: 65-6; (1887/1967), *70-1*, 120
Boahen, A.A. (1964), *87*, 100-1, 325, 339
boats, 11, 124, 227; slave ships, 64, 108, 119, 223; other ships, 83, 85-6, 251; slave seamen, 213, 222-4; drowning, 238
Bokari, rebel governor of Hadeija, 25
Bombay, African guide, 74
booty: 25, 31, 47-50, 54-6, 115, 122, 132, 163, 166, 177, 180, 249, 251-4, 256, 298, 310, 325, 348-9, 354-7, 365-6, 369-72, *et passim; khums*, fifth, 49, 173; share of woman, slave, minor, 48
Boporo, 156, 222
Borgu, 29, 34, 116, 203, 208, 220
Borku, xviii, 20, 58, 78, 168, 235-6, 342, 345
Borno, Bornu (old spelling): xvii-xix, 35-6, 124, 197, 210, 213-14, 220, 229, 241, 245-8, 257, 268-9, 274-5, 304-5, 306, 308, 333, 339, 344-5, 358, 360, 377, *et passim*; Emir of Borno, 161; raiding against, 40-1; raiding by, 49, 114, 151-2, 180, 203, 230, 244-5, 251, 252-3, 305; slaves, 17, 19-22, 30, 34-6, 60, 66-8, 82, 86, 88-9, 92, 95-6, 98-101, 112, 128, 130-3, 136, 142, 147-9, 154, 164-6, 167, 194, 197, 200-1, 203, 206, 210-1, 221-4, 231-4, 235-6, 238-9, 256, 258-61, 263-6, 282-4, 287-94, 296, 313, 322-31, 333, 335, 370; *see also* Alooma; Kuka; Lamino; markets: slave; 'numbers game'; Shaykh Umar
boundaries, borders, frontiers, 25, 56, 69, 90, 155, 161, 244, 264, 290, 298, 307, 336-7, 343
Bovill, E.W.: *Missions, xviii*, 20, 24-5, 29, 33, 73, 82, 83-4, 87, 99, 130, 132, 135-6, 149, 154, 220, 233, 244-6, 251, 292, 298, 299, 333, *384*; (1968) *131*
Bowen, T.J. (1857/1968), *85*, 212, 317, 320

Boyle, C. V. (1910-11), *240-1*, 272, 297
Brackenbury, E. A., 1924, *194*
Brahim, king of Darfur, 1874, 301
Brass, eastern Nigeria, 119-20
Brazil, Bahia, 30, 64, 68, 74-6, 89-90, 91, 153, 157, 196, 203, 223, 236, 255
Brenner, L. (1973), 7, 200, 246, 266
bride-price; *see* dowry
British: 146, 208, 317, 324; anti-slavery, 30, 52-3, 82, 90, 92, 96-7, 100, 102-3, 107-8, 175-6, 182, 187, 228-9, 314, 324, 332, 341; colonialism, xvii, 26, 45, 61-2, 71, 79, 89, 92, 133, 147, 159-61, 163, 175-6, 206, 215, 272, 291, 308, 312, 314, 341; England, 90, 94, 97, 317; London, 184; *see also* abolition, English language
Broto, 347, 355-9, 379
Bruce, James, in Sennar in 1772, 243
Bua of Korbol, tributary allies of Bagirmi, 127, 348, 358, 366, 374, 380-1
Bu Aisha, Ottoman envoy to Borno, with whom Nachtigal travelled south from Fezzan, 31, 132, 258, 340
Buba Njidda, a chief in Adamawa, 297-8
Buckor Sano, Gambian friend of Jobson, 187
Budduma, 22, 37, 40-1, 200
Buganda, *kabaka*, 106-7, 243; Kalema, 272; Mutesa, 195
Bugoman, 164, 166, 381
Bulala, 154, 201
burial involving slaves: 71, 192, 218, 320, 376-7; alive, 40, 42-3, 320; cemetery, 92; tomb, 266-7; *see also* graves
Burkomanda, eunuch-rich *mbang*, 285
Burton, Richard, 85; (1860/1961), *42*, 101, 110, 116, 165-6, 223, 226, 325-6, 404
butter, 135, 136, 259, 260, 278, 284, 301, 380; *see also* cows
Büttikofer, J. (1890), *232*, 343
Buxton, T. F. (1840/1967), *100*
Byng-Hall, F. F. W., 1908, *149*

Caillié, R. (1830/1965), *81*, 218
Cairo, 22, 86, 238, 280, 307, 312, 324, 330, 332, 346
calendars, 50
caliph, *khalifa*: Bagdad, 36; Darfur border guards, 337; *see also* Sokoto
camels, xviii, xx, 38, 58, 63, 79, 81, 91, 111, 122, 129, 130-2, 136-7, 142-4, 146,

Index

149, 158, 184, 188, 193, 212, 214, 222, 224, 229, 230, 235-6, 279, 296, 301, 303, 309, 313, 318, 319, 325, 329
Cameron, V. L. (1885), *156*, 226, 251, 252, 338
Cameroons, 43, 54, 161, 223, 230
Candler, J., and W. Burgess (1853), *203*
cannibalism, 43-4, 109, 244; alleged of Europeans, 43, 116, 133-4
Canot (1928), *22*, 108, 117-20, 133, 231, 310, 316, 326
Cape Coast, Ghana, 83, 338
Cape Mount, Liberia, 42
Cape Town, 176
caravans, 122-37, 224-7; to the Atlantic, 117-8, 120, 230-1, 316; to Bagirmi, 36, 95-6, 106, 122-30, 132, 163-6, 170-1, 227, 323, 377; on the East African coast, 109-11, 133, 135, 146, 214, 224, 226-7, 338; eastwards, 35-6, 56, 136, 307, 335-8; languages, 224, 317; pilgrimage, 12-3, 86, 228-30; within western Sudan, 103, 132, 222, 224, 230, 358, 360; trans-Saharan, xvii-xviii, 31-2, 69, 84, 87-9, 92, 99-106, 123, 129-37, 150-1, 168, 210, 214, 224, 226, 233, 247, 258, 289, 324-5, 333-5, 339-41; Tuareg women, 185; workers, free, 109-11, 226-7; *see also* slaves: as caravan workers
Castries, H. de (1923), *273*
cavalry, 46, 48, 50, 119, 154-5, 171, 230, 247-8, 290-1, 348-9, 356; armoured, 40, 247-8, 290, 348, 365-6; Pagan, 360; slave, 245, 272; *see also* horses
Cave, B. S. (1909), *182*
Cerulli, E. (1922), *116*, 255
Ceulemans, P. (1966), *109*
Chad, Lake, xviii, 22, 26, 37, 40-1, 99, 108, 231, 238, 240, 289, 290, 345, 381
chains, cords, &c., 30, 108, 120, 122, 132-3, 165, 167-71, 204, 215, 323, 325, 351, 353, 376; padlocks, 35
chickens, 50, 77, 124, 331, 349, 351, 353, 357, 373-4; *see also* animals, domestic
chiefs, 15, 42-3, 49, 80, 103, 113-14, 116, 124, 125, 140, 146, 155, 160, 179, 188, 193, 226, 264, 276-7, 300, 306, 308, 312, 337, 354, *et passim*; *see also* arnado, MacLeod (1912)
children 37, 42-3, 63, 81, 87, 119, 143, 161, 181, 185, 191-2, 217, 219, 246, 271, 288; *see also* slaves: children
China, Chinese, 177

Christians: 20, 27-9, 31, 43, 46-47, 49-50, 52-3, 54, 61, 64, 65, 67-8, 70, 74-6, 78, 80, 83, 91-2, 117, 128, 145, 185, 196, 198, 215, 221, 234, 236, 255, 295, 297, 312, 341, 352, 359, 377-8; Aladura, 92; Baptists, 85; Bible, 26, 81, 218, 367; martyrs, 46; missionaries, 8, 52-3, 64, 85, 89, 91-2, 107, 109, 157; People of the Book, 47
chronicles: 2, 4, 5-6, 11, 20, 60, 238, 243; local archives 66, 262; *see also* Arabic, Ibn Fartua. *Kano chronicle,* Kati, al-Sadi, al-Haj Said, *Tedzkiret*
Circassian, 177, 196, 199-200, 330; *see also* slaves: concubines
circumcision, 65, 284, 323; infibulation, 181
civet: *see* perfume
Clapperton, H., 30, 33, 73, 87, 132, 188, 220, 223, 230, 233, 297; (1829), 25, 30, *33*, 34, 59, 116, 118, 150, 153-4, 157, 199, 203, 208, 216, 218, 220, 221-2, 224, 230, 245, 249-50, 261, 292-3, 297, 309, 313, 328, 329-30; *see also* Bovill, *Missions;* Lander, R.
Clarkson, J. (1792/1927), 324
clerics, Muslim, 5-6, 10-1, 13, 20-1, 23, 57, 59-63, 69, 71-3, 154, 156, 184, 187, 188, 229, 239, 241, 252, 266, 281, 309; enslaved, 25-6, 308; *khatib,* preacher, 257; muezzins, 60; *murabid,* 21, 79, 360; *see also* imams, mal(l)ams, qadi
clients, 35, 58; *mawla,* 273
climate, 126, 132; *see also* cold, rain, water
cloth: 80, 98, 108, 111-2, 218, 220, 222, 259, 296, 301-2, 308, 313, 331, 372; as booty, 253; burnus, 60; ceremonial Pagan, 50-2; cotton strips, currency, 56, 260, 279, 303, 306, 331; dyeing: *see* handicrafts; garments, 18, 48, 56, 76, 80, 83, 101, 124, 151, 159, 166, 181, 200, 209, 211, 220, 231-2, 256, 302-3, 308, 312, 313, 319, 320, 323, 329, 331, 367, 369, 372, 374, 376, 378; nudity in Ramadan, 261; robes of honour, 25, 60, 188, 309, 314, 337; shawls, 234; slave dress, 68, 79, 81, 120, 131, 135, 136, 138, 143, 145, 146-7, 167, 198, 218, 233, 234, 246, 248, 250, 281, 308, 319; tailor, 55-6; turban, 309; weaving, 16, 55, 220-1; *see also* cotton
cloves, 136, 152, 217

394 Index

coffee, 35, 218, 234; tea, 35
cold, 36, 131-2, 143
compensation for slave owners, 101, 156, 176
Congo: 109; King Leopold, 230, 244
Constantinople, Istanbul 74, 83, 85, 93-5, 196, 206, 283, 292, 301, 307, 315, 332, 334, 339
cooks, cooking, 30, 35, 65, 90, 96, 152, 170, 202-7, 209-10, 222, 225, 235, 316, 329, 358, 369, 372; Isiaku, trainee, 206; butchers, 221, 369; *see also* food and drink
Cooley, W.D. (1841/1966), *38*
copper, 221
Corpus of early Arabic sources, 22, *34*, 43, 98, 103, 115, 123, 137, 181-2, 183, 193, 198, 202, 221, 257, 261, 273, 280, 282, 324, 330, *387*
corrections, 55, 137, 142, 183, 202, 219, 251, 261, 291, 299, 319, 329, 358; *see also* translation
cotton, 56, 131, 143, 246, 319
Coulson, N.J. (1956), *326*
courtiers, officials, 6, 34-5, 55-6, 96, 133, 170, 193, 204-5, 246-7, 257, 263, 272-3, 285-91, 376
cowries, 3, 61, 82, 198, 308, 314, 318, 329-30; *see also* currency
cows, cattle, oxen 33, 49, 50, 59, 60, 62-3, 66, 79-81, 104, 111, 165, 179-80, 194, 198, 212, 213, 216, 221, 236, 250, 253, 257, 260, 263, 266-7, 273, 290, 297, 302, 303, 306, 307, 308, 311, 313, 322, 331, 355, 357-8, 360, 361, 380-1; *see also* animals: domestic
Crawford, D. (1914), *139*, 196, 320
Crowther, Samuel Ajayi, 152, 157
cultural diffusion, 43, 99
currency: dinar, 181, 187; dirham, 181; ducat, 60, 309, 312, 326; *mahabub*, 333-5; *mithqal*, 192, 298, 333; money, 229, 301, 313; shilling, 61-2, 159, 256; *see also* Cloth: currency, cowries, dollars, slaves: as currency
Curtin, P.D. (1968), *69*, 152, 157, 184; and J. Vansina (1964), *99*

dagachi, rebellious Kano official, 267
Daget, S., (1988), *30*
Dahomey, 29, 39, 91; Bariba, 230
Dai, Sara tribe of, 358, 374
Daju tribe, 117, 301, 305
Dala, Dalatoa, 265

Dalamei, slave girl, 127-8, ? 319
Dallons, French slave-trader, 52
Damascus, 182, 228-9
Danakil, 101, 250, 280
Dar Fertit, vassal state neighbouring Darfur, 296-7
Darfur (or Fur), xix, 7, 13, 26, 35, 43-4, 56, 59, 69-70, 114, 117, 135-6, 148, 188, 195, 197, 205, 206-7, 219, 255, 256, 260, 263, 266-7, 269-72, 274-5, 279, 285-6, 290, 296, 299-302, 305-6, 309, 319, 321, 323, 328-9, 335, 337-8, 345-6 .
dar al-Islam, 173-6
Davidson, B., 1961, *112*
dawar, nomad household, 170
death, 117, 266-7 *et passim*; *see also* murder, punishment: capital, slaves: execution of
Deba, raid on, 23, 46
debt, 7, 22; *see also* slaves: for debt
Deherme, G. (1908), *39*, 126, 214, 283
Delafosse, M.: (1924), *187*; (1912/1972) *249*
Denham, D.: xviii, 23-5, 29, 83, 87, 99, 130, 136, 149, 245, 292; and H. Clapperton (1826) *38X*; *see also* Bovill, *Missions*
desert, 144, 203, 239; *see also* caravans: trans-Saharan, oases, Sahara
D'Ghies, Muhammad, who freed three young sisters, xviii, 87
dhimmi, protected person, tolerated non-Muslim, 15, 47
digma, 96, 265-6
Dimar, 81
Dinka, 328
diwan, tax in Darfur: 301; 'Diwan of the Sultans', 238
diya, blood money, 148-9, 184
dogs, 41, 44, 98, 193, 349, 351, 353-4, 380
dog-men, 134
Doka, Sudanese village without consuls, 338
dollars, Maria Theresa, 200, 210, 225, 259, 291, 296, 298, 316, 318, 319, 322, 326, 328-9, 333-4, 375-6, 379; *see also* currency
D'Ollone (1901), *43*, 113
Dominik, H. (1901), *214*
Dongola, 35, 136, 336
donkey, 171, 212, 215, 256, 322; *see also* animals: domestic
Dorugu, freed slave, xvii, 34, 36, 48,

Index

83-5, 90-1, 93-4, 98, 134, 138, 139-41, 167-8, 190-2, 211-12, 218-19, 225, 233-4, 267, 316-18, 324, 331
Doughty, C.M. (1888/1923), *43*, 65, 145, 146, 196, 213, 218, 228-9, 237, 404
Douglas, Mary (1964), *321*
Douin, G.H. (1936), *297*
dowry, bride-price, marriage gift: 112; including slaves, 41, 112, 149, 158, 307, 312-15; *see also* slaves: as gifts
drums: 1, 3, 40, 50, 360; Kwage the drummer, 140-1, 211; slave drummers, 218, 221-2; *see also* music
Duggu Debanga, *aqid*, the senior Wadai eunuch, 287
Duhu, Pagan village, 70, 159-60, 215
Dunama ibn Hume, sultan, 238, 239
Duncan, J. (1845), *89-90*
Dunkas, luxury slave, 234-5, 379
'dusting', 257, 265
Dutch, 88, 228-9
Duveyrier, H. (1918), *69*, 91
dwarfs, 328, 340
Dyeli Musa, 175

ear cutting, 81; *see also* slaves: changing one's master
East, R.M. (1934/1967), *25*, *188*, 249, 274, 297-8, 308
East Africa, 45, 52-3, 73, 77, 83, 84, 85-6, 100, 108-9, 116, 133, 146, 152-6, 177, 181, 182, 188, 194, 217, 223, 226, 228, 243, 251, 254, 325
education: 6, 10, 11, 19, 26, 59, 63-4, 72, 83, 85, 154, 184, 309; *madrasa*, 293; of slaves, 65-9, 91, 190, 192, 199; western, 64, 161, 312; of women, 199
Egypt: 14, 22, 36, 68, 69, 71, 86, 89, 112, 136, 154, 181, 190-1, 211, 223, 229, 239, 244, 250, 254-5, 271, 295-6, 324, 330, 335-6, 338; Copts, 338; Damietta, 309; Masr 238; Suez, 223
elephant, 312, 348; *see also* ivory
elephantiasis, 320
Ellis, A. B. (1883), *251*
emancipation: xviii, 19, 22, 47, 69, 70-83, 87, 101, 140-1, 149, 155, 173-6, 195, 196, 217, 249, 255-6; demand for, 66; denied, 57; by Europeans, 52, 63-4, 68, 90, 102-3, 107, 140, 175-6, 211; at festivals, 72-3; by gift, 45; *'itq*, 72, *'ataqa*, 82, 84, *al-mu'taqah ila ajl*, 185; letters of, 68, 82-3, 84, 90-1, 141; in Liberia, 317; after mistreatment, 146; *mukatib*, 66, 75, 186; on owner's death, 15, 16, 45, 73-5, 95, 206; after pilgrimage, 266; as punishment of slave-owner, 16, (*wajib*, necessary) 76-7, 79, 82; rejected, 139-41, 328; by rescue, 132; by self-purchase, 45, 59, 85, 156; *see also* abolition, freedmen, *mudabbar*, ransom
emblems, 251, 258, 282, 306, 348-9; *see also* flags, umbrellas
emir(ate), 26, 157, 181, 249, 272-3, 297 *et passim*; *see also* Adamawa, Madagali
Engerman, S.L., and E.D. Genovese, eds (1975), *134*
English language, 69, 311; *see also* languages
Ennedi, 20, 78-9, 168-70, 342
enslavement: 40-1, 46-55, 57, 92, 134, 138, 157, 163, 212, 222, 229; by one's own people, 102-3, 303, 375; of families, 42, 48, 87, 116, 320, 369-70; free Muslims legally exempt, 19, 252; of free Muslims, 18-32, 46, 57, 78, 117, 236, 252, 269, 298, 300, 308; Nachtigal on the brink of, 235-6; of pilgrims, 13, 26; as punishment, 21-2, 42, 115-21; re-enslavement, 8, 82-3, 85-6, 88, 90, 140-1, 163, 209; *see also* slaves: raids
Eritrea, 255
eschatology, afterlife, 42, 44, 61, 70, 72, 147, 245
Ethiopia(n), Abyssinia(n): 49-50, 52, 73, 83, 116, 181, 194, 196, 198, 218, 224, 244, 250, 254, 280-1, 330, 338; Ahmed Graan, 254; Amda Seyon, 280; Amhara, 280; Enarea, 198; Gallabat, 196, 244; Gojam, 198; Gondar, 338; Jesus I, 312; Theodore, 52, 338
eunuchs, *adim*, 6, 10, 35, 98, 112, 177, 181, 195, 196, 238, 242, 255, 259-61, 273, 280-94, 296, 301, 307, 315, 325-8, 339-40, 378; military role, 280, 285, 287, 375; castration, 280, 286-7; self-inflicted, 281, 284-6; *see also* Kurra
Europe: 36, 112, 206, 211, 291, 328, 344; Europeans, 43, 52, 93-4, 96, 120, 133-4, 234, 254-5, 338; colonialism, 2, 8, 29, 39, 63, 89-91, 94, 119, 120, 134, 161-2, 172-6, 182, 228-9, 255-6, 291, 310, 342-3; slave-traders, 21, 108, 134; travellers, explorers, xix, 83, 85, 87, 88, 89, 95-6, 223, 226, 368; *see also* individual countries

Evans-Pritchard, E. E. (1949), *91*
'evil eye', 36, 117, 259

Fadhl al-Nar, Madagali military commander, 159, 180
al-Fadl, Muhammad, Darfur king, 195, 321
Fage, J. (1969), *2*
Falaba, in Sierra Leone, 89
family: 3, 11, 13, 17-8, 20-1, 26, 41-2, 48, 61, 63, 78, 88, 102-3, 139, 145, 147, 149, 160-1, 182-3, 195, 199, 209, 215, 220, 271, 272, 278, 297, 331, 354 *et passim*; husbands, 42, 118-9, 183, 184-6, 193, 194; sisters, 60, 87, 143, 185, 195, 209; *see also* children, slaves: concubines, enslavement: of families, mothers, royal family, wives
famine: *see* food
fanfa, 215
Fansiggah, slave town, 65-6
farming: 1-3, 10, 41, 55-7, 64, 108, 162, 171, 239-41, 277, 348-9, 361-2; *fanfa*, 215; *gandu*, 217; *ijara*, 217; *rumde*, 104; by slaves, 37, 41, 55-7, 63-4, 71, 75, 93, 104, 211-18, 239-41, 244, 246; by slaves independently, 44, 155
fasher, royal square or campsite: 257, 361; el-Fasher, Darfur capital, 135-6, 335-7, 346
fasting, 76, 86, 205; Lent, 49-50; *see also* Ramadan
fatsha, highest Bagirmi dignitary: Alifa, 257-8, 275, 348-9, 352, 356, 361, 363, 366, 375, 378, 379; Araueli, 283
Fatimids, 86, 194, 239
Fellata: *see* Fulani
festivals: Muslim, 50, 92, 198, 233, 359; *konda*, 44; slave, 92
feudalism, 153
Fez, 60, 196, 221, 296, 312, 326
Fezzan: xviii, 31-2, 80, 85, 87, 96, 98-100, 103-5, 130-1, 133, 136, 139, 144, 182-3, 212, 234, 238-9, 248, 295, 298-9, 333-5, 341, 344, 360; Zawila, 98; Zella, 342; *see also* Murzuq
Finley, M. I. (1960), *150*, 342
fire, 90, 132, 348, 352, 361-2, 368-70, 372-3
firearms: 40, 52, 53, 77, 109, 111-15, 120, 123, 154, 156, 180, 198, 222, 232-3, 243-4, 248, 250-1, 254-5, 311, 319, 352-55, 362, 365-6, 369, 372; Arab gunpowder, 198; cannon, 248; Nachtigal's sole threat to fire in anger, xix, 57; *see also* weapons
firewood: 58, 197, 206-7, 308, 318, 324, 357, 373; other wood, 58, 151-2, 221-2, 232, 371-2; *siwak*, 221
Fisher, H.J. (1970), *156*, 188, 228; (1988), *30, 384;* (1990), 384
fishermen, slaves, 203, 213, 222
Fitri, region, lake, 201, 360, 381
flags, 25, 53, 348-9; *see also* emblems
Flint, J.E., and I. Geiss (1976), *153*
fodder for livestock, *see* grass
food and drink: 42, 44, 65, 68, 118, 120, 123-4, 135, 138, 147-8, 191, 193, 202-7, 209, 219, 221, 222, 231, 249, 258-61, 266, 279, 312, 357, 367, 373-4, 376-7; beans, 357; *burma*, 357; hunger, 1-2, 102-3, 122-4, 126, 130, 132, 135-7, 142, 151, 162, 164, 376, 380; milk, 147, 206, 380; peanuts, 10, 124, 217, 357, 373-4; yams, 357; *see also* alcohol, animals, butter, cooks, grain, honey, kola, palms, water
France, French: xix, 26, 39, 52, 63-4, 80, 86, 107, 113, 119, 126, 161, 211, 213, 217, 222, 250, 256, 283, 291, 293, 312, 317; Napoleon, 255
freedmen, xvii-xviii, 57, 58, 63, 83-97, 139, 146, 157, 184, 194, 211, 217, 224, 226, 228, 234, 242, 249, 251, 255, 297; *mawla*, 273; *wilaa*, 84
Freeman-Grenville: (1962 /1975), *52*, 64, 86, 115, 181, 194, 280, 296; (1962), *153*, 309; (1963), 1962, *46*
Freetown, 30, 89, 91-2, 108, 324; *see also* Sierra Leone
Fremantle, J.M. (1911), *273*
Freretown, freed slave settlement, 53
Fresnel, 270, 302
Froelich, J.-C.: (1954), *73*; (1962), *19-20*, 53, 229; (1966), *54*
Fuchs, P. (1966), *359*
fugoma, a Borno eunuch title, 288-9
Fuladoyo, Mogogoni, Mwaiba, fugitive slave colonies, 155-6
Fulani, Fulbe, Fellata: 6, 20-2, 23-5, 29-30, 63, 65-6, 71, 73, 89, 118, 132, 152, 157, 169, 183, 186, 194, 195, 212, 216, 221-2, 230, 240-1, 245, 246, 249-50, 265, 268, 272-4, 293, 297, 308, 381; Bororo, 194; Fulfulde language, 160; Tokolor, 50
Funj, kingdom, 243-4, 270
Futa Jallon, Timbo, 21, 65, 91, 117, 120,

Index

156, 184, 216, 230, 252, 310, 316
Fyfe, C. (1961), *92*; (1962), *116*-17, 156

Gaberi, 303, 347, 351, 356-7, 361, 371, 375
Gaden: (1907), *283*, 284-5, 291-4, 316, 328; (1935), *254*
galadima, 112, 194, 288, 327
Galla, 65, 116, 218, 228, 255
Galliéni, J.S. (1891), *256*
Galwa, to be emancipated, 70
Gambia, 22, 73, 115, 150, 156, 184, 187
Gaoga, 112, 154-5, 309
Garamantes, 130
Gaudefroy-Demombynes, M. (1962), *194*
genealogy, lineage, descent, ancestry: 145, 195, 221, 265, 275, 293, 381; liability to enslavement affected by, 26-7, 55, 78, 242; *see also* slaves: status
geographers, 38
Germans, Germany, xviii, 43, 53, 94, 95, 104, 158, 161, 179, 188, 223, 230, 260, 265, 291, 344; Berlin, 221
Ghadames, 37, 85, 92, 100, 118, 131, 133, 145-6, 154, 168, 185, 186, 189, 225, 240, 325, 332-3
Ghana: ancient, 5, 181; modern, 10, 83, 338
Ghat, 103, 131
ghazzia, raid, 374; *see also* slaves: raids
Gibson, A. E. M. (1903), *121*
goats, 1, 61, 161, 214, 306, 351, 353-4, 366, 373; *see also* animals: domestic
Gobir in Hausaland, 132, 198, 221, 241, 249-50, 282, 292; Bawa, 198
God, Allah: 5, 23, 58, 60-2, 72-3, 82, 117, 137-8, 141, 181, 204, 236, 238, 242-3, 245, 308, 342, 359, 377; Allahfi, God lives, 170.
Godechot, J. (1952), *31*
gold: 73, 98, 114, 137, 181, 188, 198-9, 222, 228, 281-2, 298-9, 313, 325, 333; alchemy, 229, 239; slave goldsmiths, 222
Gonja, 6, 230, 242
Gordon, C. G., 89, 280
Gourdault, J. *Tour*, 10, 42, 134, 347, 358, 368, *384*
grain, flour: 102, 104, 111, 119, 124, 209, 212, 216, 230, 246, 288, 296, 348-9, 351, 356-7, 361, 367-8, 373-4, 380-1; *dukhn*, 259, 373; *durra*, 113, 373, 379; *mudd*, a measure, 76; rice 205, 259-60; wheat, 259-60, 301
Grant, (1968), *134*, 184
grass, grazing, fodder, 37, 58, 211-2, 371
graves, 309, 315, 343; *see also* burial
Gray, J. M.: (1934), *195*; (1950), *272*; (1963), *53*, 217, 281
Gray, R. (1961), *111*
Greeks: ancient, 342; modern, 93
Green, W. A. (1974), *208*
Greene, Graham (1936), *45*
Groves, C.S. (1954/1964), *297*
Guinea, 39, 63-4, 113
guinea fowl, 352
guinea-worm, 133, 137
Gujeba, southwestern Borno frontier town, 264
gum arabic, 212-3
Gundi, principal Tummok village, 371, 375, 382
Gwari, raided for slaves in *Shaihu Umar*, 253
Gworam, Bauchi town, 25-6
Gwoza, village near Madagali, 62, 159

El-Hachaichi, 1903, 249
Hadeija, Fulani emirate, 25, 249, 273
Hadya, Muslim principality in Ethiopia, 280
Hair, P. E. H. (1963), *108*; (1965), *30*, 297; (1990), *384*
hairstyle, 136, 147, 227, 381
Haji, Muhammad el-Amin, *mbang*, 282-3
al-Hajj, Muhammad (1968), *11*, 13
Hajj Bezzem, Borno slave notable, later freed, 266, 292
al-Hajj Jibril, Usuman dan Fodio's teacher, 19
Hajj Salim, merchant, Nachtigal's friend, 55, 136-7
al-Hajj Umar al-Futiu, 57, 66, 173-5, 188, 249, 254, 293
hakim Freedman official, 70; eunuch, 281
Ham, son of Noah, Hamitic hypothesis, 26-7
Hamdun, S., and N.Q. King, 43, 182, 282, *385*; *see also* Ibn Battuta
Hamman Bindu, 159
Hamman Yaji: *xvii*, 33, 49, 59, 61-2, 64, 70, 73, 78-81, 111, 119, 122, 158, 159-62, 167, 171, 177, 179-80, 188-90, 202-6, 215, 222, 256, 306-8, 310-2, 314, 329, 332, 342-3, *385;* his sons, 59, 159, 162, 189, 311-12

398 Index

Hammu, Moroccan acrobat companion of Nachtigal's, 124-5, 128, 210, 352, 366-7, 372-3
handicrafts, 57, 218-22, 241; baskets, 222, 314, 351; cushions, 231; dyeing, 16, 43, 55, 98, 134, 246 (indigo); fans, 231; mats and carpets, 61, 231, 246, 307; needles, 95; spinning, 177, 220; tailoring, 55-6; weaving, 16, 55, 220-1; woodwork, 222; *see also* slaves: artisans
Hanson, J.H., 1996, *385*
Hargreaves, J.D. (1963), *29*, 114
harim, seclusion, 118, 185, 198-200, 240, 280, 282, 286-8, 292, 300, 379
Harley, G.W. (1941/1968), *44*
Harlow, V., and E.M. Chilver (1965), *53*
Harper's, xix, *347*, 349, 355, 362, 366
Harris (1844/1968), *50*, 101, 108, 155, 196, 198, 224, 228, 250, 254, 280-1
Harrison, J.W. (1890), *107*
Hasan, Y.F.: (1966), *86*; (1967), *296*
Hasib Allah, unsuccessful contender for Darfur throne, 271
Hassan, Alhaji, and Shuaibu Na'ibi (1962), *281*
Hausa, Hausaland: xvii, 1, 3, 6, 10, 13, 16, 25-6, 29, 33, 43, 48, 60, 73, 83, 85, 91-2, 113, 121, 132, 133, 134, 140, 145, 147, 154, 157, 167, 193, 195, 202, 212, 214, 216, 218-9, 221-5, 230, 240-2, 246, 250-1, 253, 265, 267, 273-4, 282, 305, 322, 331, 366; Daura, 16; Ghambaru district, 246; Kaduna, 206; language, xvii, 92, 121, 167-8, 317-8; Sarkin Hausawa, Madagali notable, 203-4; Zamfara, 249; *see also* Gobir, Kano, *Shaihu Umar*, Zaria
Hawa, returning freed slave woman, 92-3, 224
Hawalla, a Kanem tribe, victims of slave-raiders, 50
Hayatu, Sokoto dissident, 297
Hazaz, Nachtigal's Awlad Sulayman friend, 78
healing: xviii, 73, 284, 344, 377; doctors, 86, 142-3, 222, 333-4; medicine, 93, 380; surgery, 371; *see also* illness
Herold, J. Christopher (1963), *255*
hijrah, 10, 158, 173
al-Hilali, Muhammad, ruler of Dar Fertit, 296-7
hippopotamus hide, 123, 152, 232; *see also* leather; punishment: flogging

Hirla (or Kherallah), early Bagirmi slave settlement, 242
Hiskett, M. (1963), *18*; (1967/1997) *xvii*; *see also* Bivar, *Shaihu Umar*
Hobbio, Borno entry point from Bagirmi, 197
Hodgkin, T., (1960/1975), *245*
Hogben, S.J, and A.H.M. Kirk-Greene (1966), *25-26*, 297
Holt, P.M., 1970, *244*
honey, 160, 202, 206, 259-60, 301-2, 306
Hopkins, J.F.P., and N. Levtzion (1981), 22; *see also Corpus*
Hornemann, 298-9
horses: 25, 33, 36, 41, 60, 62, 81, 98, 104, 111-14, 123, 127, 136, 138, 140, 148, 150, 161, 165, 171, 184, 188, 189, 198, 203, 209-10, 211-12, 215, 219, 225, 231-4, 236, 243, 245-6, 249, 253, 255, 257, 258, 259, 260, 262, 276, 281, 282, 296, 297, 301-3, 306, 308-11, 313-14, 318, 319, 322, 329-31, 356, 358, 363, 365, 368, 369, 377, 379; 'pagan', 349, 358, 361; mules, 250; bridles, 98; halter, 232; harness, 309; saddles, 40, 55-6, 81, 231-3; spurs, 98, 365; stirrups, 365; *see also* cavalry, military
hospitality, 51, 140, 148, 164, 181, 205, 288; *see also* presents
Houdas, O.: (1901/1966), *20*; (1913-14/1964; Sadi), *5*, 86; 1913-4/1964; Kati), *19*
Houis, M., 1953, *64*
Hourst, 1896, *126*
housing: 36-7, 55-7, 58, 84-5, 140, 143, 211-12, 218-20; aristocratic, 35-7, 211, 215, 218-19, 231, 233-4, 256-7, 261, 276, 282, 286-8; commandeered, 371-3; fortified, 155-6; tree, 122, 347-56, 362, 370; women's, 35-7, 190-1
hunters, hunting, 162, 222, 352
Hunwick, J. O.: (1962), *218*; (1964) *27*; (1985) *29*; (1999) 27
Hurgronje, S., 1931, *67*, 122, 145, 196, 219, 228, 324

Ibadi, 137
Ibn Abi Zayd al-Gharnati: (1860), *77*; al-Qayrawani, *14*-16, 31, 47, 48, 66, 67, 74-6, 84, 117, 147, 184-6, 319-20
Ibn Battuta, xvii, 42-3, 98, 123, 182, 183, 192-3, 198, 221, 257, 261, 280-2, 309, 324, *385*
Ibn Fartua, Ahmed, Borno chronicler:

Index

(1926/1970), *49*, 228, 251, 254-5; (1928/1967), *19*, *203*; (1987), *49*, 228, 242-3, 251, 254-5.
Ibn Hawqal, 187
Ibn Khaldun, 153, 194, 228
Ibn Rashid of Hayil, 228
Ibrahim, disgraced Borno *digma*: 265-6; *malam*, 61; a son of Muhammad el-Hasin, 271
Ifemesia, C.C. (1965), *290*
Igala, overlord to Nupe, 195
ijara, 217
illness, disease: 1, 73, 92, 93, 125-6, 132, 135, 137, 165, 206, 225, 316, 376-80; dysentery, 124, 133, 376-7; epidemics, 2, 99, 132-3, 317; eyes, blindness, 124, 133; fever, malaria, 35, 130, 377, 380; guinea-worm, 133, 137; leprosy, 315, 320; madness, 320; rheumatism, 372; smallpox, 133, 167, 191-2; tuberculosis, xviii, 344; *see also* healing
Ilorin, 157, 297
imam: 61, 62, 66, 81, 122, 157, 172, 190, 203; *almami* of Futa Jallon, 91, 117, 120, 252, 310; freed slave as, 69-70; Samori, 63; *see also* clerics
India, 74, 85, 228-9, 254; Indian Ocean, 217
inheritance by, from, and of slaves, 15-7, 45, 59, 60, 71, 73, 156, 243, 321; *see also* slaves: status
insects: flies, 42; locusts, 1; termites, 372
interpreter, 96, 198, 310
iron: 108, 250, 373, 376; slave iron-workers, 222; *see also* chains, throwing-irons
Islam: conversion to, 5, 18-9, 20, 23, 27-30, 46, 48, 53-4, 64-71, 85-6, 173-5, 235, 254, 269, 273, 296, 317; influence on Pagan society, 40, 42-4, 45, 46, 53-4, 63, 70, 91-2, 109, 116-17, 242-3, 273, 305, 319-20, 352, 362
Ismail Pasha, khedive, 68, 114, 297, 335
Italians: 255, 342; Genoa, 112; Nachtigal's Piedmontese servant, 235-6
ivory, 79, 108-11, 113, 136-7, 153, 165, 214, 226, 230, 297, 298, 302, 309, 317, 319, 325, 333, 336-7, 340, 379, 382
Ivory Coast, 39, 114

Jahanka, 63
Jalo, oasis, 100, 360
Janissaries, 254
jauro, Jauro, 159-60, 189
Java, 177, 229

Jellaba, importing merchants, especially in slaves; often called Nile merchants, from north and central Nilotic Sudan, 114, 205, 276, 279, 306, 336
Jenne, 5, 8, 10
jerma toluk or *luluk*, senior Wadai officials, 276; Jerma Abu Jebrin, 276
Jews, 27, 29, 47, 185, 218
jihad, religious war, 8, 10, 20, 22, 27-30, 46-54, 66, 77, 103, 122, 157, 221, 244, 249, 254; *see also* theocracies (Muslim), al-Hajj Umar, Usuman dan Fodio
Job ben Solomon, the fortunate slave, 184
Jobson, R. (1623/1932), *73*, 115, 150, 187
Johnson, S. (1921/1956), *293*
Johnson, W. (1999), *386*
Johnston, Sir Harry (1906), *30*, 112, 251
Johnston, H.A.S. (1967), *195*, 221

Kabala District Office, Sierra Leone, 66
Kaduna, 206
kaffara, legal expiation, 76-7
'kaffering', apostasy, 20, 29
kaigamma, 264
Kala Kafra, 125, 164-5
Kake, I.B. (1979), *28*
kamkolak, very high Wadai title, 287
kamuma, 199
Kanajeji, Kano ruler, 296
Kanem, Kanembu, xvii-xix, 19, 21, 37, 50, 77, 87, 88, 99, 166, 203, 238, 242, 264-5, 276, 329, 345, 347, 360; al-Kanemi, Muhammad; 20-1, 183, 244-7, 251, 268, 283; dynasty, 7
Kano, 6, 8-10, 13, 16, 21, 25, 33, 38, 80, 91, 93, 100, 103, 112, 118, 121, 153-4, 190-1, 212, 222, 225, 236, 240, 242, 243, 267, 273, 274, 281, 296; Bala district, 212; *K. Chronicle*, 5-6, 112-3, 240, 241, 243, 267, 274, 281, 296
Kanuri, 22, 37, 134, 147, 191, 194, 201, 227, 239, 264, 327; language, 17, 135, 167-8, 219, 225, 317-18, 357
Kashella Bilal, 264-5; *kashellawa*, 264, 275, 290
Katanga, 109, 196-7, 226, 320, 331
Kati, Mahmud (1913-14/1964), *19*, 23, 60-1, 72, 112, 216, 228, 243, 269, 282
Katsina, 16, 41, 218, 242, 272, 273, 296
katurluli, Bagirmi eunuch title, 285, 375
Kawar, xix, 32, 142, 239, 319, 329, 334, 344-5

Kayor, Cayor, 119, 269, 274
Keffi, 322
Kent, R. K.: (1965), *30*, 153; (1968) *155*
Kenya, 85
Khadduri (1955), *17*, 29, 47-8
Khalil bin Ishaq, 14, *47*, 48, 59, 66, 67, 69, 75-6, 122, 149, 158, 185-6
Khamis, non-escaping tracker, 77, 139
Khartoum, 89, 111, 188, 280
Kherallah, 242
Khorasan, 86, 98
kidnapping: 3, 9, 26, 31, 41, 48, 57, 86, 107-8, 117, 120, 167, 271, 296, 338; *nkole*, 320; panyarring, 321
Kilwa, 309
Kimre, Pagan group south of Bagirmi, 52, 122, 347-55
kings, 42, 85-6, 95, 103, 181-2, 266, 309 *et passim*
Kinjalia, 221
Kirdi, Wadai patriot, 299
Kirk, Sir John, 45
Kirk-Greene, A.H.M.: (1960), *229*; and S.J. Hogben (1966) *26*; and P. Newman (1971), *xvii*, 34, 36, 48, 83-5, 91, 93-4, 98, 134, 138, 140-1, 167-8, 191-2, 211-12, 218-19, 225, 234, 267, 316-8, 322, 324, 331, *386*; *see also* Vaughan and ——
Klein, M.A. (1968), *119*, 217, 256, 273; H.S. (1969) *223*
Knetishe, Wadai military commander, 360
knives, 56, 128, 130, 221, 284
Kobe, 136, 205, 272, 319, 329, 337
Koelle, S. W.: (30); (1849) *214*, 315; (1854/1968) *62*, 108, 114; (1854/1963) *30*, 89, 296
kokenawa, sing. *kokena*, Borno State Councillors, free and slave, 263-4, 274-5
kola nuts, 6, 10, 147-8, 242, 298, 308
Koli, village and battle, 122, 253, 327, 362-71, 375
Kolokomi, the Tubu, 144
Kondeeah, Futa Jallon town, 156
Kong, Ivory Coast, 114
Kontagora, Fulani emirate, 25
Koranko, rebel slaves, 156
Korbol, *see* Bua
Kordofan, ixi, 70, 243, 336, 338
Kore, contented captive, 78, 139-41
Kotoko, 22
Koukiya, 86
Kouroubari, A. (1959), *63*, 114, 188, 331

Krapf, 1860, *52*, 64-5, 102, 338
krema, high Bagirmi official, 275
Kru, people, 45
Kuang, people, 303
Kuka, Kukawa, Borno capital: 7, 34-6, 58, 83, 87-8, 91, 94, 96, 99, 100, 105-6, 112, 113, 121, 127-8, 132, 164-5, 167, 191, 196, 197, 200, 209-10, 219, 221, 224, 225, 226, 233-5, 258, 269, 290, 317-9, 340-1, 345, 360; proposed new site at Ba Dungu, 231; market, 105-6, 121, 183-4, 202, 235, 291, 322-31, 375-6, 379
Kuka, people, 201
Kurra, Muhammad, *abu shaykh*, 195, 284-6, 290
kursi, Wadai official, usually slave, 279-80
Kutumbi, ruler of Kano, 281
Kwararafa, 296

Lacroix, P.F.: (1952), *25*, 112, 194, 297, 298; (1966), *66*
Lafia, slave-girl, 151; Mallam Lafia, 6, 8-9; *afia*, 135
lagha, Timbuktu pasha's slaves, 172
Lai, 358-9
Laing, A. G. (1825), *156*
lakes: Bangweolo, 133; Central Africa, 42, 135; *see also* individual lake names
Lamino, Kuka dignitary, 7, 9-10, 12, 34-5, 151-2, 203, 234-5, 247-8, 284, 290, 291, 317, 345
land, 9; for slave use, 216-17, 277
Lander, Richard, in Clapperton (1829), *33*, 83, 133, 188, 223-4, 230
Lange (1987), *49*, 243, 254-5
languages: African, 90; Bagirmi, 371; Dorugu, 93-4, 167-8, 219, 317-18; English, 69, 311; Ennedi, 168-70; European, 93-4; Fulfulde, 160; linguistics, 4, 89; Musgo, 45; Oriental, 96; problems, 4, 167-8, 224, 317-18; Somali, 250; Swahili, 85; Vai, 62, 108; *see also* Arabic, Hausa, Kanuri
Last, M. (1967), *172*
Lat Dyor, *damel* of Kayor, 269, 274
Law, Robin (1977), *2*
law, Muslim: xvii, 20, 26-7, 31, 45, 46-9, 52, 59, 67, 69, 71-2, 74-6, 82-3, 118, 122, 139, 146-7, 149, 172-5, 183-6, 193-4, 199, 241, 252-4, 326; courts, 21; *faqih*, 60; Hanafi, 84, 230; judicial sentences by slaves, enforced by *naqib*,

Index

145; magistrate, 277, 279, 281; Maliki law, 14-18, 47, 59, 72, 76, 117, 186; *shari'ah*, 14, 17-18, 29, 158; see also qadi
League of Nations, 229
leather, skins: 56, 108, 133, 290, 296, 302, 325, 369, 373, 376; dress, 143, 218, 246, 367-8, *see also* hippopotamus hide
Legassick, M. (1966), *114*
legends of origin, 4-5, 10, 16, 242
Leo Africanus, xvii, *34*, 60, 98-9, 112, 154-5, 196, 221-2, 282, 296, 309, 312, 326
letters, xvii, 22, 78, 124, 159-61, 244, 255; *see also* emancipation: letters of; Sokoto letters
Levtzion, N. (1963), *267*, 273; 1973, *5*; and J.F.P. Hopkins (1981) *22, 386*; *see also Corpus*
Lewis, I.M. (1966), *45*, 53-4, 64, 66, 69, 86, 109, 243, 244, 269, 274
Liberia: 30, 42-5, 111-3, 156, 222, 232, 343; Monrovia, 91, 149, 251, 317
Libya, 255; Cyrenaica, 91, 342
Lippert, J. (1899), *126*, 244; (1907) *214*
Liverpool, 90
Loël, 18th-century Bagirmi king, 256
Logon, kingdom, 45, 95, 125, 223, 227, 256, 264, 285-6, 304, 345
Lokoja, 90, 92
London, 184
Lovejoy, P.: 9, 13; (1983) *xx*, 293, *386*; (1986) *7*; and J.S. Hogendorn (1993) *xxi*, 79, 90, 175-6, 182, 205, 216, 294
Lucas, Simon, 96-7
Lugard, F.D.: (1893) *45*, 83, 85, 150, 155-6; (1906) *103*, 107-8; (1933) *84*, 115, 185, 208, 229
Lynch, H. R. (1967), *65*, 71

Ma'adan, marsh dwellers 153
Maba tribes, 270-1
Mabberate, 242
Mackay, A.M. (1890), *107*
MacLeod (1912), *22*, 37, 41, 55, 107, 244, 249
McPhee, A. (1926), *222*, 316
Madagali emirate, 61, 78, 81, 159, 161, 167, 203, 256; *see also* Hamman Yaji
Madagascar, 155
Mafara, 80, 171-2
Magaria, town near Sokoto, 216
al-Maghili, cleric c. 1500, 29
Magomi, 242
Mahdism, 12, 176, 188, 244, 324

Mahe Sarkin Mafara, 80, 171-2
Mahfuz, ruler of Harar, 50
Mahoney, F., and H. C. Idowu, (1965), *236*
mai: 194, 229, 239, 255; Mai Madubi, colonial judge, 332, 342-3
Maina Adam, Kawar dignitary, 334
Maje, tributary of Bagirmi, 303
mala, 259, 288, 289-91; *katib el-mal*, 334
mal(l)ams, 6, 26, 61-2, 94, 159, 161; *see also* clerics
Mali, ancient, 5, 11, 13, 72, 181-2, 198, 228-9, 241, 257, 261, 267, 273, 280, 330
Malta, 31, 83
Mamluks, 250
Mandara: 20-1, 82-3, 187-8, 220, 283, 292; Ali from, 88-9, 209; Dhunfa, 80-1
Mandingo, 30, 63, 73, 116, 149-50, 222
Manjafa, 124, 164
manjak, free village headman in Wadai, 277
Manning, P., 1995, *xx*, *277-8*, 294, 370
Mannix, D.P., and M. Cowley (1962), *65*
Mansa Musa, 14th-century ruler of Mali, 72, 181-2, 198, 228-9, 280, 330
Manyuema, 135, 195
maqdum, Darfur provinicial commissioner, 275
al-Maqrizi, Arab historian, 330
Maracatos, 181
Maria de Fonseca, 196
markets: 37, 58, 107-8, 124, 203, 209, 221, 222, 224, 235, 272, 374; 'exports and marketing', 98-137; slave, 18, 23, 26, 29, 46, 52, 105-6, 121, 122, 126, 136, 140, 147, 183-4, 196, 202, 236, 283, 291-2, 293, 316, 322-31, 340
Marmon, S.E., 1999, *27*
marriage: 9, 15-6, 23, 34, 41-2, 56, 58-9, 116, 118, 146, 149-50, 158, 182-3, 185-6, 202, 220, 242, 250, 261, 300, 303, 314, 343; divorce, 186; dog-men and slave girls, 134; *see also* dowry, slaves: marriage, wives
Marty, P., 1920, *63*, 91; 1926, *29*, 91, 116; 1931, *81*, 211
Masina, 63, 71, 186, 188, 199, 249
Massenya, Bagirmi capital, 54, 56, 221, 302, 315, 382
Mathew, G. (1963), *152*, 177, 254
Mauny, R. (1961/1967), *100*, 267
Mauritania, 63-4, 69, 93, 111, 147, 149, 154, 193

402 Index

Maxwell, G. (1957/1994), *153*
mbang, royal Bagirmi title, 242, 285, 381-2; *see also* Abu Sekkin
mbarma, high Bagirmi official, 275, 366, 368
Mecca, 10-1, 13, 22, 26, 46, 50, 67, 86, 145, 146, 196, 210, 218, 228-30, 238-9, 266, 283, 292, 300-1, 315-6, 324, 328
mediation, 159, 337, 382
Médicon, enslaved nephew of Borno ruler, 86
Medina, 10, 11, 13, 22, 146, 239, 281, 301, 315, 324, 328; *see also* Ahmed el-Medeni
Mediterranean, 31, 83, 94, 99-101, 135, 200, 240, 325, 333, 342, 381
Meillassoux, C. (1975), *184*
Mejabra, traders from Jalo oasis, 100, 335, 360
Mesopotamia, 152
Middle East: 4, 27, 28, 49, 67, 98; Iraq, 153; Kufa, 98; *see also* Arabia, Bagdad, Basra, Egypt, etc.
military establishments, expeditions, 54, 96, 104, 151, 159, 203, 244-5, 247-8, 251-2, 266, 269-70, 276, 285, 288, 297; *see also* cavalry, slaves: raids, slaves: soldiers
millek artan, ornang shuyukh, overseer of Wadai eunuchs, 287
Miltu, tributary to Bagirmi, 303, 381
mines, quarries, masons, 75, 218, 221, 277
Mirambo, 156, 251
mistrema, second ranking Borno eunuch, 288
mithqal, 192, 298, 333
Mode, a Gaberi region, 356-7, 359, 361
Mohamma Yaji, 'just and good' Kano ruler, Mallam Lafia, 6, 8, 9-10
Mohammedu, slave servant of Nachtigal, 57, 67-8, 83, 210-11, 287
Mokolo, 33, 179
Mombasa, 46, 53, 102, 155
Momodu Lamine, Soninke leader, 156, 188, 228, 256
money, 256, 301, 313
Monteil, C. (1924), *70*, 72, 187, 296; (1930), *267;* Monteil P.-L. (1894), *290;* Monteil, V.: (1964/1980), *331;* (1966) *269*, 274; (1967) *30*
Moore, F. (1738), *22*
Moors, Trarza, 212, 229
Morocco, Moroccan, 77, 96, 100, 178,
187, 193, 204, 210, 282, 297, 307; conquest of Songhay, 198, 218, 269, 273
Morton-Williams, P. (1964), *293*
Moses, 11, 81
mosque, 61, 65, 86, 172, 281, 312; al-Azhar, 324; muezzins, 60
Mossi, 64
mothers, 48, 54, 57, 149, 151, 183, 188, 190, 194-5, 201, 271, 323; *see also* family
Msidi, ruler of Katanga, and his white wives, 196-7
mudabbar slave, 66, 74-5
Muhammad, the Prophet: 10, 14, 17, 47, 72, 174, 218, 280, 309, 315; his birthday, 60, 359; prophets, 23, 47; *sunnah*, 14, 72
Muhammad Ali, 244
Muhammad el-Hasin (or al-Husayn), king of Darfur, 271, 274
Muhammad en-Nur, Nachtigal's final guide, 338
Muhammad al-Qatruni, Nachtigal's servant and friend, 57, 210, 236, 259
Muhammad Rimfa, ruler of Kano, 281
muhsan, legally responsible, 186
Mukasa, H. (1934), *195*
murder, 12, 15-16, 19, 58, 61, 76, 88, 96, 117-18, 128, 135, 149, 154, 161, 172, 192, 193, 196, 234, 238, 270, 327
Murki, 361, 371
Murzuq, 31, 54, 57, 82, 85, 88, 98, 105, 135, 210, 221, 224, 225, 248, 299, 325, 333-5, 339-40, 342; *see also* Fezzan
Musadu, 149, 157
Muscat, 280
Musfeia, Muslim town, 23-5 (*see also* 20-1)
Musgo: 45, 95, 203, 220, 303-4; Barqa Musgo, slave and trader, 226
music, singing, poetry: 60, 69; dance, 3, 16, 66, 92; by slaves, 69, 82, 148, 181, 198, 218, 222, 224, 313; *see also* drums
muwalladun (Burton [1860/1961], II.31, 'domestic slave'; Doughty [1888/1923], I.553, 'home-born and free-born blacks', and II.638, 'home-born persons of strange blood'; *Corpus*, 41), 255

Nachtigal's servants: 31, 52, 57, 182, 204, 208-11, 224, 226, 234-6, 319, 329, 341, 378; Giuseppi from Piedmont, 235-6; *see also* Billama, Dunkas, Hammu,

Index 403

Mandara: Ali Mohammedu, Muhammad al Qatruni, Sa'ad, Soliman el-Nager, O. (al-Naqar, U.) (1969), *11*, 26, 67, 72, 229, 239; (1972), *11*, 22, 230, 266
names, naming, nicknames, 37, 73, 94, 145, 311
Ndamm, tribe, 348, 366, 381
Negro, 27, 38, 65, 70, 78, 84, 88, 94, 96, 131, 143, 199, 323, 339
Newitt, M.D.D. (1969), *34*, 102, 222
Newman, P.: *see* Kirk-Greene, A.H.M.
newspapers, 4, 149
ngarmane, senior Bagirmi eunuch, 285, 366, 375
Ngaundere, 169, 310
Ngigmi, northernmost Borno town: 37, 221, 289, 345; Barua, 289
Ngolo, 72, 296
Ngongo Lutete, 243-4
Ngornu, 288-9
Nicolaisen, J. and I. (1997) *15*, 17, 38, 81, 145-6, 214, 217, 250, 315
Niger, river: xviii, 5, 86, 107, 126, 172, 194, 203, 224; territory, 39, 81, 211
Nigeria: 10, 19, 102-3, 147, 229; northern, xvii, 3, 12, 22, 26, 79, 89, 107, 172, 175-6, 182, 216, 331; southern, 91-2, 212; Brass, 119-20; Ibadan, 26; Lagos, 316; Nassarawa, 148-9; Okrika, 138
Nile, 53, 65, 86, 203, 337; Upper, 88
Nimro, traders' town, Wadai, 55, 279
Njeuma, M. Z., (1978), *71*
nomads, beduin, pastoralists, 15, 20, 38, 58-9, 64, 66, 69, 85, 168, 194, 213-5, 217, 226, 240
Norris, H. T. (1968), *69*, 147, 149
North Africa: xviii, 14, 28, 33, 36, 49, 85-6, 92, 100, 130, 136, 145, 154, 180, 192, 194, 221, 254, 295, 309, 316-17, 342, 344; Akli, Homria, Kabylia, Mzab, 221; Barbary 98-9; Maghrib, 181
Nubia, Nuba, 53, 86, 243-4, 295-6; Amai, Christian ruler, 312
'numbers game', 103-7
Nupe, 6, 103, 112-13, 195, 198, 220, 224, 242, 281
Nyasaland, lake, 108-9
Nyillem, 42, 358, 366, 374

oases, 100, 213, 215, 239-40, 360
oath, vow, 15, 47, 59, 75, 76, 165, 186
el-Obeid, 280, 336, 338
O'Fahey, R.S., and J.L. Spaulding (1974), 7, 263, 272, *286*
Ogilby, J. (1670), *40*, 148, 315
Okihiro, G. (1986), *7*
Olderogge, D,.A. (1957), *153*
Oliver, R. (1965), *53*, 111, 243
Oliver and Mathew (1963), *46*, 53, 152-3, 177, 217, 243, 254, 281
Oman, 85-6
Omar Lele, Darfur ruler in 1730s, 300, 305
Omdurman, 324
Omm Meshana, 336-8
oral tradition, story-telling, 2, 4, 36, 44, 55, 72, 116, 134, 179, 194, 198-9, 200
ornaments, jewellery, beads, 52, 108, 145, 166, 198, 200, 253, 281, 313-14, 319
ostriches, feathers, 136, 198-9, 296, 313, 317, 336-7, 340
Ottomans: *see* Turkey
Ouseley, W. (1800), *187*
Overweg, A., Barth's colleague, 90, 134, 234
Ozi river, slave sanctuary, 155

Pagans, non-Muslims: 16-18, 20, 22-3, 27-31, 40-7, 52-4, 65, 71, 92, 102-4, 107-8, 116-17, 121-4, 127-8, 134, 173-6, 198, 201, 227, 253, 284, 285, 297, 299, 303-4, 305, 319, 322-4, 341, 348, 351, 360-1, 366-9, 378; and Hamman Yaji, 49, 62, 64, 70, 78, 80, 119, 159-60, 179-80, 189, 306, 308-11; heathen, 58, 251, 352, 356, 377; 'kaffering', 29; 'pagan horses', 113, 123, 379; pagan slaving, 25, 29, 40-5, 71; religious specialists, 62, 93; *see also* slaves: non-Muslim owners
Palem, 362, 370-1
palm trees: 93, 146, 213, 370-1; coconut wine, 213; dates, 20, 143, 184, 191, 359
Palmer, H. R.: (1914), *73*; (1916) *198*; (1926/1970), *49*, 98-9, 238, 239 254-5; (1928/1967) *6*, *19*, *203*, 296
paper, 83, 95, 308
pasha: Egypt, 114; Fezzan, 234; Timbuktu, 23, 172; Tripoli, 25, 83, 87, 255
Passarge, S. (1895), *169*
Pate Island, 64, 155, 296
Patterson, J.R. (1926 and 1930), *327*
Peel, J.D.Y. (1968), *91-2*
Pemba, 45
perfume: 297, 308, 325; ambergris, 198, 296; civet 198, 296, 326

Persia, Persian, 27, 64, 194, 228
Petermanns Mitteilungen, 1855, 325, 333; 1868, 334; 1872, 378-9
Petragnani, E., 1928, *342*
pilgrimage, *hajj*, 11-4, 26, 60, 65, 67, 73, 86, 89, 130-1, 145, 156, 176, 181-2, 184, 188, 198, 210, 228-30, 234, 238-9, 266, 283, 292, 297, 300, 309, 330; *see also* Mecca, Medina
Pipes, D. *(1981), 317, 327*
Planhol, X. de (1959), *221*
Pliny, 130-1
poison, 196, 219
Pollaud-Dulian, M. (1967), *83*
polygamy, polygyny, 1, 184-6; *see also* marriage; slaves: concubines
Pope-Hennessy, J.L. (1967), *121*
population mobility, demographic resources: 1-14, 28, 47, 58, 90, 102, 126, 155-76, 189, 192, 239, 241, 272, 288, 305, 307, 375-7; immigration into Wadai, 35, 54-7, 136-7
Portuguese, 46, 64, 112, 115, 155, 182, 196, 217; *prazo* estates, 34, 102, 222
prayer: 5, 8, 10, 11, 20, 61, 63, 66, 76, 77, 172, 229, 233, 243, 293, 308-9; by slaves, 29-31, 35, 65, 67, 71, 75, 86; Azahar, *zuhr* prayer, 217; curse, 26-7
pregnancy: *see* slaves: reproduction
presents, alms, xviii, 12, 198-9, 258-61, 288-90, 301, 323, 326, 339-40, 344, 382; slaves as, 59-63, 283, 292-8, 301, 304, 307-21, 326-8, 334, 339-40, 376, 378-9; to slaves, 226, 245-6, 258-60, 289-90; free people given as if slaves, 22-3; *see also* dowry slaves: as gifts, tribute
Prietze, R. (1914), *148*
prisoners, exchange of, 47, 79
prisoners of war, 19-21, 27, 46-7, 54, 58, 71, 77-9, 89, 115-16, 118, 121, 144, 157, 240-1, 250, 251-2; *see also* slaves: execution of slaves: raids
punishments: 42, 115-21, 125, 148-9, 179, 186, 213, 215, 232-3, 304; by slaves, 145; amputation, 16, 229; blinding, 278; capital, 15-6, 31, 42, 44, 69, 93, 115-17, 119-20, 149, 162, 172, 186, 193, 195, 196, 200, 213, 219, 262-3, 267, 273, 277, 280, 289, 290, 333; castration, 284-7; compensation, 148-9; damnation, 72; deportation, 157, 186; different penalties for free and slave, Muslim and non-Muslim, 15-6, 21-2, 117, 186; emancipation of a slave, 16, 76-7, 79, 82; fines, 15, 79, 81, 119, 148, 159, 277, 279, 311; flogging, xviii, 15, 30, 70, 81, 117, 123, 127, 130, 152, 157, 162, 186, 191-2, 213, 314; forced labour, 215; hunger, 162; *lex talionis*, 16; prison, 70, 117, 186, 198; Quranic, 23; torture, 31, 52, 151-2, 169, 232, 290; *see also* chains, enslavement: as punishment

qadi, kadi, kadhi: 11, 18, 54, 57, 60-1, 82, 90, 117, 192, 247, 269; Hamman Yaji's, 62, 78-9, 189, 204; *see also* law: Muslim
Qairawan, 136, 153, 180; *see also* Ibn Abi Zayd
al-Qallabat, Gallabat, on Ethiopia-Sudan border, 196, 244
Qatrun, 212, 325, 341, 360; *see also* Muhammad al-Qatruni
Qor'an, 197
Quran, 14, 20, 23, 46-7, 52-3, 61, 63, 72, 77, 117, 165, 199, 228, 241, 243, 266; school, 59, 65, 68, 86, 190; *see also* Arabic, education

Rabih, Arab marauder, 126, 244, 290-1, 297
race, 4, 26-7, 64, 78, 87, 133-4, 195-7, 381; *see also* genealogy; skin colour
rain: 35, 41, 91, 123, 235, 306, 348, 357-8, 360, 361-2, 371-3, 376-7, 380; rainmaking, 67; drought, 1-2; *see also* climate, water
Ramadan: 49-50, 53, 66, 72, 76-7, 92, 204, 233, 260; *lailat al-qadr*, 92; *see also* fasting
ransom, 3, 21, 43, 47, 58, 77-80, 111, 139; *see also* emancipation
Raum, O.F. (1965), *53*
Reade, W. W. (1864), *81*, 116, 216
rebellion, 58, 221, 243, 249, 258, 267, 268-70, 272, 306; *see also* slaves: revolt
Red Sea, 11, 13, 64
refugees, fugitives, 2, 7-8, 26, 43, 58, 81, 187, 271, 283, 382; *see also* slaves: runaway
Reichert, R. (1967), *30*
research topics, 8, 94-5, 134, 172-6
rhinoceros horn, 302
Richardson, J., 99; (1848) *37-8, 50*, 67, 82-3, 85, 92, 118, 129, 131, 133, 145-6, 168, 185-6, 189, 224-5, 240, 325, 332-3; (1853) *87*, 92, 305

Rio de Janeiro, 203
rivers, 218, 223, 371; Juba, 155; Matacan, 118; Ozi, 155; Rio Pongo, 117; St Paul's, 251; *see also* Ba Ili, Benue, Niger, Nile, Shari, Zambesi
Robinson, A.E. (1926), *196*
Robinson, C.H., 121
Rochlin, S. A. (1956), *176*
Rohlfs, G.: (1874-5), *105-6*, 131, 248, 256, 265-6, 288, 333-4; (1868), *334*; (1872), *378-9*
Ronciere, de la (1919), *86*, 222, 255, 328
Rotter, G. (1967), *27*
Rouch, J. (1953), *53*, 243, 282
Rudin, H., (1938), *43*, 230
Runga, 188, 306, 313, 346
Ruxton, F. H.: (1908), *89*, 296; (1916), 72, 147

Sa'ad, a servant of Nachtigal, 31, 38, 87-9, 105, 144, 341
Sabun, king of Wadai, 302-3
sacrifice: *sadaqah*, 72-3, 266; human sacrifice, 42-3; of slaves, 40, 42-3, 73; *see also* presents
al-Sadi, Abd al-Rahman ibn Abdulah (1913-4/1964), 5, 11, 72, 86, 213, 228, 273, 282, 307
Sahara, xvii-xviii, 6, 34, 37-8, 50, 81, 83, 89, 106, 112, 148, 150-1, 164, 211-14, 221, 238-40, 315, 329, 339-42, 345; Air, 100; slave trade, 29, 49, 99-102, 342; *see also* caravans: trans-Saharan, ouses
Sahara and Sudan, xv-xix-xx, 55, 142, 202, 219, 346-7, *370*, *et passim*
Said, Alhaj, Sokoto chronicler, *20*, 252, 273, 293, 309-10; servant of Richardson, 82-3
Sakura, ruler of Mali, 273
Salih Shanqa, at al-Qallabat, 244
salt: 6, 10, 103, 108, 111, 118, 187, 222, 301; mines, 221
Sambo, founder of Fulani emirate of Hadeija, 273
Samori, 43, 63, 114, 188, 331
Sanankoro, 188
sanctuary, refuge, 3, 9, 155, 171, 172, 257
Sanderson, G.M. (1919), *109*
Sanusiyya, 13, 69, 91, 342
São Tomé, 138-9
Sara, tributary to Bagirmi: 227, 303, 348, 366; Sara of Dai, 358, 374; Sara Kumra, 374, 379, 381
sarki, title: 6, 8, 82, 163, 171, 215; Sarkin Musulmi, 163
Sarua, 303
Savage, E. (1992), xxi, *387*
Say, 94
Schultze, A. (1913/1968), 195, 200, 244, 290, 377; *see also* P.A. Benton
Schwab, G. (1947), *44-5*, 113
Seabrook, W. (1934), *221*, 293
secret societies: Bundu, 116; Komo, 50-2; Poro, 44
Segu, 26, 70, 72, 187, 188, 198, 296
Sellnow, (1964), *33-4*, 154
Senegal, 29, 39, 50, 119, 156, 256, 269
Senegambia: 10, 116, 119, 156, 173; Gamon, 156
senna, 299, 325
Sennar, 7, 154, 243, 338
servants *see:* Nachtigal's servants
settlers, 6, 11, 13, 35, 41, 54-7; *see also* slaves: colonists
sexual relations, 74, 76, 144, 177-202, 205; indiscretions, 15, 186, 191, 319; *tazahara*, 76-7; *see also* adultery
Shaihu Umar, xiii, 46, 49, 54, 57, 105, 113, 162-3, 189-92, 253, 366, *387*
Shari river, Ba Bai, Ba Logon, 166, 358-9
shari'ah: *see* law, Muslim
sharif, descendant of the Prophet, 50, 57, 61, 136, 172, 184, 218, 267; al-Habib, 309; see also Ahmed el-Medeni
al-Sharishi, 181
shaykh, shehu, 7, 11, 37, 196, 271; shaykh (a slave) of the slaves, 145; *bash-shaykh*, 306; eunuchs' title, 195, 286-7
Shaykh Umar, Borno ruler, xviii, 12, 20, 35, 36, 57, 60, 67-8, 74, 83, 96, 122, 132, 165, 200, 211, 226, 233, 247, 248, 257, 258-61, 266, 269, 284, 289, 291-2, 305, 333, 339-40, 344, 374, 379, 382
sheep, 44, 61, 73, 93, 161, 214, 259, 260, 331; *see also* animals, domestic
Shems ed-Din, Darfur messenger to Wadai, 301
Shepperson, G., 1975, 134
Sherif, Wadai king, 36, 200
Sherif ed-Din, pilgrimage leader, 13
al-Shinqiti, Ahmad bin al-Amin (1911/1953), *63*, 93, 111, 193
shitima, settima, a Borno eunuch title, 290
shoes, footwear, 367
Shuqair, Na'um (1903), *70*
Shuwa Arabs, 35, 41, 130, 252-3, 327, 329; *see also* Arabs
Sidi Mabed, oasis without slaves, 240

Sidi Mustafa, Consular Agent of Britain in Jerbah, 82
Sierra Leone, 30, 52, 66, 89, 90-2, 99, 115-17, 118, 297; *see also* Freetown
silk, 56, 198, 233
silver, 198, 281, 282, 308, 313, 316, 320
Sina, 180
skin colour: 38, 78, 152, 170, 181, 187, 236, 330, 371, 381; white men, 52, 116, 133-4, 310, 317-18, 378; *see also* race
Skinner, E. P., 1966, *64*
Slade, R., 1962, *230*, 244
Slane, Baron M. de: (1854), *153*; (1911-13/1964) *180*
Slatin, R.C. (1896), *188*, 195, 286, 298, 324
slaves, slavery:
 artisans, 218-22; *see also* handicrafts
 assimilation of, 49, 139, 141, 144-5, 147, 149, 182, 189, 192, 201-2, 241, 250
 cannibalism, victims of 43-4
 as caravan workers, 101-2, 109, 222-31; *see also* slaves: as traders
 and centralised government, 42, 240, 267-80
 changing one's master, 44-5, 81, 142, 163-4
 children, xviii, 23, 32, 36, 41-2, 48, 50, 59, 62, 64, 74, 75-6, 77-8, 102-3, 108-9, 111-12, 113, 116, 118, 124-31, 134, 139, 151, 164-5, 168-70, 179-80, 183-4, 189-90, 194-6, 200-1, 206, 234, 252, 311, 323-6, 331, 342, 353, 356, 366-71, 376, 381
 as colonists, 2, 54-7, 58, 84-6, 104, 139, 155-6, 213-14, 223, 238-42, 243, 267; *see also* settlers
 as compensation, fines, 148-9
 concubines, *surriya*, 18, 23, 76, 89, 140, 148, 152, 154, 160, 177-202, 205, 220, 243, 245, 252, 267, 270, 286, 291, 300, 309, 320, 328
 contribution to religious activity, 59-64
 as currency, 228, 316-21
 deaf-mute, xvii-xviii, 36, 87, 202, 291, 317, 328, 340
 for debt, pawning, 32, 74, 111, 116-17, 120-1, 156, 320-1
 disputed ownership of, 203-4, 331
 earnings, 58, 75, 85, 154, 156; *see also* slaves: as property owners
 educated, 64-70, 192-3

 execution of (usually adult male slaves, or sick slaves on the march), 23, 26, 41, 47-50, 71, 93, 119, 157, 179-80, 230, 251, 275, 311, 320, 325
 as executioners, 44, 267
 for export, 29, 55-6, 98-121, 182, 254, 267, 280-3, 285, 292, 306-7, 340
 free-slave distinction, 33, 39, 54-9, 74, 136-7, 144-5, 154, 184-6, 194-5, 197, 208-11, 213, 214, 225, 234, 238, 241, 263, 276-9; free-slave labour, xx, 208-211, 223, 235-6, 240, 277
 freed, *see* freedmen
 as gifts, 50, 54, 100, 127, 148, 180, 187-9, 198-9; *see also* dowry, presents
 government, royal: 6, 59, 160, 177, 227, 230, 238, 256-80, 267, 277, 348-9, 372; *lagha*, 172
 half-slaves, 59, 66, 74-5, 186, 321
 'hot' and 'cold', 56, 336
 inherited, 156; *see also* inheritance, slaves: status
 luxury, 177, 231-7, 257-8
 markets: *see* markets: slave
 marriage, 15-6, 31, 45, 58-9, 150, 182, 185-6, 193, 202, 216, 242, 250; *see also* marriage, slaves: concubines
 mortality, 89, 130-3, 230 *et passim*; *see also* slaves: execution of
 non-Muslim owners, 40-5, 64, 71, 117, 157, 175-6, 212; *prazo*, 34, 222
 numbers of: xvii, 25, 31, 33-41, 55, 61, 86-7, 99-100, 102-7, 114, 117, 131, 133, 135, 145-6, 153, 155, 179-81, 190, 198-9, 203, 214, 216, 222, 228, 230, 235-6, 238-40, 243-5, 251-2, 255-7, 260, 262, 334-5, 338, 341, 369-70, 375; 'numbers games', 106-7
 prices, 3, 30, 36, 38, 48, 52, 56, 63, 78, 86, 101-3, 111, 113-4, 125, 135, 144, 165, 181, 187, 192, 196, 200, 202, 283, 291, 318, 323, 325-31, 333, 339, 358, 375-6, 379
 as property, 7-8, 13, 45, 73, 82, 132, 143, 156, 166-7, 203-4, 230, 236; owner's property, 15
 as property owners, 17, 45, 58, 59, 74-5, 79, 81, 154, 160, 162, 173, 185, 189; *see also* slaves: earnings
 raids, 1, 3, 6, 8-9, 10, 20, 22-3, 25, 33, 40-1, 46-54, 71, 80-1, 99, 102, 103, 106, 107-8, 111, 114-15, 121-2, 126, 128, 132, 138, 140, 144, 150, 154,

Index

166, 168, 177, 179-80, 188, 189-90, 200, 201, 203, 204, 226, 251, 267, 298, 303-4, 310-1, 314, 319, 343, 345, 347-82; *see also* military
reproduction, pregnancy, infertility, 41, 48, 59, 127, 150-1, 184
return: 53, 83-97, 127, 139, 189, 315-6, 375; return to owner, 159
revolt, resistance, 30-1, 53, 58, 68, 152-8, 175, 205, 274; *see also* rebellion
runaway, 3, 7-8, 10, 13, 42, 48, 67, 77, 82, 86, 124-7, 132, 137, 142, 147, 152, 155-76, 189, 204-6, 223, 226, 244, 251, 314, 317, 327, 330, 358, 375-6; *see also* refugees
slave-owning slaves, 263
soldiers, 2, 8, 89, 102, 104, 115, 154, 156, 177, 216, 238, 242-56, 270, 272, 275, 277, 293, 294, 327, 349; *see* also military soldiers
standard Spave heights *sedasi*, 'six-span', 42, 319, 326-9, 378; *khumasi*, 182, 327-8
status: 31, 54-9, 68, 77-8, 82-3, 90, 120, 121, 139, 160, 179, 181-6, 190, 194, 196, 208-9, 213, 214, 225, 241, 245, 254, 255, 275; inheritance of, 48, 55, 250, 320, 321
towns, 33, 240
trade: 3, 10, 16, 22, 25, 26-8, 35-6, 38, 45, 50, 52, 54, 64-5, 69, 71, 84, 98-137, 177, 181-2, 196, 198, 214, 217-8, 246, 277, 281, 291-3, 304, 381 *et passim*; individual transactions 42, 68, 69, 72, 83, 123, 125, 147-9, 177, 189, 192-3 *et passim*; *see also* Atlantic slave trade, Sahara: slave trade
as traders, 75, 117, 139, 186, 213, 225-6; *see also* slaves: as caravan workers
as tribute, 89, 104, 177, 182, 187-8, 195, 230, 292-3, 295-308, 316, 375, 379, 381; *see also* tribute
virgins (not all slaves), 42, 44, 116, 181, 240, 313, 330
women and girls: 15, 23, 32, 36, 37, 41, 42, 47-50, 54, 57, 59, 60, 61, 62, 74, 79-81, 87, 92, 98, 103, 106, 109, 111, 113, 114, 117, 118, 120, 124-30, 132, 134, 135, 137, 147, 149, 151, 154, 159-62, 165-71, 177-207, 209-11, 213, 220-1, 223, 224, 225, 230, 231, 244-5, 249, 252, 255, 256, 257, 261, 281, 282, 287-8, 291, 301, 302, 306, 308, 310-12, 313-14, 318, 323-31, 337, 339, 342, 353, 355, 356, 358, 360, 367-71, 375-6 *et passim*; women captives killed, 23, 311; *see also* sexual relations, slaves: concubines, slaves: marriage etc.

Slavery 1970, xv, xx-xxi, 98, 104, 146-7, 158, 166, 172, 177-9, 183, 254, 280, 292, 299, 319, 381, 387
Smith, Adam, *Wealth of nations*, 208, 236-7
Smith, Alison, 1963, *217,* 243
Smith, Mary, 1954 (Baba of Karo), *1, 3,* 26, 72, 147, 217, 383
Smith, M.G. (1959), *154,* 272; (1964 A) *25,* 267, 272, 274, 297; (1964 B) *240,* 267, 296
Smith, R. (1965), *293*
sofas, 254
Sokoro, 303, 381
Sokoto: 7, 9, 11-13, 20, 25, 27, 30, 59, 71-2, 90, 112, 118, 121, 132, 150, 167, 172, 175-6, 180, 186, 187, 195, 199, 203, 212, 216, 220, 221-2, 230, 233, 245, 249, 252, 261, 272-3, 292, 297-8, 309, 312, 329-30; letters, xvii, 58, 80, 82, 163, 171-2, 308; Gwandu, 58
soldiers, xviii, 2, 40, 49, 69, 272, 331, 379, 381; *see also* cavalry, slaves: raids, slaves: soldiers
Soliman, servant of Nachtigal, 37, 235
Somalia, Somalis: 52, 85, 101, 250; Barder, 155; Berbera, 224; Mogadishu, 155, 181
Somraï, 42, 103, 303, 358, 371-3
song, poetry, 69, 82, 148, 245, 252, 309, 327
Songhay, 19, 22-3, 29, 53, 60-1, 86, 112, 153, 215, 229, 243, 282, 307; Gao, 112; *see also* Moroccan conquest
Soninke, 156, 256
Sonni Ali, 15th-century Songhay ruler, 22
Soqna, 82, 212
South Africa, 176
Sow, Alfa Ibrahim, 1966, *252*
Spanish, Spaniards, 108, 196; Andalus, 187, 282; Cordova, 326
Spaulding, J. *see* O'Fahey and Spaulding
spears, lances, 233, 243, 247-8, 250, 286, 287, 306, 348, 351, 353, 354, 363, 365, 368; *see also* weapons
Speke: (1863), *65,* 74, 153, 224; (1864), *52-3,* 74, 223, 226, 251

spirit possession, 16, 92-3, 224; *see also* supernatural
Stanley, H.M., 195
Stannus, H.S. (1922), *109*
state formation, 242
Stenning, D. J. (1966), *66*
Stevenson, R.C. (1966), *53*, 243, 244
strangers, foreigners, 10, 36-7, 144, 243, 250, 255, 259-61, 262, 381
succession: 271-4, 278-9, 308; eunuchs as regents, 282, 286, 290; *see also* inheritance
Sudan, Sudanese: 26-7, 56, 72, 81, 87, 93, 98, 102, 103, 111-12, 115, 126, 133, 146, 150, 153, 168, 186, 187, 189, 198, 202, 220, 222, 239, 249, 259, 263, 282, 285, 299, 309, 323, 327, 333, 340-42, 376; eastern, 88, 89, 111, 243-4, 270, 296, 338-9; Soudan, French colony, 256; Republic of, 13
Sudi, History of, 115
suicide, 67, 138-9, 142, 219
Sukur, 180, 189
Sula, 301
Suleman Solon, King of Darfur, 305
sultan, sultanate: 294; Agades, 293; Bagirmi, 249, 328; Borno, 19, 200, 203, 290-1, 355; Brumley, 251; Darfur, 69-70, 117, 299; Fezzan, 298; Kilwa, 309; Mandara, 283, 378-9; Morocco, 187; Ottoman, 101, 292; Pate, 296; Wadai, 213, 287, 302; Zanzibar, 146, 155; *see also* Sokoto
Sumatra, 177
supernatural powers: of clerics, 21, 61-2, 188; of Nachtigal, 95, 368, 377; of slaves, 93, 154, 192; of whites, 43, 133-4; witchcraft, 116-17, 119-20; *see also* amulets, spirit possession
Susu, 156
Swahili, 53, 102, 188, 243; language, 85-6
sword, 232-3, 247, 250, 309
Sy, Cheikh Tidiane (1969), *269*
Syria, 22, 255

Tabora, 138, 156, 243
Taghaza, salt mining centre, 221
Tajura, 108
Ta'if, 174
Takadda, 192, 198, 221
Takruri, 196, 244
Tanganiyka, Tanzania: 153, 156, 243; Lake, 135, 165, 214, 223, 226, 338
Tangatanga, Hajj Ahmed, 35-6, 56, 136, 148, 204, 210, 328, 337
Tarbush, Adam, leading Darfur slave official, 274, 321; tarbush, 367
Tauxier, L. (1927), *52*
taxes, taxation, 2, 7, 23, 34, 53-4, 133, 160, 214, 215, 256, 279, 281, 285, 288, 306, 333-5, 337, 374; *jizya*, 28, 47; *kharaj*, 47; *zakat*, 158; tolls, 307
Tedzkiret, *20*, 23, 172, 198, 252
telescope, Nachtigal's, 355
Tepowa, A. (1907), *120*, 138
theft, 42, 77, 88, 115-16, 118, 119, 121, 192, 279; slaves stolen, 82, 132, 166-7
Theobald, A.B. (1965), *13*, 26, 194, 263
theocracies, Muslim, 8, 10, 50, 63, 71, 172-6, 188, 243, 249, 252-4
thirst: *see* water
Thomas, H. (1997), *xx*, 28
Thompson, V., and R. Adloff (1958), *63*, 64
Thomson, J. (1881/1968), *135*, 138, 146, 154, 214, 223, 224; (1893), *133*
Thousand and One Nights, Arabian Nights, 36, 67
throwing-irons, hand-irons, 124, 247-8, 348, 351, 353-4, 363, 365, 368, 374; *see also* chains, iron, weapons
Tibati, 274
Tibesti, xviii-xix, 31, 38, 57, 77, 80, 87-8, 130-1, 133, 139, 141-4, 182, 235-6, 246, 339, 341-2, 344
Tidjikdja, Saharan town, 93, 154, 213
Tilho, J. (1911), *200*; (1920), *342*
Timbuktu, 5, 11, 13, 20-1, 23, 26, 34, 57, 63, 72, 81, 94, 100, 145, 172, 187, 198, 213, 218, 221, 293, 316, 324; Kabara port, 172
Tinne, Alexandrine, Dutch traveller, 88
Tippu Tib, slaver, 195, 244
Tirab, Muhammad, Darfur sultan, 69-70, 305-6
tobacco, 108, 228, 301
Touba, 63, 252
el-Tounsy, Muhammad, Tunisian traveller, 197, 286, *302-3*
Tour. see Gourdault
trade, traders, 5-6, 7, 16, 32, 35-6, 37, 43, 91, 98-9, 108-9, 133, 136, 140, 154, 156, 164-5, 181, 187, 210, 214, 222, 225-6, 227, 242, 243, 272, 309, 318, 336-7, 360; *see also* Jellaba, slaves: trade
translation, xv, xvii, 142, 181, 282, 311, 347, 358, 366, 367, 381; *see also* corrections

Index

trees, 123, 151, 356, 361-6; cotton –tree houses, 122, 347-56, 362, 370; *Parkia biglobosa*, 377; *see also* palm trees
Tremearne, A.J.N., (1913), *16*, 145, 193, 194, 222
tribes: 19, 20, 21, 44, 59, 71, 78, 81, 89, 95, 104, 120, 144, 145, 156, 199-201, 226, 227, 235, 239, 242, 244, 253, 264, 285, 287, 304, 306, 310, 347, 353, 360, 363 *et passim*; clans, 217; tattoo, 145
tribute, 9, 116, 175, 216; *see also* presents, slaves: as tribute
Trimingham: (1962), *154*, 216, 228, 244; (1968), *73*, 150
Tripoli, Tripolitania: xvii-xviii, 31, 37, 50, 57, 69, 83-5, 86-7, 88, 90, 94-5, 96, 100, 104, 105, 118, 132, 135-6, 139, 144, 150, 209-10, 222, 255, 290, 298-9, 307, 328, 332, 334, 335, 339-40, 344; Meshiya gardens, 84
Tsoede, Nupe ruler, 195
Tuareg, 15, 17, 23, 38, 81, 83, 88, 131, 144, 146, 150, 185, 189, 214, 217, 229, 230, 246, 250, 315, 329; Kel-Air, 81; Kelowi, 41
Tuat, 26
Tubu, Tibbo, Teda, 38, 88, 108, 141-4, 239, 246, 284, 329, 342; Daza, 366
tuburu, 254
Tukur, chief of Tibati, 274
Tummok, tributary to Bagirmi, 124, 348, 362, 366, 371, 373-5, 379, 381
Tunis, Tunisian, xviii, 31, 94, 100, 197, 333, 339; Jerbah, 82
Tunjur, Tunjer, 265, 299-300, 305
Turkey, Ottomans, 27, 31, 100, 181, 243, 248, 250, 254-5, 280, 309, 330, 332, 339; Abd el-Hamid, 292; Arabo-Turks, 255; Turco-Egyptians, 53
tuweirat, 'birds', pages at Wadai court, 261-2, 278, 286
twins, 331
Tyam, M.A. (1935), *254*

Ujiji, 165
ulama: see clerics
Ulungu, 138
al-Umari, 228, *254*, 280n.
umbrellas, 233, 258; *see also* emblems
Umm Asta Belel, Hamman Yaji's wife, 64, 70
umm al-walad, 74, 184
Unyanyembe, 138

Uncle Salih, 184
Uqba bin Nafi, 295
Usuman dan Fodio, 11, 18-21, 23, 27, 29-30, 71, 73, 172-4, 199, 252-3, 309; (1978) 173-4, 253, *387*

Vai, 108, 114, 148, 214, 314, 315; language, 62
Vansina, J., *et al.* (1964), *240*
Vaughan and Kirk-Greene (1995), *xvii*, 179, 314; *see also* Hamman Yaji
Verger (1968/1976), *30*, 64, 68, 75-6, 157, 182, 196, 236, 255, *388*
Vischer, H. (1910), *88-9*, 92-3, 130, 132, 192, 341-2
Vittou, slave refugee town, 155
Vogel, E. (d. 1856), 96, 193, 197, 234, *325*, 333
von Duisburg, A. (1942), *291*

Wadai, xix, 19, 20-1, 26, 32, 35-7, 43, 52, 54-7, 69, 88, 91, 96, 100, 117, 136-7, 148, 153, 154, 192, 193-4, 197, 200-2, 204-5, 210-11, 213, 231, 233-4, 239, 241, 248, 256, 258, 260-2, 267-71, 276-9, 284-7, 292, 294, 295, 299-303, 306, 307-8, 313, 315, 319, 323, 328, 329, 336, 342, 345, 347, 360, 381-2; *see also* population mobility: immigration into Wadai
Wadstrom, C.P. (1795/1968), *30*
Walata, 183, 198
walls, fortifications: 3, 155, 355, 359; *zariba*, 192(?), 205; *see also* Koli
Wangarawa, 11
Wanika, 102
Wanyamwezi, 42, 116, 214
war, 1, 6, 12, 24, 26, 47, 102, 103, 108, 120, 193, 242; civil, 108, 116, 152, 157, 333; *see also* slaves: raids
war-camp, 43, 51, 95, 122, 124, 126, 165, 220, 299, 357-8, 371-82
Ward, H. (1890), *109*, 111, 195
Ward, W.E.F., 1969, *108*
Washlu, castration centre, 280
water: 140, 197, 202, 211, 215, 249, 329, 371; waterbags, 44, 132; wells, 130-1, 210, 212, 215, 315, 367; thirst, 87, 123, 130-2, 193, 249, 367; *see also* climate, rain
wazir, *waziri*, vizier, xvii, 131, 163, 196, 199-200, 219, 233, 263, 291, 308, 321
weapons, 254, 367-8; bows, 250, 370; chainmail, 308; darts, 351, 354, 365; shields, 243, 248, 351, 365; *see also* fire-

arms, spears, swords, throwing-irons
Wellard, J. (1964), *342*; (1967) *221*
West Africa, 2, 71, 150, 156 *et passim*
West Indies: 7, 70, 115; Cuba, 30; Haiti (San Domingo), 153-4; Jamaica, 68; Trinidad, 92
whip, 232; *see also* punishment: flogging
Whittier, J.G., American poet, 82
Whitting, C.E. (1948) (?), *273; see* Said
Whydah 90
Wilberforce, William, 30
Wilkeson, S., 1839, *91*
Willis, J. R., 57; (1970) *66*, 174, 254; (1985) *xxi*, 26-7, *388*; (1989) *174*, 254
Wilmot, Christopher, 155
al-Wisyani, 137
witchcraft, sorcery, *see* supernatural powers
wives: 2, 3, 6, 20, 35, 41-2, 48, 56-7, 63-4, 69, 70, 76, 80, 85, 87, 103, 116, 118-19, 168, 170, 182-6, 188, 191, 193, 195, 197, 198, 201-2, 214, 216, 246, 271; royal, 116, 148, 257, 287, 319; widows, widowers, 34, 45, 184; *see also* adultery, dowry, family, housing: women's, marriage, polygamy, slaves: concubines, slaves: marriage
Woloff, 116, 269, 273
women, free, 16, 35-8, 47-8, 56-7, 205, 214, 287-8, 293; *see also* Baba of Karo wives, *et passim*
World War I, 342

Wurubo, 89

Yaji, first Muslim ruler of Kano, 243
Yakubu, peaceful Kano ruler, 5-6, 9-10, 241-2
Yamba, C. Bawa (1995), *13*
Yao, Wayao, 108-9
Ya'qub Arus, king of Wadai, *circa* 1700, 299-300
al-Ya'qubi, 98, 103, 106
Yemen, 86, 218; Emir al-, of Adamawa, 161
Yoruba 30, 85, 89, 92, 157, 175, 293, 320 330; Oyo, 2, 152, 293
yuroma, a Borno eunuch title, 288
Yusuf, sultan of Wadai, 194

Zamanei, freed female slave, 79
Zambesi, 34, 102, 222
Zammit, T. (1929), *31*
Zamzam, sister of blind Darfur king, 272; Meccan well, 315
Zanj, 65, 85-6
Zanzibar, 45, 52, 53, 65, 74, 101, 146, 153, 155, 182, 217, 280-1
Zaria, 16, 25, 133, 188, 272, 309; Queen Amina, 281
Zinder, Tanemon, 36, 140-1, 190, 219, 305, 331
Zintgraff, E. (1895), *223*, 297
Zubayr, celebrated slaver, 114; *see also* Adamawa